Covers Exam 70-059

TCP/IP

Second Edition

201 West 103rd Street, Indianapolis, Indiana 46290

Erik Rozell
Mary Pablo

MCSE TestPrep: TCP/IP, Second Edition

International Standard Book Number: 0-7357-0025-7

Library of Congress Catalog Card Number: 98-88578

Printed in the United States of America

First Printing: December, 1998

00 99 98 4 3 2 1

Trademarks

Warning and Disclaimer

EXECUTIVE EDITOR
Mary Foote

ACQUISITIONS EDITOR
Steve Weiss

DEVELOPMENT EDITOR
Howard A. Jones

MANAGING EDITOR
Sarah Kearns

PROJECT EDITOR
Jennifer Chisholm

COPY EDITOR
Daryl Kessler

INDEXER
Chris Wilcox

TECHNICAL EDITORS
Walter Glenn
Alain Guilbault

PROOFREADER
Maribeth Echard

LAYOUT TECHNICIANS
Cheryl Lynch
Jeannette McKay

Contents at a Glance

Table of Contents

About the Authors

Erik Rozell is a Microsoft Certified Trainer and Systems engineer. With a degree in Management Information Systems, Erik has implemented many solutions at several Fortune 500 companies, and has been commonly used as a source for information technology throughout the industry. Erik has over 11 years of networking experience.

Mary Pablo is a Product Specialist who deals with people who need ordinary solutions. As an Administrator and Project Manager, she is responsible for the operations of over 200 sites for a national firm. With a Bachelor of Science in Business Administration, Mary has worked for over 10 years in both financial and data management information systems.

Dedication

Erik Rozell: *To my family—Dennis, Eleanor, Denelle, Stacy, Ronda, Jasmine, Tesa, and Tara.*

Mary Pablo: *To Julius, my one and only true love. Just kidding, that's my dog; I really wanted to dedicate this to my parents—Benjamin and Aurea.*

Acknowledgments

We would like to recognize, with much appreciation, our network team—William Joseph Scully III (Bill), Dennis Rozell, and Eric Vasserman. These guys assisted with presubmission reviews of questions, materials, and research of obscure information. Thank you.

We have worked very hard to ensure that this book is a top-quality product. Howard Jones has provided excellent reviews and critical analysis of this book. Without Howard, this book would not be nearly the product it is. While on the subject of quality, I would like to also express my gratitude to our two technical editors Alain Guilbault and Walter Glenn. Thanks for all the red marks and corrections, guys. Collectively, we also wanted to extend our thanks to Emmett Dulaney, who wrote the first version of this book, which we used as guidance material.

Last, but definitely not least, we owe this entire book to Steve Weiss and his efforts in arranging an agreement with Macmillan. Steve is our Acquisitions Editor, and the key person who has brought this book to fruition. Thanks, again.

Erik Rozell ("I know this will have little meaning to most of you; however, here it goes!!!")

Thanks to Grant Freeman, the man who reminds us that you will always miss those opportunities that you do not try for. My other cohorts, Walter Polanski and John E. Schaffer—thanks for the OK. Dana Sullivan for offering an alternative solution to reality, Peter Luk, a friend long since passed and missed, and Richard (Rick) Freedman for the head start (completely missed). Hector Moreno for all the trouble that he has gotten me into, Bob Rodriguez for creating the trouble (but still a good guy), and Shaun Walsh for advice on how to get out of it all. I would also like to thank those people who have made the trip in life move a bit faster. Dino Wibowo, Elias Abughazeleh, Norm Corison, Colin Cox, John Gordon, Haijin (Jim) Hu, Frank LaChapelle, Greg Silver, Carlos Nigretti, Jeff Freilach, Jesse Hillman, Julie Baas, Laya Johnson, Steve Smith, Yuri Furman, and Andrew Harrod. Finally, I would like to congratulate my brother Stacy (Dwayne) on selecting Julie Baas to be his wife and my grandmother Molly for being so lovable.

Mary Pablo: I was going to break out a phone book; however, I have included a few select people from my life who I feel have had a heavy impact on me and helped guide me in the success of my career—John Bauer: I'm glad you want to be an MCSE. Melissa (Missy) Burnhard: Enjoying Colorado? Deanne Dorado: I'm not related to Cadillac. Bob Genest: A great conversationalist. David Klein: Wobblestone. Donna Haber-McGullam: A true friend. Friends of Hollyhock House 1997-98 Board Members: Patricia Olguin, Lisa Borque, Ted Burton, and Karen Renner. Richard Hopkins: Thanks for training Julius to sit. Judy Lau: I only have $2.17 in change today for lunch. Velko Milosevich: The Paraclete. Amparo Moreno (A.K.A. Eileen Bickford): Do you remember the ghost we saw in the hall in first grade? Hector Moreno: Enjoy the ride (by the way, thanks for the introduction). Eva Pablo: Ahhh…Daylight! James Pablo: Snowballs and Spam. Janet Pablo: Snowballs...just pop it in your mouth. Joy Pablo: Ernie, Dopey, the Hawaiian Punch guy, and Snowballs. Ruth Price: Thanks for believing in me. Randy Regner: Thanks for inspiring me to be the best I can be. Monica Richardson: Thanks for your friendship. Diane Turski: Am I really like your brother?

Tell Us What You Think!

As the reader of this book, *you* are our most important critic and commentator. We value your opinion and want to know what we're doing right, what we could do better, what areas you'd like to see us publish in, and any other words of wisdom you're willing to pass our way.

As the Executive Editor for the Certification team at Macmillan Computer Publishing, I welcome your comments. You can fax, email, or write me directly to let me know what you did or didn't like about this book—as well as what we can do to make our books stronger.

Please note that I cannot help you with technical problems related to the topic of this book, and that due to the high volume of mail I receive, I might not be able to reply to every message.

When you write, please be sure to include this book's title and author, as well as your name and phone or fax number. I will carefully review your comments and share them with the author and editors who worked on the book.

Fax: 317-581-4663

Email: `certification@mcp.com`

Mail: Mary Foote
Executive Editor
Certification
Macmillan Computer Publishing
201 West 103rd Street
Indianapolis, IN 46290 USA

Introduction

The *MCSE TestPrep* series serves as a study aid for people preparing for Microsoft Certification exams. The series is intended to help reinforce and clarify information with which you are already familiar by providing sample questions and tests, as well as summary information relevant to each of the exam objectives. Note that this series is not intended to be the only source for your preparation, but rather a review of information with a set of practice tests that can be used to increase your familiarity with the exam questions. Using books in this series with the complementary *MCSE: Training Guide* books can increase the likelihood of your success when taking a certification exam.

Who Should Read This Book

The *TCP/IP, Second Edition* book in the *MCSE TestPrep* series is intended specifically for students who are in the final stages of preparing for Microsoft's Windows NT TCP/IP (70-059) exam, which is one of the core exam electives in the MCSE Microsoft Windows NT 4.0 Track program.

How This Book Helps You

This book provides a wealth of review questions similar to those you will encounter in the actual exam, categorized by the objectives published by Microsoft for the exam. Each answer is explained in detail in the "Answers and Explanations" sections. The "Further Review" sections provide additional information that is crucial for successfully passing the exam. The full-length practice exams at the end of the book help you determine whether you have mastered the skills necessary to successfully complete the Microsoft exam. The practice exams also identify areas that you need to study further before taking the actual exam.

How to Use This Book

This book series is designed to be used at the final stages of exam preparation. When you feel as though you're fairly well prepared for the exam, use this book as a test of your knowledge. Each objective is covered by a minimum of 10 questions. Start by using the practice questions as a self-quiz. Circle what you think is the correct answer (or answers), and then check your answers against the answer key. Identify the questions you missed, and look them up in the "Answers and Explanations" sections. Here you find the question repeated, the correct answer(s) identified, and a thorough explanation of the answer. You can hit the "Further Review" section if you missed several questions for one objective. After following this process for each objective, you will know on which topics your comprehension is sufficient and which objectives require continued study. This is the best study tool available to help you reinforce what you already know and identify areas that require more work.

After you have taken the practice tests and feel confident in the material on which you were tested, you should be ready to schedule your exam. Use this book for a final quick review just before taking the test to ensure that all the important concepts are set in your mind. Appendix C, "Fast Facts," summarizes key information you need to know about each objective. This feature is excellent for last-minute review before you take the exam.

Hardware/Software Recommendations

MCSE TestPrep: TCP/IP, Second Edition is meant to help you review concepts with which you already have training and experience. In order to make the most of the review, you should have as much background and experience as possible. The best way to do this is to combine studying with working on real networks by using the products on which you will be tested. The following list provides a description of the minimum computer requirements you need to build a good practice environment.

- Any computer on the Microsoft Hardware Compatibility List
- 486DX 33MHz or better (Pentium recommended)
- A minimum of 16MB of RAM (32MB recommended)
- 125MB (or more) of free disk space (160MB for RISC-based systems)
- 3.5-inch 1.44MB floppy drive
- VGA (or Super VGA) video adapter
- VGA (or Super VGA) monitor
- Mouse or equivalent pointing device
- Two-speed (or faster) CD-ROM drive
- Presence on an NT Network
- Windows NT Server software

What Exam 70-059 Covers

Just as other Microsoft exams are, the Windows NT TCP/IP exam is organized by category, with objectives and subobjectives in each. The following sections address the Microsoft objectives for the exam that was current at the time of printing of this book. Be aware that the objective may change at any time. It is wise to check out the preparation guide for the exam on the Microsoft Web site.

Planning

Given a scenario, identify valid network cofigurations.

Installation and Configuration

Given a scenario, select the appropriate services to install when using Microsoft TCP/IP on a Microsoft Windows NT Server computer.

On a Windows NT Server computer, configure Microsoft TCP/IP to support multiple network adapters.

Configure scopes by using DHCP Manager.

Install and configure a WINS server. Requirements include the following:

- Import files to WINS.
- Run WINS on a multihomed computer.
- Configure WINS replication.
- Configure static mappings in the WINS database.

Configure subnet masks.

Configure a Windows NT Server computer to function as an IP router. Requirements include the following:

- Install and configure the DHCP Relay Agent.

Install and configure the Microsoft DNS Server service on a Windows NT Server computer. Requirements include the following:

- Integrate DNS with other name servers.
- Connect a DNS server to a DNS root server.
- Configure DNS server roles.

Configure HOSTS and LMHOSTS files.

Configure a Windows NT Server computer to support TCP/IP printing.

Configure SNMP.

Connectivity

Given a scenario, identify which utility to use to connect to a TCP/IP-based UNIX host.

Configure a RAS server and dial-up networking for use on a TCP/IP network.

Configure and support browsing in a multiple-domain routed network.

Monitoring and Optimization

Given a scenario, identify which tool to use to monitor TCP/IP traffic.

Troubleshooting

Diagnose and resolve IP addressing problems.

Use Microsoft TCP/IP utilities to diagnose IP configuration problems.

Identify which Microsoft TCP/IP utility to use to diagnose IP configuration problems.

Diagnose and resolve name resolution problems.

GOOD LUCK!

As you approach the final stages of your exam preparation, New Riders wishes you the best of luck. If you should find after using this *TestPrep* tool that you need further study in a particular area, look into purchasing a New Riders *Training Guide, Second Edition*, a complete, thorough, and accurate study guide. If you would like to try computerized testing, check out New Riders' *Top Score* software simulation suite in the software or computer book section of your neighborhood bookstore. It includes an exclusive test engine that mimics Microsoft styles and an NT Simulator!

Keep us posted on your success. There is a registration card in the back of the book. Fill it out and fax or send it in. We'd love to hear from you. Good luck on your exam!

CHAPTER 1

TCP/IP Basics and Planning

OBJECTIVES

This chapter helps you prepare for the exam by covering the following objectives:

Given a scenario, identify valid network configurations.

- On paper, almost any solution can be made to sound feasible and correct. However, to an expert, flaws can be found and corrections can be made such that a network performs better than one that is proposed by an individual or group that is not properly familiar with more acceptable methods. Identifying these solutions can be a vast time-saver.

Given a scenario, select the appropriate services to install when using Microsoft TCP/IP on a Microsoft Windows NT Server computer.

- The efficiency on a network depends on a correct configuration and minimal number of services running on a server. Under certain conditions, some services should be used while others should not. This section makes specific reference to what items to install and when.

Networks today are a complication of different protocols and topologies that link various systems together. In building a network, we typically are concerned with four components: computer hardware (network adapters), operating systems, topologies (physical connections), and protocols.

The components of a network are generally designed with a particular framework, or architecture, in mind. Although they may vary from vendor to vendor, this fundamental architecture defines how all components of a machine, operating system, and protocol fit together.

All computers in a network environment rely on network protocols to enable them to communicate with one another. Network protocols are designed and written to fit into the overall computing framework, or architecture, of the operating system running on a machine.

TCP/IP is one of many protocols; however, it is of a special interest because it is by far the most popular of all networking protocols and the one upon which the Internet is built.

The second half of this chapter focuses on planning—that is, designing networks and designating the appropriate services to use.

PRACTICE QUESTIONS

GIVEN A SCENARIO, IDENTIFY VALID NETWORK CONFIGURATIONS

1. **Several programmers are discussing the design of a new application to be written for your company and a heated debate ensues over whether the application should use Windows Sockets or NetBIOS. Some programmers think TCP/IP supports Windows Sockets only, some think NetBIOS only, and half think TCP/IP supports both Windows Sockets and NetBIOS. Who is correct in this argument?**

   A. Programmers who say Windows Sockets only

   B. Programmers who say NetBIOS only

   C. Programmers who say neither

   D. Programmers who say both

2. **One of your users' calls cannot connect to the network. The user can't log on to the NT domain and can't use Network Neighborhood. As part of your trouble-shooting routine, you find out that the user can ping every IP address on the network successfully. In addition, the user seems to be able to FTP, HTTP, and telnet without a problem. Which of the following do you think might be the source of the error?**

   A. NetBIOS API isn't functioning properly.

   B. DNS isn't configured.

   C. Telnet is an unpredictable program.

   D. Windows Sockets aren't functioning properly.

3. **Which of the following are Network Modeling Structures? Choose all that apply.**

   A. DOD

   B. Microsoft Network Interface Structure

   C. OSI

   D. ISO

4. **What function occurs at the Physical layer?**

   A. Cables and connections

   B. Network adapter drivers loaded

   C. Transportation of data

   D. Applications run here

5. **What function occurs at the Data Link layer?**

   A. Cables and connections

   B. Network adapter drivers loaded

   C. Transportation of data

   D. Applications run here

6. **What TCP/IP component is present at the Network layer?**

A. IP

B. TCP

C. UDP

D. FTP

E. HTTP

7. **What components of TCP/IP are present at the Transport layer? Choose all that apply.**

A. Cables and connections

B. UDP

C. TCP

D. FTP

E. All of the above

8. **What function occurs at the Session layer?**

A. Connections to remote systems are managed.

B. IP addresses are assigned.

C. Transportation of data.

D. Control of user data on a per-user login under Windows NT.

9. **What is the primary responsibility of the Presentation layer?**

A. Conversion of data formats

B. Management of connections

C. Presentation of applications to users

D. Network diagram imaging

10. **The Application layer supports which of the following? Choose the best answer.**

A. TCP

B. FTP

C. DOS

D. Hardware addressing

E. Connectivity to remote systems

11. **Which of the following properly lists all four layers of the DOD model?**

A. Network Access, Internet, Host to Host, Process/Application

B. DataLink, Host to Host, Internet, Presentation

C. Physical, Interlink, Host Transport, Application

D. IP, TCP, UPD, API

12. **With respect to the Network and Transport layers of the OSI model, which of the following shows DOD layers in order?**

A. Internet, Host to Host

B. Host to Host, Internet

C. IP, TCP

D. Internet, Session

13. **At what layers would you find the following: SMTP, ICMP, Frame Relay, and TCP?**

A. 4, 2, 2, 3

B. 4, 3, 2, 3

C. 4, 2, 1, 3

D. 3, 2, 1, 3

14. **Which of the following is not present at the Network Access layer?**

A. Hardware address

B. Network driver

C. Cabling

D. Routers

15. **Paul is having trouble connecting to another network segment on the other side of a router. Despite repeated attempts to route packets to the other side, Paul is unsuccessful. In an attempt to help Paul, you will need to determine which layer is responsible for the routing of IP packets. Which layer would that be?**

    A. Network layer

    B. Transport layer

    C. Internet layer

    D. Application layer

16. **Which of the following is not a property of IP?**

    A. Routability

    B. 32-bit addressing

    C. Fragmenting and reassembly

    D. Time-to-Live (TTL) freshness stamping

    E. None of the above

17. **Which of the following is a local broadcast?**

    A. 134.57.0.0

    B. 134.57.255.255

    C. 255.255.255.255

    D. 0.0.0.0

18. **Several machines on the network use DHCP and WINS to get their IP address information and to resolve NetBIOS names to IP addresses. What protocol allows these machines to resolve an IP address to a hardware address?**

    A. Internet Control Protocol

    B. DHCP address resolution manager

    C. WINS address resolution manager

    D. Address Resolution Protocol

19. **During the troubleshooting of a problem, you take a *trace* (capture the network traffic) to discover what is going on. As you are analyzing the packets, you discover a redirect packet that appears to have come from a router. Which protocol can generate such a packet?**

    A. Transmission Control Protocol

    B. User Datagram Protocol

    C. Internet Group Management Protocol

    D. Internet Control Message Protocol

20. **Which of the following explains Internet Group Management Protocol?**

    A. It is used to verify connectivity to a system.

    B. It allows a group of systems to act as one while receiving broadcast data.

    C. It is a workgroup chat protocol.

    D. It is a method by which addresses may be consolidated.

21. **Which two communications protocols are present at the Host to Host layer of the DOD model?**

    A. IP

    B. TCP

    C. ICMP

    D. UDP

22. **For what type of application is UDP more desirable than TCP?**

    A. High security

    B. Internet radio

    C. Web browsing

    D. Large file data transfers

23. **You're talking with a few of the programmers in your department about an application they are working on. They tell you it is designed to use a connection-oriented protocol to communicate over the network. Which protocol in the TCP/IP protocol suite provides connection-oriented communications?**

    A. Transmission Control Protocol

    B. User Datagram Protocol

    C. Internet Control Message Protocol

    D. Address Resolution Protocol

24. **Kristin in the advertising department is writing a very important document in Word. She must transfer it immediately to the remote office. Which of the following protocols is the best protocol for this type of transfer?**

    A. Universal Datagram Protocol

    B. Internet Group Protocol

    C. Transmission Control Protocol

    D. Secured Access Link Protocol

25. **As far as communications are concerned, why are sliding windows and acknowledgments important to TCP/IP?**

    A. Sliding windows allow the protocol to shield itself against unwanted communication while acknowledging or accepting communication.

    B. Sliding windows are used to allow a buffer and the time frame for a system to communicate, whereas acknowledgments certify that a message has been received correctly.

    C. Sliding windows is a made-up term; however, acknowledgments are used to certify communications.

    D. None of the above are correct.

26. **With many TCP/IP applications running simultaneously, how does TCP/IP know which application to send inbound data to?**

    A. By IP address

    B. By port and socket

    C. By host name

    D. By URL

27. **Which of the following is not a Network API?**

    A. WinSocks

    B. Sockets

    C. NetBIOS

    D. NetBEUI

ANSWER KEY

1. D
2. A
3. A-C
4. A
5. B
6. A
7. B-C
8. A
9. A
10. B
11. A
12. A
13. C
14. D
15. C
16. E
17. B
18. D
19. D
20. B
21. B-D
22. B
23. A
24. C
25. B
26. B
27. D

ANSWERS & EXPLANATIONS

GIVEN A SCENARIO, IDENTIFY VALID NETWORK CONFIGURATIONS

1. Several programmers are discussing the design of a new application to be written for your company and a heated debate ensues over whether the application should use Windows Sockets or NetBIOS. Some programmers think TCP/IP supports Windows Sockets only, some think NetBIOS only, and half think TCP/IP supports both Windows Sockets and NetBIOS. Who is correct in this argument?

D. Programmers who say both

1. CORRECT ANSWER: D

Both Windows Sockets and NetBIOS are supported. Consider the fact that Microsoft's Operating system is NetBIOS based for its internal commands, but must have Windows Socket compatibility for those that are external (or expressly designed for TCP/IP); both sets of APIs are supported.

2. One of your users' calls cannot connect to the network. The user can't log on to the NT domain and can't use Network Neighborhood. As part of your troubleshooting routine, you find out that the user can ping every IP address on the network successfully. In addition, the user seems to be able to FTP, HTTP, and telnet without a problem. Which of the following do you think might be the source of the error?

A. NetBIOS API isn't functioning properly.

2. CORRECT ANSWER: A

The most likely cause is that NetBIOS isn't functioning properly. Remember that multiple APIs are used to compose the Microsoft suite of TCP/IP services. Those services include both NetBIOS and Windows Sockets support. When you communicate to the Internal Microsoft Network, communications are performed via NetBIOS services. However, in situations where communications are performed externally, the connections are established through the Windows Sockets configuration.

Advantages of TCP/IP Implementation

An administrator has many choices when deciding the protocol platform for which they want their network to operate. Windows NT includes support for TCP/IP, IPX, NetBEUI, AppleTalk, DLC, and many others. Given that your network will operate with the Internet, TCP/IP is generally required. Microsoft's implementation of TCP/IP provides the following advantages:

- **An industry-standard protocol.** Because TCP/IP is not maintained or written by one company, it is not proprietary or subject to as many compatibility issues as other protocols. The Internet community as a whole decides whether a particular change or implementation is worthwhile. Naturally, this process slows down the implementation of new features and characteristics compared to how quickly a particular company might make changes. However, this process guarantees that changes are well thought out and provide functionality with most, if not all, other implementations of TCP/IP. A set of publicly available specifications can be referenced at any time over the Internet, detailing how the protocol suite should be used and implemented.
- **A set of utilities for connecting dissimilar operating systems.** Many connectivity utilities have been written for the TCP/IP suite, including the File Transfer Protocol (FTP) and Terminal Emulation Protocol (Telnet). Because these utilities use the Windows Sockets API, connectivity from one machine to another does not depend on the network operating system used on either machine. For example, a Microsoft FTP client could access a UNIX FTP server to transfer files without either party having to worry about compatibility issues. This functionality also enables a Windows NT machine running a Telnet client to access and run commands on an IBM mainframe running a Telnet server, for example.
- **A scalable, cross-platform client/server architecture.** Consider what happened during the initial development of applications for the TCP/IP protocol suite. Vendors wanted to be able to write their own client/server applications. For example, SQL and Simple Network Management Protocol (SNMP) fit this relationship. The specification for how to write applications was also up for public review. Which operating systems would be included?

Users everywhere wanted to be able to take advantage of the connectivity options promised through the use of TCP/IP regardless of the operating system they were currently running. Therefore, the Windows Sockets API was established so that applications using the TCP/IP protocol could write to a standard, agreed-upon interface. Because the contributors included everyone, and therefore every kind of operating system, the specifications for Windows Sockets on TCP/IP were written to make the operating system transparent to the application. Microsoft TCP/IP includes support for Windows Sockets and for connectivity to other Windows Sockets–compliant TCP/IP stacks.

- **Access to the Internet.** TCP/IP is the de facto protocol of the Internet and allows access to a wealth of information that can be found at thousands of locations around the world. Creative alternatives have been established to allow connections to the Internet as IP addresses have become more scarce and security issues surrounding access have become more prevalent. However, all these implementations use gateways or firewalls that act on behalf of the requesting machines.

3. Which of the following are Network Modeling Structures? Choose all that apply.

A. DOD

C. OSI

3. CORRECT ANSWERS: A-C

Both DOD and OSI are network models. The OSI model is a seven-layer model, whereas the DOD contains four layers. These two models are roughly translatable to each other.

Network Modeling Structures

A network is basically comprised of four components: computer hardware (network adapters), operating systems, topologies (physical connections), and protocols. These items are collectively arranged into a hierarchy model that facilitates a developer's ability to write just their application without the concern of developing other components. For instance, a programming company can design a file transfer server without having to also design the network, the wiring, and so forth.

There are two prevalent structures that are commonly noted among the programming community. The first is the OSI model. This is a model by which almost any network is designed and the base for which most applications are developed. The second model is the Department of Defense (DOD) Model, which is a predecessor to the OSI model. The OSI model has the advantage of more detail and structure than the DOD model that TCP/IP was designed upon. Although the TCP/IP protocol suite maps to only the four-layer DOD model, these four layers provide the same functionality as the seven layers of the Open Systems Integration (OSI) model.

The OSI Model

The OSI model divides networking tasks into seven fundamentally different layers to make it easier for the industry to move forward and evolve. With the tasks segregated into functional units, a person writing the code for a network card doesn't have to worry about what applications are going to be run over it; conversely, a programmer writing an application doesn't have to worry about who manufactured the network card. However, to make this system work, everything must be written to comply with the boundary specifications between each of the seven layers of the model.

Each layer is isolated from the others where the area between each level is a common boundary layer. For instance, between layer 1 and layer 2 is a boundary that both layers must be able to support. These boundary layers enable one layer of the networking model to communicate and share valuable and necessary information with the layer above or below it. In fact, each time a layer passes data to the layer below, the sending layer adds information to it; similarly, each time a layer receives data, it strips off its own information and passes the rest up the protocol stack.

One of the most common and useful ways to describe the networking model is to imagine the process a letter goes through to get to its destination.

Messages from one layer are packaged and placed into the next layer. Each step of the process has little to do with the preceding or following step. The kind of envelope has nothing to do with either the language in which the message is written or its content. In the same way, the actual address on the envelope—be it California, Florida, or Hawaii—has absolutely nothing to do with the color of the envelope. The only common link between the address and the message is the envelope itself. Finally, the method of delivery—whether the postal service uses a boat, plane, or train—doesn't matter, as long as the envelope gets to its destination address. Each layer depends on the other layers, but is only mildly related to the functionality of the others.

Remember that this is a solution that allows programmers and developers to openly model applications. Not all levels of the model will constantly be used by all layers. In fact, the purpose of any layer may simply be to forward information up the chain.

4. What function occurs at the Physical layer?

A. Cables and connections

4. CORRECT ANSWER: A

At the Physical layer, the physical network wires exist. Wires are connected to Network adapters. These network adapters are at the Physical layer as well.

The first layer of the OSI model is the Physical layer. This layer is the only one truly connected to the network in the sense that it is the only layer concerned with how to interpret the voltage on the wire—the 1s and 0s. This layer is responsible for understanding the electrical rules associated with devices and for determining what kind of medium is actually being used (cables, connectors, and other mechanical distinctions). TCP/IP does not function at the physical level, leaving these tasks instead for the network cards to handle.

5. What function occurs at the Data Link layer?

B. Network adapter drivers loaded

5. CORRECT ANSWER: B

The second layer of the OSI model is the Data Link layer. This layer is responsible for the creation and interpretation of different frame types based on the actual physical network being used. For instance, Ethernet and token-ring networks support different and numerous frame types, and the Data Link layer must understand the difference between them.

This layer is also responsible for interpreting what it receives from the Physical Layer, using low-level error detection and correction algorithms to determine when information needs to be re-sent. Network protocols, including the TCP/IP protocol suite, do not define physical standards at the Physical or Data Link layer, but instead are written to make use of any standards that may currently be in use.

The boundary between the Data Link layer and Network layer defines a group of agreed-upon standards for how protocols communicate and gain access to these lower layers. As long as a network protocol is appropriately written to this boundary layer, the protocols should be able to access the network regardless of what media type is being used.

6. What TCP/IP component is present at the Network layer?

A. IP

6. CORRECT ANSWER: A

Internet Protocol (IP) is the network transport component that operates at the Network layer. This is also the layer in which the IP address resides.

The third layer of the OSI model is the Network layer. This layer is mostly associated with the movement of data by means of addressing and routing. It directs the flow of data from a source to a destination, despite the fact that the machines may not be connected to the same physical wire or segment, by finding a path or route from one machine to another.

If necessary, this layer can break data into smaller chunks for transmission. This step is sometimes necessary when transferring data from one type of physical network to another, for instance, token-ring (which supports larger frame sizes) to Ethernet (which supports smaller frame sizes). Of course, it is also responsible for reassembling those smaller chunks into the original data after the data has reached its destination. A number of protocols from the TCP/IP protocol suite exist in this layer, but the network protocol that is responsible for routing and delivery of packets is the IP protocol.

7. What components of TCP/IP are present at the Transport layer? Choose all that apply.

B. UDP

C. TCP

7. CORRECT ANSWERS: B-C

Both TCP and UDP are present at the Transport layer. These are the connection (TCP) and connectionless (UDP) transports that are available to TCP/IP-based applications and services.

The fourth layer of the OSI model is the Transport layer. This layer is primarily responsible for guaranteeing delivery of packets transmitted by the Network layer, although it does not always have to do so. Depending on the protocol being used, delivery of packets may or may not be guaranteed. When it is responsible to guarantee the delivery of packets, the Transport layer does so through various means of error control, including verification of sequence numbers for packets and other protocol-dependent mechanisms. TCP/IP has two protocols at this layer of the model: Transmission Control Protocol (TCP) and User Datagram Protocol (UDP). UDP may be used for nonguaranteed delivery of packets, and TCP may be used to guarantee the delivery of packets.

8. What function occurs at the Session layer?

A. Connections to remote systems are managed.

8. CORRECT ANSWER: A

The Session layer manages connections to remote systems. This layer supports application programming interfaces and therefore overlaps into the layers above it under TCP/IP.

The fifth layer of the OSI model is the Session layer. This layer is responsible for managing connections between two machines during the course of communication between them. The Session layer determines whether it has received all pertinent information for the session and whether it can stop receiving or transmitting data. This layer also has built-in error correction and recovery methods. TCP/IP uses two Application Programming Interfaces (APIs)—Windows Sockets and NetBIOS—to determine whether all information has been sent and received between two connected machines.

9. What is the primary responsibility of the Presentation layer?

A. Conversion of data formats

9. CORRECT ANSWER: A

The Presentation layer is primarily concerned with the conversion of one data format to another. This allows incompatible data to be placed with others. Commonly, this is seen in Windows technologies such as OLE (Object Linking and Embedding), which involves taking an object from one application and placing it in another.

The sixth layer of the OSI model is the Presentation layer. This layer is primarily concerned with the conversion of data formats from one machine to another. One common example is the sending of data from a machine that uses the ASCII format for characters to a machine that uses the EBCDIC format for characters, typically IBM mainframes. (EBCDIC and ASCII are standards for translating characters to hexadecimal code.) Letters, numbers, and symbols in one format must be translated when communicating with machines using a different format. The Presentation layer is responsible for picking up differences such as these and translating them to compatible formats.

10. The Application layer supports which of the following? Choose the best answer.

B. FTP

10. CORRECT ANSWER: B

The Application layer is used as a go-between for the computer and users. Of all examples listed, FTP is the only choice that fits this layer's criteria. Keep in mind that due to the way in which TCP translates from the DOD model to the OSI model, FTP is present at layers below as well.

The seventh layer of the OSI model is the Application layer. This is the last layer of the model, and it acts as the arbiter or translator between users' applications and the network. Applications that want to use the network to transfer data must be written to conform to networking APIs supported by the machine's networking components, such as Windows Sockets and NetBIOS. After the application makes an API call, the Application layer determines with which machine it wants to communicate, whether a session should be set up between the communicating machines, and whether the delivery of packets needs to be guaranteed.

11. Which of the following properly lists all four layers of the DOD model?

A. Network Access, Internet, Host to Host, Process/Application

11. CORRECT ANSWER: A

The four layers of the DOD model are Network Access, Internet, Host to Host, and Process/Application. Each of these layers acts in accordance with how a network logically functions. For example, the Network access layer is used for cables, drivers, and hardware. As you compare this to the OSI model, you will note many similarities such that it almost would not matter which model you examine. However, it is important that you understand both models and which layers are equivalent to each other.

12. With respect to the Network and Transport layers of the OSI model, which of the following shows DOD layers in order?

A. Internet, Host to Host

12. CORRECT ANSWER: A

The Network layer is equivalent to the Internet layer of DOD while the Transport layer is equal to the Host to Host layer. These layers are key to the transport of TCP/IP messages–IP (Internet Protocol) is present at the Internet layer, while TCP and UDP are present at the Host to Host.

The DOD Model—Four Layers of TCP/IP

TCP/IP maps to a four-layer architectural model. This model is called the Internet protocol suite or DOD model and is broken into the Network Interface, Internet, Transport, and Application layers. Each layer corresponds to one or more layers of the OSI model. The Network Access layer of TCP/IP corresponds to the Physical and Data Link layers of OSI.
The Internet layer corresponds to the Network layer of the OSI model. The Host to Host layer corresponds to the Transport layer of OSI, and the Application layer corresponds to the Session, Presentation, and Application layers of the OSI model.

Each of the four layers of the TCP/IP model is responsible for all the activities of the layers to which it maps.

The Network Access Layer (#1)

The Network Access layer is responsible for communicating directly with the network. It must understand the network architecture being used, such as token ring or Ethernet, and provide an interface allowing the Internet layer to communicate with it. The Internet layer is responsible for communicating directly with the Network Access layer.

The Internet Layer (#2)

The Internet layer is primarily concerned with the routing and delivery of packets through the Internet Protocol (IP). All the protocols in the Transport layer must use IP to send data. The Internet Protocol includes rules for how to address and direct packets, fragment and reassemble packets, provide security information, and identify the type of service being used. However, because IP is not a connection-based protocol, it does not guarantee that packets transmitted onto the wire will not be lost, damaged, duplicated, or out of order. This task is the responsibility of higher layers of the networking model, such as the Transport layer or the Application layer. Other protocols that exist in the Internet layer are the Internet Control Messaging Protocol (ICMP), Internet Group Management Protocol (IGMP), and the Address Resolution Protocol (ARP).

The Host to Host Layer (#3)

The Host to Host layer maps to the Transport layer of the OSI model and is responsible for providing communication between machines for applications. This communication can be connection based or nonconnection based. The primary difference between these two types of connections is whether a mechanism exists for tracking data and guaranteeing the delivery of the data to its destination. TCP is the protocol used for connection-based communication between two machines providing reliable data transfer. UDP is used for nonconnection-based communication with no guarantee of delivery.

The Process/Application Layer (#4)

The Process/Application layer of the Internet protocol suite is responsible for all the activities that occur in the Session, Presentation, and Application layers of the OSI model. Numerous protocols have been written for use in this layer, including SNMP, FTP, Simple Mail Transfer Protocol (SMTP), as well as many others.

The interface between each of these layers is written to have the capability to pass information from one layer to the other.

The interface between the Network Access layer and the Internet layer does not pass a great deal of information, although it must follow certain rules. Namely, it must listen to all broadcasts and send the rest of the data in the frame up to the Internet layer for processing, and if it receives any frames that do not have an IP frame type, they must be silently discarded.

The interface between the Internet layer and the Host to Host layer must be able to provide each layer full access to information such as the source and destination addresses, whether TCP or UDP should be utilized in the transport of data, and all other available mechanisms for IP. Rules and specifications for the Transport layer include giving the Transport layer the capability to change these parameters or to pass parameters it receives from the Application layer down to the Internet layer. The most important thing to remember about all of these boundary layers is that they must use the agreed-upon rules for passing information from one layer to the other.

The interface between the Host to Host layer and the Application layer is written to provide an interface to applications, whether they are using the TCP or UDP protocol for transferring data. The interface uses the Windows Sockets and NetBIOS APIs to transfer parameters and data between the two layers. The Application layer must have full access to the Transport layer to change and alter parameters as necessary.

A comparison of the DOD Model to the OSI Model can be observed in the following table. Note that this is an approximate translation of the two models and in some areas there may be some overlap.

DOD Model	*OSI Model*
Layer 1—Network Access	Layer 1—Physical Layer 2—Data Link
Layer 2—Internet	Layer 3—Network
Layer 3—Host to Host	Layer 4—Transport
Layer 4—Process/ Application Layer	Layer 5—Session Layer 6—Presentation Layer 7—Application

13. At what layers would you find the following: SMTP, ICMP, Frame Relay, and TCP?

C. 4, 2, 1, 3

13. CORRECT ANSWER: C

SMTP can be found at layer 4, ICMP at layer 2, Frame Relay at layer 1, and TCP at layer 3. In general, you will find very little difference in what is found in layers 2 and 3 between applications and uses for TCP/IP. Layer 1 generally describes your network topology and layer 4 usually reflects your suite of TCP/IP programs—FTP, SMTP, SNMP, RSH, Web Browsers, and so on.

How TCP/IP Is Built on the DOD Model

The layers provide guidelines only; the real work is done by the protocols that are contained within the layers. Although each layer is designed to operate independently of others, there is some overlap. Six primary protocols are associated with TCP/IP:

- Internet Protocol (IP)
- Internet Control Message Protocol (ICMP)
- Address Resolution Protocol (ARP)
- Internet Group Management Protocol (IGMP)
- Transmission Control Protocol (TCP)
- User Datagram Protocol (UDP)

The following table represents how TCP/IP is built upon the DOD model. Note that at each layer, specific components related only to that layer are present. For example, the Network Access layer will contain hardware specific materials not directly attached to any protocol. This table is not a complete list of all elements present at each level.

DOD Model	*Components Present at Each Layer*
Layer 1—Network Access	Ethernet, Token Ring, FDDI, Arcnet, Frame Relay, and so on
Layer 2—Internet	IP, ICMP, BootP, ARP, RARP
Layer 3—Host to Host	TCP, UDP
Layer 4—Application	LPD, SMTP, Telnet, FTP, NFS, X Window, Gopher, WWW, and so on

14. Which of the following is not present at the Network Access layer?

D. Routers

14. CORRECT ANSWER: D

Routers work based on directing an IP address. As you should recall, IP addressing is performed at the Internet layer.

DOD Layer 1—Network Access

When we refer to the Network Access layer of TCP/IP, we are primarily focusing on physically linking systems together. This layer also takes into account the hardware address of the Network Interface Card by which every machine may be uniquely identified. It is important to realize that this hardware address is located at the Network Access level because it is primary to the operation of any networking protocol.

15. Paul is having trouble connecting to another network segment on the other side of a router. Despite repeated attempts to route packets to the other side, Paul is unsuccessful. In an attempt to help Paul, you will need to determine which layer is responsible for the routing of IP packets. Which layer would that be?

C. Internet layer

15. CORRECT ANSWER: C

The Internet layer is the layer to select. You should note while reading each section of the OSI and TCP/IP layers, which functions correspond. This information is useful when trying to determine where in a chain a breakdown is occurring.

DOD Layer 2—Internet

This second layer of the TCP/IP structure is where all of the busywork of TCP/IP is performed. At this layer, we find a number of protocols, including IP, ICMP, BootP, ARP, and RARP. Each protocol has a specific task and may utilize one of the other protocols at this layer. The most used and most famous protocol at this level is Internet Protocol (IP).

16. Which of the following is not a property of IP?

E. None of the above

16. CORRECT ANSWER: E

TCP/IP is a fully scalable, routable, 32-bit protocol that supports fragmentation and reassembly, and Time-to-Live (TTL) freshness stamping. The overall structure of TCP is similar to IPX, whereas a protocol such as NetBEUI supports few of these features and is not routable.

Internet Protocol (IP)

A number of protocols are found in the Internet layer, including the most important protocol in the entire suite, the Internet Protocol, or IP. The Transport layer cannot communicate at all without communicating through IP in the Internet layer.

Addressing

The most fundamental element of the IP is the address space that IP uses. Each machine on a network is given a unique 32-bit address called an *Internet address* or *IP address.* A 32-bit address is one in which four individual numbers are used. Each number in the address can range from 0 to 255. An example of an IP address might be 134.57.8.253. The numbers in this example are somewhat random; however, the actual numbers that are found on the Internet are not.

Addresses are divided into five categories, called *classes.* The currently defined classes are labeled A, B, C, D, and E. An address given to a machine is derived from classes A, B, or C, depending on the network to which the system belongs. The class is determined by the first number of the IP address—class A uses addresses that range from 1 to 126, B from 128 to 191, and C from 192 to 223. The other two classes are not widely used—class D addresses are used for combining machines into one functional group; class E addresses are considered experimental and are not currently available.

For now, the most important concept to understand is that each machine requires a unique address and IP is responsible for providing communication between two machines. The whole concept behind uniquely identifying machines is to be able to send data to one machine and one machine only, even if the IP stack has to broadcast at the Physical layer.

Technologies such as Ethernet, which use a common wire or hub for all nodes, will hear traffic not bound for other workstations. If IP receives data from the Network Access layer that is addressed to another machine or is not a broadcast, IP's directions are to silently discard the packet and not continue processing it.

The IP layer receives information in the form of *packets* from the Transport layer (either TCP or UDP). Data is then sent in what is commonly referred to as a *datagram*. The size of a datagram depends on the type of network that is being used, such as token ring or Ethernet. If a packet has too much data to be transmitted in one datagram, it is broken into pieces and transmitted through several datagrams. Each of these datagrams has to then be reassembled by TCP or UDP.

IP addresses are assigned by organizations called *ISPs* (Internet Service Providers). ISPs sell/rent IP address ranges to companies for the purpose of having active addresses on the Internet. Anytime a system accesses the Internet, the routers (on the Internet) understand how to deliver their packets according to unique addresses. Considering the lack of addresses, many companies that use an ISP will receive only a single address and use a proxy server or firewall with address translation capabilities to retrieve data on the Internet. Networks that are using such devices should always use the private address ranges because they are not routable across the Internet, do not interfere with active sites, and are secure. These ranges are listed as follows:

Class	*Private IP Address Range*
A	10.0.0.0
B	172.16– 31.0.0
C	192.168.0.0

Fragmentation and Reassembly

The Internet Protocol will send a message (datagram) up only to the maximum size that a topology will allow. As such, fragmentation and reassembly occur when data is too large to be transmitted on the underlying network. Combining a token-ring and Ethernet network is the most common example. Token-ring networks support much larger frame sizes and therefore support larger datagram sizes. Alternatively, the Transport layer may send the Internet layer more data than one datagram can handle. In either of these cases, IP must break down the data into manageable chunks through a process called *fragmentation*.

After data is fragmented, each datagram gets a fragment ID, identifying it in the sequence so that each fragment can be reassembled at the destination machine. This whole process is transparent to the user.

After the fragments have been received and reassembled at the destination machine, the data can be sent up to the higher layers for processing.

Routability

IP is responsible for routing IP datagrams from one network to another. Machines on a network can be configured to support routing. With routing, when a machine receives a datagram that is neither addressed to it nor is a broadcast, the machine must determine where the datagram should be sent so that it can reach its destination. Not all machines on a TCP/IP network are routers. But all routers can forward datagrams from one network to another. Connections to the Internet are often through some form of router.

When you consider that all networks are assigned a network number, then we can understand how routing works. Suppose, for instance, that you wanted to send a message from a network 134.57.0.0 to one that is 161.209.0.0. The transmitting machines are not located on the same network and must forward messages to routers (also called *gateways*) that can send a message to the correct next logical step in reaching a destination.

Time to Live

The Time-to-Live (TTL) specification is set in Windows NT to a default of 128. This setting represents 128 hops, 128 seconds, or a combination of the two. Each time a router handles a datagram, it decrements the TTL by a minimum of one. If a datagram is held up at a router for longer than one second before it is transmitted, the router can decrement the TTL accordingly (by more than one).

One way to visualize how the TTL works is to think of a deadly poison. Each time a datagram is sent out on to the network, it is injected with this deadly poison. The datagram has only the length of time specified in the TTL to get to its destination and receive the antidote for the poison. If the datagram gets routed through congested routers, traffic jams, narrow bandwidth communication avenues, and so on, it might not make it. If the TTL expires before the datagram reaches its destination, it is discarded from the network.

Although this concept may seem strange at first, in reality it prevents datagrams from running around a network indefinitely, wreaking havoc with bandwidth and the synchronization of data. Imagine a scenario in which 100 datagrams are sent to a machine. Twenty-five of them have to be re-sent because the retransmit timer on the sending machine expired. After the communication is complete and the session broken down, suddenly 25 packets appear out of nowhere hitting the destination machine. These 25 packets may have been rerouted through some extremely slow network path and were never discarded. At least in this case, the destination machine can just ignore the datagrams. However, in routed environments it would be pretty easy to set up infinite loops where packets would bounce between two routers indefinitely.

TCP, UDP, and IP work together to provide both connection-oriented and nonconnection-oriented communication. These three protocols work together to provide communication between two machines.

17. Which of the following is a local broadcast?

B. 134.57.255.255

17. CORRECT ANSWER: B

The 134.57 portion of the address designates the locality, and 255.255 states that the destination is a broadcast.

Broadcasts

Despite the fact that IP was designed to be able to send packets directly to a particular machine, at times it is preferable to send a message to all machines connected to a physical segment. IP supports broadcasts at the Internet layer; if IP receives a broadcast datagram from the Network Access layer, IP must process the packet as if the packet had been addressed to IP itself.

The destination for a broadcast is usually 255. The number of times that this number appears in an IP address will vary according to the size of the network that you are broadcasting to, as well as the subnet mask. Suppose that you were on a network that was defined as 134.57.0.0 with a mask of 255.255.0.0; a broadcast to the entire network would be a message sent to 134.57.255.255. Although these numbers probably will not mean much to you at this point, by the end of the next chapter, all should be clear.

18. Several machines on the network use DHCP and WINS to get their IP address information and to resolve NetBIOS names to IP addresses. What protocol allows these machines to resolve an IP address to a hardware address?

D. Address Resolution Protocol

18. CORRECT ANSWER: D

The Address Resolution Protocol (ARP) resolves IP addresses to hardware addresses. You should note that WINS is a service for resolving NetBIOS names to IP addresses, whereas DHCP is a service that is used to configure TCP/IP parameters at a workstation.

Address Resolution Protocol (ARP)

Unless IP is planning to initiate a full broadcast on the network, it has to have the physical address of the machine to which it is going to send datagrams. For this information, it relies on ARP. ARP is responsible for mapping IP addresses to the corresponding hardware address of the machine to which the IP address is assigned. This way, whenever IP needs a physical address for a particular IP address, ARP is used to determine it. After an address has been resolved, it is stored in memory.

ARP is responsible for finding a map to a local physical address for any local IP address that IP may request. If ARP does not have a map in memory, it has to find one on the network. ARP uses local broadcasts to find physical addresses of machines and maintains a cache in memory of recently mapped IP addresses to physical addresses. Although this cache does not last indefinitely, it enables ARP to not have to broadcast every time IP needs a physical address.

As long as the destination IP address is local, ARP performs a local broadcast for that machine and returns the physical address to IP. IP, realizing that the destination IP address is local, simply formulates the datagram with the IP address above the physical address of the destination machine.

A problem occurs, however, when the ARP needs to resolve an address that is on a remote network. Because ARP operates so closely to the Network Access layer, it is really only good for finding local physical addresses—even in environments where routers exist. ARP never reports a physical address that exists on a remote network to IP.

To send a packet to another network, the router is required to listen to the packet and forward it. The only way for the router to listen to the packet is to either do a broadcast or send the packet to the router's physical address. IP is intelligent enough to realize that the destination IP address is on a remote network and that the datagram must be sent to the router. To send the packet to the router, ARP must be used to determine the physical address of the router.

When routing packets, IP asks ARP whether it has the physical address of the router, not of the destination machine. This technique is one of the more subtle and elegant features of the TCP/IP suite in that it cleverly redirects packets based on the layer that is being communicated with. After IP receives the physical address of the router from ARP, IP formulates the datagram, placing the destination IP address directly above the router's physical address.

Under Windows NT, ARP can be used directly via the ARP command. This command is valid for viewing the ARP table, adding static entries, and manually determining the hardware address of another system. Note that addresses are automatically added to the ARP table; however, each entry is valid for only ten minutes.

A twist on the ARP protocol is its counterpart Reverse Address Resolution Protocol (RARP). RARP works in a manner opposite of ARP in that it converts physical addresses to IP addresses rather than the other way around.

19. During the troubleshooting of a problem, you take a *trace* (capture the network traffic) to discover what is going on. As you are analyzing the packets, you discover a "redirect" packet that appears to have come from a router. Which protocol can generate such a packet?

D. Internet Control Message Protocol

19. CORRECT ANSWER: D

The Internet Control Message Protocol (ICMP) can generate the packet described. Although ICMP is typically used for diagnostic purposes, this protocol is also known to be used to validate paths.

Internet Control Message Protocol (ICMP)

ICMP is part of the Internet layer and is responsible for reporting errors and messages regarding the delivery of IP datagrams. It can also send "source quench" and other self-tuning signals during the transfer of data between two machines without the intervention of the user. These signals are designed to fine-tune and optimize the transfer of data automatically. ICMP is the protocol that warns you when a destination host is unreachable or informs you how long it took to get to a destination host.

ICMP messages can be broken down into two basic categories: error messages and general queries. Error messages include the following:

- **Destination unreachable**—ICMP generates the destination unreachable error message when an IP datagram is sent out and the destination machine either cannot be located or does not support the designated protocol. For instance, a sending machine may receive a destination host unreachable message when trying to communicate through a router that does not know to which network to send a datagram.
- **Redirect**—The first important thing to realize about redirect messages is that these are sent only by routers in a TCP/IP environment, not individual machines. A machine may have more than one default gateway defined for redundancy. If a router detects a better route to a particular destination, it forwards the first packet it receives but sends a redirect message to the machine to update its route tables. In this way, the machine can use the better route to reach the remote network.

- `Source quench`—Sometimes a machine has to drop incoming datagrams because it has received too many to process. In this case, a machine can send a source quench message to the source, telling the source to slow down transmission. The source quench message can also be sent by a router between the source and destination machines that is having trouble routing all the packets in time. Upon receiving a source quench message, the source machine immediately reduces its transmissions. However, it continues to try to increase the amount of data to the original quantity.
- `Time exceeded`—The time exceeded error message is sent by a router whenever it drops a packet because the TTL expired. This error message is sent to the source address to notify the machine of a possible infinite routing loop or that the TTL is set too low to get to the destination.

ICMP also includes general message queries. The two most commonly used are the following:

- Echo request
- Echo reply

The most familiar tool for verifying that an IP address on a network actually exists is the *Packet Internet Groper (PING)* utility. This utility uses the ICMP echo request and reply mechanisms. The *echo request* is a simple directed datagram that asks for acknowledgment that a particular IP address exists on the network. If a machine with this IP address exists and receives the request, it is designed to send an ICMP *echo reply*. This reply is sent back to the destination address to notify the source machine of its existence. The PING utility reports the existence of the IP address and how long it took to get there. The PING utility is common to Windows NT and provides several options including the capability to extend the time of a PING timeout.

20. Which of the following explains Internet Group Management Protocol?

B. It allows a group of systems to act as one while receiving broadcast data.

20. CORRECT ANSWER: B

The Internet Group Management Protocol (IGMP) protocol is used in conjunction with class D network addresses to allow systems to receive broadcast data as a single unit.

Internet Group Management Protocol (IGMP)

IGMP is a protocol and set of specifications that enables machines to be added and removed from IP address groups, utilizing the class D range of addresses. IP allows the assignment of class D addresses to groups of machines so that they may receive broadcast data as one functional unit. Machines can be added and removed from these units or groups, or be members of multiple groups.

Most implementations of the TCP/IP protocol stack support IGMP on the local machine; however, routers designed to broadcast IGMP messages from one network to another are still in the experimental stage. Routers are designed to initiate queries for multicast groups on local network segments to determine whether they should be broadcasting on that segment. If at least one member of an IGMP group exists or responds with an IGMP response, the router processes IGMP datagrams and broadcasts them on the segment.

21. Which two communications protocols are present at the Host to Host layer of the DOD model?

B. TCP

D. UDP

21. CORRECT ANSWERS: B-D

TCP and UDP are the two protocols that are present at the Host to Host layer. These protocols provide connection- and connectionless-based services.

22. For what type of application is UDP more desirable than TCP?

B. Internet radio

22. CORRECT ANSWER: B

UDP is connectionless-based; therefore, if you missed a music note, for example, it would not matter. Its low overhead makes it extremely useful in such purposes.

DOD Layer 3—Host to Host

This third layer of the TCP/IP structure is used exclusively for two protocols: TCP and UDP. Although it would appear the TCP is the only protocol that is used, more often than not UDP is used as well. Each protocol serves a purpose and the suite would be incomplete without the capabilities of the other.

23. You're talking with a few of the programmers in your department about an application they are working on. They tell you it is designed to use a connection-oriented protocol to communicate over the network. Which protocol in the TCP/IP protocol suite provides connection-oriented communications?

A. Transmission Control Protocol

23. CORRECT ANSWER: A

The Transmission Control Protocol (TCP) is connection oriented. That is to say that where communication is established between two systems and a requirement exists such that they must be constantly linked, information will be sent through the TCP stack.

24. Kristin in the advertising department is writing a very important document in Word. She must transfer it immediately to the remote office. Which of the following protocols is the best protocol for this type of transfer?

C. Transmission Control Protocol

24. CORRECT ANSWER: C

The Transmission Control Protocol would be best for this type of transfer. The best feature about this transport is its guarantee of delivery. Unlike its counterpart (UDP), if data is sent via TCP, the sender is completely aware whether the destination system has received the message.

User Datagram Protocol (UDP)

UDP is a nonconnection-based protocol and does not require a session to be established between two machines before data is transmitted. UDP packets are still delivered to sockets or ports, just as they are in TCP. But because UDP does not create a session between machines, it cannot guarantee that packets will be delivered, delivered in order, or retransmitted if the packets are lost. Given the apparent unreliability of this protocol, you may wonder why UDP was developed.

One of the main reasons for its development is that sending a UDP datagram involves very little overhead. A UDP datagram has no synchronization parameters or priority options. It doesn't have to keep track of sequence numbers, retransmit timers, delayed acknowledgment timers, and retransmission of packets. All that exists is the source port, destination port, the length of the data, a checksum for verifying the header, and then the data. UDP is quick and extremely streamlined functionally; it's just not guaranteed. Therefore, UDP is perfect for communications that involve broadcasts, general announcements to the network, or real-time data.

Another good use for UDP is in streaming video and streaming audio. Not only does the nonguaranteed delivery of packets enable more data to be transmitted (because a broadcast has little to no overhead) but also the retransmission of a packet is pointless. In a streaming broadcast, users are more concerned with what's coming next than with trying to recover a packet or two that may not have made it. Compare the situation to listening to a music CD and a piece of dust gets stuck in one of the little grooves. The small omission is usually imperceptible; your ear barely notices and your brain probably filled in the gap for you. Imagine instead that your CD player decides to guarantee the delivery of that one piece of data that it can't quite get and ends up skipping and skipping indefinitely. This technique can definitely ruin your day; in fact, dealing with an occasional packet dropping out provides a much more fulfilling listening experience. Thankfully, UDP was developed for applications to use in this fashion.

Transmission Control Protocol (TCP)

TCP is a connection-based protocol and requires the establishment of a session before data is transmitted between two machines. TCP packets are delivered to sockets or ports. Because TCP sets up a connection between two machines, it is designed to verify that all packets sent by a machine are received on the other end. If, for some reason, packets are lost, the transmitting machine resends the data. Because a session is established and delivery of packets is guaranteed, using TCP to transmit packets involves additional overhead. Also, because communications is two way, a technology known as sliding windows, discussed later in this chapter, is used.

The structure of TCP is similar to that of a phone call. Each participant is aware of the connection to the other (as in connection-based), the listening party acknowledges the receipt of information, and usually there is a window of opportunity for each party to communicate back (as in sliding windows). The key points to remember are that TCP/IP is connection-oriented and each packet received is acknowledged. Each of the features of TCP is discussed in the following sections.

Connection-Orientation Communication

TCP is a connection-based protocol that establishes a connection, or *session*, between two machines before any data is transferred. TCP exists within the Transport layer, between the Application layer and the IP layer, providing a reliable and guaranteed delivery mechanism to a destination machine. Connection-based protocols guarantee the delivery of packets by tracking the transmission and receipt of individual packets during communication. A session is able to track the progress of individual packets by monitoring when a packet is sent, in what order it was sent, and by notifying the sender when the packet is received so the sender can send more.

The first step in the communication process is to send a message indicating a desire to synchronize the systems. This step is equivalent to dialing a phone number and waiting for someone to answer. The second step is for the machine to send an acknowledgment that it is listening and willing to accept data. This step is equivalent to a person answering the phone and then waiting for the caller to say something. The third step is for the calling machine to send a message indicating that it understands the receiving machine's willingness to listen and that data transmission will begin now. This is equivalent to the caller having the understanding that the person on the other side has time to talk (as opposed to hearing, "I can't talk now, call me back later.").

After the TCP session has been created, the machines begin to communicate just as people do during a phone call. In the example of the telephone, if the caller uses a cellular phone and some of the transmission is lost, the user indicates she did not receive the message by saying, "What did you say? I didn't hear that." This message tells the sender to resend the data.

Included in the header are sections defining the sequence numbers and acknowledgment numbers that help verify the delivery of a datagram. A datagram or packet is simply the data that is being transferred to the destination machine. This data often has to be broken up into smaller pieces (datagrams) because the underlying network can transmit only a limited amount of data at one time.

Other parameters include the `SYN` and `FIN` options for starting and ending communication sessions between two machines, the size of the window to be used in transferring data, a checksum for verifying the header information, and other options that can be specific implementations of TCP/IP.

The last part of the frame is the actual data being transmitted. A full discussion of these parameters is beyond the scope of this book or the TCP/IP test. More academic texts and Requests for Comment (RFCs) on the Internet describe in fuller detail the specifications for each parameter.

The initialization of a TCP session is often called the *three-way handshake.* Both machines agree on the best method to track how much data is to be sent at any one time, acknowledgment numbers to be sent upon receipt of data, and when the connection is no longer necessary because all data has been transmitted and received. It is only after this session is created that data transmission begins. To provide reliable delivery, TCP places packets in sequenced order and requires acknowledgments that these packets reached their destination before it sends new data. TCP is typically used for transferring large amounts of data or when the application requires acknowledgment that data has been received. Given all the additional overhead information that TCP needs to keep track of, the format of a TCP packet can be somewhat complex.

25. As far as communications are concerned, why are sliding windows and acknowledgments important to TCP/IP?

B. Sliding windows are used to allow a buffer and time frame for a system to communicate, whereas acknowledgments certify that a message has been received correctly.

25. CORRECT ANSWER: B

Sliding windows are used to increase communications efficiency; acknowledgments are used to certify communications.

Sliding Windows

TCP uses the concept of *sliding windows* for transferring data between machines. In the UNIX environment, sliding windows are often referred to as *streams*. Each machine has both a send window and a receive window that it uses to buffer data and make the communication process more efficient. A window represents the subset of data that is currently being sent to a destination machine and is also the amount of data that is being received by the destination machine. At first, this method seems redundant, but it really isn't. Not all data that is sent is guaranteed to be received, so both machines must keep track of the data. A sliding window allows a sending machine to send the window data in a stream without having to wait for an acknowledgment for every single packet.

A receiving window allows a machine to receive packets out of order and reorganize them while it waits for more packets. Reorganization may be necessary because TCP uses IP to transmit data, and IP does not guarantee the orderly delivery of packets. By default, window sizes in Windows NT are a little more than 8KB, representing eight standard Ethernet frames. Standard Ethernet frames are a little more than 1KB apiece.

Packets do not always make it to their destination, however. TCP has been designed to recover in the event that packets are lost along the way, perhaps by busy routers. TCP keeps track of the data that has been sent out, and if it doesn't receive an acknowledgment for that data from the destination machine in a certain amount of time, the data is re-sent. In fact, until acknowledgment for a packet of data is received, further data transmission is halted completely.

Acknowledgments

Acknowledgments ensure the reliable delivery of packets. As the receiving window receives packets, it sends acknowledgments to tell the sending window that the packets arrived intact. When the sending window receives acknowledgments for data it has sent, it slides the window to the right so that it can send any additional data stored in memory. But it can slide over only by the number of acknowledgments it has received. By default, a receive window sends an acknowledgment for every two sequenced packets it receives.

As long as the acknowledgments begin flowing back regularly from the receiving machine, data flows smoothly and efficiently. However, on busy networks, packets can get lost and acknowledgments may be delayed. Because TCP guarantees delivery and reliability of traffic flow, the window cannot slide past any data that has not been acknowledged. If the window cannot slide beyond a packet of data, no more data beyond the window is transmitted, TCP eventually has to shut down the session, and the communication fails.

Each machine is therefore instructed to wait a certain amount of time before either retransmitting data or sending acknowledgments for packets that arrive out of sequence. Each window is given a timer: The send window has the retransmit timer and the receive window has the delayed acknowledgment timer. These timers help define what to do when communication isn't flowing very smoothly.

In the sending window, a retransmit timer is set for each packet, specifying how long to wait for an acknowledgment before assuming that the packet did not get to its destination. After this timer has expired, the send window is instructed to resend the packet and wait twice as long as the time set on the preceding timer. The default starting point for this timer is approximately three seconds but is usually reduced to less than a second almost immediately.

Each time an acknowledgment is not received, the retransmit timer doubles. For instance, if the retransmit timer started at approximately one second, the second retransmit timer is set for two seconds, the third for four seconds, and the fourth for eight seconds, up to a fifth attempt that waits 16 seconds. The number of attempts can be altered in the Registry, but if after these attempts an acknowledgment still cannot be received, the TCP session is closed and errors are reported to the application.

In the receiving window, a delayed acknowledgment timer is set for those packets that arrive out of order. Remember, by default an acknowledgment is sent for every two sequenced packets, starting from the left side of the window. If packets arrive out of order (if, for instance, packets 1 and 3 arrive but packet 2 is missing), an acknowledgment for two sequenced packets is not possible. When packets arrive out of order, a delayed acknowledgment timer is set on the first packet in the pair.

In the preceding example, a timer is set on packet 1. The delayed acknowledgment timer is hard-coded for 200 milliseconds, or one-fifth the retransmit timer. If packet 2 does not show up before the delayed acknowledgment timer expires, an acknowledgment for packet 1, and only packet 1, is sent. No other acknowledgments are sent, including those for packets 3 through 8 that might have appeared. Until packet 2 arrives, the other packets are considered interesting but useless. As data is acknowledged and passed to the Application layer, the receive window slides to the right, enabling more data to be received. Again, though, if a packet doesn't show up, the window is not enabled to slide past it.

26. With many TCP/IP applications running simultaneously, how does TCP/IP know which application to send inbound data to?

B. By port and socket

26. CORRECT ANSWER: B

The port and socket information is used to determine communication internal to the TCP/IP stack to applications.

DOD Layer 4—Process/Application

A variety of protocol utilities function at the application layer of the DOD model. These applications include (but are not limited to) Line Printer Daemon, Simple Mail Transport Protocol, Telnet, File Transfer Protocol, Network Filing System, X Window, Gopher Services, and WWW. Each utility or application at this layer functions by defining its usage according to a port number assignment. Before proceeding further, it is necessary that you have an understanding of how these applications function via ports and how a developer can create applications without the concern of the underlying infrastructure through the use of APIs, Sockets, and WinSocks.

Ports and Sockets

The communication process between the Transport layer and the Application layer involves identifying the application that has requested either a reliable or unreliable transport mechanism. Port assignments are the means used to identify application processes to the Transport layer. Ports identify to which process on the machine data should be sent for further processing. Specific port numbers have been assigned, specifically those from 1 to 1023, by the Internet Assigned Numbers Authority (IANA). These port assignments are called the *well-known ports* and represent the ports to which standard applications listen. An example of commonly known ports includes the following:

TABLE 1.1 COMMONLY KNOWN PORTS

1 *service name*	*2* *port #/protocol*	*3* *aliases*	*4* *#comment*
echo	7/tcp		
echo	7/udp		
discard	9/tcp	sink null	
discard	9/udp	sink null	
systat	11/tcp		
systat	11/tcp	users	
daytime	13/tcp		
daytime	13/udp		
netstat	15/tcp		
qotd	17/tcp	quote	
qotd	17/udp	quote	
chargen	19/tcp	ttytst source	
chargen	19/udp	ttytst source	
ftp-data	20/tcp		
ftp	21/tcp		
telnet	23/tcp		
smtp	25/tcp	mail	
time	37/tcp	timserver	
time	37/udp	timserver	

1	*2*	*3*	*4*
service name	***port #/protocol***	***aliases***	***#comment***
rlp	39/udp	resource	# resource location
name	42/tcp	nameserver	
name	42/udp	nameserver	
whois	43/tcp	nicname	# usually to sri-nic
domain	53/tcp	nameserver	# name-domain server
domain	53/udp	nameserver	
nameserver	53/tcp	domain	# name-domain server
nameserver	53/udp	domain	
mtp	57/tcp	# deprecated	
bootp	67/udp	# boot program server	
tftp	69/udp		
rje	77/tcp	netrjs	
finger	79/tcp		

Regardless of platform or implementation of TCP/IP, a list of these ports can typically be found in the `services` file. In the case of Windows NT, this file is located in `%Systemroot%\SYSTEM32\DRIVERS\ETC`. Note that format of the services file typically uses the following template:

```
# Format:
# <service name>  <port number>/<protocol>
➥[aliases...]   [#<comment>]
```

▼ NOTE

Note that any material on a line that follows a pound symbol (#) is always noted as a comment.

Defining these standard port numbers helps eliminate guessing to which port an application is listening so that applications can direct their queries or messages directly. Port numbers above the well-known port range are available for running applications, and work in exactly the same way. In this case, however, the client or user must be able to identify to which port the application is connecting. Ports can be used by both TCP and UDP for delivering data between two machines. Ports themselves do not care whether the data they receive is in order or not, but the applications running on those ports might.

To identify both the location and application to which a stream of data needs to be sent, the IP address (location) and the port number (application) are often combined into one functional address called a *socket*. Sockets are described further in the following section.

27. Which of the following is not a Network API?

D. NetBEUI

27. CORRECT ANSWER: D

NetBEUI is a transport protocol. Although it does accept data, it is not, in a local sense of the other options in the list, an equal API as much as it is a service.

The Network APIs, Windows Sockets, and NetBIOS

The Application layer provides the interface between applications and the transport protocols. Microsoft supports two APIs for applications to use: Windows Sockets and NetBIOS. This functionality is included because Microsoft networks still use NetBIOS for much of the internal networking within the Windows NT operating system. It is also used because it provides a standard interface to a number of other protocols. TCP/IP, NetBEUI, and NWLink all have a NetBIOS interface to which applications can be written to use networking protocols. Strict UNIX flavors of TCP/IP may not support the NetBIOS interface and may support only Windows Sockets as their API; Microsoft's implementation of TCP/IP therefore includes support for both.

The Windows Sockets interface defines an industry-standard specification for how Windows applications communicate with the TCP/IP protocol. Derived from the UNIX version known as SOCKS (4.3a), this specification contains definitions for how to use the transport protocols and how to transfer data between two machines, including the establishment of connection-oriented sessions (TCP three-way handshake) and nonconnection-oriented datagrams (broadcasts). The Windows Sockets API also defines how to uniquely address packets destined for a particular application on another machine.

The concept of a *socket* (the combination of the TCP/IP address and the port number) is a common example of the relative ease of uniquely identifying a communications path. Because of the ease and standardization of the Windows Sockets specifications, this API is enjoying a tremendous amount of exposure and success, particularly in Internet applications.

▼ NOTE

Do not confuse a socket with the UNIX Sockets API. The Sockets API is a programming interface, whereas a socket is used to uniquely identify a program running on a network.

Windows Sockets uniquely identify machines through their IP address, so machine names in the TCP/IP environment are entirely optional. Given that it is tremendously more difficult for users to remember a hundred IP addresses than to remember some form of an alias for these machines, a name space was created to help identify machines on a TCP/IP network. A *name space* is a hierarchical naming scheme that uniquely identifies machine aliases to IP addresses.

This scheme allows two machines to have the same alias as long as the machines are in different domains. This approach is very useful for people, but it is entirely unnecessary for applications because they can use the IP address. However, this naming scheme enables you to use any alias you want to establish a connection to a particular machine. As long as the name resolution method (DNS, hosts file) returns a valid IP address, a communication path can be created. The IP address is what's most important.

With the NetBIOS API, the IP address is only part of the information necessary to establish communication between two machines, and the name of the machine is required.

The NetBIOS API was developed on local area networks and has evolved into a standard interface for applications to use to access networking protocols in the Transport layer for both connection-oriented and nonconnection-oriented communications. NetBIOS interfaces have been written for the NetBEUI, NWLink, TCP/IP, and other protocols so that applications need not worry about which protocol is providing the transport services. (Any protocol that NT uses will have a Transport Driver Interface to translate between the NetBIOS world of NT and the native abilities of the protocol.) Because each of these protocols supports the NetBIOS API, all the functionality for establishing sessions and initiating broadcasts is provided. Unlike Windows Sockets, NetBIOS requires not only an IP address to uniquely identify a machine but a NetBIOS name as well.

Every machine on a network must be uniquely identified with a NetBIOS name. This name is required for establishing a NetBIOS session or sending out a broadcast. When using names through a NetBIOS session, the sending machine must be able to resolve the NetBIOS name to an IP address. Because both an IP address and name are needed, all name resolution methods have to supply the correct IP address before successful communication can occur.

The Microsoft TCP/IP stack supports connection-oriented and nonconnection-oriented communications established through either of these popular APIs. Microsoft includes *NetBT* (NetBIOS over TCP/IP) for applications that want to use the NetBIOS API over a TCP/IP network. This small, seemingly insignificant piece of software prevents your machine from having to run two protocols, one for Windows Sockets and one for NetBIOS. By providing NetBT with Microsoft's TCP/IP protocol stack, all NetBIOS calls an application may initiate are supported.

PRACTICE QUESTIONS

GIVEN A SCENARIO, SELECT THE APPROPRIATE SERVICES TO INSTALL WHEN USING MICROSOFT TCP/IP ON A WINDOWS NT SERVER COMPUTER

1. **To install TCP/IP support on Windows NT Server 4.0, which utility in the Control Panel must you select?**

   A. Services

   B. System

   C. Network

   D. Hardware

2. **After having chosen the utility in question 1, which tab must you then select?**

   A. Protocols

   B. Adapter

   C. Bindings

   D. Information

3. **When manually configuring TCP/IP, which of the following fields are required entries? Select two.**

   A. IP address

   B. TCP address

   C. Subnet mask

   D. Default gateway

4. **IIS enables you to share information with any type of computer that can use the TCP/IP protocol. IIS includes which three servers?**

   A. FTP

   B. Gopher

   C. SMTP

   D. WWW

5. **Which server enables you to share your printers with UNIX-based hosts?**

   A. Dynamic Host Configuration Protocol

   B. Line Printer Daemon

   C. DHCP relay agent

   D. WINS

   E. SNMP

6. **Which server provides automatic configuration of remote hosts?**

   A. Dynamic Host Configuration Protocol

   B. Line Printer Daemon

   C. DHCP relay agent

   D. WINS

7. **Selecting which service prevents you from needing to supply TCP/IP configuration information?**

   A. WINS

   B. DNS

   C. DHCP

   D. PDC

8. What is the primary purpose of the DHCP relay agent?

A. To provide name resolution

B. To track TCP/IP performance

C. To extend the DHCP service across subnets

D. To allow UNIX-based hosts to print on Windows NT printers

9. What does the SNMP acronym stand for?

A. System Network Monitoring Protocol

B. Simple Network Monitoring Protocol

C. System Network Management Protocol

D. Simple Network Management Protocol

10. Which service should you use to track the performance of your TCP/IP protocols?

A. Dynamic Host Configuration Protocol

B. Line Printer Daemon

C. DHCP relay agent

D. SNMP

11. Which service resolves host names to IP addresses?

A. DNS

B. DHCP

C. WINS

D. BDC

12. Which service resolves NetBIOS names to IP addresses?

A. DNS

B. DHCP

C. WINS

D. BDC

13. Which server provides a centralized method of name management?

A. Dynamic Host Configuration Protocol

B. Line Printer Daemon

C. DHCP relay agent

D. WINS

14. Which add-on service can be used to automatically route data between Windows NT with multiple network adapters and existing routers?

A. DNS

B. RIP

C. WINS

D. SNMP

15. Which of the following allows remote users to access the network via dial-up connection?

A. RAS

B. Line Printer Daemon

C. DHCP relay agent

D. RIP

ANSWER KEY

1. C
2. A
3. A-C
4. A-B-D
5. B
6. A
7. C
8. C
9. D
10. D
11. A
12. C
13. D
14. B
15. A

ANSWERS & EXPLANATIONS

GIVEN A SCENARIO, SELECT THE APPROPRIATE SERVICES TO INSTALL WHEN USING MICROSOFT TCP/IP ON A WINDOWS NT SERVER COMPUTER

1. To install TCP/IP support on Windows NT Server 4.0, which utility in the Control Panel must you select?

C. Network

1. CORRECT ANSWER: C

Begin installation from the Network icon in the Control Panel. When you double-click this icon, you are able to modify the installed network services, protocols, network adapters, bindings, and so on.

2. After having chosen the utility in question 1, which tab must you then select?

A. Protocols

2. CORRECT ANSWER: A

You must select the Protocols tab to add TCP/IP. After the Protocols tab is displayed, click ADD and select TCP/IP.

3. When manually configuring TCP/IP, which of the following fields are required entries? Select two.

A. IP address

C. Subnet mask

3. CORRECT ANSWERS: A-C

If a computer will be configured with static addresses, you must specify the IP address and Subnet mask fields. This assumes that you are communicating to the local network only. If the question had asked you to select three, you would also include the default gateway, which is required to communicate to different networks.

4. IIS enables you to share information with any type of computer that can use the TCP/IP protocol. IIS includes which three servers?

A. FTP

B. Gopher

D. WWW

4. CORRECT ANSWERS: A-B-D

IIS includes FTP, Gopher, and WWW servers. Note that IIS 4.0 no longer includes the Gopher service; however, Microsoft has added NNTP (News) and SMTP (Mail). For the TCP/IP exam, you will not be required to know IIS in detail. For this reason, further explanation is left to the IIS TestPrep books.

5. Which server enables you to share your printers with UNIX-based hosts?

B. Line Printer Daemon

5. CORRECT ANSWER: B

The Line Printer Daemon (LPD) enables you to share your printers with UNIX-based hosts. By using this service, the NT system emulates the printer service that is typically available under UNIX.

Line Printer Daemon (LPD)

Line Printer Daemon (LPD) enables you to share your printers with many different types of hosts, including mainframes and UNIX-based hosts. This service allows an administrator to directly communicate with a network printer that utilizes a TCP/IP address. This service is extremely important for integration; however, in NetBIOS-based networks, or when working with network printers that connect with other protocols such as DLC, the LPD service is not worthy of installation.

6. Which service provides automatic configuration of remote hosts?

A. Dynamic Host Configuration Protocol

6. CORRECT ANSWER: A

DHCP provides automatic configuration of remote hosts. DHCP has many requirements, including support by the network hardware itself. However, after DHCP is configured, this service eliminates a number of problems traditionally inherent to manually assigning addresses.

7. Selecting which service prevents you from needing to supply TCP/IP configuration information?

C. DHCP

7. CORRECT ANSWER: C

The DHCP service prevents you from needing to manually enter TCP/IP configuration information. In order to use this setting, you must have a DHCP server configured with the proper information and valid addresses.

8. What is the primary purpose of the DHCP relay agent?

C. To extend the DHCP service across subnets

8. CORRECT ANSWER: C

The DHCP relay agent extends the capabilities of the DHCP service by allowing it to work across various subnets. This service is required when you have a router that does not forward DHCP/BOOTP requests.

Dynamic Host Configuration Protocol (DHCP)

Dynamic Host Configuration Protocol (DHCP) is a service for automatically configuring IP information for clients. This service works well for practically any environment. When working with DHCP, administrators typically experience fewer configuration problems with nodes getting assigned wrong information;

however, if the DHCP server were to fail, after the lease period of an address expires, users would no longer be able to communicate with one another. Typically, a server can be placed back into service, or the DHCP service can be added to a different server. This is not a painless process, however; switching servers can have problems with duplicate address issues if a different or reserved range is not available. If, while planning your network, you find that you have very few machines, or many that require special configurations, such as differing DNS information, multiple IP addresses to a single network interface card, and so forth, this service may not be desirable. The type of environment in which DHCP would not be beneficial usually is comprised of few users and few workstations. In most cases, DHCP is a must.

9. What does the SNMP acronym stand for?

D. Simple Network Management Protocol

9. CORRECT ANSWER: D

One problem that most people who are new to TCP/IP experience is acronym translation. People often confuse SNMP with SMTP and assume that it stands for Simple Network Mail Protocol or something of the sort. Considering that the Microsoft exam will use acronyms as if they were words, you should be able to recognize them.

10. Which service should you use to track the performance of your TCP/IP protocols?

D. SNMP

10. CORRECT ANSWER: D

SNMP is used to track the performance of your TCP/IP protocols. It should be used to ensure that a network is not reaching capacity, to judge expansion, and to assist in avoiding and detecting faults.

Simple Network Management Protocol (SNMP)

Simple Network Management Protocol (SNMP) is an add-on agent that allows Windows NT to report information to a Management program such as Open View, Net View, and so on. This service is very important in the management of devices in larger environments. Typically, smaller and midsize firms will not find much value in using this service.

However, after a network grows beyond 100 users or five servers, most administrators find that SNMP reduces the amount of effort that they must commit to guaranteeing service levels.

11. Which service resolves host names to IP addresses?

A. DNS

11. CORRECT ANSWER: A

The DNS server resolves host names to IP addresses. This service can be thought of as a centralized hierarchical version of the HOSTS file. With the DNS service, only one location is required to be maintained. Also, if you're using the Microsoft implementation of the DNS, it can work with WINS to use a reverse lookup (using WINS).

Domain Name Server (DNS)

Domain Name Server (DNS) is a hierarchical name-resolution system. Whereas the WINS server enables you to find NetBIOS names, the DNS server works with host names, which means that you can integrate your systems into the Internet or resolve hosts on the Internet. This service is great for integrating with other platforms such as UNIX, in which you a have a number of workstations. However, in smaller to mid-size networks where there are only one to five systems that are addressed by their host names, usually this service is not very effective. For example, a company that is based on a Microsoft Network that has two UNIX servers would probably be best off to use a host file at the workstation or perhaps using WINS with static entries (it is a host name). The host file, for example, could be updated via a login script. The exception to the decision of using a DNS is if you are connecting to the Internet and want to have a local DNS either for direct control of your own server's IP address publication, or if you are attempting to get better name resolution performance.

12. Which service resolves NetBIOS names to IP addresses?

C. WINS

12. CORRECT ANSWER: C

The WINS server resolves NetBIOS names to IP addresses. However, the requirement is that clients must be configured to register themselves with a WINS server. If multiple WINS servers are involved, these servers must replicate their databases to ensure full resolution support.

13. Which server provides a centralized method of name management?

D. WINS

13. CORRECT ANSWER: D

WINS server provides a centralized method of name management that is both flexible and dynamic. Although LMHOSTS performs the resolution of NetBIOS names, WINS is more up-to-date when configured for an entire network and is easier to manage. Unlike LMHOSTS, which is a flat file processed by a client, WINS is an active service that maintains a database that is processed by the server hosting the WINS service.

Windows Internet Name Service (WINS)

Windows Internet Name Service (WINS) is a service for locating resources on the network and resolving NetBIOS names to IP addresses. This service is used in mid- to large-sized network environments, but may optionally be used by smaller ones as well. WINS' key efficiency is in reducing network traffic by providing a single location by which clients can find resource information. WINS' information is dynamically updated by clients and requires minimal administrative support.

This service eliminates the need of sending every system on a network a message to report on their available service and resources. In smaller networks where only a single segment exists, that is perhaps 10 to 20 workstations, this service is not very useful.

14. Which add-on service can be used to automatically route data between Windows NT with multiple network adapters and existing routers?

B. RIP

14. CORRECT ANSWER: B

Router Information Protocol (RIP)

Router Information Protocol (RIP) for IP is a service by which a multihomed Windows NT server can be configured as a router that shares information with other routers. This service is beneficial when other routers exist that are also running RIP. However, if other routers are configured with other routing protocols such as OSPF, IGRP, EGRP, static, and so on, this protocol will serve no purpose. If a network contains no other routers, then this service is not very useful, either. If your network is completely routed by Windows NT with static tables, and is near a level of complexity that tables are a chore for an administrator to configure, however, this service can be quite useful.

15. Which of the following allows remote users to access the network via dial-up connection?

A. RAS

15. CORRECT ANSWER: A

Remote Access Service (RAS)

Remote Access Service (RAS) provides dial-up networking and remote access service to clients. This service is extremely useful in smaller companies for traveling users and in mid- to large-size companies that have light loads on this service. RAS functions by allowing users to connect their systems via dial-up connection such that their workstations will appear to the network as if they were physically connected to it. This is not the same as a remote control functionality such as with Symantec's PC Anywhere and others of the sort. As the number of users increases, this service tends to lose its functionality. Although RAS can be extended with devices such as DIGI PORTS (which provides additional serial ports), typically environments that require large numbers of users to have simultaneous access are better with products such as Shiva's LAN rover or Cisco's Access Server, for example.

FURTHER REVIEW

INTRODUCTION TO TCP/IP—BASIC THEORY

TCP/IP is an industry-standard suite of protocols designed to be routable, robust, and functionally efficient. TCP/IP was originally designed as a set of WAN protocols for the express purpose of maintaining communication links and data transfer between sites in the event of an atomic/nuclear war. Since those early days, development of the protocols has passed from the hands of the U.S. Government to the Internet community.

The evolution of these protocols from a small four-site project into the foundation of the worldwide Internet has been extraordinary. But despite more than 25 years of work and numerous modifications to the protocol suite, the inherent spirit of the original specifications is still intact.

Planning

When installing the TCP/IP protocol, you have the choice of installing and using several different services that work with it. The following table describes the services that you may want or need to install:

TCP/IP Component	*Purpose*	*Details*
Internet Information Server (IIS)	FTP, WWW, and Gopher Server services	Covered in its own certification exam.
Windows Internet Naming Service (WINS)	Used in the resolution of NetBIOS names and network browsing	Chapter 3
Domain Name Server (DNS)	Used in the resolution of host names	Chapter 4
Dynamic Host Configuration Protocol (DHCP)	Used to automatically configure TCP/IP clients and devices	Chapter 5
IP Router Information Protocol (RIP)	Allows Windows NT to act as an automatically configuring router in RIP environments	Chapter 6
Line Printer Daemon (LPD)	Supports printing in TCP/IP-based environments	Chapter 7
Remote Access Service (RAS)	Provides dial-up and remote network connectivity	Chapter 8
Simple Network Management Protocol (SNMP)	Used to gather statistics and manage network components and devices	Chapter 9

CHAPTER SUMMARY

This chapter discussed a number of technologies and theories that are key to your understanding of the TCP/IP protocol suite. While Microsoft does not address any part of this chapter directly to its test objectives, rest assured that these items will be the foundation upon which all the objectives will come together.

When reviewing the section on networking, the key points to remember are the wiring structures and the networking protocols. In short, Wiring Architecture + Hardware Protocol = Topology. Each component offers pros and cons. The best choice for a situation is unique to its environment. Obviously, if you favored a technology such as Ethernet and the environment was already running Token Ring, you would not rework the situation for one system.

As you look onward and are in the process of comparing the OSI and DOD models, it is important to focus on what happens at each layer and understand as a process why networking happens in that order. Regardless of which model you look at, you will find that they both follow a similar pattern.

Finally, TCP/IP basics provide the key components to the lowest level of operations in networking. While it would appear that there is a widespread amount of information present, realize that these are the tools that are necessary to connect machines of different operating systems together. Do not overlook the TCP/IP utilities and technologies by comparing them to other protocols such as IPX.

Remember that TCP/IP is a way to connect different operating systems independently, whereas a technology such as IPX has many of its utilities embedded directly into the operating system that it supports. A classic example would include copying a file from a remote site. With TCP/IP, the technology is File Transfer Protocol (FTP), but with IPX, it must have a shell or redirector to convert the `COPY` command to the foreign system. This is not practical when the command is valid only on filing systems of a homogeneous variety.

CHAPTER REVIEW

REVIEW QUESTIONS

Note: The additional Chapter Review section that ends each chapter is unique to this member of the *New Riders TestPrep, Second Edition* series. We've included it to more fully and fairly cover the unique aspects of TCP/IP in relation to its mastery in preparation for the MCSE examination.

1. **In your environment, you have a Windows NT machine that seems to not be responding to PING requests using an IP address. You want to make sure that the machine's configuration is appropriate for the network. Which of the following options would you need to check?**

   A. IP address

   B. Subnet mask

   C. Default gateway

   D. DNS

2. **You've noticed a significant increase in the amount of time it takes to reach your remote offices. You think one of your routers may not be functioning. Which utility would you use to find the pathway a packet takes to reach its destination?**

   A. WINS

   B. DNS

   C. TRACERT

   D. Network monitor

3. **You have a machine that seems to be able to communicate with other machines on its same local subnet, but whenever you try to reach destinations on a remote network, the communications fail. What is the most likely cause of the problem?**

   A. IP address

   B. Subnet mask

   C. Default gateway

   D. WINS

4. **You've set up a simple routed environment in which one router is central to three subnets, meaning that the router can see each of the three segments. No default gateway has been assigned because there doesn't seem to be any reason to do so. If a router doesn't know where to send a packet and no default gateway has been assigned, what will the router do with the packet?**

   A. Drop the packet

   B. Store the packet for later processing

   C. Broadcast on the local network

   D. Use ARP to locate another pathway

5. **You want your Windows NT routers to share information on the network so that you don't have to continually update the route tables manually. What protocol do you need to install to allow this to happen?**

A. DNS

B. RIP

C. OSPF

D. WINS

6. Ten machines on your network have stopped communicating with other machines on remote network segments. The router seems to be working properly, but you want to make sure the route table has not been modified. What utilities can you use to view the route table on your Windows NT router?

A. Route

B. Netstat

C. PING

D. Rttable

7. Your environment consists of both LAN and WAN connections spread out over five continents. You've begun an expansion that has added a number of routers to your already large organization. Your network currently uses RIP as the routing protocol, but as new network segments are being added, routers on each end of your network insist that they can't see each other and that they are unreachable. What seems to be the problem?

A. The routers aren't made by Microsoft.

B. The RIP protocol can't share route table information.

C. The RIP protocol can't support more than 15 hops.

D. Routers aren't designed for WAN connections.

8. When installing and testing a brand-new Windows NT router, you notice that the router routes packets to any network to which it is physically attached but drops packets to networks (seven of them) to which it is not attached. What would be the easiest way to make sure the router performs its function for those other networks?

A. Disable IP routing.

B. Enable IP filtering on all ports.

C. Change the IP address bindings.

D. Add a default gateway.

9. After adding a network segment (131.107.7.0) for a new wing, you discover that your route tables need to be altered. In this case, you simply need to add a new entry for this segment, but you want to make sure that the entry survives a reboot. The gateway that will be servicing the route is 131.107.2.1. Which of the following commands would you choose for the addition?

A. `route change 131.107.2.0 131.107.7.0`

B. `route add 131.107.7.0 mask 255.255.255.0 131.107.2.1`

C. `route -p add 131.107.2.1 mask 255.255.255.0 131.107.7.0`

D. `route -p add 131.107.7.0 mask 255.255.255.0 131.107.2.1`

10. Last year, one of your major concerns was connectivity problems associated with having only one router in your environment that could route packets between subnets.

This year, your budget enabled you to add a second router to provide some backup for your primary router. Windows NT is smart enough to utilize dead gateway detection, but during your test of this feature, it didn't work at all. What might you have forgotten to configure for dead gateway detection to work?

A. Dead gateway detection must use RIP, so RIP must be installed on each router.

B. Each host machine must be configured with the IP addresses of both routers before dead gateway detection is used.

C. Static route table entries must be configured on the routers so that they can communicate with each other.

D. Every application must be individually tailored to perform dead gateway detection because they are initiating the communication.

11. **After checking a route table, you notice that it is missing a very important route to one of your network segments. Before you can add the route to your router's table, however, you need to know what pieces of information to use the route utility?**

A. Network ID

B. Netmask

C. MAC address

D. Gateway address

12. **Your organization uses primarily Microsoft operating systems and you want to provide reverse DNS lookup for the hosts in your organization for servers on the Internet. Your organization uses DHCP to assign IP addresses. How can you provide reverse lookup capabilities?**

A. Reserve a DHCP address for each client and enter this information into the DNS server.

B. Set up the clients to use DNS for WINS resolution.

C. Add an @ IN WINS record in the DNS database.

D. This is not possible.

13. **Your organization currently uses a UNIX server for DNS. The server is fully configured using BIND files. In which two ways can you configure your Microsoft DNS server so you will not need to reenter any information?**

A. Set up Microsoft DNS as the Primary and transfer the zone to the UNIX system.

B. Set up Microsoft DNS as the Secondary and transfer the zone from the UNIX system.

C. Configure the Microsoft DNS server as an IP Forwarder.

D. Configure the Microsoft DNS server as a Caching Only server.

14. **Which of the following is *not* part of a Fully Qualified Domain Name? Choose all that apply.**

A. Type of organization

B. Host name

C. Company name

D. CPU type

15. What are the benefits of DNS? Select all that apply.

A. It allows a distributed database that can be administered by a number of administrators.

B. It allows host names that specify where a host is located.

C. It allows WINS clients to register with the WINS server.

D. It allows queries to other servers to resolve host names.

16. With what non-Microsoft DNS platforms is Microsoft DNS compatible?

A. Only UNIX DNS servers that are based on BIND

B. Only UNIX DNS servers that are based on the DNS RFCs

C. UNIX DNS servers that are either BIND based or RFC based

D. Only other Microsoft DNS servers

17. In the DNS name `www.microsoft.com`, what does `microsoft` represent?

A. The last name of the host

B. The domain in which the host is located

C. The IP address of the building in which the host is located

D. The directory in which the host name file is located

ANSWER KEY

1. A-B-C
2. C
3. C
4. A
5. B
6. A-B
7. C
8. D
9. D
10. B
11. A-B-D
12. C
13. B-C
14. D
15. A-B-D
16. C
17. B

REVIEW ANSWERS

1. In your environment, you have a Windows NT machine that seems to not be responding to PING requests using an IP address. You want to make sure that the machine's configuration is appropriate for the network. Which of the following options would you need to check?

A. IP address

B. Subnet mask

C. Default gateway

1. CORRECT ANSWERS: A-B-C

The fact that the system is not responding might indicate a problem with the system itself. Assuming that you are able to successfully ping other systems, use IPCONFIG (Windows NT) or WINIPCFG (Windows 95/98) to review the IP address, subnet mask, and default gateway.

2. You've noticed a significant increase in the amount of time it takes to reach your remote offices. You think one of your routers may not be functioning. Which utility would you use to find the pathway a packet takes to reach its destination?

C. TRACERT

2. CORRECT ANSWER: C

When a network has multiple routes to a destination, it is often useful to know which path is used so that faults can be found. Use TRACERT to follow the progress of a packet as it is passed between points of your network. When the packet fails to go any further, check the router for a proper path to the destination system.

3. You have a machine that seems to be able to communicate with other machines on its same local subnet, but whenever you try to reach destinations on a remote network, the communications fail. What is the most likely cause of the problem?

C. Default gateway

3. CORRECT ANSWER: C

When your workstation can communicate locally but not remotely, the first thing to check is the default gateway. If missed, no remote communications can take place. As a secondary item, you should then check the subnet mask to verify that it matches that which is specified for that network. If a system is missed, it might think that a remote system is local and never send a packet to the gateway.

4. You've set up a simple routed environment in which one router is central to three subnets, meaning that the router can see each of the three segments. No default gateway has been assigned because there doesn't seem to be any reason to do so. If a router doesn't know where to send a packet and no default gateway has been assigned, what will the router do with the packet?

A. Drop the packet

4. CORRECT ANSWER: A

When a message is sent on a local network, it is broadcast to the capacity of the entire wire (unless switched). Any systems also attached to that cable will hear the message. If the message is not specifically destined for it, or a broadcast address, the message will be dropped.

5. You want your Windows NT routers to share information on the network so that you don't have to continually update the route tables manually. What protocol do you need to install to allow this to happen?

B. RIP

5. CORRECT ANSWER: B

Because you are working with Windows NT routers, your choices are limited to static or RIP. If, for example, these were Cisco routers, you might consider a different technology such as OSPF.

6. Ten machines on your network have stopped communicating with other machines on remote network segments. The router seems to be working properly, but you want to make sure the route table has not been modified. What utilities can you use to view the route table on your Windows NT router?

A. Route

B. Netstat

6. CORRECT ANSWERS: A-B

Either Netstat or Route has the capability to view the routing table. If any changes are to be made to the table, use the `route` command. The PING utility is excellent for verifying connectivity through the router. Rttable is not a valid Windows NT utility or command.

7. Your environment consists of both LAN and WAN connections spread out over five continents. You've begun an expansion that has added a number of routers to your already large organization. Your network currently uses RIP as the routing protocol, but as new network segments are being added, routers on each end of your network insist that they can't see each other and that they are unreachable. What seems to be the problem?

C. The RIP protocol can't support more than 15 hops.

7. CORRECT ANSWER: C

One of the key limitations of RIP is its inability to operate over 15 hops. For this reason, RIP is mainly designed as a small- to mid-size company solution. Although the hop limitation may seem unreasonable, this does prevent router loops and other router-related issues.

8. When installing and testing a brand-new Windows NT router, you notice that the router routes packets to any network to which it is physically attached but drops packets to networks (seven of them) to which it is not attached. What would be the easiest way to make sure the router performs its function for those other networks?

D. Add a default gateway.

8. CORRECT ANSWER: D

The problem with the router is not so much the problem of filters or bindings, but one of routing. Clearly, if some packets are passing, those that are not must be sent to the default gateway for further processing when no other path is defined.

9. After adding a network segment (131.107.7.0) for a new wing, you discover that your route tables need to be altered. In this case, you simply need to add a new entry for this segment, but you want to make sure that the entry survives a reboot. The gateway that will be servicing the route is 131.107.2.1. Which of the following commands would you choose for the addition?

D. `route -p add 131.107.7.0 mask 255.255.255.0 131.107.2.1`

9. CORRECT ANSWER: D

Using the `route` command, you want to permanently add the path of 131.107.7.0 by using a mask of 255.255.255.0, which should be serviced by 131.107.2.1. When building the command, first set the options, then the destination followed by the mask, and then complete the command by defining which address performs the servicing.

10. Last year, one of your major concerns was connectivity problems associated with having only one router in your environment that could route packets between subnets. This year, your budget enabled you to add a second router to provide some backup for your primary router. Windows NT is smart enough to utilize dead gateway detection, but during your test of this feature, it didn't work at all. What might you have forgotten to configure for dead gateway detection to work?

B. Each host machine must be configured with the IP addresses of both routers before dead gateway detection is used.

10. CORRECT ANSWER: B

The only way a dead gateway can be detected is if it is defined as a gateway at each router. In that way, if a failure can be found, the other gateway can take over for the dead partner.

11. After checking a route table, you notice that it is missing a very important route to one of your network segments. Before you can add the route to your router's table, however, you need to know what pieces of information to use the route utility?

A. Network ID

B. Netmask

D. Gateway address

11. CORRECT ANSWERS: A-B-D

You should recall that the `route` command is based upon sending information to a network which is defined by both the Network ID and Subnet or Netmask. Additionally, you must define which address will service this route (gateway address). Because ARP is used, the hardware address should be reasonably transparent to this type of operation and therefore not used.

12. Your organization uses primarily Microsoft operating systems and you want to provide reverse DNS lookup for the hosts in your organization for servers on the Internet. Your organization uses DHCP to assign IP addresses. How can you provide reverse lookup capabilities?

C. Add an @ IN WINS record in the DNS database.

12. CORRECT ANSWER: C

Microsoft offers a custom DNS feature for the reverse look-up feature that is designated at @ IN WINS. Using this designation, the Internet-based servers will query the Microsoft DNS, which then performs the reverse lookup. The Internet-based DNS will never be aware of the WINS service. Essentially, this functions as a reverse zone in the DNS server.

13. Your organization currently uses a UNIX server for DNS. The server is fully configured using BIND files. In which two ways can you configure your Microsoft DNS server so you will not need to reenter any information?

B. Set up Microsoft DNS as the Secondary and transfer the zone from the UNIX system.

C. Configure the Microsoft DNS server as an IP Forwarder.

13. CORRECT ANSWERS: B-C

The DNS server can be configured for zero maintenance by setting it as a Secondary or as an IP Forwarder. DNS servers that are set as Primary are the entry point for data for a given zone.

14. Which of the following is *not* part of a Fully Qualified Domain Name? Choose all that apply.

D. CPU type

14. CORRECT ANSWER: D

A fully qualified domain name includes the name of the host such as `WWW`, the domain or company name such as `MICROSOFT`, and the type of organization such as `COM` for company. When we combine our example, it reads `WWW.MICROSOFT.COM`.

15. What are the benefits of DNS? Select all that apply.

A. It allows a distributed database that can be administered by a number of administrators.

B. It allows host names that specify where a host is located.

D. It allows queries to other servers to resolve host names.

15. CORRECT ANSWERS: A-B-D

A DNS provides a hierarchical name resolution that allows for replication (zone transfers), and recursive lookups to other systems. This service is completely independent of WINS; however, DNS may be linked in Microsoft environments for reverse lookups.

16. With what non-Microsoft DNS platforms is Microsoft DNS compatible?

C. UNIX DNS servers that are either BIND based or RFC based

16. CORRECT ANSWER: C

The answer is truly inclusive of everything. If a DNS is BIND- or RFC-based for standardization of transfers and record types, the DNS is compatible. Based on a standard, it is obviously compatible with its own type as well.

17. In the DNS name `www.microsoft.com`, what does `microsoft` represent?

B. The domain in which the host is located

17. CORRECT ANSWER: B

A fully qualified domain name is specified as `HOST.DOMAIN.ORG`_type. In this case, `microsoft` is the company or domain name.

CHAPTER 2

Configuring Subnet Masks

As a network grows in size, it becomes less practical to maintain a single large network, and much more beneficial to design smaller ones. In the implementation of TCP/IP, smaller networks are defined as *subnets* or *subnetworks*. This chapter focuses on why you might want to divide your networks, how dividing a network provides better efficiency, and how these divided networks come together to appear as one.

In a logical sense, the Internet can be thought of as one big global-based network; however, it is actually several networks that have been combined to function together. Many of the networks that are linked to the Internet are actually collections of even smaller networks themselves. For example, a company such as Boeing may have a presence on the Internet with all subdivisions as **`Boeing.com`**. However, Boeing's networks also include the smaller networks of its subsidiaries, such as McDonnell Douglas, Rocketdyne, and so forth.

Clearly, you can see that the Internet is already divided. As a network is divided further, you will observe the capability for better management, less traffic, better performance, and less required equipment.

OBJECTIVE

This chapter helps you prepare for the exam by covering the following objective:

Configure subnet masks.

- This chapter reviews subnet masks and how they are configured.

PRACTICE QUESTIONS

CONFIGURE SUBNET MASKS

1. Given IP addresses that begin with 192, 127, 92, and 150, which of the following lists best describes classes of these networks?

A. Class C, Reserved, Class A, Class B

B. Class B, Class A, Class A, Class B

C. Class C, Class A, Class A, Class C

D. Reserved, Class A, Class D, Class B

2. What does 240 translate to in binary?

A. 11110000

B. 00011110

C. 00001111

D. 11100000

3. What does 224 translate to in binary?

A. 11110000

B. 00011110

C. 00001111

D. 11100000

4. What does 192 translate to in binary?

A. 11000000

B. 00111110

C. 00001111

D. 00000011

5. What part of 192.168.10.51 is the Network ID, assuming a default subnet mask?

A. 192

B. 192.168.10

C. 10.51

D. 51

6. When performing an Andding function on 192.168.10.5 and 255.255.255.0, what is the result?

A. 192.168.10.0

B. 192.168.10

C. 0.0.0.5

D. 447.423.265.5

7. Which of the following best illustrates the default subnet mask for a class A, B, and C Network?

A. 0.0.0.0, 0.0.0.1, 0.0.1.1

B. 255.255.255.0, 255.255.0.0, 255.0.0.0

C. 255.0.0.0, 255.255.0.0, 255.255.255.0

D. 255.255.0.0, 255.255.255.0, 255.255.255.255

8. **With an IP address of 201.142.23.12, what is your default subnet mask?**

 A. 0.0.0.0

 B. 255.0.0.0

 C. 255.255.0.0

 D. 255.255.255.0

9. **With an IP address starting at 200, you currently have 10 subnets. What subnet mask should you use to maximize the number of available hosts?**

 A. 192

 B. 224

 C. 240

 D. 248

 E. 252

10. **With an IP address of 100, you currently have 80 subnets. What subnet mask should you use to maximize the number of available hosts?**

 A. 192

 B. 224

 C. 240

 D. 248

 E. 252

11. **With an IP address of 100, you currently have only eight subnets, but anticipate adding two more subnets next year. What subnet mask should you use to maximize the number of available hosts?**

 A. 192

 B. 224

 C. 240

 D. 248

 E. 252

12. **With an IP address set starting with 150, you currently have six offices that you are treating as subnets. Plans are in place to open 10 more offices before the end of the year. What subnet mask should you use to satisfy the needed number of subnets and maximize the number of hosts available at each site?**

 A. 192

 B. 224

 C. 240

 D. 248

 E. 252

13. **On a class C network with a subnet mask of 192, how many hosts are available?**

 A. 254

 B. 62

 C. 30

 D. 14

 E. 2

14. **On a class C network with a subnet mask of 192, how many subnets are available?**

 A. 254

 B. 62

 C. 30

 D. 14

 E. 2

15. On a class B network, how many hosts are available at each site with a subnet mask of 248?

A. 16,382

B. 8,190

C. 4,094

D. 2,046

E. 1,022

16. On a class B network, how many subnets are available with a subnet mask of 248?

A. 2

B. 6

C. 30

D. 62

E. 126

ANSWER KEY

1. A	5. B	9. C	13. B
2. A	6. A	10. E	14. E
3. D	7. C	11. C	15. D
4. A	8. D	12. D	16. C

ANSWERS & EXPLANATIONS

CONFIGURE SUBNET MASKS

1. Given IP addresses that begin with 192, 127, 92, and 150, which of the following lists best describes classes of these networks?

A. Class C, Reserved, Class A, Class B

1. CORRECT ANSWER: A

The 192 falls in the class C range, 127 falls in the class A range, however is a reserved address, 92 is a class A network and 150 is a class B address. Note that if you converted these numbers to binary, you would observe a pattern such that anything that begins 0 is class A, 10 is class B, 110 is class C, and 1110 is class D.

2. What does 240 translate to in binary?

A. 11110000

2. CORRECT ANSWER: A

See explanation to question 4.

3. What does 224 translate to in binary?

D. 11100000

3. CORRECT ANSWER: D

See explanation to question 4.

4. What does 192 translate to in binary?

A. 11000000

4. CORRECT ANSWER: A

Subnet Masks, Host IDs, and Network IDs

Simply put, *subnetting* is a mechanism for using some bits in the host ID octets as a subnet-id. Without subnetting, an IP address is logically interpreted as two fields:

```
Network-id + Host-id
```

With subnetting, an IP address is logically interpreted as three fields:

```
Net-id + Subnet-id + Host-id
```

Subnets are created in a TCP/IP internetwork by applying a filter that is used to determine which part of an IP Address is a component of the network-id and which is part of the host-id. This process is commonly referred to as subnet addressing or subnetting.

▼ **NOTE**

The term *network* is used when it is not necessary to distinguish between individual subnets and internetworks. A *subnet* is simply a subdivision of a network. The term *subnetworking* or *subnetting* is used when a single network ID is subdivided into multiple network IDs by applying a custom subnet mask.

The subnet mask, like the IP address, is a 32-bit number often shown in dotted decimal notation. When shown in binary notation, the subnet mask has a 1 bit for each bit corresponding to the position of the network ID in the IP address, and a 0 bit for each bit corresponding to the position of the host ID in the IP Address (in binary notation). An example of a subnet mask is 11111111 11111111 00000000 00000000, which is 255.255.0.0 in dotted decimal notation.

A binary number is made up of bits. A bit can be either a 1 or a 0, in which 1 represents TRUE and 0 represents FALSE. All computer operations are performed by using binary numbers because the bits are easily represented by electrical charges. Huge binary numbers are usually fairly meaningless to the average person, so the computer converts them to more human-friendly states such as decimal numbers and characters.

Any decimal number can be represented in binary notation, using 1s and 0s. Each bit with a 1 represents 2 raised to the power of n–1 [2×(n–1)], where n is the position of the bit from the right. Each bit with a 0 represents a 0 in decimal notation as well. The decimal number results from adding together all the 1 bits after converting each to 2×(n–1).

(A binary conversion chart can be found in this chapter's "Further Review" section.)

For example, the binary number 100 is 2×2, which means the decimal equivalent is 4.

The binary number 101 would be 2×2 + 0 + 2×0, or 5 in decimal notation.

With TCP/IP, 8-bit binary numbers are often used in IP addresses, also called *octets* or *bytes*. The following is an example:

11111111

Each bit in position *n* from the right gives a value of $2\times(n\text{-}1)$. Therefore, the first bit represents a 1, the second bit a 2, the third a 4, the fourth an 8, and so on, so that you have the following representations:

1 1 1 1 1 1 1 1	(binary)
128+64+32+16+8+4+2+1 = 255	(decimal)

Keep in mind that any 0 bits do not add to the total, so the following representations are equal:

1 1 0 0 1 0 0 1	(binary)
128+64+0 +0 +8+0+0+1 = 201	(decimal)

Memorizing the decimal equivalent number of each character in the 8-bit number is much simpler. Remembering the value 201 is easier than remembering 11001001.

▼ NOTE

The following table is the Decimal to Binary positional values:

1	1	1	1	1	1	1	1
128	64	32	16	8	4	2	1

The preceding table makes it extremely easy to convert between binary and decimal quickly. Consider the following number:

01111111

This binary example should be easily recognized as 127, by taking the maximum value (255) and subtracting the missing digit (128). Likewise, consider this example:

11011111

This binary value is quickly converted to 223 by subtracting the value of the missing digit (32) from the maximum value (255).

The 0 bits of the subnet mask essentially mask out, or cover up, the host ID portion of an IP address. Thus, the subnet mask is used to determine on which network or subnet the address being referred to is found. When one host sends a message to another host, the TCP/IP protocol must determine whether the hosts are on the same subnet and can communicate by broadcasts or whether they are on different subnets and the message should be sent via a router to the other subnet. You cannot determine without the subnet mask whether two IP addresses are on the same subnet just by looking at the IP addresses. For example, if the host at 192.20.1.5 sends a message to the host at 192.20.6.8, you cannot determine whether it should be sent by broadcast or to a router connecting to another subnet.

The answer depends on the subnet mask being used on the network. Suppose the subnet mask is 255.255.255.0; then the network ID of the first host would be 192.20.1 and the network ID of the second host would be 192.20.6, which are on different subnets. Therefore, the two hosts must communicate via a router. On the other hand, if the subnet mask were 255.255.0.0, then both hosts would be on subnet 192.20 and could communicate by using local broadcasts and local address resolution.

When the subnet mask is one of 255.0.0.0, 255.255.0.0, or 255.255.255.0, it is fairly obvious which part of the IP address is the network ID. (These subnet masks are the defaults for class A, B, and C networks, respectively.) However, which part of the IP address is the network becomes less apparent when other subnet masks are used (such as 255.255.248.0). In this case, if both the IP address and subnet mask are converted to binary, then the answer becomes more apparent. (The 1 bits of the subnet mask correspond to the network ID in the IP address.)

By figuring out what subnet a host is on from the IP address and subnet mask, routing a packet to the proper destination becomes easier. Fortunately, all you have to do is supply the proper IP addresses with one subnet mask for the entire internetwork, and the software determines which subnet the destination is on.

If the destination address is on a different subnet than that of the sender, then it is on a remote network and the packet is routed appropriately, usually by being sent to the default gateway.

If a network has a small number of hosts and they are all on the same segment without any routers, they are likely given the same network ID (the network portion of an IP address). If the network is larger, however, with remote segments connected by routers (an internetwork), then each individual subnet needs a different network ID. Therefore, when assigning IP addresses and subnet masks, the network administrator must know how many subnets are required and the maximum number of hosts that are on each subnet.

Depending on the subnet mask, the internetwork can have either many different network IDs with a smaller number of hosts on each subnet or a smaller number of network IDs with a larger number of hosts on each subnet. The reasons for these results become clearer as you read further. The following table shows the maximum number of hosts and subnets available per the number of bits used.

Additional Bits Required	*Number of Possible Subnets*	*Maximum C Hosts*	*Maximum B Hosts*	*Maximum A Hosts*	*Subnet Mask*
0	0	254	65,534	16,777,214	0
1	invalid	invalid	invalid	invalid	invalid
2	2	62	16,382	4,194,302	192
3	6	30	8,190	2,097,150	224
4	14	14	4,094	1,048,574	240
5	30	6	2,044	524,286	248
6	62	2	1,022	262,142	252
7	126	invalid	510	131,070	254
8	254	invalid	254	65,534	255

5. What part of 192.168.10.51 is the Network ID?

B. 192.168.10

5. CORRECT ANSWER: B

Purpose of Subnet Masks

By specifying the correct subnet mask for addresses, you are telling the TCP/IP software which part of the address refers to the host and which part refers to the specific subnet on which the host is located. As mentioned previously, the IP address and subnet mask are made up of four 8-bit octets that are most often shown in decimal, rather than binary, format for ease of reading. Here's an example of an IP address and subnet mask in binary format:

IP address	11001000 00010100 00010000 00000101
Subnet mask	11111111 11111111 11111111 00000000
Network ID	11001000 00010100 00010000 00000000
Host ID	00000000 00000000 00000000 00000101

Notice that the network ID is the portion of the IP address corresponding to a bit value of 1 in the subnet mask.

In the preceding example, you could have a maximum of 254 different hosts on the network 192.20.16 (192.20.16.1 through 192.20.16.254). If you wanted to have more hosts on one network, then you have to use a different addressing scheme. For example, using a subnet mask of 255.255.0.0 gives the following results:

IP address	192.20.16.5
Subnet mask	255.255.0.0
Network ID	192.20
Host ID	16.5

▼ NOTE

A common convention in TCP/IP is to omit the trailing zero octets in a network ID and the leading zero octets in a host ID. Therefore, the network ID 192.20 represents 192.20.0.0, and the host ID 16.5 represents 0.0.16.5.

Because the host ID in this example is a 16-bit value, you can have (256 × 256) – 2 hosts on the network 192.20. The two addresses that must be subtracted from the possibilities are 0 (consisting of all 0s) and 255 (consisting of all 1s)—both reserved addresses. The 0 is used to define the network, whereas 255 is a broadcast address for all computers in the network.

A host ID cannot have all bits set to either 1 or 0 because these addresses would be interpreted to mean either a broadcast address or "this network only." Thus the number of valid addresses will be $(2 \times n) - 2$, where n is the number of bits used for the host ID.

▼ NOTE

Common practice dictates that address bits cannot be all 1s or 0s. In reality, if—and only if—the routers on the network support extended prefixing addressing, addresses of all 1s or 0s are possible. Both the software and the routers must support RIP V2, and you must disallow the possibility of traffic over any older, incompatible routers.

Cisco routers, NetWare 4.*x*, and Windows NT support the extended prefixing address (although they often call it a *zero network*). Contrary to the principles of RFC 950, these products permit the use of all-0 and all-1 subnets. However, even one NetWare 3.*x* system anywhere on your network, or any older router, means that you cannot use the 0-network option. Therefore, for all practical purposes, you should consider 0s and 1s off limits.

6. When performing an Andding function on 192.168.10.5 and 255.255.255.0, what is the result?

A. 192.168.10.0

6. CORRECT ANSWER: A

The result of adding 192.168.10.5 to 255.255.255.0 is 192.168.10.0. This number explains the network ID. While the answer may appear correct without the fourth octet, technically while performing this function, without the fourth octet in place the answer is incomplete.

Combining IP Address and Subnet Mask

Take note of how a subnet mask is used to determine which part of the IP address is the network ID and which part is the host ID. TCP/IP does a binary calculation by using the IP address and the subnet mask to determine the network ID portion of the IP address.

The computation TCP/IP performs is a logical bitwise AND of the IP address and the subnet mask. The calculation sounds complicated, but all it means is that the octets are converted to binary numbers and a logical AND is performed whose result is the network ID. Recall that in the preceding example the network ID is the portion of the IP address corresponding to a bit value of 1 in the subnet mask.

Performing a bitwise AND on two bits results in 1 (or TRUE) if the two values are both 1. If either or both of the values are not 1, then the result is 0 (or FALSE).

Any logical AND with a 0 results in 0.

See the following list for examples:

1 AND 1 results in 1.

1 AND 0 results in 0.

0 AND 1 results in 0.

0 AND 0 results in 0.

In the first example of this section, the IP address 192.20.16.5 is ANDed with the subnet mask 255.255.255.0 to give a network ID of 192.20.16. The following minitable shows the calculation:

	Decimal Notation	*Binary Notation*
IP address:	192 20 16 5	11000000 00010100 00010000 00000101
Subnet mask:	255 255 255 0	11111111 11111111 11111111 00000000
IP address *and* subnet mask	192 20 16 0	11000000 00010100 00010000 00000000

Determining the network ID is very easy if the subnet mask is made up of only 255 and 0 values. Simply *mask,* or cover up, the part of the IP address corresponding to the 0 octet of the subnet mask. For example, if the IP address is 15.6.100.1 and the subnet mask is 255.255.0.0, then the resulting network ID is 15.6. You cannot use a subnet mask with only 255 and 0 values if you need to subdivide your network ID into individual subnets.

7. Which of the following best illustrates the default subnet mask for a class A, B, and C network?

C. 255.0.0.0, 255.255.0.0, 255.255.255.0

7. CORRECT ANSWER: C

See explanation to question 8.

8. With an IP address of 201.142.23.12, what is your default subnet mask?

D. 255.255.255.0

8. CORRECT ANSWER: D

The first octet 201 signifies a class C network. Therefore, the default subnet mask for a class C network is 255.255.255.0.

Default Subnet Masks

Default masks are usually assigned by the ISP vendor, based on the class network in question. The following table shows the subnet mask that appears in the subnet mask field when an IP address is selected:

Default Subnet Masks

Class	*IP Address*	*Default Subnet Mask*
A	001.x.y.z to 126.x.y.z	255.0.0.0
B	128.x.y.z to 191.x.y.z	255.255.0.0
C	192.x.y.z to 223.x.y.z	255.255.255.0

Thus, by using the default mask, the emphasis is on the number of hosts available, and nothing more, as the following table illustrates:

Maximum Number of Networks and Hosts per Network in TCP/IP

Class	*Using Default Subnet Mask*	*Number of Networks*	*Number of Hosts per Network*
A	255.0.0.0	126	16,777,214*
B	255.255.0.0	16,384	65,534*
C	255.255.255.0	2,097,152	254*

*The number of hosts is equal to the number of bit permutations (0 or 1) multiplied by the number of bit places (8-bit maximum per octet) minus 2. So 11111111 is 256 – 2 = 254.

If the hosts on your internetwork are not directly on the Internet, then you are free to choose the network IDs that you use. For the hosts and subnets that are a part of the Internet, however, the network IDs you use must be assigned by InterNIC (the Internet Network Information Center).

If you are using network IDs assigned by InterNIC, then you cannot choose the address class you use (and you can bet you will be given class C addresses). In this case, the number of subnets you use is normally limited by the number of network IDs assigned by InterNIC, and the number of hosts per subnet is determined by the class of address. Fortunately, by choosing the proper subnet mask, you can subdivide your network into a greater number of subnets with fewer possible hosts per subnet.

Many companies today with Internet requirements are avoiding the addressing constraints and security risks of having hosts directly on the Internet by setting up private networks with gateway access to the Internet. Having a private network means that only the Internet gateway host needs to have an Internet address. For security, a firewall can be set up to prevent Internet hosts from directly accessing the company's network.

9. With an IP address starting at 200, you currently have 10 subnets. What subnet mask should you use to maximize the number of available hosts?

C. 240

9. CORRECT ANSWER: C

A subnet mask of 240 will make 14 hosts available on each subnet of a class C network. That is to say that if you were to convert 240 to binary, you would have 11110000.

Because you are concerned with the quantity of hosts, you would observe $2^4 - 2 = 14$. Note that the 4th power is the count of the number of zeros in the mask. When applied to an IP address, these bits can either be 0 or 1. That is 0000, 0001, 0010, and so on. The number of bit permutations that can come from 4 bits is 16. Remember that you must always subtract 2 so that you do not have a host with a 0- or 255-equivalent address.

10. With an IP address of 100, you currently have 80 subnets. What subnet mask should you use to maximize the number of available hosts?

E. 252

10. CORRECT ANSWER: E

A subnet mask of 255.252.0.0 will make 262,142 hosts available on each subnet of a class A network. Again with the concentration on hosts, you are interested in the number of 0s in the subnet mask. That is to say that 255.252.0.0 is equal to 11111111.11111100.00000000.00000000 in binary. There are 18 0s. If you were to take 2 to the 18th power, you would find that there are 262,144 possible permutations on the 0 and 1 combinations. Subtracting 2 addresses for all 0s and for all 1s, we would find 262,142 valid addresses.

11. With an IP address of 100, you currently have only eight subnets but anticipate adding two more subnets next year. What subnet mask should you use to maximize the number of available hosts?

C. 240

11. CORRECT ANSWER: C

A subnet mask of 240 will make over 1 million hosts available on each subnet of a class A network. In calculating this value, observe that the mask is 255.240.0.0. Recalling that the 0 in the subnet mask is equivalent to 256 permutations of addresses, you then must determine how many possibilities exist for 240. First, convert it to binary for 11110000. Because $2^4 = 16$, you see that the entire mask supports $(16 \times 256 \times 256) - 2$ or 1,048,574 hosts. A faster way to make this calculation is take the subnet mask - 11111111.11110000.00000000.00000000 and count the number of 0s. Then calculate $2^{20} - 2$.

12. With an IP address set starting with 150, you currently have six offices that you are treating as subnets. Plans are in place to open 10 more offices before the end of the year. What subnet mask should you use to satisfy the needed number of subnets and maximize the number of hosts available at each site?

D. 248

12. CORRECT ANSWER: D

On a class B network, a subnet mask of 248 will provide for up to 30 subnets and 2,046 hosts on each. That is to say when the mask—255.255.248.0 is applied, the number of host addresses that are available are (8 × 256) – 2, or 2046 hosts. Notice that we calculated the 8 from the 248 binary number of 11111000, which is 2 possibilities per bit (0 or 1) and 3 positions (2 × 2 × 2) = 8. A faster way to calculate these would be to count the number of 0s in the binary subnet mask — 11. Then calculate 2^{11}-2.

13. On a class C network with a subnet mask of 192, how many hosts are available?

B. 62

13. CORRECT ANSWER: B

On a class C network, 62 hosts are available at each subnet with a subnet mask of 192. Simply put, a mask of 192 in binary is 11000000 or $2^6 - 2$ (as in 6 zeros minus the 2 reserved addresses per network).

14. On a class C network with a subnet mask of 192, how many subnets are available?

E. 2

14. CORRECT ANSWER: E

On a class C network, two subnets are available with a subnet mask of 192. This question may have fooled you if you calculated for the number of hosts; in this case, rather than figuring the number of 0s, you must calculate based on the number of 1s. For 192, you would observe that 11000000 is ($2^2 - 2$, or 2. Remember that a class C network with a 192 mask is "spelled out" as 255.255.255.192.

15. On a class B network, how many hosts are available at each site with a subnet mask of 248?

D. 2,046

15. CORRECT ANSWER: D

On a class B network, 2,046 hosts are available on each subnet with a subnet mask of 248. In other words, 255.255.248.0 is 11111000 or 2^3 = (8 × 256) – 2, or 2,046 hosts.

16. On a class B network, how many subnets are available with a subnet mask of 248?

C. 30

16. CORRECT ANSWER: C

On a class B network, 30 subnets are available with a subnet mask of 248. Watch the wording: You must calculate for the number of subnets rather than hosts—that is, 255.255.248.0 produces 11111000 or $2^5 - 2 = 30$. Remember that because you are assigned a class B network, you are calculating only for the number of addresses you can make for your network, not all networks. That is why you practically ignore the first two octets for a class B subnet mask.

FURTHER REVIEW

CONFIGURE SUBNET MASKS

Table 2.1 is a handy binary conversion chart. Trying to memorize it is not recommended, but it can be useful for checking your own decimal-to-binary conversion practice.

TABLE 2.1 BINARY CONVERSION CHART

Decimal	*Binary*	*Decimal*	*Binary*
0	0000 0000	23	0001 0111
1	0000 0001	24	0001 1000
2	0000 0010	25	0001 1001
3	0000 0011	26	0001 1010
4	0000 0100	27	0001 1011
5	0000 0101	28	0001 1100
6	0000 0110	29	0001 1101
7	0000 0111	30	0001 1110
8	0000 1000	31	0001 1111
9	0000 1001	32	0010 0000
10	0000 1010	33	0010 0001
11	0000 1011	34	0010 0010
12	0000 1100	35	0010 0011
13	0000 1101	36	0010 0100
14	0000 1110	37	0010 0101
15	0000 1111	38	0010 0110
16	0001 0000	39	0010 0111
17	0001 0001	40	0010 1000
18	0001 0010	41	0010 1001
19	0001 0011	42	0010 1010
20	0001 0100	43	0010 1011
21	0001 0101	44	0010 1100
22	0001 0110	45	0010 1101
46	0010 1110	75	0100 1011
47	0010 1111	76	0100 1100
48	0011 0000	77	0100 1101
49	0011 0001	78	0100 1110
50	0011 0010	79	0100 1111
51	0011 0011	80	0101 0000
52	0011 0100	81	0101 0001
53	0011 0101	82	0101 0010
54	0011 0110	83	0101 0011
55	0011 0111	84	0101 0100
56	0011 1000	85	0101 0101
57	0011 1001	86	0101 0110
58	0011 1010	87	0101 0111
59	0011 1011	88	0101 1000
60	0011 1100	89	0101 1001
61	0011 1101	90	0101 1010
62	0011 1110	91	0101 1011
63	0011 1111	92	0101 1100
64	0100 0000	93	0101 1101
65	0100 0001	94	0101 1110
66	0100 0010	95	0101 1111
67	0100 0011	96	0110 0000
68	0100 0100	97	0110 0001
69	0100 0101	98	0110 0010
70	0100 0110	99	0110 0011
71	0100 0111	100	0110 0100
72	0100 1000	101	0110 0101
73	0100 1001	102	0110 0110
74	0100 1010	103	0110 0111

Decimal	*Binary*	*Decimal*	*Binary*	*Decimal*	*Binary*	*Decimal*	*Binary*
104	0110 1000	137	1000 1001	170	1010 1010	203	1100 1011
105	0110 1001	138	1000 1010	171	1010 1011	204	1100 1100
106	0110 1010	139	1000 1011	172	1010 1100	205	1100 1101
107	0110 1011	140	1000 1100	173	1010 1101	206	1100 1110
108	0110 1100	141	1000 1101	174	1010 1110	207	1100 1111
109	0110 1101	142	1000 1110	175	1010 1111	208	1101 0000
110	0110 1110	143	1000 1111	176	1011 0000	209	1101 0001
111	0110 1111	144	1001 0000	177	1011 0001	210	1101 0010
112	0111 0000	145	1001 0001	178	1011 0010	211	1101 0011
113	0111 0001	146	1001 0010	179	1011 0011	212	1101 0100
114	0111 0010	147	1001 0011	180	1011 0100	213	1101 0101
115	0111 0011	148	1001 0100	181	1011 0101	214	1101 0110
116	0111 0100	149	1001 0101	182	1011 0110	215	1101 0111
117	0111 0101	150	1001 0110	183	1011 0111	216	1101 1000
118	0111 0110	151	1001 0111	184	1011 1000	217	1101 1001
119	0111 0111	152	1001 1000	185	1011 1001	218	1101 1010
120	0111 1000	153	1001 1001	186	1011 1010	219	1101 1011
121	0111 1001	154	1001 1010	187	1011 1011	220	1101 1100
122	0111 1010	155	1001 1011	188	1011 1100	221	1101 1101
123	0111 1011	156	1001 1100	189	1011 1101	222	1101 1110
124	0111 1100	157	1001 1101	190	1011 1110	223	1101 1111
125	0111 1101	158	1001 1110	191	1011 1111	224	1110 0000
126	0111 1110	159	1001 1111	192	1100 0000	225	1110 0001
127	0111 1111	160	1010 0000	193	1100 0001	226	1110 0010
128	1000 0000	161	1010 0001	194	1100 0010	227	1110 0011
129	1000 0001	162	1010 0010	195	1100 0011	228	1110 0100
130	1000 0010	163	1010 0011	196	1100 0100	229	1110 0101
131	1000 0011	164	1010 0100	197	1100 0101	230	1110 0110
132	1000 0100	165	1010 0101	198	1100 0110	231	1110 0111
133	1000 0101	166	1010 0110	199	1100 0111	232	1110 1000
134	1000 0110	167	1010 0111	200	1100 1000	233	1110 1001
135	1000 0111	168	1010 1000	201	1100 1001	234	1110 1010
136	1000 1000	169	1010 1001	202	1100 1010	235	1110 1011

TABLE 2.1 CONTINUED

Decimal	*Binary*	*Decimal*	*Binary*
236	1110 1100	246	1111 0110
237	1110 1101	247	1111 0111
238	1110 1110	248	1111 1000
239	1110 1111	249	1111 1001
240	1111 0000	250	1111 1010
241	1111 0001	251	1111 1011
242	1111 0010	252	1111 1100
243	1111 0011	253	1111 1101
244	1111 0100	254	1111 1110
245	1111 0101	255	1111 1111

Defining Networks by IP Address

Communication in a TCP/IP network is based on sending messages back and forth between computers and network devices. The messages contain sender and recipient addresses, known as IP addresses. The IP addresses are in an octet-based form, such as 100.34.192.212. The first octet dictates the class of network that is being referred to, and as such, administrators can use three classes:

- **01–126** class A
- **128–191** class B
- **192–223** class C

Thus, the address 100.34.192.212 is clearly a class A address, whereas 220.34.192.212 is a class C address. The class is important because it indicates the maximum number of hosts that a network can have according to the following rules:

- **Class A** 16,777,214 hosts
- **Class B** 65,534 hosts
- **Class C** 254 hosts

The class ranges are determined according to the first octet in an IP address. The way that this is determined is according to how the number is written in binary. That is to say that all numbers in the A range will have the first octet beginning with a 0. Then the B range will be 10, and the C 110. Suppose you are examining the C range of 192 to 223. 192 in binary is 11000000, whereas 223 is 11011111. Note that both binary numbers begin with 110, as do all class C addresses.

Although the existing shortage of addresses has made it impossible to obtain a class A address for some time, imagine the difficulties inherent in trying to network 16 million hosts on a single segment—it is virtually impossible. At the same time, networking 254 hosts, although not impossible, can be done on a single segment. Typically, hosts are spread out across several physical locations, often within the same building, campus, or other geographical area. For that reason, and to make routing practical and possible, subnets are used to divide the network (and network numbers) into smaller portions.

Subdividing a Network

Internetworks are networks made up of individual segments connected by routers. The reasons for having distinct segments are as follows:

- To permit physically remote LAN connections.
- To mix network technologies, such as Ethernet and token ring, on a single logical network.
- To allow an unlimited number of hosts to communicate, regardless of the underlying topology.

- To reduce network congestion because broadcasts and local network traffic are limited to the local segment.

Each segment is a subnet of the internetwork and requires a unique network ID. If you have only one network ID—for example, if you have an InterNIC-assigned Internet network ID—then you must subdivide this network ID into other network IDs—a process known as *subnetting* or *subnetworking*.

The following five steps explain the process involved in subnetting a network:

Step 1: Determine the Number of Network IDs Required

The first step in subnetting a network is to determine the number of subnets required, making sure to plan for future growth. A unique network ID is required for each of the following:

- Each subnet
- Each WAN connection

Step 2: Determine the Number of Host IDs per Subnet Required

Determine the maximum number of host IDs that are required on each subnet along with any planned future growth. A host ID is required for each of the following:

- Each TCP/IP computer network interface card.
- Each TCP/IP printer network interface card.
- Each router interface on each subnet. For example, if a router is connected to two subnets, then it would require two host IDs and, therefore, two IP addresses.

Step 3: Define the Subnet Mask

The next step is to define for the entire internetwork one subnet mask that gives the desired number of subnets and allows enough hosts per subnet.

As shown previously, the network ID of an IP address is determined by the 1 bits of the subnet mask shown in binary notation. To increase the number of network IDs, you need to add more bits to the subnet mask.

Suppose InterNIC assigns you a class B network ID of 129.20. By using the default class B subnet mask 255.255.0.0, you have one network ID (129.20) and about 65,000 valid host IDs (129.20.1.1 through 129.20.255.254). Now suppose you want to subdivide the network into four subnets.

First, consider the host 129.20.16.1 using the subnet mask 255.255.0.0. In binary notation, it is represented as follows:

IP address
10000001 00010100 00010000 00000001
Subnet mask
11111111 11111111 00000000 00000000
Network ID
11000000 00010100

Remember that the 1 bits in the subnet mask correspond to the network ID bit in the IP address.

By adding bits to the subnet mask, you increase the bits available for the network ID and thus create a few more combinations of network IDs.

Suppose, finally, that you add 3 bits to the subnet mask. The result increases the number of bits defining the network ID and decreases the number of bits that define the host ID. Thus, you have more network IDs but fewer hosts on each subnet.

The new subnet mask is as follows:

Subnet Mask			
11111111	11111111	11100000	00000000
Decimal			
255	255	224	0

The 3 extra bits in the network ID give you six different network IDs. You cannot use all 0s or all 1s because they are reserved for the broadcast address. The former implies "this network only," and the latter would be the same as the subnet mask. Examples of network IDs include the following:

11000000	00010100	001
11000000	00010100	010
11000000	00010100	011
11000000	00010100	100
11000000	00010100	101
11000000	00010100	110

Now summarize the preceding example by using decimal notation. By applying the new subnet mask of 255.255.224.0 to the network ID 129.20, you create six new network IDs: 129.20.32, 129.20.64, 129.20.96, 129.20.128, 129.20.160, and 129.20.192.

Note that if you used only two additional bits in the subnet mask, you would be able to have only two subnets. The network IDs that result in the preceding example are as follows:

10000001	00010100	01	(129.20.64)
10000001	00010100	10	(129.20.128)

Therefore, you must use enough additional bits in the new subnet mask to create the desired number of subnets, while still allowing for enough hosts on each subnet.

After you determine the number of subnets you need to create, you can calculate the subnet mask as follows:

1. Convert the number of subnets to binary format. You may want to use the Windows Calculator in Scientific view.

   The number of bits required to represent the number of subnets in binary is the number of additional bits that you need to add to the default subnet mask.

2. Convert the subnet mask back to decimal format.

Suppose you are assigned a class B network ID of 192.20 and you need to create five subnets.

Converting 5 into binary format results in 00000101, or simply 101. By ignoring the 0 bits to the left of the leftmost 1, the required number of bits is 3.

Therefore, you need to add 3 bits to the default subnet mask. The default subnet mask for a class B network is 255.255.0.0.

In binary notation, the result is as follows:

Default subnet mask 11111111 11111111 00000000 00000000

Adding 3 bits results in the following subnet mask:

11111111 11111111 11100000 0000000 or 255.255.224.0 in decimal notation.

Step 4: Determine the Network IDs to Use

The next step is to determine the subnet network IDs that are created by applying the new subnet mask to the original assigned network ID. Any or all of the resulting subnet network IDs are used in the internetwork. Aside from using a table, you may use either method listed in the following sections to compute the Network ID value. The first describes a manual solution, "Defining the Network IDs Manually." The second provides a handy shortcut, "Shortcut for Defining the Network IDs."

Defining the Network IDs Manually

The network ID for each subnet is determined by using the same number of bits as were added to the default subnet mask in the previous step. To define each subnet network ID, follow these steps:

1. List all possible binary combinations of the bits added to the default subnet mask.
2. Discard the combinations with all 1s or all 0s. All 1s or all 0s are not valid as network IDs; all 1s are the same as the subnet mask, and all 0s imply "this network only" as a destination.
3. Convert the remaining values to decimal notation.
4. Append each value to the original assigned network ID to produce a subnet network ID.

Using the previous example, you were assigned a class B network ID of 129.20 and created at least five subnets. You needed to add 3 bits to the default subnet mask to create the subnets. The new subnet mask was then 255.255.224.0, or in binary:

Subnet Mask:
11111111 11111111 11100000 00000000

Listing all combinations of the additional bits gives the following:

000
001
010
011
100
101
110
111

Discarding the values 000 and 111 and converting the remaining combinations to decimal format, you have the following:

.32.
.64.
.96.
.128.
.160.
.192.

Appending the preceding values to the original assigned network ID gives the following new subnet network ID:

129.20.32
129.20.64
129.20.96
129.20.128
129.20.160
129.20.192

All the new subnet network IDs use the subnet mask 255.255.224.0.

Shortcut for Defining the Network IDs

Using the preceding method becomes tedious when more than 3 bits are added to the default subnet mask because the technique requires listing and converting many bit combinations. You can use the following shortcut for defining the subnet network IDs:

1. List the octet added to the default subnet mask in binary notation.
2. Convert the rightmost 1 bit of this value to decimal notation, which is the incremental value between each subnet value, known as *delta* (D).
3. The number of subnet network IDs that are created is two fewer than two to the power of *n*, where *n* is the bits used in step 1 (number of subnets = $2^n - 2$).
4. Append "Delta" to the original network ID to give the first subnet network ID.
5. Repeat step 4 for each subnet network ID, incrementing each successive value by "Delta."

Using the previous example, you were assigned a class B network ID of 129.20 and created at least five subnets. You needed to add 3 bits to the default subnet mask to create the subnets.

The bits you added to the default subnet mask are 11100000.

The rightmost bit converted to decimal (00100000) is 32. Thus the incremental value, delta, is 32.

There are $2^3 - 2 = 6$ subnets created.

The subnets created are as follows:

Begin Value	End Value
129.20.0	129.20.32
129.20.32	129.20.64
129.20.64	129.20.96
129.20.96	129.20.128
129.20.128	129.20.160
129.20.32	129.20.192

If you increment the last subnet network ID once more, the last octet matches the last octet of the subnet mask (224) and thus is an invalid network ID.

Step 5: Determine the Host IDs to Use

The final step in subnetting a network is to determine the valid host IDs and assign IP addresses to the hosts.

The host IDs for each subnet start with the value .001 in the last octet and continue up to one less than the subnet ID of the next subnet. Keep in mind that the last octet cannot be .000 or .255; these are reserved for broadcast addresses.

Finally, the valid IP addresses for each subnet are created by combining the subnet network ID with the host ID.

By using the subnets in the previous example, the range of IP addresses for each subnet would be as follows:

Subnet	First IP Address	Last IP Address
129.20.32.0	129.20.32.1	129.20.63.254
129.20.64.0	129.20.64.1	129.20.95.254
129.20.96.0	129.20.96.1	129.20.127.254
129.20.128.0	129.20.128.1	129.20.159.254
129.20.160.0	129.20.160.1	129.20.191.254
129.20.192.0	129.20.192.1	129.20.223.254

Supernetting

In certain implementations, a special condition might exist, which involves the subnet mask actually using fewer bits than the standard class mask allows. For example, suppose that you had multiple class C networks that included 192.53.168-174.0. Rather than defining a router with a table that included multiple networks with a mask of 255.255.255.0, a single network could be specified by using a mask of 255.255.248.0.

If you were to perform the math, you would find that supernetting allows a company that is too small for a class B network and too big for a class C network to function without having to waste excess addresses between classes. In the preceding example, the mask of 255.255.248.0 translates to providing the consolidation of six networks over the standard mask. That is to say that the Node ID now has 11 bits, or 11111111.11111111.11111000.00000000. Simply count the number of 0s in the third octet, multiple each to the power of 2, then subtract two from the result. So, 11111000 is $2^3 - 2$, or 6.

Supernetting requires a technology defined by RFC1519 called Classless Inter-Domain Routing (CIDR). As a technology, supernetting is somewhat uncommon; however, because it does exist, it is worthy of mention.

CHAPTER SUMMARY

Subnetting is a methodology of dividing a network into smaller segments. These smaller segments produce greater efficiency and allow for stronger management. A network IP address uniquely identifies a system. The first part defines the network, whereas the later part of the address defines the host. To determine which part of the address is used for network or host, examine the subnet mask. Because all calculations are performed in binary, anywhere a 1 appears in the subnet mask network ID, and anywhere a 0 appears is considered part of the host ID. So a subnet mask with 255.255.0.0 would define the first two octets for the network work and the last two for the host. Moreover, a mask of 255.255.240.0 would define the first 2 octets and 4 additional bits (11111111.11111111.1111) as network and the last octets with 4 additional bits (0000.0000000) as host. Note that when these binary numbers are combined, they are equal to the decimal subnet mask 255.255.240.0.

Supernetting is an inverse technology that works in the opposite manner from subnetting. Rather than borrowing addresses bits from the node ID, supernetting borrows from the network ID.

CHAPTER REVIEW

REVIEW QUESTIONS

Note: The additional Chapter Review section that ends each chapter is unique to this member of the *New Riders TestPrep, Second Edition* series. We've included it to more fully and fairly cover the unique aspects of TCP/IP in relation to its mastery in preparation for MCSE examination.

1. **You have a network ID of 134.57.0.0 and you need to divide it into multiple subnets in which at least 600 host IDs for each subnet are available. You desire to have the largest amount of subnets available. Which subnet mask should you assign?**

    A. 255.255.224.0

    B. 255.255.240.0

    C. 255.255.248.0

    D. 255.255.252.0

    E. 255.255.255.255

2. **You have a network ID of 134.57.0.0 with 8 subnets. You need to allow the largest possible number of host IDs per subnet. Which subnet mask should you assign?**

    A. 255.255.224.0

    B. 255.255.240.0

    C. 255.255.248.0

    D. 255.255.252.0

    E. 255.255.255.255

3. **You have a network ID of 192.168.10.0 and require at least 25 host IDs for each subnet, with the largest amount of subnets available. Which subnet mask should you assign?**

    A. 255.255.255.192

    B. 255.255.255.224

    C. 255.255.255.240

    D. 255.255.255.248

    E. 255.255.255.255

4. **You have a class A network address 10.0.0.0 with 40 subnets, but are required to add 60 new subnets very soon. You would like to still allow for the largest possible number of host IDs per subnet. Which subnet mask should you assign?**

    A. 255.240.0.0

    B. 255.248.0.0

    C. 255.252.0.0

    D. 255.254.0.0

    E. 255.255.255.255

5. **Your company, ABC Law, has offices located in three different cities. You have one class C network address, which you have divided among the sites evenly. Each site has no more than five attorneys and six secretaries; however, your company's growth may require support for up to 25 users per site. Additionally, ABC Law plans to expand into two more cities in the next six months. Which subnet mask should you assign to support all sites and the maximum number of users per site?**

   A. 255.255.255.0

   B. 255.255.255.192

   C. 255.255.255.224

   D. 255.255.255.248

   E. 255.255.255.255

6. **Your company is building a new plant with 24 different sales offices with over 150 users per location. Each location must be able to communicate with one another continuously. You need to come up with a TCP/IP addressing scheme for your company. Knowing that your address is 172.16.0.0, how many network IDs must you allow for when you define the subnet mask for the network? Select all that apply.**

   A. One for each subnet

   B. One for each host ID

   C. One for each router interface

   D. One for each WAN connection

   E. One for each network adapter that is installed on each host

ANSWER KEY

1. D	3. B	5. C
2. B	4. D	6. A-D

REVIEW ANSWERS

1. You have a network ID of 134.57.0.0 and you need to divide it into multiple subnets in which at least 600 host IDs for each subnet are available. You desire to have the largest amount of subnets available. Which subnet mask should you assign?

D. 255.255.252.0

1. CORRECT ANSWER: D

Knowing that you need 600 host IDs per subnet, you must calculate that $2^x > 600$ which is to say, the number of bits that must be reserved for a host such that there can be more than 600. Consider that 8 bits is 2^8-2 = 254 nodes, 9 bits is 2^9-2 = 510, and 10 bits is 2^{10}-2 = 1022 hosts. Each time you calculate for this, you are figuring 2 to the power of the number of bits—in this case, 10. Applying this, you find that 10 bits reserved for a host ID is a mask of 255.255.252.0

2. You have a network ID of 134.57.0.0 with 8 subnets. You need to allow the largest possible number of host IDs per subnet. Which subnet mask should you assign?

B. 255.255.240.0

2. CORRECT ANSWER: B

The first consideration that you must observe is that you have a class B network with 8 subnets. In order to have 8 subnets, you must have 4 bits reserved in the 3rd octet. That is to say that 2^4-2 = 14 possible subnets. Applying 4 bits in the third octet yields a mask of 255.255.240.0

3. You have a network ID of 192.168.10.0 and require at least 25 host IDs for each subnet, with the largest amount of subnets available. Which subnet mask should you assign?

B. 255.255.255.224

3. CORRECT ANSWER: B

If you are working with a class C network, note that you can work with only the 8 bits of the fourth octet. Calculating that $2^x > 25$, calculate that 5 bits yields 30 clients (don't forget to subtract 2 from 2^5). If you apply this to the default mask, you get a mask of 255.255.255.224

4. You have a class A network address 10.0.0.0 with 40 subnets, but are required to add 60 new subnets very soon. You would like to still allow for the largest possible number of host IDs per subnet. Which subnet mask should you assign?

D. 255.254.0.0

4. CORRECT ANSWER: D

To calculate this subnet mask for this class A network, you must figure out the number of required networks. That is the 40 existing and 60 planned (100 total) subnets. Calculating that $2^x < 100$, you find that 7 bits allows this situation. Therefore, a mask of 255.254.0.0 will suffice.

5. Your company, ABC Law, has offices located in three different cities. You have one class C network address, which you have divided among the sites evenly. Each site has no more than five attorneys and six secretaries; however, your company's growth may require support for up to 25 users per site. Additionally, ABC Law plans to expand into two more cities in the next six months. Which subnet mask should you assign to support all sites and the maximum number of users per site?

C. 255.255.255.224

5. CORRECT ANSWER: C

The first step to solving this problem is to determine the maximum number of users and the maximum number of hosts. From reading the scenario, you must have 25 users per site at five sites. To maintain 25 users calculate $2^x > 25$. Reserving 5 bits yields 30 hosts ($2^5 = 32 - 2$) and six subnetworks. Effectively, a mask of 255.255.255.224 produces this result.

6. Your company is building a new plant with 24 different sales offices with over 150 users per location. Each location must be able to communicate with one another continuously. You need to come up with a TCP/IP addressing scheme for your company. Knowing that your address is 172.16.0.0, how many network IDs must you allow for when you define the subnet mask for the network? Select all that apply.

A. One for each subnet

D. One for each WAN connection

6. CORRECT ANSWERS: A-D

With the exception of third-party solutions, which have a workaround for proving address to router WAN connections, you must have one network ID for each subnet, and one for each WAN connection. Keep in mind that TCP/IP can communicate only to an address on the same network and must use a router to talk with others. On the Internet, a link may have the capability to communicate with many other routers; effectively, you have a network in which each node is a router (gateway).

In this chapter, you will learn how Microsoft Windows NT systems address one another and how their names are resolved to IP addresses. When reviewing this section, be sure to note that we are specifically dealing with NetBIOS names and their functions with Windows NT. You should pay close attention to the types of services that are available for name resolution, where they operate, and how they are configured.

CHAPTER 3

NetBIOS Naming and WINS

OBJECTIVES

This chapter helps you prepare for the exam by covering the following objectives:

Configure and support browsing in a multiple domain-routed network.

- TCP/IP is designed to function in a *wide area network* (or *WAN*) which may be separated by routers or other networking equipment. Because Microsoft's implementation of TCP/IP includes NetBIOS naming, it must be able to resolve those names over a wide area network. Also, when outside of the home domain, name resolution must also be able to occur on remote domains.

Install and configure a WINS server.

- WINS is Microsoft's key solution to NetBIOS name resolution. Although reasonably straightforward, WINS must be configured and installed correctly in order to function at its fullest.

continues

OBJECTIVES (continued)

Import LMHOSTS files to WINS.

- LMHOSTS files are a local method for NetBIOS name resolution and location of Domains. This section explains how this file should be configured.

Run WINS on a multihomed computer.

- Multihomed computers are configurations that require special considerations as to how NetBIOS names are handled. Because a NetBIOS name is linked to a hardware address whenever multiple addresses are present, certain support prerequisites must be fulfilled.

Configure WINS replication.

- To provide balancing and fault tolerance, Microsoft's WINS can be configured to duplicate its database with a partner. Depending on the network environment, replication parameters will vary.

Configure static mappings in the WINS database.

- Because not all systems participate as WINS clients, they must undergo a special procedure to ensure that other systems on the network can still communicate with them. Essentially, these static entries will provide the register information that the client system does not.

PRACTICE QUESTIONS

CONFIGURE AND SUPPORT BROWSING IN A MULTIPLE-DOMAIN ROUTED NETWORK

1. **Which of the following best describes the list of computers on the network that users view when accessing Network Neighborhood?**

   A. A browse list

   B. A browse table

   C. A resource list

   D. A resource table

2. **The list of network resources viewed while in Network Neighborhood can be distributed on Microsoft and NetWare networks using what protocol?**

   A. TCP/IP

   B. NetBIOS

   C. PPP

   D. IPX/SPX

3. **The browse list is compiled by which of the following? Select the best answer.**

   A. A static resource table

   B. LMHOSTS files

   C. WINS servers

   D. A Master Browser

4. **To whom does the Master Browser distribute the browse list?**

   A. Primary Domain Controllers

   B. Backup Browsers

   C. Windows-based clients

   D. NT servers

5. **From whom does the client access the browse list?**

   A. Primary Domain Controllers

   B. Backup Browsers

   C. Windows-based clients

   D. NT servers

6. **Which of the following enables users to search for availability of network resources without knowing the exact location of the resources?**

   A. Browsing through Network Neighborhood

   B. The `Net Use` command

   C. The `Net View` command

   D. The `Net Search` command

7. **Master and Backup Browsers are determined by which of the following? Select the best answer.**

   A. Primary Domain Controllers

   B. WINS servers

   C. Elections

   D. Polling

8. All other factors being equal, which of the following machines on a network is most likely to be the Master Browser?

A. Windows 95 workstation

B. Windows NT workstation

C. Windows NT Server

D. Windows for Workgroups workstation

9. A Windows 95 computer can be configured to maintain or to not maintain browse lists by configuring which of the following? Select the best answer.

A. The File and Printer Sharing service

B. The Share Level Security tab

C. The `LMHOSTS` file

D. The Network Neighborhood properties

10. Under what circumstances would a Windows 95 machine be set up as a Master Browser?

A. Always

B. Never

C. When elected

D. When polled

11. What would be one reason to prevent a Windows 95 machine from being a Master Browser or Backup Browser?

A. When performance load is critical

B. When connected to a NetWare server

C. When user-level security is configured

D. When you have failed to register the machine with the local polling server

12. To have Windows 95 automatically determine whether the computer is needed as a browse server, which option should you select?

A. Enabled: May Be Master

B. Enabled: Must Be Master

C. Master: Enabled

D. Master: May Be Enabled

13. To prevent the computer from maintaining browse lists for the network, which option should you select?

A. Enabled: May Not Be Master

B. Enabled: Must Not Be Master

C. Master: Disabled

D. Master: May Not Be Enabled

14. Selecting the Enabled: May Not Be Master option has what effect on browsing the network?

A. Stops all LMANNOUNCE messages, effectively stopping browsing

B. Prevents the computer from browsing the network resources

C. Requires the re-enabling of the service before browsing can take place

D. Does not prevent the computer from browsing the network resources

15. To prevent the computer from using the browse service altogether, what option should you select?

A. NOT

B. DISABLED

C. INVALID

D. LMANNOUNCE NO

16. To give the computer priority in browse elections, which option should you select?

A. Enabled: May Be Master

B. Enabled: Must Be Master

C. Enabled: Preferred Master

D. Master: Enabled

17. If a server name doesn't appear on the browse list, what is one possible cause?

A. The server is on a different domain.

B. The Master Browser hasn't updated the Backup Browser.

C. The Master Browser hasn't updated the server.

D. The Master Browser is currently processing other requests.

18. You are running a Windows NT 4.0 server that is currently the Primary Domain Controller, and you have a multiple domain network. What browser roles does the server have?

A. Backup Browser

B. Master Browser

C. Potential Browser

D. Domain Master Browser

19. Which one of these situations is true regarding Master Browser to Backup Browser synchronization?

A. The Master Browser copies the updates to the Backup Browser.

B. The Backup Browser copies the updates to the Master Browser.

C. The Master Browser copies the updates from the Backup Browser.

D. The Backup Browser copies the updates from the Master Browser.

20. If you have a domain set up with two Windows 95 computers, three Windows NT Workstations computers, three Windows NT server computers, and four Windows for Workgroups computers, which is the third Backup Browser for this domain?

A. Windows 95

B. Windows for Workgroups

C. Windows NT Workstation

D. No computer can fill this role

21. Which of the following is in charge of continually updating the browse list and managing the database of network servers on domains and workgroups?

A. Backup Browser

B. Master Browser

C. Potential Browser

D. Browser Browser

22. Which of these statements is *not* true about the `DomainAnnouncement` packet?

A. It has the name of a domain.

B. It has the name of the Master Browser for that domain.

C. It specifies whether the Master Browser is a Windows NT server or workstation.

D. If it is a Windows NT server, it specifies the version number of the server.

23. You have a network with five different subnets, each with its own Master Browser. The network administrator wants to be able to see resources of each subnet at the same time. Which process allows for this?

A. Directed datagram

B. Directed telegram

C. Replication

D. Synchronization

24. If a domain announcement is sent out to a domain and the domain does not respond, how long is it before the remote domain is removed from the browse list?

A. Four announcement periods

B. Three announcement periods

C. Two announcement periods

D. Five announcement periods

25. Suppose you have a network with three subnets: subnet A, subnet B, and subnet C. What happens if the Domain Master Browser on subnet A goes down?

A. Browsing is restricted to each subnet.

B. Subnet B can see C but not A.

C. Subnet C can see B but not A.

D. All subnets continue browsing normally.

26. How is it possible to browse across routers without the use of WINS, DNS, HOSTS, or LMHOSTS? Select the best answer.

A. You can browse using Network Neighborhood.

B. You can use an IP-enabled router.

C. You can use a NetBIOS-enabled router.

D. You can manually update the ARP cache file.

27. What does the `#PRE` statement in an `LMHOSTS` file do?

A. Prepares a name to load into memory

B. Preloads an entry into cache

C. Permanently caches a preloaded file

D. Identifies comment lines

28. When should you put the addresses of the other Master Browsers into the `LMHOSTS` file as well as into the Domain Master Browser?

A. If the Domain Master Browser is busy, you have to change your `LMHOSTS` file to access the new Domain Master Browser.

B. If the Domain Master Browser goes down, you do not have to change your `LMHOSTS` file to access the new Domain Master Browser.

C. If your `LMHOSTS` file is unavailable, you have to update your Domain Master Browser list.

D. When your server has more free space than others.

29. Which method of updating across routers does WINS use to take the place of an `LMHOSTS` file over a network?

A. Dynamically

B. Statically

C. Manually

D. None

30. Which two additional Windows NT network services initiate a broadcast in a domain, but not across routers?

A. Logging in and passwords; PDC-to-PDC replication

B. Directory replication and authentication

C. Logging in and passwords; PDC-to-BDC replication

D. Remote execution and file transfer utility usage

31. The `LMHOSTS` file is mainly used on a network with non-WINS clients specifically for what job?

A. Resolving NetBIOS names to MAC-level address

B. Resolving a NetBIOS name to an IP address

C. Resolving an IP address to Internet names

D. Routing BOOTP information

ANSWER KEY

1. A	9. A	17. B	25. A
2. D	10. C	18. B-D	26. C
3. D	11. A	19. D	27. B
4. B	12. A	20. C	28. B
5. B	13. A	21. B	29. A
6. A	14. D	22. D	30. C
7. C	15. B	23. A	31. B
8. C	16. C	24. B	

ANSWERS & EXPLANATIONS

CONFIGURE AND SUPPORT BROWSING IN A MULTIPLE-DOMAIN ROUTED NETWORK

1. Which of the following best describes the list of computers on the network that users view when accessing Network Neighborhood?

A. A browse list

1. CORRECT ANSWER: A

The browse list is viewed when accessing Network Neighborhood. This list contains a set of names and the association of services which the name represents. Because it is inefficient for the workstation to maintain this list, it is stored on a Master Browser.

2. The list of network resources viewed while in Network Neighborhood can be distributed on Microsoft and NetWare networks using what protocol?

D. IPX/SPX

2. CORRECT ANSWER: D

Microsoft and NetWare networks can use IPX/SPX to distribute browse lists throughout a domain. NetWare networks do not have browse lists per se for their servers, but rather for the workstations when sharing has been enabled. TCP/IP can also be used for distributing browser lists; however, this is not a valid communication protocol for NetWare except when running NetWare 5.0.

3. The browse list is compiled by which of the following? Select the best answer.

D. A Master Browser

3. CORRECT ANSWER: D

The Master Browser of the segment/protocol/workgroup/domain compiles the browse list. This makes browsing a convenient, one-stop operation.

4. To whom does the Master Browser distribute the browse list?

B. Backup Browsers

4. CORRECT ANSWER: B

When the Master Browser has compiled the browse list, it distributes the list to the Backup Browsers. This function facilitates load balancing. Fault tolerance is also available in that a re-election of a master will occur which may use data on the Backup Browser.

5. From whom does the client view the browse list?

B. Backup Browsers

5. CORRECT ANSWER: B

When a client requires access to the browse list, it obtains it from a Backup Browser so that the Master Browser does not become overloaded with requests from all the computers.

6. Which of the following enables users to search for availability of network resources without knowing the exact location of the resources?

A. Browsing through Network Neighborhood

6. CORRECT ANSWER: A

Browsing through the Network Neighborhood allows users to search for available resources without specifying their exact location. This function is similar to running the DOS `dir` command except that the directory is networked-based and security is restrictive.

What Are Browsing and Browse Lists?

It's important not only to know an easy way to share a network resource but also to know which network resources are accessible. Microsoft has made the process of viewing these resources available through browsers. These browsers actually compile a list (called a *browse list*) which is then downloaded by requesting clients. One main computer is designated to collect and update a browse list. This not only frees the other systems on the network from having to constantly find resources, but it also reduces network traffic by using a single source to locate all network resources. Under certain conditions— which may be predefined or overidden by an administrator—additional systems may be designated as backup browsers (to a master browser) in order to help distribute the load of systems making requests for the systems list. Those that are not providing browse lists maintain only a short list containing the most recently accessed resources.

Browsing Tools

A simple example of how browsing is employed is the Network Neighborhood icon on the desktop. When you open Network Neighborhood, it provides a list of the network resources available in your local workgroup or domain which include, but are not limited to, printers, fax capabilities, CD-ROMs, and other drives or applications. The "Entire Network" selection provides the ability to see resources outside of the default workgroup or domain.

When you open a remote domain or workgroup, you are in the process of browsing. This is not unlike window shopping in the real world when, for example, you might go to the mall and browse through the shops until you find exactly what you want. The same process applies to the network, but now you are browsing network resources—remote files, printers, CD-ROMs. When you use the Network Neighborhood for browsing, you are using the graphical view method or *graphical user interface* (GUI). You may also browse network resources from the command prompt by using the `Net View` command. After you specify the server name, a list appears showing the resources available on that specific server. Note that this command uses a Universal Naming Convention to describe a resource, that is, the server name preceded by two backslashes (\\Server).

For example:

```
C:\users\default>net view \\instructor
```

results in the following:

```
Shared resources at \\instructor


Share name    Type          Used as   Comment

---------------------------------------------------
cdrom          Disk
MSDOS          Disk
NETLOGON      Disk                      Logon server share
Public         Disk
SQLSETUP       Disk
WGPO           Disk
The command completed successfully.
```

System Roles and NetBIOS Conventions

Certain predefined roles must be addressed with certain names. The computer that has the resource you are trying to access may be referred to as the *host computer*. While you are trying to access its resources, this computer is also playing the role of a *server* because it is providing a service: the sharing of its resources. The person trying to access the host computer is in the role of a *client.* Remember, a computer may play the roles of both client and server at the same time. If, for example, you are trying to access a printer on a remote computer while someone is using your shared CD-ROM, you are then acting as both client and server; that is, you are simultaneously sharing a resource and accessing a remote one.

Anytime a resource—drive, printer, and so forth—is shared, it will appear on the browse list, which is available to everyone on the network. Even if you do not have permission to use the resource, it will still appear on your browse list. The browse list displays all available network resources, not just the network resources that are available to you. There are ways of limiting access to the resource to specific clients (by setting permissions directly on the resource you are sharing), but there is no way to control the browse list itself. Your list is not specific to you; it is the entire list for either your workgroup, domain, or network. (The exception, however, is shares that end with a dollar sign ($) are not visible.)

A delay time in updating the browse list may make it appear incomplete or it may contain items that you cannot access, even though you have been given the correct permissions. In effect, the server you attempt to access is either not available anymore (which results in your being denied access to a server you had previously been allowed to access), or the server does not appear in the browse list.

Direct Communication with a NetBIOS Resource

By directly working with a resource, the browse list delay problem can be avoided. Using the exact name of the network host that contains the resource that you want to access, this workaround is similar to the `Net View` command but with a graphical interface.

The following steps demonstrate how to directly access a computer and to bypass any browser list delay problems:

1. Click the **Start** button.
2. Click **Find**.

3. Click **Computer**.
4. Type in the name of the server you are trying to find.
5. Click **Find Now**.

Alternatively, you can go to the Start menu, choose **Run**, and enter the **\\computername**.

You should then see a list of resources available on that system.

The direct approach bypasses browsing and resolves the NetBIOS name to an IP address. It is especially helpful when a new resource has been made available but may not have appeared on any browse list, or when you want to see whether a resource to which you are being denied access is really currently available on the network. You can also use the `Net Use` command at the command prompt to specify the remote resource you are going to access. The `Net Use` command is typically used with the previously described `Net View` command; whereas the `Net View` command lists only that server's shared resources, the `Net Use` command actually attaches you to the resource.

7. Master and Backup Browsers are determined by which of the following? Select the best answer.

C. Elections

7. CORRECT ANSWER: C

The decision of which computers are Master and Backup Browsers is determined through browse elections. This process may be determined in part by manual settings made by an administrator. In this case, you might think of it as a fixed election.

8. All other factors being equal, which of the following machines on a network is most likely to be the Master Browser?

C. Windows NT Server

8. CORRECT ANSWER: C

Windows NT computers are favored over Windows 95 computers to be browsers. As a part of the hierarchy among operating systems, it is assumed that a Windows NT system is better equipped with hardware that supports browsing with minimal impact to the user.

9. A Windows 95 computer can be configured to maintain or to not maintain browse lists by configuring which of the following? Select the best answer.

A. The File and Printer Sharing service

9. CORRECT ANSWER: A

A Windows 95 computer can be configured to maintain or to not maintain browse lists by configuring the File and Printer Sharing service. Further settings are available though the registry which provide fine-tuning. However, these settings typically should not be altered because they may have a great impact on the system. For the registry setting for your operating system, visit Microsoft's home page at **www.microsoft.com** and look at their knowledge base.

10. Under what circumstances would a Windows 95 machine be set up as a Master Browser?

C. When elected

10. CORRECT ANSWER: C

Normally, you let the browser elections automatically determine which computers are the browsers.

11. What would be one reason to prevent a Windows 95 machine from being a Master Browser or Backup Browser?

A. When performance load is critical

11. CORRECT ANSWER: A

If you do not want the potential performance load on a Windows 95 computer that can result from browsing, you can configure the computer to never be a browser.

12. To have Windows 95 automatically determine whether the computer is needed as a browse server, which option should you select?

A. Enabled: May Be Master

12. CORRECT ANSWER: A

To have Windows 95 automatically determine whether the computer is needed as a browse server, select **Enabled: May Be Master**. This is useful when you have limited hardware and are concerned about availability.

13. To prevent the computer from maintaining browse lists for the network, which option should you select?

A. Enabled: May Not Be Master

13. CORRECT ANSWER: A

To prevent the computer from maintaining browse lists for the network, select **Enabled: May Not Be Master**. This option is desirable when you do not want to add any potential loads to a system. In some cases where network traffic is extreme, clients may have difficulty talking to a master and would be better served if others provided support.

14. Selecting the Enabled: May Not Be Master option has what effect on browsing the network?

D. Does not prevent the computer from browsing the network resources

14. CORRECT ANSWER: D

Selecting the **Enabled: May Not Be Master** option does not prevent the computer from browsing the network resources.

15. To prevent the computer from using the browse service altogether, what option should you select?

B. DISABLED

15. CORRECT ANSWER: B

Select the **DISABLED** option to prevent the computer from using the browse service. This is useful to secure your network and to keep users from accessing areas that they shouldn't.

16. To give the priority in browse elections, which option should you select?

C. Enabled: Preferred Master

16. CORRECT ANSWER: C

To give the computer a higher weighting for the browse elections, select **Enabled: Preferred Master**. This option assists an administrator in balancing traffic and creating a predictable environment.

17. If a server name doesn't appear on the browse list, what is one possible cause?

B. The Master Browser hasn't updated the Backup Browser.

17. CORRECT ANSWER: B

The most likely cause of the server name not appearing on the browse list is that the Master Browser has not updated the Backup Browser. A workaround to this situation is to access the server directly rather than through the browser list.

18. You are running a Windows NT 4.0 server that is currently the Primary Domain Controller, and you have a multiple domain network. What browser roles does the server have?

B. Master Browser

D. Domain Master Browser

18. CORRECT ANSWERS: B-D

The Primary Domain Controller can be a Master Browser and Domain Master Browser.

19. Which one of these situations is true regarding Master Browser to Backup Browser synchronization?

D. The Backup Browser copies the updates from the Master Browser.

19. CORRECT ANSWER: D

The Backup Browser duplicates information from the Master Browser in the same manner as a BDC backs up a PDC. The only difference is that clients do not access the browse list from the Master Browser. The Master Browser offers clients a list of backup browsers.

20. If you have a domain set up with two Windows 95 computers, three Windows NT Workstations computers, three Windows NT server computers, and four Windows for Workgroup computers, which is the third Backup Browser for this domain?

C. Windows NT Workstation

20. CORRECT ANSWER: C

A Windows NT Workstation is the most likely choice for the third Backup Browser in the situation given. Each operating system is given a weight for use in an election. When determining which computer will be a browser, it is awarded to the system with the highest tally.

21. Which of the following is in charge of continually updating the browse list and managing the database of network servers on domains and workgroups?

B. Master Browser

21. CORRECT ANSWER: B

The Master Browser is in charge of continually updating the browse list. Others, such as backup browsers, simply download the information or have the functionality to do the task, but don't. Because only the Master Browser performs this function, there is less of a drain on network resources.

Browsing Roles

The role of a browser will vary while running on a network. The following list describes these roles:

- **Master Browser**—Collects and maintains the master list of available resources in its domain or workgroup as well as the list of names, not resources, in other domains and workgroups. Distributes the browse list to Backup Browsers.
- **Backup Browser**—Obtains its browse list from the Master Browser and passes this list to requesting clients.
- **Domain Master Browser**—Fulfills the role of a Master Browser for its domain as well as coordinating and synchronizing the browse lists from all other Master Browsers for the domains that reside on remote networks. A Domain Master Browser is required per domain to maintain the list and make the list available to browsers on other domains.
- **Potential Browser**—A computer that could be a Master, Backup, or Domain Master Browser, if needed, is currently not enabled and does not hold a browse list.
- **Non-Browser**—A computer that does not maintain a browse list.

How Roles Are Assigned

Windows NT Workstation, Windows NT Server, Windows for Workgroups, and Windows 95/98 can all perform these browsing roles. However, only a Windows NT Server acting as a Primary Domain Controller (PDC) may occupy the role of the Domain Master Browser. In a LAN, the Domain Master Browser is also the Master Browser.

Windows NT Workstation and Windows NT Member Servers can become Backup Browsers if there are three Windows NT server-based computers not already filling these roles for the workgroup or domain.

To determine and control the roles in which your computers are participating as browsers, you must look in the Registry. By understanding some default rules and invoking a little user intervention, you can control the browsing environment to a certain extent. By default, Windows NT and Windows 95 are set to auto—meaning either one has the potential to fill a browsing role. The Master Browser is chosen through an *election process*, which is based on the following criteria:

- A Windows NT-based computer takes precedence over a Windows 95 or Windows for Workgroups computer. Windows 95 will take priority over Windows for Workgroups. This hierarchy is true at any time. Even if a Windows 95 machine has been on for two years, as soon as a Windows NT computer comes online, an election will be held. The Windows NT computer will always win because of its higher priority rating.
- If the two operating systems are equal, the computer that has been turned on longer will win the election and will become the new Master Browser.
- If none of the above criteria fit, the server with a NetBIOS name of lowest alphabetical lettering will win the election. For example, if the contest is between Argyle and Zot, the server named Argyle will become the next Master Browser.

Controlling Your Browser Role

To control the browser role that your computer is playing for a Windows NT Server and Windows NT Workstation, you can change the IsDomainMaster Registry setting to a true or yes to force your computer to be the Master Browser. This setting is found in the following Registry subkey:

```
\HKEY_LOCAL_MACHINE\SYSTEM\CurrentControlSet\Services
➥\Browser\Parameters
```

To control your browser role for Windows 95, the File and Print Sharing for Microsoft Networks service is required. Browsing roles can be implemented through the following steps:

1. Right-click **Network Neighborhood**.
2. Choose **Properties**.
3. Select the **File and Print Sharing for Microsoft Networks** service if you have it installed. If it is not installed, you are not currently participating in browsing. You can install the service by clicking the **Add** button, selecting **Microsoft**, and then adding **File and Print Sharing for Microsoft Networks**.
4. Choose **Properties**.
5. Select **Browse Master**, which is set to Automatic by default; you can either enable or disable it.

These are the only controls you have for configuring the browser roles of your computers. So you could turn IsDomainMaster Registry off on all but the specific machines that you want to participate in browsing. If one of those machines goes down, however, there goes your browsing. You cannot directly control Backup Browsers and can only set them to auto with one set to IsDomainMaster.

Understanding the Cost of Browsing

The first cost of browsing is the bandwidth consumed by network traffic. The second is that browsing reduces the performance of the system that acts as a Master Browser.

This performance degradation may be noticeable on slower systems such as a 486/66, but not as noticeable on most newer machines, such as a Pentium II 300. Anything the computer does will affect its performance in some way, but remember that being a Browse Master means keeping an updated list of network resources. The number of network resources that the Browse Master needs to track obviously will affect that computer's performance accordingly. The best you can do to minimize this performance degradation is to minimize the number of computers sharing network resources. Doing so keeps the browse list short, thereby relieving the strain on the Master Browser.

Windows NT Browsing Services

Most of what happens in the browsing process happens automatically, without any intervention. Sometimes, however, problems develop, and understanding the browsing process can help you find solutions.

The browsing services have three main break points, or sections, in Windows NT:

1. Collecting information for the browse list
2. Distributing the browse list itself
3. Servicing browser client requests for the list

22. Which of these statements is not true about the `DomainAnnouncement` packet?

D. If it is a Windows NT server, it specifies the version number of the server.

22. CORRECT ANSWER: D

The DomainAnnouncement packet carries the name of a domain, the name of the Master Browser, and whether the Master Browser is a server or workstation.

Collecting the Browse List

The first important part of being able to browse network servers is the collection of the browse list itself. The Master Browser continually updates its browse list to include the current network servers available. This update process is continual because as servers appear and disappear, the Master Browser must constantly revise its browse list. This process happens every time a computer that has something to share is turned on and every time one that is sharing resources is turned off.

The Master Browser obtains a list of servers in its own domain or workgroup, as well as a list of other domains and workgroups, and updates these servers with network resources to the browse list as changes are made. Much of this process has to do with browser announcements.

When a computer that is running a server service is turned on, it announces itself to the Master Browser which then adds this new resource to its browse list. This step happens whether or not the computer has resources to share. When a computer is shut down properly, it announces to the Master Browser that it is leaving; again, the Master Browser updates its list accordingly.

Master Browsers also receive DomainAnnouncement packets from other domains and place these packets in their own local browse lists. DomainAnnouncement packets contain the following information:

- The name of the domain.
- The name of the Master Browser for that domain.
- Whether the browser is a Windows NT Server or Windows NT Workstation computer.
- If the browser is a Windows NT Server computer, it is the Primary Domain Controller for that domain.

Distributing the Browse List

Another important part of browsing is the distribution of the previously collected browse list. The extent of this distribution depends largely on the size of the network. A Master Browser broadcasts a message every so often to let the Backup Browsers know the Master Browser is still around. If the Master Browser does not send this message, the network holds an election process to elect a new Master Browser. Also, if a Master does not reply to a request, a client may also trigger an election.

The Master Browser holds the list of network resources. The Backup Browser contacts the Master Browser and copies the list from the Master Browser. Therefore, the Backup Browsers are the active components, intermittently contacting the passive Master Browser for the updated list.

23. You have a network with five different subnets, each with its own Master Browser. The network administrator wants to be able to see resources of each subnet at the same time. Which process allows for this?

A. Directed datagram

23. CORRECT ANSWER: A

A directed datagram enables you to see resources for each subnet at the same time. Keep in mind that as you work with TCP/IP, all materials aside from routing must be directed. With a protocol such as NetBEUI, multiple subnets must be bridged and therefore the matter of being directed does not apply.

24. If a domain announcement is sent out to a domain and the domain does not respond, how long is it before the remote domain is removed from the browse list?

B. Three announcement periods

24. CORRECT ANSWER: B

A remote domain is removed from the browse list when it does not respond to an initial announcement after three announcement periods (which occur within 45 minutes). Remember that the timeout for servers is every 12 minutes, not 15 as with domains and workgroups.

25. Suppose you have a network with three subnets: subnet A, subnet B, and subnet C. What happens if the Domain Master Browser on subnet A goes down?

A. Browsing is restricted to each subnet.

25. CORRECT ANSWER: A

If a domain's Master Browser goes down, browsing is restricted to each subnet. This problem occurs only if a NetBIOS-enabled router is not in use.

26. How is it possible to browse across routers without the use of WINS, DNS, HOSTS, or LMHOSTS? Select the best answer.

C. You can use a NetBIOS-enabled router.

26. CORRECT ANSWER: C

You can use a NetBIOS-enabled router to browse across routers. If this service is not available on the router, the only other possible solution would be to use a third-party proxy device. However, at that point, you would have been better off to just simply use WINS.

Browsing over Subnets

Within Windows NT, every local subnet—a collection of computers separated by a router—is its own browsing area. This browsing area is complete with its own Master Browser and Backup Browsers. Subnets hold browser elections for their own subnet. Therefore, if you have multiple subnets on your internetwork, it needs a Domain Master Browser to permit browsing over more than just one subnet. In addition, each subnet needs at least one Windows NT controller to register with the Domain Master Browser to support multiple-subnet browsing.

Generally, broadcasts do not go through a router; the router needs to be enabled to allow passing of broadcasts (137 and 138 UDP are the NetBIOS ports). If a domain has multiple subnets, each Master Browser for each subnet uses a directed datagram called a *MasterBrowserAnnouncement.* The MasterBrowser Announcement tells the Domain Master Browser that the subnet Master Browser is available and what it has on its browse list. Because they are directed, these datagrams pass through the routers which enables these updates to occur.

The Domain Master Browser adds all the subnet Master Browser lists to its own browse list, providing a complete browse list of the entire domain, including all subnets. This process occurs, by default, every 15 minutes to ensure regular list updates. The timing of the MasterBrowserAnnouncement is controlled through the registry by the HKEY_LOCAL_MACHINE\system\currentcontrolset\services \browser\parameters\MasterPeriodicity setting in Windows NT 4. Prior to Windows NT 4, the timing was not adjustable. Windows NT workgroups and Windows for Workgroups are not able to send a MasterBrowserAnnouncement packet, and therefore cannot span these multiple subnets or have a complete list—thus the need for Windows NT domain controllers to allow for multiple-subnet browsing.

Browser Announcement Periods

When the Master Browser first comes online, it sends out a DomainAnnouncement once a minute for the first 5 minutes and then once every 15 minutes after that. If the domain does not respond by sending out its own DomainAnnouncement for three successive announcement periods, the domain is removed from the Master Browser list. In this scenario, it is possible that a domain or workgroup may remain on the list for up to 45 minutes after it becomes unavailable.

Do not confuse the removal of a Domain or Workgroup from the browser list with that of a server or workstation. A server or workstation will be removed from the Master Browser if it does not receive a server announcement for three periods (which occurs every 12 minutes). It is therefore possible for a server to appear on a browse list for up to 36 (3×12) minutes after it originally becomes unavailable.

Domain Master Browser Failure

In the event of a Domain Master Browser failure, users on the entire network are limited to their own individual subnets, assuming that a Master Browser for their subnet exists. If a subnet doesn't have a Master Browser, no browsing is possible. Without a Domain Master Browser, no complete overall browse list exists of the entire domain, and within three announcement periods, all other servers not on the local subnet are removed from the browse list. You then must either promote a Backup Domain Controller to perform the role of Domain Master Browser or bring the downed Domain Master Browser back online before the time limit expires for its three announcements. Remember the Backup Domain Controller does not automatically promote itself, and after a new Domain Master Browser is elected, it will take time to collect the browse list from all the different subnets. There is no way you can force the browse list to move faster.

Servicing Client Browser Requests

The final browsing service process is the actual servicing of client requests. Now that a browse list exists and has been distributed, clients have something to access.

The process follows these steps:

1. The client tries to access a domain or workgroup using Microsoft Internet Explorer. In doing so, it contacts the Master Browser of the domain or workgroup that it is trying to access.
2. The Master Browser gives the client a list of three Backup Browsers.
3. The client then asks for the server from one of the Backup Browsers.
4. The Backup Browser provides the list of servers in the relevant domain or workgroup.
5. The client chooses a server and obtains a list of that server's shared resources.

This process can occasionally cause some conflict if the Master Browser has a resource in its list, but the Backup Browser has not updated itself yet and the client connects to that Backup Browser and looks for the current list. The resource is not yet listed in the backup browse list, which is another reason why items that are not available may appear on the list or may not be on the list at all.

Browsing in an IP Internetwork

The major obstacle in browsing an IP internetwork is that browsing relies on broadcast packets. Because routers generally do not forward these broadcast packets, a browsing problem is created for collecting, distributing, and servicing the client request for browse lists. As such, packets are not forwarded and you are unable to browse in an internetwork environment without a local domain controller. In effect, you have very limited or no browsing capabilities.

Note that DomainAnnouncement allows only for Master Browsers to talk to the Domain Master Browser. The problem occurs when this function cannot take place.

27. What does the #PRE statement in an LMHOSTS file do?

B. Preloads an entry into cache

27. CORRECT ANSWER: B

The #PRE statement in the LMHOSTS file preloads an entry into the NetBIOS name cache.

28. When should you put the addresses of the other Master Browsers into the LMHOSTS file as well as into the Domain Master Browser?

B. If the Domain Master Browser goes down, you do not have to change your LMHOSTS file to access the new Domain Master Browser.

28. CORRECT ANSWER: B

The domains of other Master Browsers should be placed in the LMHOSTS file to access new Domain Master Browsers in case your Domain Master Browser goes down.

29. Which method of updating across routers does WINS use to take the place of an LMHOSTS file over a network?

A. Dynamically

29. CORRECT ANSWER: A

WINS updates dynamically, whereas LMHOSTS is static.

30. Which two additional Windows NT network services initiate a broadcast in a domain, but not across routers?

C. Logging in and passwords; PDC-to-BDC replication

30. CORRECT ANSWER: C

Broadcasts can be initiated by users logging in, as well as by PDC-to-BDC replication.

31. The LMHOSTS file is mainly used on a network with non-WINS clients specifically for what job?

B. Resolving a NetBIOS name to an IP address

31. CORRECT ANSWER: B

The LMHOSTS file resolves remote IP addresses to NetBIOS names. Note that local addresses can either be resolved by the local name cache or broadcast.

Internetworking Browser Solutions

There are a few possible solutions to the problem of being able to browse in an IP internetwork; for example, the use of a UDP port 137\138-enabled router and an LMHOSTS file.

IP Router

Configuring a router to forward NetBIOS name broadcasts eliminates problems associated with browsing across subnets. In effect, all broadcasts and network resource requests appear to all client computers as if the broadcasts are all on the same subnet. Master Browsers have their own lists as well as those of the other domains and workgroups, so when a client makes an inquiry for a browse list, the list can be provided for any domain or workgroup. Note that solutions that make routers bridge network traffic, such as BOOTP-enabled routers, are not good solutions because they increase traffic on the entire network.

LMHOSTS File

An LMHOSTS file can be used to eliminate subnet issues by providing a client with the ability to issue directed traffic rather than broadcasts. In other words, NetBIOS names can be resolved locally, thereby providing access to resources on remote subnets. This allows communication between Master Browsers on remote subnets and the Domain Master Browser.

Using an `LMHOSTS` file is a workable solution but has some special requirements. For example, the `LMHOSTS` file must be on each subnet's Master Browser with an entry to the Domain Master Browser. It must also be updated manually any time there are changes to the LMHOSTS list. The `LMHOSTS` file needs to be placed in the `winntroot\system32\drivers\etc` directory on NT systems and in the windows folder in Windows for Workgroups, Windows 95 and Windows 98. (See the sample TCP/IP files for reference.) The LMHOSTS list is a regular text file that can be created using any text editor. There is no file extension, and Windows NT will look for and reference the file in this location whenever it needs to.

To work across a subnet, the `LMHOSTS` file needs the following two items:

- IP address and computer name of the Domain Master Browser
- The domain name preceded by `#PRE` and `#DOM:`

```
129.62.101.5     server1           #PRE #DOM:try
129.62.101.17    server2           #PRE
129.62.101.25    server3           #PRE
```

The `#PRE` statement preloads the specific line it is on into the NetBIOS name cache as a permanent entry, making it easily available without having to first access the domain.

`#DOM:<domain_name>` supports logon validation over a router, account synchronization, and, in this case, browsing. Every time the computer sends a broadcast to a domain, it also sends the broadcast to every computer that has a `#DOM:` in its `LMHOSTS` file. These types of broadcasts do go across routers, but are not sent to workgroups. The many difficulties to watch out for are discussed in the following subsections.

LMHOSTS File Problems

The most common problems you might have with the `LMHOSTS` file are the following:

- The NetBIOS name is misspelled.
- The IP address is incorrect.

- An entry is not listed for that host.
- There are too many entries for a host where only the first entry is used. For example, if the `LMHOSTS` file has multiple entries for the same host computer, only the first one listed will be used.
- The `LMHOSTS` file is in the incorrect location and is not being read.
- The `LMHOSTS` file is out-of-date with respect to its listings.

Note that the `LMHOSTS` file can be created with any standard text editor. If using Notepad, remember to discard the `.txt` extension.

Domain Master Browser

For the Domain Master Browser, you need an `LMHOSTS` file that is set up with entries pointing to each of the remote subnet Master Browsers. You should also have a `#DOM:` statement in each of the Master Browsers' `LMHOSTS` files that points to each of the other subnet Master Browsers. If any of them gets promoted to the Domain Master Browser, you then do not have to change all your `LMHOSTS` files.

Duplicate Names

If a duplicate LMHOSTS entry for a single domain is found, the Master Browser decides which one relates to the Domain Master Browser by querying each IP address for each entry it has. None of the Master Browsers respond; only the Domain Master Browser does. Therefore, the Master Browser narrows down the list of duplicates, and because only the real one responds, the Master Browser communicates with the one that responds and proceeds to exchange browse lists.

The WINS Solution

WINS helps to solve the problem of NetBIOS broadcast difficulties by dynamically registering the IP address and NetBIOS name and keeping track of them in a database. Keeping these computer names in its database greatly enhances the network performance. Whenever there is a need to find a server, clients access the WINS server rather than broadcasting on the network. Accessing the WINS server directly is a more efficient approach when looking for network resources. In addition, this approach makes updating much easier because you do not have to manually configure anything.

Domain Browser

If a computer is configured as a WINS client, the Domain Master Browser periodically queries the WINS server to update its database comprised of all the domains listed in the WINS database, thereby providing a complete list of all the domains and subnets. The list will in effect contain only domain names and IP addresses, not the names of the Master Browsers of each particular subnet.

Client Access

When a client needs access to a network resource, it calls the WINS server directly and asks for a list of domain controllers. WINS provides a list of up to 25 domain controllers, referred to as a *Domain group*. A client is then able to access a domain controller without a network broadcast.

PRACTICE QUESTIONS

INSTALL AND CONFIGURE A WINS SERVER, IMPORT LMHOSTS FILES TO WINS, CONFIGURE WINS REPLICATION, CONFIGURE STATIC MAPPINGS IN THE WINS DATABASE

1. **WINS must be installed on which version of Windows NT Server?**

   A. 3.1 or greater

   B. 3.5 or greater

   C. 3.51 or greater

   D. 4.0 or greater

2. **WINS can be installed on which of the following? Select all that apply.**

   A. Windows NT Workstation

   B. Member server

   C. Backup Domain Controller

   D. Primary Domain Controller

3. **To use WINS, what do clients need to know about the WINS server? Select the best response.**

   A. Host name

   B. Subnet mask

   C. Default gateway

   D. IP address

4. **Which of the following can be WINS clients? Select all that apply.**

   A. Windows NT Server 3.5

   B. Windows NT Workstation 3.5

   C. Windows 95

   D. Microsoft Network Client 2.0 for MS-DOS

   E. LAN Manager 2.2c for MS-DOS

5. **You can register a non-WINS client with a WINS server by performing what task?**

   A. Adding a static entry to the WINS database

   B. Creating a reservation for the entry

   C. Modifying the scope to exclude the address

   D. Manually editing the cache

6. **With entries added for non-WINS clients, a WINS client can resolve more names without having to look up the entries in what file?**

   A. `HOSTS`

   B. `SERVICES`

   C. `LMHOSTS`

   D. `NETWORKS`

7. **On which platforms can you install a WINS server? Select all that apply.**

   A. On a Windows NT 3.51 member server

B. On a Windows NT 4.0 Workstation running the WINS proxy agent

C. On a Windows NT 4.0 Backup Domain Controller

D. On a Windows NT 4.0 Primary Domain Controller

8. How many WINS servers should be installed?

A. One primary for each subnet and one secondary for every two subnets

B. One primary for every 2,000 clients and one secondary for every additional 2,000 clients

C. One primary and one secondary for every 10,000 clients

D. One primary and one secondary for each domain

9. Where does a client first look to resolve a NetBIOS name?

A. In the NetBIOS cache on the WINS server

B. In the NetBIOS cache on the WINS proxy agent

C. In the NetBIOS cache on the primary Domain Controller

D. In the NetBIOS cache on the client

10. What types of names are registered by WINS clients? Select all that apply.

A. The computername

B. The domain name of a domain controller

C. Share names created on that computer

D. The names of network services

11. When does a WINS client try to renew its registration?

A. After three days

B. One day before the registration expires

C. Every 24 hours

D. When half of the registration life has expired

12. Where should a WINS proxy agent be located?

A. On the same subnet as non-WINS clients

B. On the same subnet as the DHCP server

C. On the same subnet as the DNS server

D. On the same subnet as the DHCP relay agent

13. How can the WINS clients of one WINS server resolve the addresses of clients registered with another WINS server?

A. The WINS server can be configured for recursive lookup to the other WINS server.

B. The WINS server can be a replication partner of the other server.

C. The client can be configured with the address of the other WINS server as its secondary WINS server.

D. The WINS servers automatically synchronize their databases.

14. Static entries are added through which of the following? Select the best answer.

A. Entry Manager

B. ARP cache

C. HOSTS file

D. WINS Manager

15. How can you add entries for non-WINS clients to a WINS server's database? Select all that apply.

A. Configure the WINS server to be a pull partner for a DNS server

B. Import an `LMHOSTS` file

C. Install the WINS proxy agent on the segment with non-WINS clients

D. Add the entries with WINS Manager

16. How do you configure replication to occur at specified intervals?

A. Configure a WINS server to be a pull partner

B. Use the `AT` command to schedule replication

C. Configure a WINS server to be a push partner

D. Edit the ReplIntrvl parameter in the Registry

17. How can you configure a WINS server to automatically replicate its database with any other WINS servers?

A. Specify All servers as push partners for replication

B. Turn on the Migrate On/Off switch in WINS Manager

C. Change the UseSelfFndPnrs parameter in the Registry to `0`

D. Turn off the Replicate Only with Partners switch in WINS Manager

18. Which replication option is best for WINS servers separated by a slow WAN link?

A. Pull replication configured to replicate after 100 changes

B. Push replication configured to replicate after 100 changes

C. Pull replication configured to replicate at 6 a.m. and 6 p.m.

D. Push replication configured to replicate at 6 a.m. and 6 p.m.

19. Which of the following is not a valid WINS static mapping type?

A. Normal Group

B. Multihomed

C. Domain Name

D. Internet Group

E. None of the above

20. How does WINS integrate `LMHOST` entries to its database?

A. By reading automatically and dynamically from the system on which the WINS service resides

B. By using server manager and polling systems for entries so that it can determine the #DOM entries

C. By reading automatically on install, but no other time

D. By using WINS service manager and manually running an import procedure

21. By default, where does the WINS server first write changes to the database?

A. To the log file

B. To the database

C. To the Registry

D. To the temporary database

22. Where can you see a record of WINS server error messages? Select the best answer.

A. In the Windows NT System Event log

B. In the ERROR.LOG file in the WINS directory

C. In the Windows NT Application Event log

D. In the error log in WINS Manager

23. What does a WINS server do if it receives a name registration request for a host name already in its database?

A. It replaces the old entry with the newer one.

B. It queries the host of the existing registration to see whether the registration is still valid.

C. It denies the registration request.

D. It adds the registration as an alternative address for the existing name.

24. How do you install a WINS proxy agent?

A. From Control Panel, select **Network**, then choose **Services**.

B. From Control Panel, select **Add Programs**.

C. By changing a Registry entry.

D. By running the Network Client Administration tool from the WINS program group.

25. How does a client decide which WINS server to use? Select all that apply.

A. The first WINS server that responds to a broadcast

B. The WINS server that WINS an election

C. The primary WINS server configured in TCP/IP

D. The primary WINS server specified in the DHCP scope options

26. What happens to a name registration when the host crashes?

A. The WINS server marks the record as released after it queries the client at half of TTL.

B. The name is marked as released after three renewal periods are missed.

C. The name is scavenged after the registration expires.

D. The name is released after the TTL is over.

27. Where is WINS configuration information stored?

A. In the `\WINNT\SYSTEM32\WINS` directory

B. In the Registry

C. In the `WINS.CFG` file in the `WINNT` directory

D. In the `J50.CHK` file in the `WINS` directory

28. How do you configure automatic backup of the WINS database?

A. Use the AT command to schedule the backup.

B. Specify the name of the backup directory in WINS Manager.

C. Specify the backup interval in WINS Manager.

D. Install a tape device through Control Panel, SCSI Adapters.

ANSWER KEY

1. B	8. C	15. B-D	22. C
2. B-C-D	9. D	16. A	23. B
3. D	10. A-B-D	17. D	24. C
4. A-B-C	11. D	18. C	25. C-D
5. A	12. A	19. E	26. D
6. C	13. B	20. D	27. B
7. A-C-D	14. D	21. A	28. B

ANSWERS & EXPLANATIONS

INSTALL AND CONFIGURE A WINS SERVER, IMPORT LMHOSTS FILES TO WINS, CONFIGURE WINS REPLICATION, CONFIGURE STATIC MAPPINGS IN THE WINS DATABASE

1. WINS must be installed on which version of Windows NT Server?

B. 3.5 or greater

1. CORRECT ANSWER: B

WINS must be installed on a Windows NT Server version 3.5x or 4.0. Although it is possible to use third-party solutions on a platform such as Windows NT Workstation, the Microsoft components work only on the server.

2. WINS can be installed on which of the following? Select all that apply.

B. Member server

C. Backup Domain Controller

D. Primary Domain Controller

2. CORRECT ANSWERS: B-C-D

You can install WINS on any configuration of Windows NT Server—a member server, a Backup Domain Controller, or a Primary Domain Controller. WINS operates as an independent service beyond domains with the exception of administrator management.

3. To use WINS, what do clients need to know about the WINS server? Select the best response.

D. IP address

3. CORRECT ANSWER: D

Until WINS clients are configured with the IP address of the WINS server, they cannot register their names or use the WINS server for name resolution.

4. Which of the following can be WINS clients? Select all that apply.

A. Windows NT Server 3.5

B. Windows NT Workstation 3.5

C. Windows 95

4. CORRECT ANSWERS: A-B-C

Any Microsoft Windows System capable of networking can be a WINS client.

5. You can register a non-WINS client with a WINS server by performing what task?

A. Adding a static entry to the WINS database

5. CORRECT ANSWER: A

Because not all clients will participate with the WINS server, but will still require name resolution, you should register them with a WINS server by adding a static entry to the WINS database. This will also serve to protect other systems from attempting to duplicate a system's NetBIOS name.

6. With entries added for non-WINS clients, a WINS client can resolve more names without having to look up the entries in what file?

C. LMHOSTS

6. CORRECT ANSWER: C

With entries added for non-WINS clients, a WINS client can resolve more names without having to look up the entries in an `LMHOSTS` file. This functionality is extremely useful when you must integrate with a foreign network and do not desire to merge the two completely together. Also, if you need to assign temporary names, such as in a test environment, this would also allow their resolution.

7. On which platforms can you install a WINS server? Select all that apply.

A. On a Windows NT 3.51 member server

C. On a Windows NT 4.0 Backup Domain Controller

D. On a Windows NT 4.0 Primary Domain Controller

7. CORRECT ANSWERS: A-C-D

You can install a WINS server on any Windows NT Server platform. Keep in mind that WINS is a special service that will not function under lower operating systems such as Windows 95 or Windows for Workgroups.

8. How many WINS servers should be installed?

C. One primary and one secondary for every 10,000 clients

8. CORRECT ANSWER: C

You should have one primary and one secondary WINS server for every 10,000 WINS clients. Although the secondary server is not required, it can serve as a backup if the primary WINS server goes down.

9. Where does a client first look to resolve a NetBIOS name?

D. In the NetBIOS cache on the client

9. CORRECT ANSWER: D

A client always tries to resolve a NetBIOS name through its own name cache. Assuming that a client is configured as a Hybrid (H-Node) or Peer (P-Node) resolution system—if the entry is not found, then the client sends a name resolution request to the WINS server. The WINS server looks in the WINS database for the resolution at that point.

10. What type of names are registered by WINS clients? Select all that apply.

A. The computername

B. The domain name of a domain controller

D. The names of network services

10. CORRECT ANSWERS: A-B-D

All networking services register with WINS. A domain controller must also register its domain name with WINS, along with its computer name, so clients of that domain can log on. These services are described in the 16th character of the NetBIOS name.

11. When does a WINS client try to renew its registration?

D. When half of the registration life has expired

11. CORRECT ANSWER: D

A client first tries to renew its registration when half of the time to live has expired. Although the default time to live is six days, the more correct answer is half of the TTL because the default TTL could have been changed.

Installing and Configuring a WINS Server

WINS must be installed on a Windows NT Server version 3.5x or 4.0. WINS servers on any version are compatible with the others; that is, you can mix a Windows NT 3.51 WINS server with a Windows NT 4.0 WINS server, including using them as replication partners. You can install WINS on any configuration of Windows NT Server—a member server, a Backup Domain Controller, or a Primary Domain Controller. The WINS server should have a static TCP/IP address with a subnet mask and default gateway along with any other TCP/IP parameters required for your network (such as a DNS server address). You can assign a DHCP address to the WINS server (the address should be reserved so the WINS server always receives the same address), but using a static address is the recommended option. Also, you should specify a WINS server address; in this case, the address is the same machine.

The WINS service is installed as a network service. After it is installed, it is immediately available for use. However, until WINS clients are configured with the TCP/IP address of the WINS server, they cannot register their names or use the WINS server for name resolution. In fact, if no clients are configured with this WINS server's address, the WINS database remains empty unless you add static entries or set up replication with another WINS server.

WINS Clients

Almost any Microsoft client capable of networking can be a WINS client:

- Windows NT Server 3.5x, 4.0
- Windows NT Workstation 3.5x, 4.0
- Windows 95
- Windows for Workgroups with TCP/IP-32
- Microsoft Network Client 3.0 for MS-DOS
- LAN Manager 2.2c for MS-DOS

However, only the Windows-based clients can register their names with the WINS server. The DOS-based clients can use the WINS server for name resolution, but you must add static entries for DOS clients to the WINS server so their names can be resolved.

To enable these clients for WINS, the address of the primary WINS server must be specified on the client. The client can also have the address of a secondary WINS server configured. The client can either have this configuration information manually entered at the client or it can receive the configuration information with its TCP/IP address from a DHCP server.

Configuring a Client for WINS

Microsoft TCP/IP systems including Windows for Workgroups, Windows NT, Windows 98, and Windows 95 can be configured as WINS clients. For those using NT, 95, and 98, the following instructions will manually configure a WINS client:

1. Specify the WINS server address as part of the TCP/IP configuration.
2. Open the TCP/IP properties in the Protocol tab of the Network Properties dialog box (opened with Control Panel, Network).
3. Select the WINS tab in the TCP/IP Properties dialog box and simply specify the address of a primary WINS server. If you are using a secondary WINS server (recommended for every 10,000 clients), you should also type in the IP address of the secondary WINS server.

DHCP & WINS

Clients can automatically be configured to operate with WINS via Microsoft's DHCP server (discussed in Chapter 5, "DHCP"). To configure a DHCP client to be a WINS client, you must add two properties to the DHCP scope created on the DHCP server. Under the DHCP scope options, add the following parameters:

- **`044 WINS/NBNS Servers`**—Configure this parameter with the address of the primary WINS server and a secondary WINS server if desired.
- **`046 WINS/NBT Node`**—By default, this parameter is set to `1`, a b-node broadcast. WINS clients use h-node broadcasts, so you must change the value of this parameter to `8`.

12. Where should a WINS proxy agent be located?

A. On the same subnet as non-WINS clients

12. CORRECT ANSWER: A

You should locate a WINS proxy agent on each subnet that has non-WINS clients. Non-WINS clients resort to b-node broadcasts to resolve NetBIOS names, yet these broadcasts are typically forwarded by routers. The only way to have the request forwarded to a WINS server is to have a WINS proxy agent on the subnet so it can hear the broadcast.

Configuring WINS to Be Used by Non-WINS Clients

A WINS server interacts in two ways with WINS clients.First, it registers the names of those clients. Second, it answers requests for name resolutions (name queries). You can enable both functions for non-WINS clients through additional configuration.

13. How can the WINS clients of one WINS server resolve the addresses of clients registered with another WINS server?

B. The WINS server can be a replication partner of the other server.

13. CORRECT ANSWER: B

WINS clients register their addresses only with the primary WINS server. If the registration succeeds, the clients won't attempt to contact the secondary WINS server. WINS servers copy entries to their replication partners, but it doesn't happen automatically; the copying process must be configured.

14. Static entries are added through which of the following? Select the best answer.

D. WINS Manager

14. CORRECT ANSWER: D

With the exception of fine-tuning—which may be performed through the registry editor—all control of the WINS server including static entries are made through the WINS Manager.

15. How can you add entries for non-WINS clients to a WINS server's database? Select all that apply.

B. Import an LMHOSTS file

D. Add the entries with WINS Manager

15. CORRECT ANSWERS: B-D

An LMHOSTS file can be imported to a WINS server, which adds all the entries in the LMHOSTS file as static entries in the WINS database. You can also add static entries through WINS Manager. A WINS server can be a replication partner only with another WINS server, not a DNS server. A WINS proxy agent can help non-WINS clients resolve NetBIOS names, but non-WINS clients cannot automatically register their names with a WINS server even if a WINS proxy agent is installed.

Using the WINS Manager

As you install WINS, a WINS Manager tool is added to the Administrative Tools group. You can use this tool to manage the local WINS server and remote WINS servers as well. You can use WINS Manager to view the WINS database, add static entries to the database, configure push and pull partners for replication, and back up and restore the WINS database.

WINS Manager Configuration Dialog

You can use the WINS Manager configuration dialog box to configure how long entries will stay in the WINS database. The following four parameters control the life of entries:

- **Renewal Interval**—The interval given to a WINS client after it successfully registers its name. The client begins renewing the name registration when half this time has expired. The default is six days.
- **Extinction Interval**—The amount of time that must pass before the WINS server marks a released entry as extinct. An extinct entry is not immediately deleted. The default is six days. The time until removal is controlled by the Extinction Timeout parameter.
- **Extinction Timeout**— The amount of time WINS waits before removing (scavenging) entries that have been marked extinct. The default is six days.
- **Verify Interval**—The interval at which the WINS server verifies that names in its database from other servers are still valid. The default is 24 days and cannot be set below this value. This parameter applies if WINS servers are set up for replication.

Initial Replication Configuration

You can configure whether the WINS server replicates with its replication partners when it starts. To do this, check the Initial Replication option under Pull Parameters on the WINS server Configuration dialog box and a pull replication partner will replicate on startup. You can also specify the number of times the pull partner tries to contact the other WINS server since the pull partner does the startup replication.

For a push partner, you can also configure it to replicate upon startup by checking the Initial Replication option under Push Parameters. You can also specify that the push partner replicates when it has an address change.

Advanced Configuration Options

You can turn on or turn off the logging of entries to the WINS database. This log file records changes that are made to the WINS database before they are made. By default, logging is turned on, which gives the WINS server a backup via the log file. If you turn off the logging, the WINS server registers names more quickly, but you lose the backup support of the log file. These settings are configured through the WINS Advanced Configuration dialog box.

The following are the advanced settings you can configure:

- **Log Detailed Events**—This option makes the logging of WINS events in Event Viewer verbose. That is, you get more detailed information from the log file, but at the cost of a slight performance degradation.
- **Replicate Only with Partners**—By default, WINS replicates only with other WINS servers that are specifically configured as push or pull partners. If you want the WINS server to replicate automatically, you must turn off this setting.
- **Backup on Termination**—If you set this option, the WINS database is automatically backed up when the WINS service is stopped. However, the database is not backed up when the Windows NT Server is shut down.
- **Migrate On/Off**—If this switch is on, static entries that have the same address as a WINS client requesting registration are overwritten. This option is helpful if you are converting a computer from a non-Windows NT machine to one with the same TCP/IP address. To have addresses resolved for this non-Windows NT machine in the past, you may have added a static entry to the WINS database. With the option on, the new dynamic entry can overwrite the old static entry. It is usually best to turn off this switch after you have migrated (upgraded) the new Windows NT machine. This switch is off by default so static entries are not overwritten.

- **Starting Version Count**—This option specifies the largest version ID number for the database. Each entry in the database is assigned a version ID. Replication is based on the version ID. A replication partner checks its last replicated entries against the version IDs of the records in the WINS database. The replication partner replicates only records with a later version ID than the last records it replicated from this partner. Usually, you don't need to change this parameter. However, if the database becomes corrupted, you may need to adjust this number so a replication partner replicates the proper entries.
- **Database Backup Path**—When the WINS database is backed up, it is copied to a local hard drive. This entry specifies the path to a directory on a local drive where the WINS backups are stored. This directory can also be used to automatically restore the WINS database. You must specify a local drive path.

16. How do you configure replication to occur at specified intervals?

A. Configure a WINS server to be a pull partner

16. CORRECT ANSWER: A

Only pull partners can have replication occur at specified times. Push replication occurs after a specified number of changes have been made to the WINS database. The ReplIntrvl parameter in the Registry doesn't exist.

17. How can you configure a WINS server to automatically replicate its database with any other WINS servers?

D. Turn off the Replicate Only with Partners switch in WINS Manager

17. CORRECT ANSWER: D

A WINS server can automatically replicate with any other WINS server. However, WINS is configured by default to replicate only with specified partners. You must turn off this parameter to enable the automatic replication.

18. Which replication option is best for WINS servers separated by a slow WAN link?

C. Pull replication configured to replicate at 6 a.m. and 6 p.m.

18. CORRECT ANSWER: C

The best way to manage traffic on a slow WAN link is to schedule replication during slow traffic times. The only type of replication that supports scheduling is pull replication.

Configuring WINS Replication

Because WINS clients are configured to communicate only with specified WINS servers, the database on each WINS server may not have entries for all the WINS clients in the network. WINS clients cannot resolve addresses registered with another WINS server unless the registrations from that server are somehow copied (replicated) to the client's WINS server. To resolve this problem, Microsoft allows you to configure a WINS server so that it replicates its database (including static entries) with another WINS server. After you enable replication, clients seeking name resolution can see not only entries from their server, but also entries of the replication partners. Remember that clients register their names with the WINS server for which the clients are configured. WINS registrations are not done through broadcasts (in fact, one of the main benefits of WINS is the reduction of broadcast traffic).

To set replication, you must configure a WINS server as a push partner or a pull partner. A *push partner* sends its entries to another server; for example, you can send a copy of the database from this WINS server to the other WINS server. A *pull partner* retrieves entries from another server; for example, one server can receive a copy of the database from another WINS server.

Note that Replication does not occur unless both WINS servers are properly configured (that is, as replication partners or to function with non-partners).

Most WAN implementations will use a pull partner across slow wide area network (WAN) links because you can configure a pull partner to replicate at specific times (when usage is low). For example, you could make the WINS server on each side of the WAN link a pull partner with the other WINS server, perhaps replicating at midnight. This setup is known as *pull-pull replication.*

Faster WAN links typically function better with the WINS servers set as push partners. Push partners replicate when a specified number of changes, or updates, are made to the database. These updates can happen fairly frequently and are rarely large since they replicate only a few changes. For two WINS servers to have identical databases, they must be configured to be push and pull partners of each other.

You can configure a replication partner in several ways:

- When the WINS server starts, you can configure it as either a push or a pull partner.
- At a specified interval, such as every 24 hours. This option applies to pull replication.
- When a push partner reaches a specified number of changes to the database. These changes include name registrations and name releases. When this threshold is reached, the push partner notifies all its pull partners that it has changes for replications.
- Manually. You can force replication from the WINS Manager.

WINS can automatically replicate with other WINS servers if your network supports multicasting. By default, every 40 minutes each WINS server sends a multicast to the address 224.0.1.24. Any servers found through this multicast are automatically configured as push and pull partners with replication set to occur every two hours. If the routers on your network do not support multicasting, the WINS servers see only other servers on the same subnet.

You can turn off this multicasting feature by editing the Registry in the following location:

```
HKEY_LOCAL_MACHINE\System\CurrentControlSet\Services\
➥NetBT\Parameters
```

In the Registry, change the value of `UseSelfFndPnrs` to `0`. Change the value of `McastIntvl` to a large number.

19. Which of the following is *not* a valid WINS static mapping type?

E. None of the above.

19. CORRECT ANSWER: E

All of the mapping types listed are valid WINS static entries. These entries are used to group categories of systems together so that they can be appropriately handled. For example, a multihomed system will show its name registered twice. The second registration is not rejected because this condition is registered by the type.

Configuring Static Mappings in the WINS Database

You can register a non-WINS client with a WINS server by adding a static entry to the WINS database. With entries added for non-WINS clients, a WINS client can resolve more names without having to look up the entries in an LMHOSTS file. In fact, by adding entries for all non-WINS clients, you can eliminate the need for an LMHOSTS file. Static entries are added through the WINS Manager.

There are several types of static mappings. The following table summarizes the types that you can add.

TABLE 3.1 TYPES OF STATIC MAPPINGS

Type of Mapping	*Explanation*
Normal Group	Group names don't have an address; rather the WINS server returns 255.255.255.255 (the broadcast address). This type of mapping forces the client to broadcast on the local subnet to resolve the name.
Multihomed	A multihomed name is used to register a computer with more than one network card. It can contain up to 25 addresses.
Domain Name	In Windows NT 3.51, the Domain Name mapping was known as an Internet Group. This entry contains a maximum of 25 IP addresses for the Primary or Backup Domain Controllers in a domain. This type of mapping enables client computers and servers to locate a domain controller for logon validation and pass through authentication.
Internet Group	An Internet Group mapping name is a user-defined mapping used to store addresses for members of a group other than a domain (such as a workgroup).

20. How does WINS integrate LMHOST entries to its database?

D. By using WINS service manager and manually running an import procedure

20. CORRECT ANSWER: D

To import an LMHOSTS file into the WINS database, you must use the WINS manager. When performing this operation, typically you should verify that you are duplicating systems that are already in the WINS database.

Importing LMHOSTS Files to WINS

The `LMHOSTS` file is a static file that can be used in place of WINS for NetBIOS name resolution. If you have been using `LMHOSTS` files and decide to implement WINS, you can copy entries from an `LMHOSTS` file to a WINS server. Any entries copied this way are considered static entries. To copy the entries, follow these steps:

1. Choose **Start**, **Programs**, **Administrative Tools**.
2. From the Administrative Tools menu, choose **WINS Manager.**
3. From the Mappings menu in WINS Manager, choose **Static Mappings.**
4. Choose the **Import Mappings** button.
5. Browse to find the `LMHOSTS` file you modified and then choose that file.
6. Choose **Open**.
7. Note the names from the `LMHOSTS` file have been added to the static mappings.
8. Close the Static Mappings dialog box.
9. From the Mappings menu, choose **Show Database**.
10. Note that the mappings you added from the `LMHOSTS` file are now in the WINS database.

21. By default, where does the WINS server first write changes to the database?

A. To the log file

21. CORRECT ANSWER: A

The WINS database is a transactional database in which changes are first written to a log file and then to the database. This technique gives the database a backup source for all its changes.

22. Where can you see a record of WINS server error messages? Select the best answer.

C. In the Windows NT Application Event log

22. CORRECT ANSWER: C

WINS writes its error messages to the Windows NT Event log. However, because WINS uses a JET (or *Joint Engine Technology*) database to store its entries, messages are written in the Application log instead of the System log.

23. What does a WINS server do if it receives a name registration request for a host name already in its database?

B. It queries the host of the existing registration to see whether the registration is still valid.

23. CORRECT ANSWER: B

When a WINS server receives a registration request that conflicts with an existing entry, the server tries to resolve the conflict by querying the owner of the original registration. If the owner responds, the WINS server denies the new registration request. If the owner doesn't respond, the WINS server successfully registers the client and replaces the old entry with the new one.

24. How do you install a WINS proxy agent?

C. By changing a Registry entry.

24. CORRECT ANSWER: C

You must change a Registry entry to turn on the WINS proxy agent for an existing WINS client. When that client reboots, it notes the new Registry setting and makes that client a WINS proxy agent.

25. How does a client decide which WINS server to use? Select all that apply.

C. The primary WINS server configured in TCP/IP

D. The primary WINS server specified in the DHCP scope options

25. CORRECT ANSWERS: C-D

A WINS client communicates only with WINS servers for which the client is configured. You can configure these WINS servers in one of two ways. You can manually specify a WINS server with the primary WINS server address in TCP/IP. Or, you can specify the primary WINS server address through the scope options of DHCP for clients that receive their TCP/IP addresses from DHCP.

26. What happens to a name registration when the host crashes?

D. The name is released after the TTL is over.

26. CORRECT ANSWER: D

After a client registers its NetBIOS name with a WINS server, it is the client's responsibility to renew that registration. The WINS server does not initiate any registration renewals with clients. The registration is released if not renewed by the time the TTL expires. However, the entry is not scavenged until the Extinction Interval and the Extinction Timeout have expired.

27. Where is WINS configuration information stored?

B. In the Registry

27. CORRECT ANSWER: B

The WINS database, with its associated files, is stored in the `\WINNT\SYSTEM32\WINS` directory. However, the WINS configuration information is stored in the Registry.

28. How do you configure automatic backup of the WINS database?

B. Specify the name of the backup directory in WINS Manager.

28. CORRECT ANSWER: B

You can back up the WINS database only through the WINS Manager. After you specify the path of the backup directory, backups automatically take place every 24 hours. The only backup interval you can specify is 24 hours. However, you can do a manual backup through WINS Manager.

Files Used for WINS

Like the critical component of your network, you must be able to locate and identify the crucial elements of the WINS service. The WINS database is stored in the path `\WINNT\SYSTEM32\WINS`, and several files make up the WINS database:

- **WINS.MDB**—The WINS database.
- **WINSTMP.MDB**—A temporary working file used by WINS. This file is deleted when the WINS server is shut down normally, but a copy could remain in the directory after a crash.
- **J50.LOG**—The transaction log of the WINS database.
- **J50.CHK**—A checkpoint file used by the WINS database. This file is equivalent to a cache for a disk drive.

Backing Up the WINS Database

The database can be backed up automatically when WINS shuts down. You also can schedule backups or manually start a backup. All these backups are copied to the backup directory specified in the Advanced Configuration options. You can manually start a WINS backup from the Mappings menu in the WINS Manager. To automatically schedule backups, configure the path for a backup directory. After you set this path, the WINS server automatically backs itself up every 24 hours.

You should also back up the WINS subkey in the Registry. This subkey has the configuration settings for WINS, but does not contain any entries from the WINS database. The regular backup for WINS makes a copy of the database.

Restoring the WINS Database

You can restore the WINS database from the backup files. To restore the database, from the **Mappings** menu in WINS Manager, choose **Restore database**.

WINS also can automatically restore the database. If the WINS service detects a corrupted database on startup, WINS automatically restores a backup from the specified backup directory. If you suspect the database is corrupt, you can stop and start the WINS service from **Control Panel**, **Services** to force this automatic restoration.

Compacting the WINS Database

You can compact the WINS database to reduce its size. However, WINS under Windows NT 4.0 is designed to automatically compact the database, so you shouldn't have to compact it. To force a manual compaction of the database, use the JETPACK utility in the `\WINNT\SYSTEM32\WINS` directory. (The WINS database is a JET database, so this utility packs that database.) To pack the database, you must first stop the WINS service. You cannot pack an open database. Then type the following command:

```
jetpack WINS.mdb temp.mdb
```

This command compacts the database into the file `temp.mdb`, copies the compacted database to WINS.mdb, and deletes the temporary file. After the database is compacted, you can restart the WINS service from **Control Panel**, **Services**.

FURTHER REVIEW

INSTALL AND CONFIGURE A WINS SERVER, IMPORT LMHOSTS FILES TO WINS, CONFIGURE WINS REPLICATION, CONFIGURE STATIC MAPPINGS IN THE WINS DATABASE

What Is NetBIOS Naming?

Regardless of the underlying protocol, all Windows NT servers use a basic naming system known as NetBIOS (Network Basic Input Output System) naming. NetBIOS naming is a component of a basic set of commands (NetBIOS) that are used to communicate with applications and operating systems in a networked environment. A NetBIOS name can take the form of a string which is up to 15 characters in length. Internally, a 16th character (in hexadecimal) is used to describe a service. Using NetBIOS names, Windows NT allows a workstation to connect to other resources, browse the network, and perform network functions. Examples of a NetBIOS name in action are the NET VIEW and NET USE commands. These commands take the form of command `\\system_resource\share`.

Most administrators commonly confuse NetBIOS with NetBEUI, although the two are not the same. NetBEUI (NetBIOS Extended User Interface) is a network protocol that has been specifically designed to operate with NetBIOS APIs. Aside from this fact, NetBIOS is not a networking protocol option as are NetBEUI, IPX, TCP/IP, DLC, and so on, but rather it is a method for addressing network resources.

When working with NetBEUI, NetBIOS support is automatically provided. However, when working with other protocols such as IPX and TCP/IP, support is added above the transport layer of the OSI model. Under TCP/IP, NetBIOS support is referred to as NetBIOS over TCP/IP (NBT). While working under the direction of TCP/IP, all NetBIOS names are treated similarly in manner to host names (explained in the next chapter) in that they are linked to IP addresses which must be resolved.

The main method by which clients on a Windows NT network connect to resources is known as browsing. Browsing is the listing of NetBIOS names in order to select a resource or to access data. Before we move forward in the process of how these names are resolved, we must first examine how they function.

Understanding WINS

WINS is used to map NetBIOS (computer) names to IP addresses dynamically. In the absence of a WINS server, the same function can be performed with LMHOSTS files, but the files are static and do not incorporate changes. A WINS server will automatically collect information for all clients configured to operate with it. When the client starts up, it sends a registration request to the WINS server.

After a client registers its NetBIOS name with a WINS server, the client is responsible for renewing its registration. The WINS server does not initiate any registration renewals with clients. The registration is released if not renewed by the time the TTL expires. However, the entry is not scavenged until the Extinction Interval and the Extinction Timeout have expired.

WINS writes its error messages to the Windows NT Event log. However, because WINS uses a *Joint Engine Technology* (JET) database to store its entries, messages are written in the Application log instead of the System log.

You can also enable non-WINS clients to use a WINS server to resolve NetBIOS names by installing a *WINS proxy agent*. By definition, a non-WINS client cannot directly communicate with a WINS server to resolve a name. The non-WINS client resolves names by resorting to a b-node broadcast. If you install a WINS proxy agent, it forwards any broadcasts for name resolution to the WINS server. The proxy agent must be located on the same subnet as non-WINS clients so the proxy agent receives the broadcast for name resolution.

When a non-WINS client broadcasts a name resolution request, a proxy agent that hears the broadcast checks its own NetBIOS name cache to see whether an entry exists for the requested name. If the entry doesn't exist, the proxy agent adds an entry to the cache for that name with the status of "pending." The proxy agent then sends a name resolution request for the same name to the WINS server. After the WINS server responds with the name resolution, the proxy agent adds the entry to its cache and then removes the pending status from the entry. The proxy agent does not forward the response to the non-WINS client making the request.

When the non-WINS client broadcasts another request for the name resolution, the proxy agent now finds an entry for the name in its cache and can respond to the non-WINS client with a successful name resolution response.

The WINS proxy agent also forwards registration requests to the WINS server. However, registration requests for non-WINS clients are not added to the WINS server's database. The WINS server uses these forwarded registration requests to check for any potential conflicts in its database with the requested name registration. You must still add static entries to the WINS database so that names of non-WINS clients can be resolved.

You must place a WINS proxy agent on each subnet where non-WINS clients are located so those clients have access to the WINS server. Because those clients resolve names only by using broadcasts which are not typically routed, those broadcasts never go beyond the subnet. With a proxy agent on each subnet, broadcasts on each subnet can then be forwarded to the WINS server. You can have two proxy agents on a subnet, but you shouldn't exceed this limit. Even having more than one proxy agent on a subnet can generate excessive work for the WINS server because each proxy agent forwards name resolution and name registration requests to the WINS server. The WINS server has to respond to duplicate messages from proxy agents if more than one proxy agent is on a subnet.

Any Windows-based WINS client can be a WINS proxy agent. To configure a Windows NT server or workstation to be a proxy agent, you must turn on a parameter in the Registry. This proxy agent cannot be a WINS server. Windows 95 and Windows for Workgroups computers are more easily configured by turning on a switch in the TCP/IP configuration.

After you configure a WINS client to be a proxy agent, you must reboot the machine for this change to take effect. No other configuration is needed for this proxy agent. This WINS client remains a proxy agent until you turn off the proxy agent parameter and reboot the computer.

CHAPTER SUMMARY

Each system in a network TCP/IP Network is addressed by at least one common name, which is symbolic for its IP Address. This common name can be either the NetBIOS or host name. Although NetBIOS naming is not identical to that of host naming, both names must be resolved. A NetBIOS name is up to 15 characters and is usable interchangeable of protocol (IPX, TCP/IP, NetBEUI) with the NET command. Host names, on the other hand, are used with TCP/IP commands and are completely interchangeable with their IP address.

The methodologies for resolving NetBIOS names include broadcasting, checking the local store of known addresses, performing lookups on the DNS, requesting resolution for a NetBIOS naming system, and parsing through the LMHOST and host files. Regardless of which service is used, the goal is still to determine what the IP address of a system is.

The most important tool for resolving NetBIOS names in mid- and large-scale networks are the WINS servers. These servers offer the least administrative overhead, the best capabilities for locating resources on a network, and the most control over functionality.

The important aspect to remember from this section is what NetBIOS naming is, how it is resolved, and how these names are integrated into the Windows NT operating system.

CHAPTER REVIEW

REVIEW QUESTIONS

Note: The additional Chapter Review section that ends each chapter is unique to this member of the *New Riders TestPrep, Second Edition* series. We've included it to more fully and fairly cover the unique aspects of TCP/IP in relation to its mastery in preparation for MCSE examination.

1. **How does a WINS server gather entries to add to its database?**

   A. It examines each packet sent on the network.

   B. It receives a copy of the browse list from the Master Browser on each network segment.

   C. WINS clients send a name registration to the WINS server.

   D. It retrieves a copy of the computer accounts in each domain.

2. **You need your WINS-enabled clients to communicate with a UNIX computer that is not registered in the WINS database. What should you do?**

   A. Configure the default gateway address of the WINS server as the IP address of the UNIX computer

   B. Add a static mapping for the name and the IP address of the UNIX computer to the WINS database

   C. Ensure that the WINS server and the UNIX computer are located on the same subnet

   D. Add the IP address and the NetBIOS name of the WINS server to the LMHOSTS file on the UNIX computer

3. **You want your two WINS servers to replicate their databases. How should you do this?**

   A. Configure the Directory Replicator service to start automatically, then configure the primary WINS server to replicate to the secondary WINS server

   B. Configure each WINS server as a WINS client of the other WINS server

   C. Install and configure DHCP on each WINS server

   D. Configure each WINS server both as a push partner and as a pull partner of the other WINS server

4. **You have 80 Windows NT workstations and 100 Windows 95 workstations. You need all your Microsoft Windows-based computers to be able to resolve computernames without using an LMHOSTS file. Which service should you use?**

   A. DHCP with WINS/DNS DLL Extensions

   B. DNS

   C. DNS with NetBIOS Name Extensions

D. WINS with Explorer Extensions DLL

E. WINS

5. Your company has a TCP/IP network consisting of four subnets with one NT domain. One subnet has the PDC whereas the other three each have a BDC. You want all clients to be able to browse all subnets automatically. The service must have a mechanism for automatic configuration, the capability to collect and hold client information, and be manageable at the NT interface. What service should you use?

A. FTP

B. DHCP

C. DNS

D. WINS

E. SNMP

6. There are three subnets, named A, B, and C. Each has 75 Windows 95/98 computers. There is a PDC on subnet A and a BDC on subnet C, both configured as WINS servers. All computers on subnet A and subnet B are configured to use the PDC on subnet A as their WINS server. All computers on subnet C are configured to use the BDC on subnet C as the WINS server. Computers on subnet C cannot connect to workstations on the other two subnets. What should you do?

A. Specify the WINS server on subnet A as the secondary WINS server on all computers on subnet C

B. Configure the two WINS servers as replication partners

C. Specify the WINS server on subnet C as the secondary WINS server on all computers on subnet A and subnet C

D. Configure each computer to register with both of the WINS servers

ANSWER KEY

1. C
2. B
3. D
4. E
5. D
6. B

REVIEW ANSWERS

1. How does a WINS server gather entries to add to its database?

C. WINS clients send a name registration to the WINS server.

1. CORRECT ANSWER: C

Designing a WINS server helps eliminate traffic by having clients directly send information to it rather than by broadcast. The only way that a WINS server can effectively gather information is when it is sent by a client.

2. You need your WINS-enabled clients to communicate with a UNIX computer that is not registered in the WINS database. What should you do?

B. Add a static mapping for the name and the IP address of the UNIX computer to the WINS database

2. CORRECT ANSWER: B

In many Microsoft configurations, the WINS server is used to resolve host names either directly or looped through the DNS. Because these systems are not WINS clients, they must be manually added as static entries to the WINS database.

3. You want your two WINS servers to replicate their databases. How should you do this?

D. Configure each WINS server both as a push partner and as a pull partner of the other WINS server

3. CORRECT ANSWER: D

When given the blanket guidelines to simply replicate two databases, the best full replication method is to configure each server as both a push and pull partner of the other.

4. You have Windows 80 NT workstations and 100 Windows 95 workstations. You need all your Microsoft Windows-based computers to be able to resolve computernames without using an LMHOSTS file. Which service should you use?

E. WINS

4. CORRECT ANSWER: E

WINS is the primary and best management tool for resolving NetBIOS names. A DNS can be used, but it is a manual process which can be slower because the DNS is queried after a WINS server when resolving NetBIOS names.

5. Your company has a TCP/IP network consisting of four subnets with one NT domain. One subnet has the PDC whereas the other three each have a BDC. You want all clients to be able to browse all subnets automatically. The service must have a mechanism for automatic configuration, the capability to collect and hold client information, and be manageable at the NT interface. What service should you use?

D. WINS

5. CORRECT ANSWER: D

The WINS service is the best solution for working in multiple subnet configurations. Because all clients send directed information, the WINS service provides automatic configuration to all subnets regardless of broadcast traffic.

6. There are three subnets, named A, B, and C. Each has 75 Windows 95/98 computers. There is a PDC on subnet A and a BDC on subnet C, both configured as WINS servers. All computers on subnet A and subnet B are configured to use the PDC on subnet A as their WINS server. All computers on subnet C are configured to use the BDC on subnet C as the WINS server. Computers on subnet C cannot connect to workstations on the other two subnets. What should you do?

B. Configure the two WINS servers as replication partners

6. CORRECT ANSWER: B

By configuring the two WINS servers as replication partners, all systems on the network should be able to see all clients. Keep in mind that either replication must be triggered to happen immediately or you must wait for the database to build based on your configuration of push/pull parameters.

CHAPTER 4

Host Naming and DNS

As mentioned in the previous chapter, two types of names—NetBIOS and host names—are commonly assigned to a Windows NT system. The purpose behind name resolution is to simplify system access by providing users with a name that is easy to remember.

With the importance of naming in mind, a number of devices have been created for their resolution to IP addresses. The main service that resolves host names, however, is known as the *DNS* (or *Domain Name System*). This is just one of many ways a name may be resolved, as you will soon discover.

As you read through this chapter, you will note that the majority of the support for host naming comes from the legacy of installations in the UNIX world. This is evident in everything from the naming format to the directory placement.

The key points of this chapter are the understanding of what a host name is, how they are resolved, and how to configure Windows NT in such an environment.

OBJECTIVES

This chapter helps you prepare for the exam by covering the following objectives:

Install and configure the Microsoft DNS server service on a Windows NT server computer.

- Microsoft's Implementation of TCP/IP includes a full-featured DNS. Installation and configuration of the DNS is key to host name resolution.

Integrate DNS server with other name servers.

- In addition to Microsoft's DNS, other name services such as WINS can be integrated with the DNS so that the static capabilities of the DNS are enhanced by the dynamic functions of WINS.

Connect a DNS server to a DNS root server.

- When connecting to the Internet, you must configure your DNS to function in a hierarchy.

continues

Objectives (continued)

DNS servers are set so that the root has authority over lower DNS systems. Connecting to these services allows a domain name to be controlled on a local level and referenced by others.

Configure DNS server roles.

- The size of a DNS database can become immense. Often, it is desirable to offload some of the DNS requests or create a situation where name resolution becomes fault tolerant.

Configure HOSTS and LMHOSTS files.

- The HOSTS and LMHOSTS file are used in a structured manner which is compatible among all platforms. This chapter explains in detail how these files function and are configured for name resolution.

PRACTICE QUESTIONS

CONFIGURE HOSTS AND LMHOSTS FILES

1. **HOSTS file entries are limited to how many characters?**
   A. 8
   B. 255
   C. 500
   D. Unlimited
2. **Entries in the HOSTS file are limited to what number?**
   A. 8
   B. 255
   C. 500
   D. Unlimited
3. **Which of the following files in Windows NT, prior to 4.0, is case sensitive?**
   A. HOSTS
   B. LMHOSTS
   C. ARP
   D. FQDN
4. **Which address is the loopback address?**
   A. 0.0.0.1
   B. 127.0.0.0
   C. 127.0.0.1
   D. 255.255.255.255
5. **Which of the following files is used for NetBIOS name resolution?**
   A. HOSTS
   B. LMHOSTS
   C. ARP
   D. FQDN
6. **To work around the problems and issues of individually maintaining HOSTS files on each machine, you should use which of the following NT services?**
   A. DHCP
   B. DNS
   C. WINS
   D. NIS

ANSWER KEY

1. B
2. D
3. A
4. C
5. B
6. B

ANSWERS & EXPLANATIONS

CONFIGURE HOSTS AND LMHOSTS FILES

1. HOSTS file entries are limited to how many characters?

B. 255

1. CORRECT ANSWER: B

When TCP/IP parses a HOSTS file, only the first 255 characters are read per line. Further details are not recommended and are typically ignored.

2. Entries in the HOSTS file are limited to what number?

D. Unlimited

2. CORRECT ANSWER: D

Because there are no limits to the number of hosts that you can communicate with, there is also no limit to the number that can be placed in the HOSTS file. However, be forewarned that very long HOSTS files can take their toll on slower systems; a number of problems can arise trying to keep entries current.

3. Which of the following files in Windows NT, prior to 4.0, is case sensitive?

A. HOSTS

3. CORRECT ANSWER: A

Prior to Windows NT 4.0, Microsoft followed TCP/IP protocol as implemented on UNIX systems where case matters. Because there is only one system with a given name per domain, the HOSTS file is no longer case sensitive.

4. Which address is the loopback address?

C. 127.0.0.1

4. CORRECT ANSWER: C

The loopback address is 127.0.0.1. This address is used to verify that the TCP/IP stack is working. For example, suppose that a client can't ping across the network. To figure out where the failure is occurring, the next logical step would be to send a Ping to the client to verify that the transport is working. In such cases, the problem is usually with the network rather than the client.

What Is Host Name Resolution?

When talking about host name resolution, we are referring to the translation of a system or resource name into an IP address. Although this concept is relatively straightforward, it is commonly confused with IP address resolution. When dealing with resolution, remember that name resolution is used to determine an IP address and IP resolution is used to find the MAC address of a system.

A number of services are available to facilitate name resolution. Network-based services include DNS, WINS, and NIS. The main service for resolving these names under Windows NT and UNIX is the DNS, which we will discuss shortly. WINS is limited in that it will resolve a name only if it corresponds to a NetBIOS name. When working under Windows NT, NIS is not used and therefore is not discussed here. However, for future reference, think of NIS as you would a DNS server, but with security features.

Local name resolution is far more primitive than its Network-based counterparts. In fact, they are limited to text-based tables and broadcasting. In most implications of TCP/IP, the local text file which is used to resolve host filenames is known as the HOSTS file. This file, like its NetBIOS counterpart LMHOSTS (discussed in Chapter 3, "NetBIOS Naming and WINS"), is static, but registers changes as soon as the file is updated and saved.

Configure HOSTS Files

The HOSTS file is an ASCII text file that statically maps local and remote host names and IP addresses. It is located in *systemroot*\System32\Drivers\etc.

The HOSTS file is case sensitive in Windows NT versions prior to 4.0 and on other operating systems and is limited to 255 characters per entry with an unlimited number of entries. It is used by Ping and other utilities to resolve host names locally and remotely. One HOSTS file must reside on each host, and the file is read from top to bottom. As soon as a match is found for a host name, the reading stops. For that reason, when the file contains duplicate entries, the latter ones (those lower on the list top to bottom) are always ignored and the most frequently used names will be (or should be placed) near the top of the file.

The following is an example of the default HOSTS file:

```
# Copyright (c) 1993-1995 Microsoft Corp.
#
# This is a sample HOSTS file used by Microsoft
➥TCP/IP for Windows NT.
#
# This file contains the mappings of IP addresses to
➥host names. Each
# entry should be kept on an individual line. The
➥IP address should
# be placed in the first column followed by the
➥corresponding host name.
# The IP address and the host name should be
➥separated by at least one
# space.
#
# Additionally, comments (such as these) may be
➥inserted on individual
# lines or following the machine name denoted by a
➥'#' symbol.
#
# For example:
#
#      102.54.94.97     rhino.acme.com          #
➥source server
#       38.25.63.10     x.acme.com              #
➥x client host

127.0.0.1        localhost
```

The first thing you'll notice in this file is that the pound sign (#) indicates a comment. When the system reads the file, the system ignores every line beginning with a comment. When a # appears in the middle of a line, the line is read only up to the sign. To use this example on a live system, the first 17 lines should be deleted or moved to the end of the file to keep them from being read every time the file is referenced.

The second thing to note is the entry:

```
127.0.0.1        localhost
```

This is a loopback address, present in every host. It references the internal card, regardless of the actual host address, and can be used to verify that things are working properly internally before further testing down the wire.

Within the HOSTS file, fields are separated by whitespace that can be either tabs or spaces. As mentioned earlier, a host can be referred to by more than one name; to do that, separate the entries on the same line with whitespace, as shown in the following example:

```
127.0.0.1        me loopback localhost
199.9.200.7      SALES7 victor
199.9.200.4      SALES4 nikki
199.9.200.3      SALES3 cole
199.9.200.2      SALES2 victoria
199.9.200.1      SALES1 nicholas
199.9.200.5      SALES5 jack
199.9.200.11     ACCT1
199.9.200.12     ACCT2
199.9.200.13     ACCT3
199.9.200.14     ACCT4
199.9.200.15     ACCT5
199.9.200.17     ACCT7
```

The aliases are other names by which the system can be referenced. Here, "me" and "loopback" do the same as "localhost," whereas "nicholas" is the same as "SALES1." If an alias is used more than once, the search stops at the first match because the file is searched sequentially.

5. Which of the following files is used for NetBIOS name resolution?

B. LMHOSTS

5. CORRECT ANSWER: B

Aside from using NetBIOS Cache, WINS, or a broadcast, the LMHOSTS file is the only other native NetBIOS name resolution solution. This file is used for converting a NetBIOS name to an IP address much as a HOSTS file converts host names to IP addresses.

Configure LMHOSTS Files

Whereas the HOSTS file contains the mappings of IP addresses to host names, the LMHOSTS file contains the mappings of IP addresses to Windows NT computer names. When speaking of Windows NT computer names, the inference is to NetBIOS names or the names that would be used in conjunction with NET USE statements.

The following is an example of the default version of this file:

```
# Copyright (c) 1993-1995 Microsoft Corp.
#
# This is a sample LMHOSTS file used by the
➥Microsoft TCP/IP for Windows
# NT.
#
# This file contains the mappings of IP addresses to
➥NT computernames
# (NetBIOS) names.  Each entry should be kept on an
➥individual line.
# The IP address should be placed in the first
➥column followed by the
# corresponding computername. The address and the
➥computername
# should be separated by at least one space or tab.
➥The "#" character
# is generally used to denote the start of a
➥comment (see the exceptions
# below).
#
# This file is compatible with Microsoft LAN Manager
➥2.x TCP/IP lmhosts
# files and offers the following extensions:
#
#       #PRE
#       #DOM:<domain>
#       #INCLUDE <filename>
#       #BEGIN_ALTERNATE
#       #END_ALTERNATE
#       \0xnn (nonprinting character support)
#
# Following any entry in the file with the
➥characters "#PRE" will cause
# the entry to be preloaded into the name cache. By
➥default, entries are
# not preloaded, but are parsed only after dynamic
➥name resolution fails.
#
# Following an entry with the "#DOM:<domain>" tag
➥will associate the
# entry with the domain specified by <domain>. This
➥affects how the
# browser and logon services behave in TCP/IP
➥environments. To preload
# the host name associated with #DOM entry, it is
➥necessary to also add a
# #PRE to the line. The <domain> is always
➥preloaded although it will not
# be shown when the name cache is viewed.
#
```

```
# Specifying "#INCLUDE <filename>" will force the RFC
➥NetBIOS (NBT)
# software to seek the specified <filename> and parse
➥it as if it were
# local. <filename> is generally a UNC-based name,
➥allowing a
# centralized lmhosts file to be maintained on a
➥server.
# It is ALWAYS necessary to provide a mapping for
➥the IP address of the
# server prior to the #INCLUDE. This mapping must
➥use the #PRE directive.
# In addition the share "public" in the example
➥below must be in the
# LanManServer list of "NullSessionShares" in order
➥for client machines to
# be able to read the lmhosts file successfully.
➥This key is under
# \machine\system\currentcontrolset\services\
➥lanmanserver\parameters\nullsessionshares
# in the registry. Simply add "public" to the list
➥found there.
#
# The #BEGIN_ and #END_ALTERNATE keywords allow
➥multiple #INCLUDE
# statements to be grouped together. Any single
➥successful include
# will cause the group to succeed.
#
# Finally, nonprinting characters can be embedded in
➥mappings by
# first surrounding the NetBIOS name in quotations,
➥then using the
# \0xnn notation to specify a hex value for a
➥nonprinting character.
#
# The following example illustrates all of these
➥extensions:
#
# 102.54.94.97     rhino         #PRE #DOM:
➥networking  #net group's DC
# 102.54.94.102    "appname  \0x14"
➥#special app server
# 102.54.94.123    popular            #PRE
➥#source server
# 102.54.94.117    localsrv           #PRE
➥#needed for the include
#
# #BEGIN_ALTERNATE
# #INCLUDE \\localsrv\public\lmhosts
# #INCLUDE \\rhino\public\lmhosts
# #END_ALTERNATE
```

```
#
# In the above example, the "appname" server
➥contains a special
# character in its name, the "popular" and
➥"localsrv" server names are
# preloaded, and the "rhino" server name is
➥specified so it can be used
# to later #INCLUDE a centrally maintained lmhosts
➥file if the "localsrv"
# system is unavailable.
#
# Note that the whole file is parsed including
➥comments on each lookup,
# so keeping the number of comments to a minimum
➥will improve performance.
# Therefore, it is not advisable to simply add
➥lmhosts file entries onto the
# end of this file.
```

Once again, the pound sign (#) indicates comments, and the file is read sequentially on each lookup, so limiting the size of the comment lines at the beginning of the file is highly recommended.

A number of special commands can be used in the file to load entries into a name cache, which is scanned on each lookup prior to referencing the file. (By default, entries are not preloaded, but are parsed only after dynamic name resolution fails.) Using these commands will decrease your lookup time and increase system efficiency.

6. To work around the problems and issues of individually maintaining HOSTS files on each machine, you should use which of the following NT services?

B. DNS

6. CORRECT ANSWER: B

The DNS is the primary service for centralized resolution of host names. Although NIS offers similar functions in a secured manner, it is not an NT service. As for WINS, remember that it is primarily focused as a NetBIOS name solution, not host name resolution.

What Is a DNS and What Does It Do?

DNS (which stands for *Domain Name System*) is one way to resolve host names in a TCP/IP environment. In non-Microsoft environments, host names are typically resolved through HOSTS files or DNS. In a Microsoft environment, WINS and broadcasts are also used. DNS is the primary system used to resolve host names on the Internet.

DNS began when the Internet was only a small network established by the Department of Defense for research. This network linked computers at several government agencies with a few universities. The host names of the computers in this network were registered in a single HOSTS file located on a centrally administered server. Each site that needed to resolve host names downloaded this file. Few computers were being added to this network, so the HOSTS file wasn't often updated. The different sites only had to download this file periodically to update their own copies. As the number of hosts on the Internet grew, managing all the names through a central HOSTS file became more and more difficult. The number of entries was increasing rapidly, changes were being made frequently, and the server with the central HOSTS file was being accessed more and more often by Internet sites trying to download a new copy.

DNS was introduced in 1984 as a way to resolve host names without relying on one central HOSTS file. With DNS, the host names reside in a database that can be distributed among multiple servers, decreasing the load on any one server and also allowing more than one point of administration for this naming system. The name system is based on hierarchical names in a tree-type directory structure. DNS allows more types of registration than the simple host-name-to-TCP/IP-address mapping used in HOSTS files and allows room for future defined types. Because the database is distributed, it can support a much larger database than can be stored in a single HOSTS file. In fact, the database size is virtually unlimited because more servers can be added to handle additional parts of the database.

PRACTICE QUESTIONS

INSTALL AND CONFIGURE THE MICROSOFT DNS SERVER SERVICE ON A WINDOWS NT SERVER COMPUTER, INTEGRATE DNS SERVER WITH OTHER NAME SERVERS, CONNECT A DNS SERVER TO A DNS ROOT SERVER, CONFIGURE DNS SERVER ROLES

1. **Which of the following static files is used to map IP addresses to host names on a Windows NT Server computer?**

    A. LMHOSTS

    B. HOSTS

    C. WINS

    D. DNS

2. **On a UNIX-based server/host, which file is used to statically map aliases to IP addresses?**

    A. LMHOSTS

    B. HOSTS

    C. WINS

    D. DNS

3. **Where can you find the files needed to install DNS?**

    A. On the Windows NT 4.0 Server Resource Kit

    B. On the BackOffice CD

    C. On the Windows NT 4.0 Server CD

    D. On the DNS CD

4. **Which of the following services dynamically resolves NetBIOS-to-IP resolution?**

    A. DNS

    B. DHCP

    C. WINS

    D. LMHOSTS

5. **What would the reverse lookup zone be called for a server with the IP address of 149.56.85.105?**

    A. 105.85.56.149.in-addr.arpa

    B. 149.56.85.105.in-addr.arpa

    C. 56.149.in-addr.arpa

    D. 149.56.in-addr.arpa

6. **What is the purpose of the Domain Suffix Search Order?**

    A. When you look for a host name, entries here can be used to complete the FQDN.

    B. When you look for a NetBIOS name, entries here can be used as the NetBIOS Scope ID.

    C. Allows your computer to be in more than one domain at a time.

    D. Tells your systems which Windows NT domains to search when looking for a logon server.

7. Which of the following can be a master server for a UNIX DNS server that is the secondary server for a zone? Select all that apply.

A. Any Windows NT DNS server with a primary zone

B. Any UNIX server with a primary zone

C. Any Windows NT DNS server with a secondary zone

D. Any Windows NT DNS server with a zone that doesn't use WINS lookup

8. Which of the following best describes the order in which you should configure the DNS server?

A. Install the server, create the zone, enter all the records, create the reverse lookup zone, and add the WINS records.

B. Install the server, create the reverse lookup zone, add the zone information, add the WINS lookup records, and add the other hosts.

C. Create the DNS server database files using a text editor, install the server, and verify the information.

D. Install the DNS server and then transfer the zone from the WINS server.

9. You have installed and tested the Microsoft DNS server configuration. Later you remove and reinstall the service in preparation for configuring the DNS server with the real information. What must you do to make sure the DNS server starts cleanly?

A. Remove the files from the `%winroot%\system32\dns` directory.

B. Reinstall Windows NT.

C. Also remove and reinstall the WINS server.

D. Nothing, the configuration will work fine.

10. How can zone files be modified? Select all that apply.

A. With NSLOOKUP

B. By editing the zone files with a text editor

C. With DNS Manager

D. With DNSCnfg

11. Which of the following `NSLOOKUP` commands provides a list of all the mail servers for the domain nt.com?

A. `NSLOOKUP -t MX nt.com`

B. `NSLOOKUP -a MX nt.com`

C. `NSLOOKUP -h nt.com`

D. `NSLOOKUP -m nt.com`

12. How do you configure a client to use DNS to resolve a host name before using other methods?

A. Query for a host name longer than 15 characters.

B. Move DNS up in the Host Resolution Order dialog box.

C. A client always searches DNS last.

D. Configure the DNS to advertise itself to DNS clients.

13. What kind of query does a DNS client make to a DNS server?

A. A reverse lookup query

B. An iterative query

C. A recursive query

D. A resolver query

14. If you do not specify the host name and domain in the TCP/IP configuration before installing DNS, what happens during the DNS installation?

A. An NS record is not created on the server.

B. DNS doesn't install.

C. Default values are used to create NS and SOA records.

D. You cannot create any zones on the server.

15. You have a computer called WEB-SERVER with a TCP/IP address of 148.53.66.45 running Microsoft Internet Information Server. This system provides the HTTP and FTP services for your organization on the Internet. Which of the following sets of entries is correct for your database file?

A. www IN A 148.53.66.45
ftp IN A 148.53.66.45

B. www IN A 148.53.66.45
ftp IN A 148.53.66.45
webserver CNAME www

C. webserver IN A 148.53.66.45
www CNAME webserver
ftp CNAME webserver

D. 45.66.53.148 IN PTR webserver

16. Your user is on a computer called prod172. The IP address of the computer is 152.63.85.5, and the computer is used to publish to the World Wide Web for the domain gowest.com. Which entries should you find in the database file? Select the best answer.

A. prod172 IN MX 152.63.85.5

B. www cname 152.63.85.5

C. prod172 IN A 152.63.85.5
www CNAME 152.63.85.5

D. prod172 IN A 152.63.85.5
www CNAME prod172

17. What is the purpose of a HINFO record?

A. Provides host information including the username

B. Provides host information including CPU type

C. Provides host information including BIOS version

D. Provides host information including hard disk size

18. What record must be added to a zone file to alias a host to another name?

A. An A record

B. An SOA record

C. A CNAME record

D. A PTR record

19. What information is contained in an MX record? Select all that apply.

A. A Preference entry.

B. The mail server name.

C. The WWW server name.

D. There is no such record.

20. When you are configuring your DNS server, where do you configure the length of time that an entry will be cached on your server?

A. Set the TTL in the DNS Manager properties on your server.

B. Set the TTL in the cache file on the remote server.

C. Set the TTL in the Registry under HKEY_LOCAL_MACHINE\SYSTEM\CurrentControlSet\Services\TCPIP\Parameters.

D. Set the TTL in the remote server in the SOA record.

21. What is the name of the file that a DNS will use in order to locate DNS servers higher than itself on the Internet hierarchy?

A. DNS.

B. Cache.DNS

C. InterNET.DNS

D. HOSTS.DNS

22. Which of the following are roles for which you can configure your DNS server? Select all that apply.

A. Primary

B. Tertiary

C. Backup

D. IP Forwarder

23. How does a caching-only DNS server build a database of host records?

A. The caching server downloads a copy of zone files into its cache from master servers when the caching server starts.

B. Entries from the local cache file are read into cache.

C. The server captures the results of queries as they are sent across the network.

D. The server makes queries.

24. What is the use of the cache file on a DNS server?

A. It has records for DNS servers at top-level domains.

B. It provides initial values to the DNS cache.

C. It specifies the TTL for cached entries.

D. It specifies the amount of memory and its location for DNS caching.

25. How do you create a Primary DNS server?

A. Install DNS on a Primary Domain Controller

B. Configure the DNS server to be a primary server in the Server Properties

C. During DNS installation, specify that it is to be a primary server

D. Create a primary zone

26. Where can a secondary server obtain a copy of the zone file?

A. Only from the primary server for the zone

B. From any server that has a copy of the zone file

C. Only from the master server for the zone

D. Only from the top-level DNS server for the domain

27. How can you configure a secondary server to receive changes to zone files as soon as they are made?

A. Decrease the refresh interval on the secondary server.

B. Turn on the Notify feature on the primary server.

C. Configure the primary server with push replication.

D. Make the primary server the master server for the secondary.

28. You have several secondary DNS servers on one side of a slow WAN link. How should you configure the master server for these secondary servers to minimize traffic over this slow WAN link?

A. Have all the secondary servers on one side of the link use one master server on the other side of the link.

B. Have one secondary server use the primary server on the other side of the link as the master. Other secondary servers use the secondary on their side of the link as the master.

C. Use a caching-only server as the master.

D. Configure DNS for pull replication scheduled during low traffic times.

29. You are attempting to troubleshoot name resolution problems. What is the proper order for name resolution?

A. Name Cache, DNS Server, HOSTS File, Broadcast

B. Local Host Name, HOSTS File, DNS, WINS, Broadcast, LMHOSTS

C. WINS, DNS, LMHOSTS File, HOSTS File, Local Host Name

D. Broadcast, DNS, WINS, Local Host Name, HOSTS File

ANSWER KEY

1. B	9. A	17. B	25. D
2. B	10. B-C	18. C	26. B
3. C	11. A	19. A-B	27. B
4. C	12. A	20. D	28. B
5. C	13. C	21. B	29. B
6. A	14. A	22. A-D	
7. B-D	15. C	23. D	
8. B	16. D	24. A	

ANSWERS & EXPLANATIONS

INSTALL AND CONFIGURE THE MICROSOFT DNS SERVER SERVICE ON A WINDOWS NT SERVER COMPUTER, INTEGRATE DNS SERVER WITH OTHER NAME SERVERS, CONNECT A DNS SERVER TO A DNS ROOT SERVER, CONFIGURE DNS SERVER ROLES

1. Which of the following static files is used to map IP addresses to host names on a Windows NT Server computer?

B. HOSTS

1. CORRECT ANSWER: B

Requiring no external services, the HOSTS file is used to statically map host names to IP addresses. When frequently accessing a system, this is often faster than relying on the DNS.

2. On a UNIX-based server\host, which file is used to statically map aliases to IP addresses?

B. HOSTS

2. CORRECT ANSWER: B

In the same manner as Windows NT, UNIX uses a HOSTS file to statically map IP addresses to host and alias names. Commonly, a system will be referred to in a workgroup by an alias. When only a few people need a solution to resolve the alias, then a HOSTS file can also be useful.

3. Where can you find the files needed to install DNS?

C. On the Windows NT 4.0 Server CD

3. CORRECT ANSWER: C

DNS used to be part of the Resource Kit for Windows NT 3.51; it was not included in the Windows NT source files. With Windows NT 4.0, DNS is included in the Windows NT source files.

4. Which of the following services dynamically resolves NetBIOS-to-IP resolution?

C. WINS

4. CORRECT ANSWER: C

This is kind of a "gotcha!" question in that you may have expected the answer to be DNS. The important thing to remember is that WINS is used to provide dynamic NetBIOS-to-IP resolution, whereas a DNS is configured manually to provide HOST-to-IP resolution.

5. What would the reverse lookup zone be called for a server with the IP address of 149.56.85.105?

C. 56.149.in-addr.arpa

5. CORRECT ANSWER: C

Only the network portion of the IP address is used to specify reverse lookup zones. Then the IP network address is listed in reverse order to match the specific-to-general naming scheme used by DNS.

6. What is the purpose of the Domain Suffix Search Order?

A. When you look for a host name, entries here can be used to complete the FQDN.

6. CORRECT ANSWER: A

When working inside our own environments, typically we will simply shorten machine names to exclude the domain, although the full name includes it. When trying to resolve these names, a suffix must be applied so that it is looked up by the DNS. The suffix search order simply provides a list of which domains to begin the search in.

7. Which of the following can be a master server for a UNIX DNS server that is the secondary server for a zone? Select all that apply.

B. Any UNIX server with a primary zone

D. Any Windows NT DNS server with a zone that doesn't use WINS lookup

7. CORRECT ANSWERS: B-D

UNIX servers can be primary or secondary servers for Windows NT DNS servers. However, a UNIX server should never be secondary for a zone on a Windows NT server that has WINS lookup enabled. Enabling WINS lookup adds a record to the file that is not compatible with UNIX implementations of DNS.

The Structure of DNS

Some host name systems, like NetBIOS names, use a flat database. With a flat database, all names exist at the same level, so there can't be any duplicate names. These names are like Social Security numbers—every participant in the Social Security program must have a unique number. Because Social Security encompasses all workers in the United States, it must use an identification system that uniquely identifies each individual in the United States.

DNS names are located in a hierarchical paths, like a directory structure. You can have a file called TEST.TXT in C:\ and another file called TEST.TXT in C:\ASCII. In a network using DNS, you can have more than one server with the same name, as long as each is located in a different path.

DNS Domains

The InterNIC controls the top-level domains. These have names like *com* (for businesses), *edu* (for educational institutions such as universities), *gov* (for government organizations), and *org* (for nonprofit organizations). There are also domains for countries. You can visit the InterNIC Web site at `http://www.internic.com/`. Table 4.1 summarizes common Internet domains.

TABLE 4.1 COMMON INTERNET DOMAINS

Name	*Type of Organization*
Com	Commercial organizations
Edu	Educational institutions
Org	Nonprofit organizations
Net	Networks (the backbone of the Internet)
Gov	Nonmilitary government organizations
Mil	Military government organizations
Num	Phone numbers
Arpa	Reverse DNS
Xx	Two-letter country code

DNS Host Names

To refer to a host in a domain, use a fully qualified domain name (FQDN), which completely specifies the location of the host. An FQDN specifies the host name, the domain or subdomain the host belongs to, and any domains above that in the hierarchy until the root domain in the organization is specified. On the Internet, the root domain in the path is something like "com," but on a private network the top-level domains may be named according to some internal naming convention. The FQDN is read from left to right, with each host name or domain name specified by a period. The syntax of an FQDN follows:

```
host name.subdomain. ... .domain
```

An example of an FQDN is `www.microsoft.com`, which refers to a server called "www" located in the subdomain called "microsoft" in the domain called "com." Referring to a host by its FQDN is similar to referring to a file by its complete directory path. However, a complete filename goes from general to specific, with the filename at the rightmost part of the path. An FQDN goes from specific to general, with the host name at the leftmost part of the name. Fully qualified domain names are more like actual addresses on an envelope. An address starts with the most specific information: who is to receive the letter. Then the address specifies the house number in which the recipient lives, the street on which the house is located, the city where the street is located, and finally, the most general location, the state in which that city is located.

Zone Files

The DNS database is stored in files called *zones.* It's possible, even desirable, to break the DNS database into a number of zones. Breaking the DNS database into zones was part of the original design goals of DNS. With multiple zones, the load of providing access to the database is spread among a number of servers. Also, the administrative burden of managing the database is spread out because different administrators manage only the parts of the DNS database stored in their own zones. A zone can be any portion of the domain name space; it doesn't have to contain all the subdomains for that part of the DNS tree. Zones can be copied to other name servers through replication. With multiple zones, smaller amounts of information are copied when zone files are replicated than would be the case if one zone file held the entire domain.

Reverse Lookup

Looking up an IP address to find the host name is exactly the same as looking up an FQDN using a DNS server (only backward). An FQDN starts with the specific host and then the domain; an IP address starts with the network ID and then the host ID. Because you want to use DNS to handle the mapping, both must go the same way, so the octets of the IP address are reversed. That is, 148.53.66.7 in the inverse address resolution is 7.66.53.148.

Now that the IP address is reversed, it is going the same way as an FQDN and the address can be resolved using DNS. You need to create a zone with a particular name. To find the name, take the assigned portion of the address—for example, in 148.53.66.7 the portion that was assigned is 148.53, and for 204.12.25.3 it is 204.12.25. Next, create a zone in which these numbers are reversed and to which you add in-addr.arpa—that is, 53.148.in-addr.arpa or 25.12.204.in-addr.arpa, respectively.

8. Which of the following best describes the order in which you should configure the DNS server?

B. Install the server, create the reverse lookup zone, add the zone information, add the WINS lookup records, and add the other hosts

8. CORRECT ANSWER: B

Using the proper procedure ensures that methods are followed and that the setup is put correctly in place. The correct sequence for configuring a DNS is to install the server, create the reverse lookup zone, add the zone information, add the WINS lookup records, and add the other hosts. Any additional steps such as updating BIND files and so forth can then be performed.

Installing and Configuring DNS

The system on which you install the DNS service must be running Windows NT Server and needs to have a static IP configuration. Installing the DNS server is the same as installing any other network service. The steps are as follows:

1. Open the Network Settings dialog box (right-click Network Neighborhood and choose Properties).
2. On the Services tab, click Add and then select Microsoft DNS Server.
3. Click OK to add the service. When prompted, enter the directory in which your Windows NT source files are located.
4. Choose Close from the Network Settings dialog box and, when prompted, restart your system.

You have now installed the DNS server. To verify that the service is correctly installed, check the **Services** icon in the

Control Panel to ensure the Microsoft DNS server is listed and has started.

Using Existing BIND Files

If you already have a series of BIND files set up on an existing DNS server, you can use these files to configure the Microsoft DNS server. To do that, follow these steps:

1. Install the Microsoft DNS service (see the preceding section for instructions).
2. Stop the DNS service (from the Control Panel, choose the Services icon, click Microsoft DNS, and click Stop).
3. Copy the BIND files to the `%winroot%\System32\DNS` directory.
4. Start the DNS service (from the Control Panel, choose the Services icon, click Microsoft DNS, and click Start).
5. Use DNS Manager to verify that your entries are there.

9. You have installed and tested the Microsoft DNS server configuration. Later you remove and reinstall the service in preparation for configuring the DNS server with the real information. What must you do to make sure the DNS server starts cleanly?

A. Remove the files from the `%winroot%\system32\dns` directory.

9. CORRECT ANSWER: A

There are a number of reasons that you might want to reinstall a DNS. Knowing which files to remove and what changes are necessary to reinstall the service can save an administrator time during the reinstallation of the NT server. In this case, you should remove the files from the `%winroot%\system32\dns` directory.

Reinstalling Microsoft DNS Server

A quick note should be made here in case you need to reinstall the DNS server. When you start adding zones to a Microsoft DNS server, by default it switches to starting from the Registry rather than from the DNS files and makes a note of this in the boot file. Removing the server (before you reinstall) does not remove the existing file; therefore, when you reinstall the DNS server, it assumes the boot file is valid and tries to read it. This procedure causes several errors in the Event Log and causes the DNS not to start.

Therefore, if you need to remove the DNS server, you should remove the boot file from the DNS directory. The original file is in the directory %winroot%\system32\dns\backup, and you can copy the files from there; however, the server continues to boot from the Registry.

If you need to enable the system to boot from files, you must use the Registry editor to open HKEY_LOCAL_MACHINE\SYSTEM\CurrentControlSet\Services\DNS\Parameters and delete the value `EnableRegistryBoot`.

The DNS Administration Tool

Adding the DNS server also adds the DNS administration tool. This tool makes configuring and maintaining the DNS server very simple. It also provides single-seat administration because you can add several DNS servers.

First, you must add the DNS server that you want to manage. Follow these simple steps:

1. Start DNS Manager by choosing Start, Programs, Administrative Tools, DNS Manager.
2. In the left pane of DNS Manager, right-click Server List.
3. Choose New Server from the menu.
4. In the DNS server box, enter the name or IP address of the server you want to add.

Now that you have added the server, you can configure it and add entries. The DNS server needs to be configured for the role that it plays in the overall system, and you should know what the server you are configuring will be used for.

Creating a Subdomain

Many organizations are broken down into smaller groups that focus on one area of the business. Other organizations are dispersed geographically. In either case, the company may decide that it wants to break down its main domain into subdomains.

This task is simple in Microsoft's DNS server. Choose the parent domain (`scrimtech.com`, for example) and then right-click. Choose New Domain and enter the subdomain name in the dialog box. A subdomain will appear with the parent's name as a suffix. For example, `beta.microsoft.com` would be the beta subdomain at Microsoft.

If the subdomain is handled on another server, enter NS records for each of the other servers. If it is handled locally, simply add the records that are required.

Updating DNS Startup Files

After you have added several records to the DNS server, you should update the information in the files on the system. Even if the server boots from the Registry, the database (zone) files are stored. To do so, choose DNS from the menu and then choose Update Server Data Files. The files update automatically when the server is shut down or when you exit DNS Manager.

DNS Manager Preferences

As a final note, you can set the following three options under Options, Preferences that affect the behavior of DNS Manager.

- **Auto Refresh Statistics**—Enables you to configure the statistics screen to automatically update information.
- **Show Automatically Created Zones**—Shows the zones that are automatically created. These are used for internal purposes only.
- **Expose TTL**—Enables you to expose the TTL for entries in your cache. (You can view these by double-clicking **cache** and then double-clicking the subfolders.)

10. How can zone files be modified? Select all that apply.

B. By editing the zone files with a text editor

C. With DNS Manager

10. CORRECT ANSWERS: B-C

NSLOOKUP enables you to examine the entries in zone files, but not to make any changes. Zone files are simply text files, so they can be edited. DNS Manager is the Windows interface used to modify zone files. There is no utility called DNSCnfg.

11. Which of the following NSLOOKUP commands provides a list of all the mail servers for the domain nt.com?

A. `NSLOOKUP -t MX nt.com`

11. CORRECT ANSWER: A

`NSLOOKUP -t MX nt.com` produces the desired results. Note that the MX variable designates mail servers (exchanges) and nt.com identifies the NT domain.

NSLOOKUP

In addition to a DNS server, Windows NT 4.0 also has a tool that uses the DNS and enables you to verify that it is working. The `NSLOOKUP` command line is

```
nslookup [-option ...] [computer-to-find ¦ -
➥[server]]
```

You can use the `NSLOOKUP` command to query the DNS server from the command line (see Table 4.2 for a list of switches), or you can start an interactive session with the server to enable you to query the database. For our purposes, look only at the command line.

TABLE 4.2 COMMAND-LINE SWITCHES FOR THE NSLOOKUP COMMAND

Switch	*Description*
-option	Allows you to enter one or more commands from the command line. A list of the commands follows. For each option you want to add, enter a hyphen (-) followed immediately by the command name. Note that the command-line length needs to be fewer than 256 characters.
Computer to find	This is the host or IP address about which you want to find information. It is processed using the default server or, if given, using the server that is specified.

The following list provides the options that are available with the `NSLOOKUP` command.

- **-t querytype**—Lists all records of a given type. The record types are listed under querytype.
- **-a**—Lists all the CNAME entries from the DNS server.
- **-d**—Dumps all records that are in the DNS server.

- `-h`—Returns information on the DNS server's CPU and operating system.
- `-s`—Returns the well-known services for hosts in the DNS domain.

12. How do you configure a client to use DNS to resolve a host name before using other methods?

A. Query for a host name longer than 15 characters.

12. CORRECT ANSWER: A

DNS is always tried last in the host name resolution methods unless the host name is longer than 15 characters. In that case, DNS is tried first because other methods, like WINS, simply resolve NetBIOS names, which are limited to 15 characters. DNS can resolve fully qualified domain names that can be much longer than 15 characters. You cannot manually change the order in which the host name resolution methods are used.

Enabling DNS on the Client

After the DNS server has been installed and configured, the client systems must be set to use it. To enable Windows clients to use the DNS server, you can add the address of the DNS server to each station (manually), or you can set the DNS server option on the DHCP server.

For Windows NT (and Windows 95/98), you can use the following procedure to set the DNS server address:

1. Open the TCP/IP Settings dialog box. (Open the Network Settings dialog box; from the Protocol tab, double-click TCP/IP.)
2. On the DNS tab, enter the required information. As a minimum, you must enter the IP address of a DNS server. Descriptions of the other options on this tab follow:
   - **Host Name**—The name of the local host. This entry is the same as the NetBIOS name by default; however, you can change it. (If you select a different name, you are warned that if the NetBIOS name is

ever changed, the host name is set to the new NetBIOS name. If you use WINS to create a dynamic DNS, the NetBIOS name and the host name must be the same.)

- **Domain**— The Internet domain to which the system belongs. This entry is combined with the host name to create the FQDN name or this system.
- **DNS Service Search Order**—The IP address of one or more DNS servers that you use. They are tried in the order given.
- **Domain Suffix Search Order**—When you search for another host—for example, if you enter **`FTP sparky`**—the system first looks for "sparky" as the name in the DNS server. If "sparky" is not in your current domain, then that system will not be found and you would have to enter **`FTP sparky.scrimtech.com`**. If you work with servers at **`scrimtech.com`** frequently, you can add the domain scrimtech.com into this area, and if the address is not resolved from "sparky," a second query for sparky.scrimtech.com is automatically sent.

3. Click OK to close the TCP/IP settings. (If you are installing TCP/IP, you will need to enter the path to the Windows NT source files.)
4. Choose Close from the Network Settings dialog box and restart your system. (This step is not absolutely required, but generally it is recommended to ensure that the values are correctly set.)

You can also use the DNS server in place of the WINS server for resolving NetBIOS names. To do so, you need to change the settings on the WINS tab in the TCP/IP configuration. Specifically, you need to select the option to use DNS to resolve host names.

13. What kind of query does a DNS client make to a DNS server?

C. A recursive query

13. CORRECT ANSWER: C

Clients make recursive queries to servers; that is, the server must give the client a positive or negative response, not a referral to another server. Servers make iterative queries of one another, which enable the servers to respond with a pointer to another server. Reverse lookup queries are made by a server that needs to know the host name for a given IP address. The term *resolver query* isn't used in DNS.

Integrating DNS with Other Name Servers (WINS)

Microsoft's DNS impersonation provides the capability to integrate with WINS. During the installation process, the last tab in the zone configuration dialog box is the WINS tab. You can use WINS to resolve DNS queries by telling the server to use the WINS server as a secondary source if the initial DNS query fails. Remember, for this process to work, the hosts must use the same name for both their NetBIOS name and the host name, and they must register with the WINS server.

The following options are available:

- **Use WINS Resolution**—Check this box to enable the DNS server to query the WINS server for queries it receives and cannot resolve from its own database.
- **Settings Only Affect Local Server**—Normally a temporary entry is added to the domain when this resolution method is used. Selecting this option allows only the current server to see these entries.
- **WINS servers**—Here you need to enter the address of at least one WINS server. This server is queried in the order entered.

From the WINS tab, you can also open the Advanced Options dialog box. You may need to use a few other settings in this dialog box.

The options available are described in the following list:

- **Submit DNS Domain as NetBIOS Scope**—Some organizations use the NetBIOS scope ID to limit the number of hosts you can see using NetBIOS. The WINS server responds with the address only if matching scope IDs are used. Therefore, this option enables you to use the domain name as the NetBIOS scope.
- **Cache Timeout Value**—Length of time the DNS server keeps the information that it gets from the WINS server.
- **Lookup Timeout Value**—Length of time the DNS server waits for a resolution from the WINS server.

14. If you do not specify the host name and domain in the TCP/IP configuration before installing DNS, what happens during the DNS installation?

A. An NS record is not created on the server.

14. CORRECT ANSWER: A

The host name and domain values are used to create default records when the server is installed. You may have to create these records later so the DNS server can communicate with its clients and other servers, but you can still install DNS and create zones. If the values aren't specified, only the SOA record is created automatically.

15. You have a computer called WEB-SERVER with a TCP/IP address of 148.53.66.45 running Microsoft Internet Information Server. This system provides the HTTP and FTP services for your organization on the Internet. Which of the following sets of entries is correct for your database file?

C. webserver IN A 148.53.66.45
www CNAME webserver
ftp CNAME webserver

15. CORRECT ANSWER: C

The information shown in the answer (C) is the correct and proper format.

16. Your user is on a computer called prod172. The IP address of the computer is 152.63.85.5, and the computer is used to publish to the World Wide Web for the domain gowest.com. Which entries should you find in the database file? Select the best answer.

D. prod172 IN A 152.63.85.5
www CNAME prod172

16. CORRECT ANSWER: D

The information shown in the answer (D) is the correct and proper format.

17. What is the purpose of a HINFO record?

B. Provides host information including CPU type

17. CORRECT ANSWER: B

The HINFO record provides host information including CPU type. This is useful for management conditions where TCP/IP is used as the de facto management tool. For example, if experiencing difficulties with FTP services to a particular system, you could examine the HINFO record to determine whether this is an incompatibility with the operating system or whether it is just the configuration.

18. What record must be added to a zone file to alias a host to another name?

C. A CNAME record

18. CORRECT ANSWER: C

A CNAME record is a Canonical Name record used to create aliases. An A record is used to register the real host name. An SOA record contains the authority information for the zone file. A PTR record exists only in reverse lookup zones and maps the IP address to a host name, not the host name to an IP address.

19. What information is contained in an MX record? Select all that apply.

A. A Preference entry.

B. The mail server name.

19. CORRECT ANSWERS: A-B

An MX record contains a Preference entry and the mail server name. When configuring email services such as Exchange to receive messages from the Internet, you must specify an MX record so that other SMTP email systems know where email should be delivered.

20. When you are configuring your DNS server, where do you configure the length of time that an entry will be cached on your server?

D. Set the TTL in the remote server in the SOA record

20. CORRECT ANSWER: D

To limit the length of time that an entry will be cached, set the TTL in the remote server in the SOA record. This allows records to either remain longer for faster name resolution or be removed more quickly for greater freshness.

Adding HOSTS

Now that the domain has been created and the WINS resolution is set up, you need to add the records that the WINS resolution cannot handle. Essentially, this is any non-WINS client that you have on your network, as well as any host that has an alias.

Adding a host record (or any record) is simple. All you need to do is right-click the domain (or subdomain) to which you want to add the record. A menu appears from which you can choose New Host.

When you choose New Host, you see a dialog box. Enter the host name and the IP address in this dialog box. You need only the host name because the domain or subdomain you clicked is assumed.

An option to Create Associated PTR Record also exists. This option enters the required information for the reverse lookup zone for this host, but you have to create the reverse lookup zone before you can use it.

Adding Other Records

The main purpose of a DNS server is to resolve a host name to an IP address. However, organizations may also want other types of information, such as the address of your mail server. You can add several types of records to the DNS server. The following list describes these other records:

- **A**—A host entry, exactly the same as that entered in the previous section.
- **AAAA**— Also a host entry; however, with AAAA you can enter an IPng address (the new version of TCP/IP that will use 128-bit addresses rather than 32-bit).
- **AFSDB**—Gives the address of an Andrew File System (AFS) database server or a Distributed Computing Environment (DCE) authenticated name server.
- **CNAME**—The canonical name is an alias that points one name such as WWW to another such as Web.

CNAME is one of the most common records that you need to enter.

- **HINFO**—Enters machine information about a host, which allows other hosts on the network to find out CPU type and operating system information.
- **ISDN**—Enables you to map an entry to an Integrated Services Digital Network (ISDN) phone number rather than to an IP address. This record is used with a Route Through (RT) record (discussed in a moment) to automate routing over dial-up ISDN.
- **MB**—An experimental record type used to associate an email ID with a particular host ID.
- **MG**—Like an MB record, the MG is experimental; it associates an MB record with a mail group that could be used for mailing lists.
- **MINFO**—Another experimental record, MINFO enables you to enter the mail information about the person responsible for a given Mail record.
- **MR**—Another experimental record which provides the Mail records the same service that CNAME entries provide for host names—aliases.
- **MX**—You need to enter at least one MX record. The MX record directs incoming connections for mail to a mail server. You may enter more than one MX record. If you do, the system uses the preference number to determine the order in which to try them (lowest first).
- **NS**—A Name Server record. It is used to find the other name servers in the domain.
- **PTR**—The Pointer record is part of the reverse lookup zone and is used to point the IP address at the host name.
- **RP**—Where you enter the name (or names) of the people responsible for the domain for which the server provides resolution. You can enter multiple RP record entries of this type.

- **RT**—Route Through points at another record in the DNS database. The RT record provides information on how to get to a host using dial-up ISDN or X.25.
- **SOA**—As already discussed, the Start of Authority record provides the basic configuration for a zone.
- **TXT**—The Text record is a way of associating text information with a host. This record can provide information about the computer (in addition to the information in an HINFO entry) or other information such as the location.
- **WKS**—Provides the capability to indicate which Well Known Services are running on a particular host. These match the service and protocols that are listed in the services file (%winroot%\System32\drivers\etc) below port 256.
- **X25**—Similar to the ISDN entry, X25provides the capability to map a name to an X.121 name.

Adding these records is similar to adding a host record. Right-click the domain or subdomain and choose New Record.

21. What is the name of the file that a DNS will use in order to locate DNS servers higher than itself on the Internet hierarchy?

B. Cache.DNS

21. CORRECT ANSWER: B

The name of the file used to locate a higher DNS on the Internet is Cache.DNS. This file contains a list that is used when a name cannot be resolved within the zone specified on a given DNS.

Connecting a DNS Server to a DNS Root Server

DNS includes a cache file that has entries for top-level servers of the Internet domains. If a host name cannot be resolved from local zone files, DNS uses the cache file to look for a higher-level DNS server to resolve the name. If your organization has only an intranet without any Internet access, you should replace this file with one that lists the top-level DNS servers in your organization. This file is called `cache.dns` and is located at `\winnt\system32\dns`.

The latest version of this file can be downloaded from InterNIC at **ftp://rs.internic.net/domain/named.cache**.

22. Which of the following are roles for which you can configure your DNS server? Select all that apply.

A. Primary

D. IP Forwarder

22. CORRECT ANSWERS: A-D

Primary and IP Forwarder are both DNS roles, as are Caching Only and Secondary.

Configuring DNS Server Roles

The roles that a server can take include that of a Primary and Secondary DNS server, an IP Forwarder, or a caching-only server. The last can resolve addresses, but does not host any domains or subdomains (zones).

23. How does a caching-only DNS server build a database of host records?

D. The server makes queries.

23. CORRECT ANSWER: D

A caching-only server starts without any entries in its cache. It builds entries by making queries on behalf of clients to other DNS servers. When the results are returned from other DNS servers, the caching-only server adds these entries to its cache.

24. What is the use of the cache file on a DNS server?

A. It has records for DNS servers at top-level domains.

24. CORRECT ANSWER: A

The cache file has entries for the top-level servers for Internet domains. On an intranet, this file must be modified to reflect the top-level servers in the local organization.

Configuring for Caching Only

You don't have to do much to run a server as a caching-only server. The caching-only server does not host any zones. It simply starts off empty and holds only those names that are requested from it. To obtain the name of a host, a caching-only server will reference other servers above it.

Configuring as an IP Forwarder

An IP Forwarder is also a caching-only server; however, you need to configure it with the address of another DNS server (another Microsoft DNS server or any other DNS—for example, the one from your ISP). By configuring an IP address, you are specifying the upstream capabilities of the server to resolve names from. This configuration is fairly simple, and the only information you require is the IP address of the upstream DNS server. Follow these steps:

1. Right-click the server in the Server list and select Properties.
2. On the Forwarders tab, check the Use Forwarders box.
3. If the server is to only use the services of the other system, select Operate as Slave Server. (If you don't select this option, the server attempts to resolve through the forwarder; however, it then uses an iterative query if that fails.) Enter the address or addresses of the DNS servers to which this one should forward queries.
4. If desired, set a time-out for the request.
5. Click OK to close the dialog box.

25. How do you create a Primary DNS server?

D. Create a primary zone

25. CORRECT ANSWER: D

The designation Primary Server means that the DNS server is the primary server for a zone file. It can also be the secondary server for another zone file. In other words, the role of a DNS server is determined on a zone-by-zone basis.

Creating a Primary DNS Server

As a primary DNS, changes that are made to the DNS database are reflected outward to other DNS servers. For example, a company maintains its own DNS and wants to add mail services. The DNS entries for the mail service must be made on the primary DNS server so that they can be distributed elsewhere upon request.

Because the purpose of DNS is to resolve names to IP addresses, you need to enter the addresses into the DNS server so other users can find your hosts. Do this by creating a zone in the DNS server and entering the information that you want to make available to the world. Here's how to create a zone:

1. Right-click the server that hosts the zone in the Server list.
2. Choose New Zone.
3. From the dialog box that appears, choose Primary. Then choose Next.
4. Enter the name of the domain (or subdomain) for which you are creating a zone on the next screen. Then press the Tab key. (This step automatically enters a zone filename; if you are adding an existing zone file, enter the name of the file that has the information—it must be in the `%winroot%\System32\DNS` directory.) When the information is in, click Next.
5. Choose Finish.

That is all there is to creating a zone. Now you can configure the zone and add the host (and other) records. This, in effect, sets the DNS as primary.

Setting Up and Reviewing the SOA Record

Configuring a zone is straightforward. In essence, the information that you are entering here includes details for the Start of Authority (SOA) record and information about using WINS. The following steps show you how to set up the information:

1. Right-click the zone you want to configure. Choose Properties from the menu. The Properties dialog box should appear and present the basic zone information.
2. Click the SOA Record tab to bring up the information about the SOA.
3. Edit the information in the SOA record. You can change the following fields:

- **Primary Name Server DNS Name**—The name of the primary name server that contains the files for the domain. Note that only the host name is entered and then a period which means this domain (for example, NS1 is NS1.ScrimTech.com.).
- **Responsible Person Mailbox DNS Name**—The email address of the person who is in charge of the DNS. (Note, as in the Primary Name Server, you need to enter only the email address—followed by a period—if the email address is within this domain.)
- **Serial Number**—A version ID that is assigned to the zone. The number is updated whenever you make changes to the database so that the secondary servers know that changes were made and can retrieve the new information.
- **Refresh Interval**—Tells the Secondary servers how often they should check their version number with the primary servers to see whether they need to transfer the zone information again.
- **Retry Interval**—Tells how long the Secondary server should wait before retrying the Primary server if the Secondary server could not connect at the time given in Refresh Interval.
- **Expire Time**—Sets the length of time a Secondary server continues to give out information on this zone after not being able to connect with the Primary server.
- **Minimum Default TTL**—When a DNS server performs an iterative query to resolve a name, the name is cached. This value sets the duration that other DNS servers are allowed to keep the information about records that your DNS server resolves for them.

4. Click the Notify tab. (This is not really part of the SOA; however, it is added here because it deals with the Secondary servers.)

5. Enter the IP addresses of all Secondary servers that should be notified when a change is made.
6. If desired, you can choose Only Allow Access from Secondaries Included on Notify List, which restricts the servers that can retrieve your zone information.
7. Click OK to accept the changes you have made. (The WINS tab is covered in the next section.)

26. Where can a secondary server obtain a copy of the zone file?

B. From any server that has a copy of the zone file

26. CORRECT ANSWER: B

A secondary server can obtain a copy of the zone file from a primary server, or from a secondary server that has a copy of the zone file. The server from which the secondary server obtains the copy is its master server. However, zones do not have master servers. A zone may have five secondary servers, each receiving a copy of the zone file from another secondary server in the zone. A zone file can have any number of master servers.

27. How can you configure a secondary server to receive changes to zone files as soon as they are made?

B. Turn on the Notify feature on the primary server.

27. CORRECT ANSWER: B

If the Notify feature is turned on, the primary server notifies the secondary servers as soon as a change is made to the zone file. Decreasing the refresh interval keeps the secondary server more up-to-date, but it doesn't necessarily update the zone file soon after changes are made. Push replication is used for WINS servers. If the primary server is the master, it provides a copy of the zone file to the secondary server. However, the primary server will not provide changes any faster unless the Notify feature is turned on. The Notify feature is the key to quick updates.

28. You have several secondary DNS servers on one side of a slow WAN link. How should you configure the master server for these secondary servers to minimize traffic over this slow WAN link?

B. Have one secondary server use the primary server on the other side of the link as the master. Other secondary servers use the secondary on their side of the link as the master.

28. CORRECT ANSWER: B

The best way to reduce traffic is to have the zone file passed one time across the link and then distributed to the other servers on that side of the link. Using a caching-only server is another strategy that can be used across a slow WAN link, but the caching-only server never gets a copy of any zone files. Pull replication is used for WINS, not for DNS.

Setting Up the Secondary DNS Server

After you configure your server, you need to add a Secondary server. Adding this server provides redundancy and also splits the workload among the servers. (You can have several Secondary servers if you want.) Once configured, a secondary server will obtain information for a master DNS server (primary or secondary). Note that a master DNS server is simply any DNS that is a source of information for your secondary. Follow these steps to configure a secondary server:

1. In DNS Manager, right-click the server to be configured as a Secondary server.
2. Choose New Zone from the context menu. From the New Zone dialog box, choose Secondary.

▼ NOTE

This screen asks for the zone name and the server from which to get zone files. A handy option is the capability (as seen here) to drag the hand over another server listed in DNS Manager to automatically pick up the information.

If the Primary DNS server is not a Microsoft DNS server, you will need to enter the information manually.

3. Click the Next button, and you can enter the information for the file. This information should already be entered, and you should click Next to accept the defaults.

4. The next screen asks you to identify the IP master for the zone. This information should already be filled in for you.
5. The last screen tells you that you are finished. Click Finish to close this screen.

29. You are attempting to troubleshoot name resolution problems. What is the proper order for name resolution?

B. Local Host Name, HOSTS File, DNS, WINS, Broadcast, LMHOSTS.

29. CORRECT ANSWER: B

The correct order for host name resolution is Local Host Name, HOSTS File, DNS, WINS, Broadcast, LMHOSTS. Keep in mind that the order for name resolution with NetBIOS names are different.

THE BIG PICTURE OF HOST NAME RESOLUTION

Now that we have reviewed the technologies behind host name resolution, we can examine how name resolution takes place. Be sure to note while reviewing this section how NetBIOS Name Resolution varies as compared to host names.

Step	*Host Name Resolution*	*NetBIOS Name Resolution*
1	Local Host Name	NetBIOS Name Cache
2	HOSTS File	NetBIOS Name Server (WINS)
3	DNS Server	Broadcast
4	NetBIOS Name Server (WINS)	LMHOSTS File
5	Broadcast	HOSTS File
6	LMHOSTS File	DNS Server

As you can see from this chart, the methods by which a NetBIOS name is resolved differs from the way the process is performed for a host name. The reason for the differences in the resolution order is because the functions behind the names are different. For example, a NetBIOS name is used for actions that directly integrate the Windows NT operating system—Net Use, Net View, and the like. On the other hand, host names are used with functions directly related to TCP/IP or are commonly associated with UNIX, FTP, PING, Telnet, LPR, and so on.

FURTHER REVIEW

INSTALL AND CONFIGURE THE MICROSOFT DNS SERVER SERVICE ON A WINDOWS NT SERVER COMPUTER, INTEGRATE DNS SERVER WITH OTHER NAME SERVERS, CONNECT A DNS SERVER TO A DNS ROOT SERVER, CONFIGURE DNS SERVER ROLES

What Is a Host Name?

A host name is an association that is used to simplify the addressing of a system. For example, a system with the IP designation 134.57.8.8 could simply be called "Ziggy." Most users can remember a name a lot easier than an IP address. For example, suppose that you were on the Web and wanted to access Toyota's home page. You can simply type in `WWW.TOYOTA.COM` and never have to know or remember the IP Address.

Unlike NetBIOS names that are limited to 15 characters, a host name can be any string up to 256 characters. During the default installation of Windows NT, both the NetBIOS and host names are set to be identical. You can view the host name at any time by viewing the TCP/IP setting in the Network section of the Control Panel or with the `HostName` command.

In many ways, host names are superior to NetBIOS names. First, any command that can be used with an IP address can have the host set in place of it. In other words, the host name and IP address in a command are interchangeable. Also, because many systems run so many processes, it often makes sense to call a system by more than one name. Systems that use TCP/IP may have one or more names which are often referred to as *aliases*. Aliases are useful for systems running multiple applications as well as helping redirect traffic when merging systems together.

History of Microsoft DNS/Introduction to DNS

DNS was first introduced in the Microsoft environment as part of the Resource Kit for Windows NT Server 3.51. It was not integrated with the Windows NT source files until version 4.0. Although DNS is not installed by default as part of a Windows NT 4.0 Server installation, you can specify that DNS be included as part of a Windows NT installation or you can add DNS later just as you would any other networking service that is part of Windows NT.

Microsoft DNS is based on Request for Comments (RFCs) 974, 1034, and 1035. A popular implementation of DNS is the Berkeley Internet Name Domain (BIND), developed at UC Berkeley for its version of UNIX. However BIND is not totally compliant with the DNS RFCs. Microsoft's DNS does support some features of BIND, but Microsoft DNS is based on the RFCs, not on BIND.

▼ **NOTE**

You can read these RFCs, or any other RFC, by going to the Internet Network Information Center (InterNIC) Web site at **`http://ds.internic.net/ds/rfc-index.html`**.

CHAPTER SUMMARY

In standard implementations of TCP/IP, machines are commonly addressed by their host name interchangeably with their IP address. This process is called *host name resolution.* In this instance, a name is associated to a specific IP address, then is registered with numerous potential resolution sources such as DNS server, HOSTS file, and so forth.

The most prominent source for host name resolution is the DNS. The DNS is the main network application on the Internet and among most UNIX networks for resolving names. To keep up with compatibility, Microsoft introduced Windows NT with a DNS service that is completely compliant and compatible with those that comply to the RFC standards for host name resolution servers. Knowing that the majority of Windows NT systems will exist with NetBIOS clients, Microsoft enhanced the capabilities of their DNS by allowing it to perform reverse lookups against the WIN service. This allows the DNS to appear as it is—somewhat dynamic.

Because DNS is structured, a number of configuration items can be set. For example, there is a logical placement of the server with respect to other servers with which it resolves names. Also, because each server functions at different levels, DNS may take on different roles, such as that of a caching-only service.

Although name resolution between both HOSTS and NetBIOS names appears similar, distinct differences define them according to their functionality and purpose. Since host names are designed to be interchangeable with their IP address and function in heterogeneous environments, we see that the path to resolution is different that than of NetBIOS. This is especially important to be aware of when troubleshooting systems and well worth committing to memory.

CHAPTER REVIEW

REVIEW QUESTIONS

Note: The additional Chapter Review section that ends each chapter is unique to this member of the *New Riders TestPrep, Second Edition* series. We've included it to more fully and fairly cover the unique aspects of TCP/IP in relation to its mastery in preparation for MCSE examination.

1. **Without using static host name resolution methods, you want to resolve host names on your Windows-based computers that use host names to access Windows NT Server computers. What should you do?**

   A. Install DNS and WINS. Configure DNS to use WINS.

   B. Create a centralized LMHOSTS file on one Windows NT Server computer. Configure all client computers to use this centralized HOSTS file.

   C. Create a centralized LMHOSTS file on one Windows NT Server computer. Configure all client computers to use this centralized LMHOSTS file.

   D. Install DNS and DHCP. Configure DNS to use DHCP.

2. **You have NT Servers, NT Workstations, and UNIX computers in your corporate environment. You have six DNS servers for the firefly.com domain. What should you do to configure resolution of names that are not in the DNS database (using the network's existing WINS servers)?**

   A. Configure only the primary DNS server to use WINS Resolution

   B. Configure all DNS servers to use WINS resolution

   C. Configure all DNS servers to use WINS reverse lookup

   D. Configure only the primary DNS server to use WINS reverse lookup

3. **You are setting up your Internet presence by adding IIS to a Windows NT Server computer with a host name of Bright. Firefly.com. You configure the server with the FTP and WWW service. You want all users to access the server by using either the alias ftp.firefly.com or the alias www.firefly.com. Which type of resource records must you add?**

   A. CNAME

   B. WKS

   C. MINFO

   D. MX

   E. NS

4. **For redundancy, how should you configure a backup server on a network?**

   A. As a caching-only server

   B. As a secondary server

   C. As a backup primary server

   D. In a new zone

5. Your company has asked you to configure an Internet Email System. You install Microsoft Exchange server and realize that outbound mail works, but you can't receive any inbound messages. You attempt to send messages from a dial-up account, but get a message that the server cannot be found. You performed tests and are able to ping the server from the Internet. Today is a Monday. You might want to verify the existence of which record?

A. CNAME

B. MX

C. MINFO

D. NS

E. WKS

6. You are in the process of developing a network that is to act as a private trusted intranet for several companies. This private network is to be used as a secured work area so that each company may codevelop a certain project. As an external entity to all companies, you would like to make your DNS root and master to all others. Which file on the DNS server must you modify?

A. Boot.INI

B. HOSTS

C. cache.dns

D. place.dom

E. DNS.INI

ANSWER KEY

1. A
2. B
3. A
4. B
5. B
6. C

REVIEW ANSWERS

1. Without using static host name resolution methods, you want to resolve host names on your Windows-based computers that use host names to access Windows NT Server computers. What should you do?

A. Install DNS and WINS. Configure DNS to use WINS.

1. CORRECT ANSWER: A

A key capability of the Windows NT implantation of DNS is its capability to become dynamic by performing lookups against the WINS server. As such, install DNS and WINS and configure DNS to use WINS. Note that the host name at the workstation should match the NetBIOS name (default).

2. You have NT Servers, NT Workstations, and UNIX computers in your corporate environment. You have six DNS servers for the firefly.com domain. What should you do to configure resolution of names that are not in the DNS database (using the network's existing WINS servers)?

B. Configure all DNS servers to use WINS resolution

2. CORRECT ANSWER: B

Because not all systems use host names exclusively, name resolution would be best met by configuring all DNS servers to use WINS resolution. With this, name resolution will be automated and registered while allowing UNIX systems to also perform lookups.

3. You are setting up your Internet presence by adding IIS to a Windows NT Server computer with a host name of Bright.Firefly.com. You configure the server with the FTP and WWW service. You want all users to access the server by using either the alias ftp.firefly.com or the alias www.firefly.com. Which type of resource records must you add?

A. CNAME

3. CORRECT ANSWER: A

The canonical name (CNAME) is an alias that points one name such as WWW to another such as Web. Despite that a single system may be known internally by one name, to the public it may be known by another (such as FTP, WWW, and so forth).

4. For redundancy, how should you configure a backup server on a network?

B. As a secondary server

4. CORRECT ANSWER: B

As a secondary server, your DNS will be redundant of the primary while allowing you to perform load balancing. Additional load balancing with less overhead should be performed by a caching-only server.

5. Your company has asked you to configure an Internet Email System. You install Microsoft Exchange server and realize that outbound mail works, but you can't receive any inbound messages. You attempt to send messages from a dial-up account, but get a message that the server cannot be found. You performed tests and are able to ping the server from the Internet. Today is a Monday. You might want to verify the existence of which record?

B. MX

5. CORRECT ANSWER: B

Never make the mistake of assuming that all facts are relative to a question. The MX record is always used to configure the mail exchange at the DNS.

6. You are in the process of developing a network that is to act as a private trusted intranet for several companies. This private network is to be used as a secured work area so that each company may codevelop a certain project. As an external entity to all companies, you would like to make your DNS root and master to all others. Which file on the DNS server must you modify?

C. cache.dns

6. CORRECT ANSWER: C

Because the default cache.dns points to servers on the Internet, it must be modified so that it operates locally. Any references to external servers should be removed. This file can be modified with any text editor.

CHAPTER 5

DHCP

The long-standing issue with TCP/IP has always been the proper configuration of each node. Perhaps for this reason, it was unpopular with early PC-based networks and was expected to die out. However, with the advent of the Internet, TCP/IP has a revitalized life, making it the protocol of choice among network engineers. As you will see, DHCP is the solution to the vast majority of node-based administrator problems because it provides an automated method by which TCP/IP can be configured on nodes.

OBJECTIVES

This chapter helps you prepare for the exam by covering the following objectives:

Configure scopes by using DHCP Manager.

- *Dynamic Host Configuration Protocol* (DHCP) provides automatic configuration of remote hosts, making management of a TCP/IP environment easy. DHCP Manager is used for the purpose of configuring how DHCP information is delivered to clients. This section will review how this information is configured and delivered to a client.

Install and configure the DHCP relay agent.

- *DHCP relay agent* extends the capabilities of the DHCP service by allowing it to work across various subnets.

  A key feature of Microsoft's DHCP server is its capability to work around legacy hardware that is not supportive of its features. Through the use of the DHCP relay agent, we will demonstrate this capability.

PRACTICE QUESTIONS

INSTALL AND CONFIGURE THE DHCP RELAY AGENT

1. **Where can you get the IP address for a client? Select all that apply.**
   - A. From the client
   - B. From the DHCP Server
   - C. From a scope of addresses on the RAS Server
   - D. From a WINS Server
2. **Before a client can receive a DHCP address, what must be configured on the DHCP server?**
   - A. The DHCP relay agent
   - B. A scope for the client's subnet
   - C. A scope for the server's subnet
   - D. A host name
3. **What is the effect of a lease duration of Unlimited?**
   - A. DHCP configuration options will never be updated automatically.
   - B. There is no effect.
   - C. Network traffic will increase.
   - D. Addresses cannot be shared dynamically.
4. **In what environment is it advisable to have a short lease duration?**
   - A. In static environments where addresses don't change often
   - B. When you have fewer hosts than IP addresses
   - C. In environments where you have hosts moving and many changes to IP addresses
   - D. When you have more hosts than IP addresses
5. **What portion of the DHCP process is initiated by the server?**
   - A. Lease acquisition
   - B. Lease renewal
   - C. Lease release
   - D. None
6. **How must a Windows NT Server be configured before you install a DHCP server?**
   - A. The WINS server must be installed.
   - B. The server requires a static IP configuration.
   - C. TCP/IP must not be installed.
   - D. The server must be a Backup Domain Controller.
7. **What information is required to define a scope?**
   - A. Starting and ending address and the subnet mask
   - B. Subnet ID and the number of addresses to lease
   - C. Number of hosts to be leased
   - D. The name of the scope

8. What is the difference between a global option and a scope option?

A. Global options affect all systems on the network whether DHCP clients or not.

B. Scope options are set in the DHCP Manager for individual scopes.

C. Global options affect the clients on scopes where no scope options are configured.

D. There is no difference between the options, just in how they are entered.

9. Why would you use a client reservation?

A. To provide dynamic configuration of TCP/IP options with a static IP address.

B. To be able to control all the IP addresses.

C. It is required for any host that cannot be a DHCP client but uses an address in the scope's range.

D. You cannot reserve addresses.

10. What is required for a client reservation?

A. The NetBIOS name of the client

B. The host name of the client

C. The MAC address of the client

D. The WINS address of the client

11. What happens to the client if you delete its lease?

A. It immediately stops using the address.

B. It will not be able to initialize at next startup.

C. Nothing happens until it attempts to renew the address.

D. The host stops working.

12. What is the recommended method of providing backup to the DHCP server information only?

A. Use a tape drive to back up the entire server.

B. Copy all files located in the DHCP directory and below to a save area.

C. Use the DHCP manager, click backup, and specify a directory.

D. Do nothing. Windows will automatically create a backup with no user intervention.

13. A DHCP client is located on a subnet with no DHCP servers. When it makes its broadcast for an address, its request is forwarded to a DHCP server on a remote network. Two DHCP servers exist on the remote network. Given that the DHCP servers are configured correctly, what IP address will the client receive?

A. An address on the remote network.

B. An address on the network of the device that forwarded its request to the DHCP server.

C. No address will be assigned; the DHCP server must be on the same subnet.

D. Two addresses—one which is for its network and a secondary on the remote used for renewal.

14. Which of the following clients cannot use a DHCP server? Select the best answer.

A. MS LAN Manager for DOS 2.2c

B. Windows NT Workstation

C. MS LAN Manager for OS/2 2.2c

D. Windows 95

15. How do you configure a client to use DHCP?

A. Install the DHCP client service.

B. Select the Automatic Configuration icon from the Control Panel.

C. DHCP automatically configures all clients.

D. Select Obtain IP address automatically in the TCP/IP configuration.

16. Which statements about the function of the DHCP relay agent are false? Select all that apply.

A. Forwards DHCP broadcast messages between DHCP-enabled clients and DHCP servers

B. Goes across IP routers

C. Forwards DHCP broadcasts between non-DHCP-enabled clients and DHCP servers

D. Updates routing tables

17. On which computers can the DHCP relay agent be configured? Select the best answer.

A. Windows 3.1x or greater

B. Windows 95 or greater

C. Windows NT Workstation 4.0 or greater

D. Windows NT Server

ANSWER KEY

1. A-B-C
2. B
3. A
4. C
5. D
6. B
7. A
8. B
9. A
10. C
11. C
12. D
13. B
14. C
15. D
16. C-D
17. D

ANSWERS & EXPLANATIONS

INSTALL AND CONFIGURE THE DHCP RELAY AGENT

1. Where can you get the IP address for a client? Select all that apply.

A. From the client

B. From the DHCP Server

C. From a scope of addresses on the RAS Server

1. CORRECT ANSWERS: A-B-C

When asking where an IP address can originate, we are referring to the sources of where it can be assigned. If a client specifies its address, the origin is the client. If it is a DHCP client, the source is the DHCP server. If it is a dial-up connection, an IP address can come from the client, a DHCP server, or the scope of addresses on a RAS Server.

2. Before a client can receive a DHCP address, what must be configured on the DHCP server?

B. A scope for the client's subnet

2. CORRECT ANSWER: B

A scope for the clients subnet must be configured on the DHCP server.

What DHCP Servers Can Do

To enable automatic TCP/IP configuration by using DHCP, the DHCP administrator first enters the valid IP addresses as a scope in the DHCP server database and then activates the scope. Next, the DHCP administrator enters other TCP/IP configuration information that will be given to the clients. The administrator or user then selects the **Enable Automatic DHCP Configuration** option (Obtain IP Address Automatically) on the client (found in their network configuration).

When a DHCP client starts, TCP/IP initializes and the client requests an IP address from a DHCP server by issuing a *Dhcpdiscover* packet. The Dhcpdiscover packet represents the client's IP lease request.

After a DHCP server receives the Dhcpdiscover packet, the DHCP server offers (*Dhcpoffer*) one of the unassigned IP addresses from the scope of addresses that are valid for that host.

This procedure ensures that no two DHCP clients on that subnet have the same IP address. This Dhcpoffer information is sent back to the host. If your network contains more than one DHCP server, the host may receive several Dhcpoffers. In most cases, the host or client computer accepts the first Dhcpoffer that it receives. The client then sends a *Dhcprequest* packet containing the IP address offered by the DHCP server.

Note that some clients' IP configurations and third-party IP stacks allow an option to attempt to regain a previous IP address. When this option is used, rejections may occur. This, however, is not a standard Microsoft client feature.

The DHCP server now sends the client an acknowledgment (*Dhcpack*) that contains the IP address originally sent and a lease for that address. The DHCP server leases the IP address to the DHCP client host for the specified period. The DHCP client must renew its lease before its expiration.

The renewal request is sent automatically if the host still has TCP/IP initialized, can communicate with the DHCP server, and is still on the same subnet or network. After 50% of the lease time expires, the client attempts to renew its lease with the DHCP server that assigned its TCP/IP configuration. If for some reason the DHCP server does not reply, the client will repeat attempts every two minutes. After 87.5% of the active lease period has expired, the client, if unable to contact and renew the lease with the original DHCP server, attempts to communicate with any DHCP server to renew its configuration information. If the client cannot make contact with a DHCP server and consequently fails to maintain its lease, the client must discontinue use of the IP address and begin the entire process again by issuing a Dhcpdiscover packet.

DHCPACK Phase

After the server that offers the lease receives the DHCPREQUEST message, it checks its DHCP database to ensure that the IP address is still available. If the requested lease remains available, the DHCP server marks that IP address as being leased in its DHCP database and broadcasts a DHCPACK to acknowledge that the IP address has been leased to the DHCP client.

The DHCPACK contains the same information as the DHCPOFFER, plus any optional DHCP information that has been configured for that scope as a scope option.

If the requested lease is no longer available, the DHCP server broadcasts a DHCP negative acknowledgment (DHCPNACK) containing the DHCP client's hardware address. When the DHCP client receives a DHCPNACK, it must start the lease request process over with a DHCPDISCOVER message. After receiving a DHCPACK, the DHCP client can continue to initialize TCP/IP, and it updates its Registry with the IP addressing information included with the lease. The client continues to use the leased IP address information until the lease expires, the command `ipconfig/release` is typed from a command prompt, or it receives a DHCPNACK from the DHCP server after unsuccessfully renewing its lease.

DHCP Lease Renewal

The DHCP client attempts to renew its IP address lease after 50% of its lease time has expired (or when manually requested to renew the lease by the `ipconfig/renew` command from a command prompt).

To renew the lease, a DHCP client sends a DHCPREQUEST directly to the DHCP server that gave it the original lease. Again, the DHCPREQUEST contains the hardware address of the client and the requested IP address, but this time uses the DHCP server IP address for the destination and the DHCP client IP address for the source IP address in the datagram. If the DHCP server is available and the requested IP address is still available (meaning it has not been removed from the scope), the DHCP server responds by sending a DHCPACK directly to the DHCP client. If the server is available but the requested IP address is no longer in the configured scopes, a DHCPNACK is sent to the DHCP client, which then must start the lease process again with a DHCPDISCOVER. A DHCPNACK can be sent for the following reasons:

- The IP address requested is no longer available because the lease was manually expired on the server and given to another client.

- The IP address requested has been removed from the available scopes on the DHCP server.
- The DHCP client has been physically moved to another subnet that will use a different scope on the DHCP server for that subnet. Hence the IP address changes to a valid IP address for the new subnet. If the server does not respond to the DHCPREQUEST sent after the lease is 50% expired, the DHCP client continues to use the original lease until it is seven-eighths (or 87.5%) expired. Because this DHCPREQUEST is broadcast rather than directed to a particular DHCP server, any DHCP server can respond with a DHCPACK or DHCPNACK to renew or deny the lease. Only the server holding that address in its scope, however, can ultimately renew it.

3. What is the effect of a lease duration of Unlimited?

A. DHCP configuration options will never be updated automatically.

3. CORRECT ANSWER: A

DHCP configuration options will never be updated if the lease is set to Unlimited unless the user manually asks for an update using `Ipconfig` or `WinIPCfg`. Most administrators in smaller environments find this option useful when addresses are plentiful. However, the major downfall with this option is poor retention.

4. In what environment is it advisable to have a short lease duration?

C. In environments where you have hosts moving and many changes to IP addresses

4. CORRECT ANSWER: C

Short lease durations are ideal for environments where you are moving hosts often. Suppose that you are the administrator at a sales office where 500 users are present, but only 50 IP addresses are available at any one time. Having a short lease period on the IP addresses would release them sooner and make them available to others. Ideally there should be at least one address per notebook.

5. What portion of the DHCP process is initiated by the server?

D. None

5. CORRECT ANSWER: D

All processes are initiated by the client and not the server. Although the server will track when a lease has expired so that addresses can be returned to the pool, it will make no attempts to communicate with a client.

6. How must an Windows NT Server be configured before you install a DHCP server?

B. The server requires a static IP configuration.

6. CORRECT ANSWER: B

A DHCP server cannot be a DHCP client and must have a static address. Because the DHCP server must be able to determine information such as its own subnet and so forth, it cannot be set as a client. Likewise, WINS, DHCP, Email, and Internet servers should also be set with static addresses or given permanent leases where applicable.

Planning a DHCP Implementation

As with all network services that you will use, you should plan the implementation of DHCP. Before beginning a conversion to DHCP, it is important to determine which, if any, IP addresses are available, that network hardware is supportive, and that both the client and server components meet the requirements.

Network Requirements

Your network must meet the following requirements to implement Microsoft TCP/IP using DHCP:

- The DHCP server service must be running on a Windows NT Server.
- The DHCP server must have a manually configured IP address.
- A DHCP server must be located on the same subnet as the DHCP clients, the clients subnet must have a DHCP relay agent running, or the routers connecting the two subnets involved must be able to forward DHCP (BOOTP) datagrams.
- Pools of IP addresses (that is, scopes) must be configured on the DHCP server.

The easiest way to implement DHCP is with only one DHCP server on a subnet (local network segment). If more than one DHCP server is configured to provide addresses for a subnet, then either can provide the address—there is no way to specify which server to use (as you can in WINS). Because DHCP servers do not communicate with one another, a DHCP server has no way of knowing whether an IP address is leased to a client from another DHCP server.

In other words, the IP address scopes cannot overlap or contain the same IP addresses. Although it is less complicated to rely on only one server, using two provides fault tolerance to your clients. In this case, the best solution is to place the DHCP server on different subnets.

Finally, the DHCP server must have one or more scopes created by using the DHCP server Manager application. (Choose **Start**, **Programs**, **Administrative Tools**, **DHCP Manager.**) A *scope* is a range of IP addresses available for lease by DHCP clients; for example, 200.20.5.1 through 200.20.5.20 may be a scope for a given subnet, and 200.20.6.1 through 200.20.6.50 may be a scope for another subnet.

Client Requirements

A Microsoft TCP/IP DHCP client can be any of the following Microsoft TCP/IP clients:

- Windows NT Server 3.5 or later that is not a DHCP server
- Windows NT Workstation 3.5 or later
- Windows 95 & 98
- Windows for Workgroups 3.11 running the Microsoft TCP/IP-32 software from the Windows NT Server CD-ROM
- Microsoft Network Client for MS-DOS 3.0 from the Windows NT Server CD-ROM
- LAN Manager server for MS-DOS 2.2c from the Windows NT Server CD-ROM

Clients that do not support DHCP or require a manual IP address such as for WINS, DNS, and so on, should use an address that is excluded from the active DHCP range; otherwise, DHCP may assign the address and create a duplicate.

Limitations of DHCP

Although DHCP can substantially reduce the headaches and time required to administer IP addresses, you should note a few limiting characteristics of DHCP:

- DHCP does not detect IP addresses already in use on a network by non-DHCP clients. These addresses should be excluded from any scopes configured on the DHCP server.
- A DHCP server does not communicate with other DHCP servers and cannot detect IP addresses leased by other DHCP servers. Therefore, two DHCP servers should not use the same IP addresses in their respective scopes.
- DHCP servers cannot communicate with clients across routers unless BOOTP forwarding is enabled on the router or the DHCP relay agent is enabled on the subnet.
- As with manually configured TCP/IP, incorrect values configured for a DHCP scope can cause unexpected and potentially disastrous results on the internetwork.

Other than the IP address and subnet mask, any values configured manually through the Network Control Panel applet or Registry editor of a DHCP client override the DHCP server scope settings. If you intend to use the server-configured values, be sure to clear the values from the host TCP/IP configuration dialog boxes. Enabling DHCP on the client host does not automatically clear any preexisting values with the exception of the IP address and subnet mask.

Installing the DHCP Server Service

The DHCP server service can be installed on a computer running Microsoft TCP/IP and Windows NT Server version 3.5 or later.

1. Open the Control Panel and double-click the Network icon.
2. From the Network settings dialog box, choose the Services tab and then click Add.
3. Choose the Microsoft DHCP Service from the list that appears and click OK. When prompted, enter the directory for the Windows NT source files.
4. Click Close on the Network settings dialog box and when prompted restart your computer.

The DHCP server must have a manually configured IP address, subnet mask, and default gateway. It cannot be assigned an address from another DHCP server even if an address is reserved for the DHCP server.

EXAM TIP

Here is something important to remember for the exam: A DHCP server cannot be a DHCP client.

Configuring the DHCP Server

After a DHCP server has been installed on an internetwork, you need to configure the following items:

- One or more IP address scopes (ranges of IP addresses to be leased) must be defined on the DHCP server.
- Non-DHCP client IP addresses must be excluded from the defined scopes.
- The options for the scope must be configured; for example, the default gateway for a subnet.
- IP address reservations must be created for DHCP clients requiring a specific IP address to be assigned.
- The DHCP clients must have automatic DHCP configuration enabled and should have unwanted manually configured TCP/IP parameters deleted.

7. What information is required to define a scope?

A. Starting and ending addresses and the subnet mask

7. CORRECT ANSWER: A

Starting and ending addresses and the subnet mask are required to define a scope. Regardless of the assignment of an entire subnet or not, both a start point and end point must be specified. On single address scopes, the start and end points are the same.

Configuring Scopes

For a DHCP server to lease IP addresses to DHCP clients, a range of valid IP addresses must be defined (on the server).

Each range of IP addresses is called a scope. One scope must be configured on the server for each subnet to which the DHCP server provides IP address leases. Configuring multiple scopes on a DHCP server has two benefits:

- The DHCP server can provide IP address leases to clients on remote subnets. This feature is especially useful as a backup in case another DHCP server is not available. You must ensure, however, that the scopes on each DHCP server have unique IP address ranges so that no duplicate IP addresses are on the internetwork. Microsoft recommends that 75% of IP address ranges be activated on a primary DHCP server and 25% on a backup.
- You can create separate scope options for each subnet. For example, each subnet could have a default gateway that can be configured individually for each scope.

To create a scope on a DHCP server, you must have the DHCP server service installed and running. You should also know a range of IP addresses that you can use to create a DHCP scope, as well as the IP addresses that should be excluded from that range.

Follow these steps to configure a scope on the DHCP server:

1. Start DHCP Manager (Start, Programs, Administrative Tools, DHCP Manager).
2. Select the local DHCP server "Local Machine" by clicking the entry and then by choosing Create from the Scope menu. The Create Scope dialog box is displayed. (This dialog box will be displayed automatically the first time you run the DHCP Manager.)
3. Enter the starting and ending IP addresses for the first subnet in the Start Address and the End Address fields of the IP Address Pool.
4. Type the Subnet Mask for this scope in the Subnet Mask field.

5. If required, type a single IP address or a range of IP addresses to be excluded from the IP. This is important to avoid duplicate address assignments. The IP address that is not used in the Address Pool in the Exclusion Range Start Address scope is added to the Excluded Addresses list. Choose Add. Repeat if required.

6. If you do not want the IP address leases to expire, select the Unlimited option under Lease Duration. (If you choose this option, then the configuration of the client will never be updated.) If you want to force the DHCP clients to renew their leases periodically (to ensure that the client is still using the IP address), choose the Limited To: option and type the lease duration in days, hours, and minutes. By default, the Lease Duration is three days. If you have a large ratio of available IP addresses to hosts on the network, you may want to use a longer lease duration to reduce broadcast traffic. If hosts are regularly coming and going and changing subnets on the network, such as with laptops and docking stations, you want a relatively short lease duration so the DHCP server recovers previously used IP addresses fairly quickly.

7. In the Name field, type the name to be used for referring to the scope in the DHCP Manager, for example, **`subnet 200.20.1.0`**.

8. In the Comment field, type an optional descriptive comment for the scope, for example, **`Third floor – west side`**.

8. What is the difference between a global option and a scope option?

B. Scope options are set in the DHCP Manager for individual scopes.

8. CORRECT ANSWER: B

Scope options are set for individual scopes whereas global options are set for all. When setting local options such as for WINS, typically an individual scope works best. However, if a given company has only one WINS server, it makes more sense to set it as a global option because it does not have to be retyped for each scope. This can be a real time saver and prevent a number of mistakes from occurring. It is not uncommon to assign some information globally, whereas others, such as a gateway, are assigned on a single scope basis.

Scope Options

Each DHCP scope can have several options that are configured on the client along with the IP address, such as default gateway and WINS server addresses. DHCP Manager includes many scope options that can be configured and sent to the DHCP clients; however, if TCP/IP configuration has been manually entered, then the client will ignore everything except the IP address and subnet mask.

Three types of DHCP scope options are available:

- **Global options**—set for all scopes in DHCP Manager
- **Scope options**—set for a selected scope in DHCP Manager
- **Client Options**—set for reserved addresses

Scope options are optional information that is delivered to a client along with their basic IP information. The value set in a scope option overrides a value set for the same DHCP option in a global option. Any values manually configured on the DHCP client—through the Network Control Panel applet Microsoft TCP/IP Configuration dialog box, for example—override any DHCP configured options. The common scope options supported by Microsoft DHCP clients are shown in Table 5.1.

TABLE 5.1 Scope Options Supported by Microsoft DHCP Clients

Scope Option	*Option Number*
Router	3
DNS server	6
DNS Domain Name	15
NetBIOS Name server (WINS)	44
NetBIOS Node Type	46
NetBIOS Scope ID	47

The Scope Options Configuration dialog box in the DHCP Manager application contains many other scope options (such as Time server) that can be sent to the clients along with the other TCP/IP configuration information.

The Microsoft DHCP clients, however, ignore and discard all the scope option information except for the options listed in Table 5.1.

Most of the scope options should be fairly intuitive, such as a DNS server is the IP address as is the router, and so on. However, when defining a WINS server (44), you must also define the node type (46). The type should be configured as follows:

- **B-Node (0×1)**—Broadcast for Name Resolution.
- **P-Node (0×2)**—Point-to-Point communication directly with a WINS Server.
- **M-Node (0×4)**—Mixed mode. First broadcasts, then tries the WINS server for resolution.
- **H-Node (0×8)**—Hybrid mode. First communicates with the WINS server, then broadcasts if a name is not resolved.

When configuring DHCP to deliver WINS information, generally the preferred setting is (0×8) H-Node.

To view and define options for a DHCP server, follow these steps:

1. Start the DHCP Manager tool.
2. Choose either Scope or Global from the DHCP Options menu.
3. Configure the desired DHCP options:
    1. From the unused Options list, select an option and click Add. The option is added to the Active Options list.
    2. Choose Value to display the value for the option.
    3. You can now edit the value. Three types of values can be edited: strings (such as Domain name), which you can simply enter; hexadecimal values (such as NetBIOS node type), which you can enter; and IP address ranges. For these, click Edit Array and another dialog box appears in which you can enter one or more IP addresses.

4. When all the required options are entered, click **OK** and exit DHCP Manager.

9. Why would you use a client reservation?

A. To provide dynamic configuration of TCP/IP options with a static IP address.

9. CORRECT ANSWER: A

A client reservation provides a static IP address. Let's say that you want a client to receive information such as WINS, DNS, and so forth, but want it assigned the same address each time. In this case, you would make a client reservation.

10. What is required for a client reservation?

C. The MAC address of the client

10. CORRECT ANSWER: C

The MAC address of a client must be given in order to configure a client reservation. Although you may input the host name, it is for informational purposes only and does not actually affect the client. The MAC address is, of course, used for the actual assignment.

11. What happens to the client if you delete its lease?

C. Nothing happens until it attempts to renew the address.

11. CORRECT ANSWER: C

If you delete a client's lease, nothing will happen until it attempts to renew the address. However, if the DHCP server assigns the address to another client, you will observe a duplicate address conflict.

Address Reservations

If a DHCP client requires a specific IP address to be assigned to it each time it renews its IP address lease, that IP address can be reserved for the DHCP client through the DHCP Manager tool. The following are the most common examples of clients that should have an IP address reservation:

- Servers on a network with non-WINS-enabled clients. If a server on such a network does not always lease the same IP address, the non-WINS clients might not be able to connect to the servers using NetBIOS over TCP/IP (NetBT).
- Any other host that is expected to have a specific IP address to which hosts connect.

To reserve an IP address from a scope for a specific DHCP client, follow these steps:

1. Determine the hardware address for the DHCP client with the IP address to be reserved from the scope. You can do so by typing **ipconfig/all** at a client's command prompt. A sample ipconfig/all output is shown here:

```
Ethernet adapter NDISLoop1:
        Description . . . . . . . . : MS
➥LoopBack Driver
        Physical Address. . . . . . : 20-4C-4F-
➥4F-50-20
        DHCP Enabled. . . . . . . . : No
        IP Address. . . . . . . . . :
➥200.20.1.30
        Subnet Mask . . . . . . . . :
➥255.255.255.0
        Default Gateway . . . . . . : 200.20.1.1
```

2. Start DHCP Manager and select the DHCP server to be configured.
3. Select the scope containing the IP address to be reserved.
4. Choose Add Reservations from the Scope menu. The Add Reserved Clients dialog box is displayed.
5. In the IP Address field, type the IP address to be reserved for the DHCP client.
6. In the Unique Identifier field, type the hardware address of the network card for the IP address used. The hardware address should be typed without hyphens (-).
7. In the Client Name field, type a name for the client to be used only in DHCP Manager. This value is purely descriptive and does not affect the client in any way.
8. In the Client Comments field, optionally type any comments for the client reservation.
9. Choose Add. The reservation is enabled.
10. Choose Active Leases from the Scope menu of DHCP Manager. The Active Leases dialog box is displayed and the reservations are shown.

Compacting the DHCP Database

Entries in the DHCP database are continually being added, modified, and deleted throughout the IP address leasing process. When entries are deleted, the space is not always completely filled with a new entry because of the different sizes of each entry. After some time, the database contains unused space that can be recovered by compacting the database. This process is analogous to defragmenting a disk drive.

Microsoft recommends compacting the DHCP database from once every month to once every week, depending on the size of the internetwork. This compaction increases transaction speed and reduces the disk space used by the database.

The Jetpack utility compacts the DHCP database (DHCP.mdb) into a temporary database, which is then automatically copied to DHCP.mdb and deleted. The command used is `jetpack DHCP.mdb` *`temp_name`*`.mdb`, where *`temp_name.mdb`* is any filename specified by the user, with extension .mdb.

Here's how to compact the DHCP database:

1. Stop the DHCP server service by using either the Control Panel, Server Manager, or a command prompt.
2. To stop the service from a command prompt, type **`net stop dhcpserver service`**. This command stops the DHCP server.
3. Type **`cd \`*`systemroot`*`\system32\dhcp`**, where *`systemroot`* is WINNT. This changes it to the DHCP directory.
4. Type **`jetpack dhcp.mdb temp.mdb`**. This command compacts dhcp.mdb into temp.mdb, copies it back to dhcp.mdb, and automatically deletes temp.mdb.
5. Type **`net start dhcpserver`**. This command restarts the DHCP server service.

12. What is the recommended method of providing backup to the DHCP server information only?

D. Do nothing. Windows will automatically create a backup with no user intervention.

12. CORRECT ANSWER: D

Windows will automatically back up files as required. These files are data files only. If a situation occurs in which a restore is desired, it may happen automatically or as a manual process. Backups occur at regular intervals as specified in the registry.

Backing Up the DHCP Database

By default, the DHCP database is automatically backed up at a specific interval. You can change the default interval by editing the DHCP server `BackupInterval` parameter value contained in the Registry:

```
SYSTEM\current\currentcontrolset\services\DHCPServer\
➥Parameters
```

Backing up the DHCP database enables recovery from a system crash or DHCP database corruption.

You can change the default backup interval of 60 minutes by following these steps:

1. Stop the DHCP server service from a command prompt by typing **`net stop dhcpserver`**.
2. Start the Registry editor (REGEDT32.EXE).
3. Open the `HKEY_LOCAL_MACHINE\SYSTEM\CurrentControlSet\Services\DHCPserver\Parameters` key and double-click to select BackupInterval.
4. In the Radix, make a selection, and configure the entry to the desired value. Close the Registry editor.
5. Restart the DHCP server service from a command prompt by typing **`net start dhcpserver`**.

Restoring a Corrupt DHCP Database

If the DHCP database becomes corrupt, it can be restored from a backup in one of the following ways:

- It can be restored automatically.
- You can use the RestoreFlag key in the Registry.
- You can manually replace the corrupt database file.

Automatic Restoration

The DHCP server service automatically restores the backup copy of the database if it detects a corrupt database. If the database has become corrupt, stop and restart the DHCP server service. You can do so by typing **`net stop dhcpserver`** and then **`net start dhcpserver`** at a command prompt.

Registry RestoreFlag

If a corrupt DHCP database is not automatically restored from a backup when the DHCP server service is started, you can force the database to be restored by setting the RestoreFlag key in the Registry. Follow these steps:

1. Stop the DHCP server service from a command prompt by typing **`net stop dhcpserver`**.
2. Start the Registry editor (REGEDT32.EXE).
3. Open the `HKEY_LOCAL_MACHINE\SYSTEM\CurrentControlSet\Services\DHCPserver\Parameters` key and select RestoreFlag.
4. Change the value to **1** in the data field and click OK. Close the Registry editor.
5. Restart the DHCP server service from a command prompt by typing **`net start dhcpserver`**. The database is restored from the backup, and the RestoreFlag entry in the Registry automatically resets to `0`.

Copying from the Backup Directory

You can manually replace the corrupt database file with a backed-up version by following these steps:

1. Stop the DHCP server service from a command by typing **net stop dhcpserver**.
2. Change to the DHCP directory by typing **cd *systemroot*\system32\dhcp\backup\jet**, where *systemroot* is WINNT, for example.
3. Copy the contents of the directory to the *systemroot*\system32\DHCP directory.
4. Type **net start dhcpserver** from a command prompt to restart the DHCP server service.

13. A DHCP client is located on a subnet with no DHCP servers. When it makes its broadcast for an address, the request is forwarded to a DHCP server on a remote network. Two DHCP servers exist on the remote network. Given that the DHCP servers are configured correctly, what IP address will the client receive?

B. An address on the network of the device that forwarded its requests to the DHCP server.

13. CORRECT ANSWER: B

Because a DHCP client will send an IP broadcast which consists of a source address of 0.0.0.0 and is a MAC address, it has no control over its processing. Wherever the relay agent or router forwards the request will provide an address. However, it will use the address of the device that sends the request to determine the network address. If the device is 0.0.0.0, it provides a local address. If it contains a device such as the router, it will get an address for that subnet. Even if there are two DHCP servers on the remote network, the client will use only the first address that it receives.

Using Multiple DHCP Servers

Having more than one DHCP server on a subnet is not recommended. When working with more than one server, there is no way to control which DHCP server will provide a client with an IP address lease. Any DHCP server that receives a client's DHCP request broadcast can send a DHCP offer to that client. The client usually accepts the lease offer it receives from the first DHCP server that responds.

If more than one subnet exists on a network, the general recommendation is to have a DHCP server on each subnet. This is practical only if the DHCP relay agent or routers that support the forwarding of BOOTP broadcasts are used, in which case a single DHCP server can handle the requests for DHCP addresses. For fault tolerance, a second server may be added.

A DHCP server has an IP address scope configured for each subnet to which it sends DHCP offers. If the DHCP server receives a relayed DHCP request from a remote subnet, it offers an IP address lease from the scope for that subnet. To ensure that a DHCP client can receive an IP address lease even if a DHCP server is not functioning, you should configure an IP address scope for a given subnet on more than one DHCP server. Thus, if a DHCP client cannot obtain a lease from the local DHCP server, the DHCP relay agent or router passes the request to a DHCP server on a remote network that can offer a DHCP lease to the client.

For example, consider a network with two subnets, each with a DHCP server, joined by a RFC 1542-compliant router. For this scenario, Microsoft recommends that each DHCP server contain approximately 75% of the available IP addresses for the subnet the DHCP server is on and 25% of the available IP addresses for the remote subnet. Most of the IP addresses available for a subnet can be obtained from the local DHCP server. If the local DHCP server is unavailable, the remote DHCP server can offer a lease from the smaller range of IP addresses available from the scope on the remote DHCP server.

If the range of IP addresses available is 120.50.7.10 through 120.50.7.110 for subnet A and 120.50.8.10 through 120.50.8.110 for subnet B, you can configure the scopes on each DHCP server as follows:

Subnet	*DHCP Server A*	*DHCP Server B*
A	120.50.7.10–120.50.7.84	120.50.7.85–120.50.7.110
B	120.50.8.10–120.50.8.34	120.50.8.35–120.50.8.110

▼ NOTE

You must ensure that no IP address is duplicated on another DHCP server. If two DHCP servers contain the same IP address, that IP address could potentially be leased to two DHCP clients at the same time. Therefore, IP address ranges must be split between multiple DHCP servers, as shown in the preceding example.

14. Which of the following clients cannot use a DHCP server? Select the best answer.

C. MS LAN Manager for OS/2 2.2c

14. CORRECT ANSWER: C

MS LAN Manager for OS/2 2.2c clients cannot use DHCP. This client is too old and has not been updated to include new automation features such as DHCP.

15. How do you configure a client to use DHCP?

D. Select Obtain IP Address Automatically in the TCP/IP configuration.

15. CORRECT ANSWER: D

Select Obtain IP Address Automatically in the TCP/IP configuration to configure a client to use DHCP. If any old settings that were manually typed into the TCP/IP configuration exist, no other steps are required because they will override any information delivered by DHCP.

DHCP Clients

For a client to use DHCP to obtain IP address information, automatic DHCP configuration must be enabled at the client. The procedure is slightly different for Windows NT and Windows for Workgroups clients.

Windows NT and Windows 95 As DHCP Clients

You can enable Automatic DHCP configuration either before or after Microsoft TCP/IP is installed. To ensure that the DHCP TCP/IP parameters are used instead of any configured manually on the host, you should preferably enable automatic DHCP configuration before Microsoft TCP/IP is installed. To enable automatic DHCP configuration after TCP/IP is installed, follow these steps:

1. Double-click the Network icon in Control Panel. The Network settings dialog box will be displayed.
2. Select the Protocols tab. From the list of installed protocols, select TCP/IP and choose the Properties button. The TCP/IP configuration dialog box appears.
3. Select the Enable Automatic DHCP Configuration (Obtain an IP address automatically) check box. The previous IP address and subnet mask values disappear. Ensure that all other configuration parameters you want DHCP to supply are cleared.
4. Close the TCP/IP configuration dialog box and the Network Setting dialog box. Restart the system when prompted.

Windows for Workgroups As a DHCP Client

Configuring Windows for Workgroups as a DHCP client is simple. Use the following steps:

1. Double-click the Network Setup icon in the Network program group of the Windows for Workgroups client.
2. Choose the Drivers button, select Microsoft TCP/IP, and choose the Setup button. The TCP/IP Configuration dialog box is displayed.

3. Select the Enable Automatic DHCP Configuration check box and choose Continue. The dialog box closes, and you are prompted to restart the computer.
4. Do not configure any other parameters, unless you want to override the options set in the DHCP scope—which is not recommended.

16. Which statements about the function of the DHCP relay agent are false? Select all that apply.

C. Forwards DHCP broadcasts between non-DHCP-enabled clients and DHCP servers

D. Updates routing tables

16. CORRECT ANSWERS: C-D

The job of the DHCP relay agent is to forward DHCP broadcast messages between DHCP-enabled clients and DHCP servers across IP routers. Non-DHCP enabled clients do not send DHCP broadcasts.

17. On which computers can DHCP relay agent be configured?

D. Windows NT Server

17. CORRECT ANSWER: D

The relay agent can be configured on any Windows NT Server computer. The dilemma with the relay agent is not that lower operating systems such as Windows 95/98 can't perform the function, but that Microsoft has not compiled a version of the relay agent to function with those operating systems. You can clearly see this during the install process when you add relay agent as a service under Windows NT.

Installing and Configuring the DHCP Relay Agent

The primary job of the DHCP relay agent is to forward DHCP broadcast messages between DHCP-enabled clients and DHCP servers, across IP routers. The relay agent can be configured on any Windows NT Server computer and adds very little load.

▼ NOTE

The DHCP relay agent that comes with Windows NT 4.0 is a new service that listens for DHCP broadcasts and forwards them to one or more configured DHCP servers. This process is different from an RFC1542-compliant router in that the system running the relay agent is not a router.

1. Open the Network Configuration dialog box and select the Services tab.
2. Select Add, DHCP Relay Agent. Click OK; when prompted, enter the path to the distribution files.
3. Click the Protocols tab and double-click the TCP/IP protocol.
4. On the DHCP Relay tab, enter the IP address of a DHCP server and the maximum number of hops and seconds that the relay can take.
5. Close the TCP/IP Configuration dialog box and the Network Configuration dialog box.
6. Restart the computer when prompted.

FURTHER REVIEW

INSTALL AND CONFIGURE THE DHCP RELAY AGENT

Understanding DHCP

The configuration of Microsoft TCP/IP involves knowing the correct values for several fields for each TCP/IP host and entering them manually. At the minimum, the host IP address and subnet mask need to be configured. In most cases, other parameters, such as WINS and DNS server addresses, also need to be configured on each host. DHCP relieves the need for manual configuration and provides a method of configuring and reconfiguring all the TCP/IP-related parameters.

The correct TCP/IP address must be configured on each host; otherwise, hosts on the internetwork might

- Fail to communicate
- Fail to initialize
- Cause other hosts on the internetwork to hang

DHCP is an open industry standard that enables the automatic TCP/IP configuration of DHCP client computers. The use of Microsoft's DHCP server greatly reduces the administrative overhead of managing TCP/IP client computers by eliminating the need to manually configure clients. The DHCP server also allows greater flexibility and mobility of clients on a TCP/IP network without administrator intervention. If used correctly, DHCP can eliminate nearly all the problems associated with TCP/IP. The administrator enters the valid IP addresses or ranges of IP addresses (called a *scope*) in the DHCP server database, which then assigns (or leases) the IP addresses to the DHCP client hosts.

Storing all the TCP/IP configuration parameters on the DHCP server provides the following benefits:

- The administrator can quickly verify the IP address and other configuration parameters without having to go to each host. Also, reconfiguration of the DHCP database is accomplished at one central location, thereby eliminating the need to manually reconfigure each host.
- DHCP does not lease the same IP address from a scope to two hosts at the same time; if used properly, this feature can prevent duplicate IP addresses.

▼ NOTE

DHCP cannot detect which IP addresses are already being used by non-DHCP clients. If a host has a manually configured IP address and a DHCP scope is configured with that same address, the DHCP server may lease the address to a DHCP client, creating a duplicate IP address on the network. To prevent this situation, you must exclude all manually configured IP addresses from any scopes configured on the DHCP server. Note that some newer implementations of DHCP (such as in Windows NT 4.0 Service Pack 3 and NetWare 5) attempt to check whether an address is in use prior to assigning it to a client.

- The DHCP administrator controls which hosts use which IP addresses. DHCP uses local network broadcasts to lease IP addresses to client hosts. If a second DHCP server resides on the same local network segment, the DHCP client can communicate with either server and may receive an IP address lease from the unintended DHCP server.

- The chance of clerical and typing errors is reduced because all TCP/IP configuration parameters are entered in the DHCP server database.
- Several options can be set for each DHCP scope (or globally for all scopes) that is configured on the client along with the IP address; for example, default gateway and WINS server addresses.
- An IP address may be leased for a limited time. Therefore, the DHCP client must periodically renew its lease before the lease expires. If the host is no longer using the IP address (is no longer running TCP/IP or is powered off), the lease expires and can then be assigned to another TCP/IP host. This feature is useful if the number of hosts requesting IP addresses is larger than the number of available valid IP addresses (such as when the network is part of the Internet). This practice is not recommended, however, and you should always have more IP addresses than you have clients.
- If a host is physically moved to another subnet, the DHCP server on that subnet automatically reconfigures the host with the proper TCP/IP configuration information for that subnet.

CHAPTER SUMMARY

DHCP provides the administrative functionality that TCP/IP has been missing. DHCP adds many capabilities for network management, which are difficult to maintain otherwise. Through the abilities of this protocol, TCP/IP systems can enjoy the same functionality as Plug-and-Play protocols such as IPX and NetBEUI.

DHCP delivers information that is granted to a system by a series of acknowledgments that are initiated by a client broadcast. After an IP address has been assigned, it is kept through the duration of the lease period set by the administrator. A client system can manually release an IP address at any time via local configuration utilities—WINIPCFG (Windows 95/98) or IPConfig (Windows NT/3.11). When a client has held an IP address for 50% of its total lease period, it will automatically attempt to renew its lease. If unsuccessful, a client will repeat the process over every two minutes. When 87.5% of the lease has expired, the client will then try a renewal with any DHCP server before losing its IP capabilities at the expiration deadline.

Because DHCP is a broadcast-based service, the BOOTP protocol is required to be placed on all routers which support networks with DHCP clients. In some instances, legacy network equipment may restrict or not support DHCP. To solve this problem, Microsoft created a DHCP relay agent service which can be run at any local workstation. These relay agents forward requests via routed IP past the router to the server.

CHAPTER REVIEW

REVIEW QUESTIONS

Note: The additional Chapter Review section that ends each chapter is unique to this member of the *New Riders TestPrep, Second Edition* series. We've included it to more fully and fairly cover the unique aspects of TCP/IP in relation to its mastery in preparation for MCSE examination.

1. **Your network is divided into nine subnets. You want to use DHCP to assign IP addresses to all computers on the entire network. You must make sure that the two DNS servers are configured on each computer regardless of the subnet they are located on. How should you configure DHCP?**

   A. By creating a global option

   B. By creating a client option

   C. By creating a scope option

   D. By creating a local option

2. **You want to configure the DHCP relay agent on your Windows NT Server. What information is required?**

   A. The IP address of the router to forward the DHCP request to

   B. The IP address of the DHCP server

   C. The IP address of a different DHCP relay agent of a remote subnet

   D. The computer name of the DHCP Server

3. **You have four Windows NT Servers and you want to use DHCP to give them a unique address each time the server is started. Each time they are assigned an address, you want it to be the same one. What information must you supply when you add the client reservation for each of the servers?**

   A. IP address

   B. Lease period

   C. Hardware address

   D. Subnet mask

4. **You use DHCP to assign IP addresses to all computers on your network. You want your Windows NT Servers to get the same unique IP address each time that the server is started. What should you do?**

   A. Create a client reservation for each server

   B. Create a separate scope that contains the IP address for each server

   C. Specify an unlimited lease period for the servers only

   D. Create an exclusion range of IP addresses to be assigned to the server

5. **You are a network engineer in a mid-sized company where you have three subnets. One subnet has only laptop Windows 95 computers and two subnets have Windows NT Workstations. You have one DHCP server to support all clients. You want the IP lease period for the laptops set to seven days. You want the Windows NT Workstations lease set to thirty days. Every segment is set for Ethernet with a Frame size of 1,500. What should you do?**

A. Create one DHCP scope for each subnet. Create a global option that specifies a lease period that is based on the operating system the client computer is running.

B. Create one DHCP scope for all subnets. For each workstation, create a client reservation with a 30-day lease period.

C. Create one DHCP scope for each subnet. Specify the lease period as part of the scope's configuration.

D. Create one DHCP scope for all subnets. For each computer, create an exclusion range with a unique lease period.

6. You are part of a planning commission that has been assigned the task of the IP design of the company's Windows NT Network. The network consists of five subnets. It has been determined that one DHCP server is adequate to support the 162 Windows NT Workstations and 26 Windows NT Servers. DHCP needs to assign the same IP addresses to your servers every time they are started.

The commission has determined the following scheme will be used to assign addresses:

Gateways	**1 through 19**
Clients	**20 through 99**
Server	**100 through 199**
Clients	**200 through 254**

How should this design be implemented?

A. Create one scope that is configured to exclude a range of addresses for the servers. Create a client reservation for each gateway.

B. Create one DHCP scope that is configured to reserve one range of addresses for the gateways and one range of addresses for the servers.

C. Create one DHCP scope that is configured to exclude a range of addresses for the gateways. Create a client reservation for each server.

D. Create four DHCP scopes for each range of IP addresses.

E. Create three DHCP scopes for each type of host computer.

ANSWER KEY

1. A	3. A-C	5. C
2. B	4. A	6. C

REVIEW ANSWERS

1. Your network is divided into nine subnets. You want to use DHCP to assign IP addresses to all computers on the entire network. You must make sure that the two DNS servers are configured on each computer regardless of the subnet they are located on. How should you configure DHCP?

A. By creating a global option

1. CORRECT ANSWER: A

By creating a global option, you can configure all subnets to use the same information. In this case, you are specifying that all clients use the same two DNS settings regardless of their location.

2. You want to configure the DHCP relay agent on your Windows NT Server. What information is required?

B. The IP address of the DHCP server

2. CORRECT ANSWER: B

The IP address of the DHCP server is required to forward DHCP requests. In effect, the relay agent is converting a local broadcast to a directed message.

3. You have four Windows NT Servers and you want to use DHCP to give them a unique address each time the server is started. Each time they are assigned an address, you want it to be the same one. What information must you supply when you add the client reservation for each of the servers?

A. IP address

C. Hardware address

3. CORRECT ANSWERS: A-C

First, you must determine which IP address you are assigning to each system. Then, to uniquely identify which system is to receive which IP address, you must specify the hardware (MAC) address.

4. You use DHCP to assign IP addresses to all computers on your network. You want your Windows NT Servers to get the same unique IP address each time that the server is started. What should you do?

A. Create a client reservation for each server

4. CORRECT ANSWER: A

Create a client reservation for each server to ensure that each time that server is started, it will always receive the same address. This is useful when changes in the environment occur, such as a new IP address for a WINS or DHCP server, a system can be automatically updated.

5. You are a network engineer in a mid-sized company where you have three subnets. One subnet has only laptop Windows 95 computers and two subnets have Windows NT Workstations. You have one DHCP server to support all clients. You want the IP lease period for the laptops set to seven days. You want the Windows NT Workstations lease set to thirty days. Every segment is set for Ethernet with a Frame size of 1,500. What should you do?

C. Create one DHCP scope for each subnet. Specify the lease period as part of the scope's configuration.

5. CORRECT ANSWER: C

Create one DHCP scope for each subnet. Specify the lease period as part of the scope's configuration. When reviewing a question such as this, feel free to ignore data that is irrelevant. In this case, the frame size is not of importance. The only concern that should face an administrator for this scenario is whether the router supports DHCP relay.

6. You are part of a planning commission that has been assigned the task of the IP design of the company's Windows NT Network. The network consists of five subnets. It has been determined that one DHCP server is adequate to support the 162 Windows NT Workstations and 26 Windows NT Servers. DHCP needs to assign the same IP addresses to your servers every time they are started. The commission has determined the following scheme will be used to assign addresses:

Gateways	**1 through 19**
Clients	**20 through 99**
Server	**100 through 199**
Clients	**200 through 254**

How should this design be implemented?

C. Create one DHCP scope that is configured to exclude a range of addresses for the gateways. Create a client reservation for each server.

6. CORRECT ANSWER: C

Create one DHCP scope that is configured to exclude a range of addresses for the gateways. Create a client reservation for each server. Because you have a set of addresses that are to be statically assigned, they must be included in the DHCP scope, but excluded from assignment. Then, using the hardware (MAC) address from each NIC, assign client reservations to each server.

CHAPTER 6

Windows NT and Multihomed Configurations

A computer can be connected to multiple networks for many reasons. Commonly, a system is set in multihomed configuration to support two networks that include no common media, such as Ethernet and Token Ring. However, multihomed systems are also used in the capacity of routers, bridges, firewalls, and proxy servers.

In this chapter, you should observe how Windows NT fits the role of a router and how it behaves as a workstation on two different networks. The key points to remember while progressing through this chapter are the types of multihomed systems and how they are used.

OBJECTIVES

This chapter helps you prepare for the exam by covering the following objectives:

On a Windows NT Server computer, configure Microsoft TCP/IP to support multiple network adapters.

- Windows NT server supports multiple network adapter in various configurations as part of its flexibility. This chapter's primary focus is on multihomed systems, specifically their interaction and configuration with TCP/IP.

Configure a Windows NT Server computer to function as an IP router.

- In addition to acting as a workstation on two different networks, Windows NT also has the capability to forward (route) information between them.

PRACTICE QUESTIONS

WINDOWS NT AND MULTIHOMED CONFIGURATIONS

On a Windows NT Server computer, configure Microsoft TCP/IP to support multiple network adapters. Configure a Windows NT Server computer to function as an IP router.

1. **A multihomed host must have two of which of the following?**
   A. Protocols
   B. Topologies
   C. Network cards
   D. Operating systems
2. **Which of the following best describes networks that would benefit from a multihomed host ?**
   A. Those with dissimilar physical topologies
   B. Those with dissimilar network cards
   C. Those with dissimilar operating systems
   D. Those with dissimilar protocols
3. **Which of the following best describes running WINS on a multihomed host?**
   A. Encouraged
   B. Possible, but discouraged
   C. Necessary
   D. The only way WINS can run
4. **You are configuring a network that uses OSPF on routers. Because of the high cost of the routers, you would like to use Windows NT as a router. How do you configure it?**
   A. Set it to route based on OSPF
   B. Set it to route based on RIP
   C. Set it to a static routing table
   D. The server will not work at this configuration
5. **You are configuring a Windows NT environment that consists of three networks. These networks are arranged so that one server is to route traffic between two networks (A and B) and forward traffic to a remote server that is connected via dial-up networking. Dial-up networking is not located on the router but is on subnet B. The router that defines two networks is aware of its own two networks (A and B), including the one in which the dial-up networking system resides, but is not aware of the third one (C). The remote router is aware of its network (C) and the one that includes the system where dial-up networking (B) resides. What happens when a system located on subnet A tries to establish a session with a system on subnet C?**
   A. The client times out and is unable to communicate with the remote system.
   B. The connection is established.
   C. The session is established by name only, and when trying to actually transfer data, the connection fails.
   D. The connection request generates a routing loop.

6. You are viewing the routing table and notice a number of entries that have the IP address 0.0.0.0. What does this address designate?

A. The local network

B. An error

C. Any unspecified route

D. Any local router interface

E. The default gateway

7. What tools can be used to view the routing table? Select all that apply.

A. NETSTAT

B. TRACERT

C. ROUTE

D. NBTSTAT

8. What tool can be used to determine the path that a packet takes across multiple routers?

A. NETSTAT

B. TRACERT

C. ROUTE

D. NBTSTAT

9. You are attempting to determine why a link to a remote site is slow. What information might help determine this? Select the best answer.

A. The metric

B. Default gateway

C. Byte count of the packet being sent

D. All of the above

10. On a multihomed Windows NT system, how can you configure it so that it automatically updates its routing tables by using routing information from other routers on the network? What service is required?

A. RIP for IP

B. RIP for NWLink IPX/SPX-Compatible Transport

C. The DHCP Relay Agent

D. The DHCP Service

11. You are configuring a Windows NT network to interface with an existing static and dynamic combo network. What is the first step that you should take to prepare the system in a multihomed configuration?

A. Install RIP

B. Configure TCP/IP

C. Add a second network card

D. Add static routes

ANSWER KEY

1. C	4. C	7. A-C	10. A
2. A	5. A	8. B	11. C
3. B	6. E	9. A	

ANSWERS & EXPLANATIONS

WINDOWS NT AND MULTIHOMED CONFIGURATIONS

1. A multihomed host must have two of which of the following?

C. Network cards

1. CORRECT ANSWER: C

A multihomed host must have two network cards. A network adapter can either be a traditional network interface card or an emulated adapter such as a modem.

2. Which of the following best describes networks that would benefit from a multihomed host?

A. Those with dissimilar physical topologies

2. CORRECT ANSWER: A

A good use for a multihomed host is to connect networks with dissimilar physical topologies. In this configuration, a system can send data between the two networks as a router and function as a workstation in either.

3. Which of the following best describes running WINS on a multihomed host?

B. Possible, but discouraged

3. CORRECT ANSWER: B

Running WINS on a multihomed host is possible, but discouraged. When referring to this configuration as possible, Microsoft is acknowledging support. However, by discouraging it, they are putting forward the expectation that more problems will be generated than in a standard configuration. This is due to the addressing of the server and the registration of clients.

What Is a Multihomed System?

A *multihomed computer* contains more than one network interface card (NIC) that participates on more than one network. For example, a Windows NT Server can have two NIC cards. One NIC card can have the address 192.2.2.1 and communicate with the network of hosts from 192.2.2.2 to 192.2.2.200. The other NIC card can have the address 160.2.2.1 and communicate with the network of hosts from 160.2.2.2 to 160.2.2.200.

The common object between these two networks is the multihomed host, and as such, it can act as a router between the two networks. This method is most useful when you have two different physical types of networks—such as Ethernet and Token Ring.

Normally, the WINS service should not be run on a multihomed computer because the WINS server always registers its names in the local database. Therefore, you will have a problem if you run DOS clients, because they always try the first address that they receive from the WINS server. When the WINS server registers its cards in order, the DOS client might not be able to reach resources on the WINS server from a network other than the one on which the first card is located.

4. You are configuring a network that uses OSPF on routers. Because of the high cost of the routers, you would like to use Windows NT as a router. How do you configure it?

C. Set it to a static routing table

4. CORRECT ANSWER: C

Because Windows NT does not support OSPF, and RIP would not matter since it is not used on the network, all routes would have to be configured as static.

Configuring Windows NT to Function As an IP Router

Routers use built-in tables to determine where to send a packet destined for a particular network. By default, routers know only about networks to which they are physically attached and depend on tables to inform them about networks to which they are not physically attached—either through manual configuration or dynamic configuration.

Static routers are not capable of discovering networks other than those to which they have a physical interface. If this type of router is to route packets to any other network, it has to be told manually what to do, either through the assignment of a default gateway on the router or by manually editing the route table. Microsoft Windows NT enables the user to build either a static or a multihomed router by using multiple network cards and IP addresses. In a static router environment, new changes are not reflected in the routing tables.

Dynamic routers, on the other hand, use interrouting protocols. These protocols simply provide a language for routers to communicate changes to their route tables to other routers in their environment. In this way, routing tables are built dynamically, and the administrator does not have to manually edit route tables to bring up a new network segment.

Dynamic routers cannot provide this function without routing protocols, though. The most popular routing protocols are the *Routing Information Protocol* (RIP) and *Open Shortest Path First* protocol (OSPF). RIP is a broadcast-based protocol used primarily on small- to medium-sized networks. The more sophisticated OSPF protocol is used for medium to large networks.

Microsoft Windows NT 4.0 supports the installation and use of RIP to provide dynamic routing for multihomed computers using Windows NT as the operating system. In this way, routing tables can be updated whenever any additions to a network occur. Using RIP or OSPF in a routed environment should help eliminate the need to manually edit route tables in your environment.

5. You are configuring a Windows NT environment that consists of three networks. These networks are arranged so that one server is to route traffic between two networks (A and B) and forward traffic to a remote server that is connected via dial-up networking. Dial-up networking is not located on the router but is on subnet B. The router that defines two networks is aware of its own two networks (A and B), including the one in which the dial up networking system resides, but is not aware of the third one (C). The remote router is aware of its network (C) and the one that includes the system where dial-up networking (B) resides. What happens when a system located on subnet A tries to establish a session with a system on subnet C?

A. The client times out and is unable to communicate with the remote system.

5. CORRECT ANSWER: A

In order to communicate, the router must be made aware of the remote network. In this case, the RAS server is acting as a router to the remote network which the RAS client is establishing. That the client can communicate with the local network is only one facet of being connected with a local address. On the other hand, if configured properly, the C subnet could in theory communicate to the A subnet, but not the other way around—resulting in the start of communications and the failure of transfers.

The Static Routing Environment

A typical small network environment can have two routers dividing three subnets. Each router has a standard routing table consisting of the networks to which it is attached. Router A would be connected to subnets 1 and 2 and have a routing table that reflects this information. Router B would be connected to subnets 2 and 3, and its routing table would reflect the networks on which it is currently configured.

Assume a Ping (echo request) packet is initiated by a machine on subnet 1. From the command prompt, or possibly a specific application on subnet 1, a `PING` command is issued to an IP address on subnet 3, perhaps from IP address 131.107.32.10 to 131.107.96.20. First, IP takes the destination address and compares it to the source address using the subnet mask of that machine. After the comparison is done, IP determines that this destination address is on a remote network. IP checks its internal route table to determine where it's supposed to send packets destined for a remote network. Whenever a destination address is remote, IP knows to ask ARP (Address Resolution Protocol) for the physical address of the default gateway specified in the internal route table. ARP then either returns the physical address from the ARP cache or does a local ARP broadcast for the router's physical address.

At this point, the Ping request has not yet left the sending machine. IP gathers the physical address of the router, inserts the destination address into the Ping packet, and finally transmits the packet onto the wire of subnet 1.

Because IP very smartly sends the packet on the wire in such a way that only the router would not discard the packet, the packet arrives safely at the router. The network interface on the router passes the data up its network stack to IP, where IP discovers that this packet is not destined for it.

Normally, IP on a machine would discard the packet. But this machine, a router, is a special kind of machine that has additional responsibilities, including trying to forward packets it receives to the necessary network. Router A reads the IP address of the destination and compares this destination to its own source address using its subnet mask. At this point, IP determines the network to which this packet is supposed to be sent and checks its internal route table to see what to do with packets destined for the 131.107.96.0 network. Unfortunately, this router has no entries for this network and therefore drops this packet. ICMP (Internet Control Messaging Protocol) reports an error to the machine on subnet 1, indicating that the destination address cannot be reached.

This whole process seems like a lot of work just to get an error message, especially if you know that the destination machine is working. You can get around this kind of scenario in two ways:

- Add a default gateway to the router's configuration
- Add a manual entry in the router's internal table

See what happens if you use one or both of these solutions on router A, picking up where router A decided to drop the packet. Router A has just figured out that the packet's destination address does not match its own IP address. It therefore checks its route table, looking for either a path to the 131.107.96.0 network or the IP address of its default gateway.

By configuring a default gateway, an administrator indicates to the router that if it handles a packet destined for a network it has no idea about, the router should send it to the default gateway specified and hope for the best. This can be useful if you don't want to configure 37 route table entries on a network. Merely specifying default gateways can minimize the size of your route tables and minimize the number of manual entries you have to maintain. This approach, of course, comes with the possibility of making your network a little more inefficient. Configuring a network always involves tradeoffs.

Router A now figures out that it needs to send the Ping request to the IP address of the other router based on its route table, in this case 131.107.64.2. Here is yet another conceptual gap. Router A doesn't know whether the IP address represents a router or just another machine on the network. For that matter, it might be sending this packet into "bit space." Router A trusts that the administrator was wise enough to specify an IP address of a device that will help get the packet to its final destination. As a side note, if you enter a route table entry incorrectly, the router just merrily starts sending packets to wherever you specified.

IP on router A now asks ARP to find the physical address of the next router in line. Just as on another machine, ARP either already has the physical address in cache or initiates an ARP broadcast to get it. After IP has the physical address, it reformulates the packet, addressing it to router B's physical address but leaving the original source address intact. It does not insert its own IP address as the source. If IP did this, the destination address would never respond to the original machine. The packet is transmitted onto the wire destined for router B.

Router B hears the transmission, goes through basically the same process, determines the destination address, and discovers that it can send the packet directly to the destination machine. By utilizing the same ARP and IP procedures, the packet finally arrives at the destination machine on subnet 3. The ICMP echo request is acknowledged, and ICMP formulates the ICMP echo response packet that must be sent back. Remember that up to this point, the original sending machine is patiently waiting for a response. The destination machine looks at the source address (131.107.32.10), figures out that it's remote, finds the physical address of router B to send the message back, and transmits it onto the wire.

▼ NOTE

For routing to work in a static routing environment, be sure that each router is aware of all relevant networks. Otherwise, packets will be dropped unexpectedly on their return to a destination.

Router B receives the packet, breaks it down, and tries to figure out what to do with a packet destined for the 131.107.32.0 subnet. And after all this work, router B drops the packet. Why? We made all our changes to router A in terms of a default gateway and route table entries, but we didn't do anything to router B.

To make static routing work, each router has to be updated and configured to know about other networks in the environment. Only after a default gateway or manual entry in router B's route table is configured will the packets successfully be transmitted between these two networks.

6. You are viewing the routing table and notice a number of entries that have the IP address 0.0.0.0. What does this address designate?

E. The default gateway

6. CORRECT ANSWER: E

The default gateway is identified on a router as 0.0.0.0 when you view its tables. In theory, you could specify an address; however, the disadvantage is that if addressing changed, the entire table would have to be modified. As such, most implementations will use the 0.0.0.0 specification.

Default Gateways

The two easiest ways to identify default gateways for a machine or multihomed router are through manual configuration through the IP properties sheet or as a DHCP option. You can specify more than one default gateway on a machine. Remember, however, that dead gateway detection will work only for machines initiating a TCP connection. In a routing table, the entry 0.0.0.0 identifies the default gateway(s).

Route Tables

Both machines/hosts on the network and routers use route tables to determine where packets should be sent to reach their final destination. Each router builds an internal route table every time IP is loaded during system initialization. Let's take a closer look at a route table.

Five columns of information are provided within the route table:

- **The network address**—This column represents all networks that this machine or router knows about, including entries for the default gateway, subnet and network broadcasts, universal loopback address, and default multicast address. In a route table, you can use names instead of IP addresses to identify networks. If you use names instead of IP addresses, the names are resolved using the networks file found in the \%system drive%\system32\drivers\etc directory.
- **The netmask**—This column simply identifies the subnet mask used for a particular network entry.
- **The gateway address**—This column is the IP address to which packets should be sent in order to route

packets to their final destination. Each network address may specify a different gateway address in which to send packets, particularly if more than one router is connected to one network segment. This column may also have self-referential entries indicating the IP address to which broadcasts should be sent, as well as the local loopback entries. You can also use names to identify these IP addresses. Any names used here will be resolved using the local HOSTS file on the machine.

- **Interface**—This IP address primarily identifies the IP address of the machine and identifies this IP address as the interface to the network. On a machine with one network card, only two entries appear. For any network address that is self-referential, the interface is 127.0.0.1, meaning that packets are not even sent onto the network. For all other communications, the IP address represents the network card interface used to communicate out onto the network. For multihomed machines, the interface IP address changes depending on which network address is configured on each network card. In this case, the interface identifies the IP address of the card connected to a particular network segment.
- **The metric**—The metric indicates the cost or hops associated with a particular network route. The router's job is to find the path representing the least cost or effort to get the packet to its destination. The lower the cost or hop count, the better or more efficient a particular route. On a static router, the metric for any network address will be `1`, indicating that the router thinks every network is only one router hop away. This information is obviously not true, indicating that on static routers, this column is fairly meaningless. On dynamic routers, however, this column tells a router the best possible route for sending packets.

7. What tools can be used to view the routing table? Select all that apply.

A. NETSTAT

C. ROUTE

7. CORRECT ANSWERS: A-C

The `ROUTE PRINT` command or `NETSTAT -R` will display the local routing table. These commands and switches are not case-sensitive.

Viewing the Route Table

To view the route table of a Windows NT machine/router, you can use two utilities: NETSTAT and ROUTE. To view the route table through NETSTAT, go to the command prompt and type **`netstat -r`**.

This command will only display the routing table on your machine. To view and manage the route table, including adding or changing entries, use the Route utility. To view the route table by using the `ROUTE` command, type **`Route Print`**. This will display the same information as with `NETSTAT -R`.

The default entries in a Windows NT 4.0 Route table include the following items:

- **0.0.0.0**—This entry identifies the IP address of the default gateway or the IP address to which packets will be sent if no other specific route table entry exists for a destination network. If multiple gateways are defined on a Windows NT machine, you may notice more than one entry that looks like this, specifying each default gateway that is defined.
- **127.0.0.1**—This entry is the local loopback address used for diagnostics, to make sure that the IP stack on a machine is properly installed and running.
- **Local network**—This entry identifies the local network address. It indicates the gateway and interface machine's IP address that is used whenever a packet needs to be transmitted to a local destination.
- **Local host**—This entry is used for self-referential purposes and points to the local loopback address as the gateway and interface.
- **Subnet broadcast**—This entry is a directed broadcast and is treated as a directed packet by routers. The packet is forwarded to the network where it is to be broadcast. In this case, the default entry specifies the IP address of the current machine for sending out subnet broadcasts to this machine's network.

- **224.0.0.0**—This entry is the default multicast address. If this machine is a member of any multicast groups, this and other multicast entries indicate to IP the interface used to communicate with the multicast network.
- **255.255.255.255**—This entry is a limited broadcast address for broadcasts destined for any machine on the local network. Routers that receive packets destined for this address may listen to the packet as a normal host, but do not support transmission of these types of broadcasts to other networks.

When a router looks for a destination for a particular packet, the router searches through the route table from first to last entry. After a route has been determined—meaning that a destination IP address has been found for the data—IP asks ARP for that IP address. As soon as ARP replies, the frame can be constructed and transmitted onto the wire.

Building a Static Routing Table

The `ROUTE` command has a number of other switches that you can use to manage a route table statically. Up to this point, the `PRINT` command is the only parameter that has been used. To manage a route table, however, an administrator must be able to add, delete, change, and clear route table entries. The commands are shown in the following table:

To Add or Modify a Static Route	*Function*
`route add [`*net id*`] mask [`*netmask*`][`*gateway*`]`	Adds a route
`route -p add [`*net id*`] mask [`*netmask*`][`*gateway*`]`	Adds a persistent route
`route delete [`*net id*`][`*gateway*`]`	Deletes a route
`route change [`*net id*`][`*gateway*`]`	Modifies a route
`route print`	Displays a route table
`route -f`	Clears all routes and rebuilds routes to the physically attached networks, but does not reenter the default gateway

Notice the entry that utilizes a `-p` (persistent) before the `add` parameter. By default, route table entries are kept only in memory. After a machine is rebooted, any entries that were added manually are gone and must be reentered. You can use batch files, startup scripts, or the persistent switch to reenter static routes. The persistent entry switch writes route entries into the Registry so they survive a reboot of the machine. Naturally, this method means that you don't have to create batch files or scripts, but it requires manual deletion of the routes if they change.

▼ NOTE

Route table entries are kept only in memory and will not survive a reboot unless the `-p` switch is used.

8. What tool can be used to determine the path that a packet takes across multiple routers?

B. TRACERT

8. CORRECT ANSWER: B

The trace route utility is used to determine the path that a packet takes through a network. Often, an administrator will need to determine a point of failure. By running the TRACERT utility, it is possible to see the last point at which a packet had been sent. By using this knowledge, a problem can be resolved quickly.

The TRACERT Utility

Windows NT includes the TRACERT utility, which verifies the route a packet takes to reach its destination. To use this utility, simply go to the command prompt and type **tracert** ***<IP address>***.

The result of running this utility for a destination address will probably look similar to the following output:

```
C:\>tracert www.learnix.com

Tracing route to www.learnix.com [199.45.92.97]
over a maximum of 30 hops:

  1   156 ms   156 ms   141 ms  annex.intranet.ca
➥[206.51.251.5]
```

```
  2    157 ms    156 ms    156 ms  cisco2.intranet.ca
➥[206.51.251.10]
  3    172 ms    156 ms    172 ms  spc-tor-6-
➥Serial3-3.Sprint-Canada.Net [206.186.248.85]
  4    156 ms    172 ms    187 ms  204.50.128.17
  5    171 ms    172 ms    157 ms  205.150.206.97
  6    172 ms    172 ms    297 ms
➥h5.bb1.tor2.h4.bb1.ott1.uunet.ca [205.150.242.70]
  7    172 ms    171 ms    172 ms  max1.ott1.uunet.ca
➥[205.150.233.2]
  8    188 ms    203 ms    218 ms  router.learnix.ca
➥[199.71.122.193]
  9    203 ms    218 ms    235 ms  sparky
➥[199.45.92.97]

Trace complete.
```

The result shows how each router traversed to a destination, as well as how long it took to get through each particular router. The time it takes to get through a particular router is calculated by using three algorithms that are displayed for each router hop. The IP address of each router traversed also appears. If an FQDN is available, it appears as well.

The TRACERT utility is useful for two primary diagnostic purposes:

- It detects whether a particular router is not functioning along a known path. For instance, suppose a user knows that packets on a network always go through Texas to get from Florida to California, but communication seems to be dead. A TRACERT to a California address shows all the hops up to the point where the router in Texas should respond. If it does not respond, the time values are marked with asterisks (*), indicating a non-functioning path.
- This utility also determines whether a router is slow and possibly needs to be upgraded or helped by adding routes on the network. You can make this determination simply by looking at the time it takes for a packet to get through a particular router. If a particular router is deluged by packets, its return time may be significantly slower than that of any of the other hops, indicating it should be upgraded or helped in some way.

9. You are attempting to determine why a link to a remote site is slow. What information might help determine this? Select the best answer.

A. The metric

9. CORRECT ANSWER: A

The metric tells an administrator the number of routers the packet must go through. In general, the higher the number, the slower the connection will appear.

10. On a multihomed NT system, how can you configure it so that it automatically updates its routing tables by using routing information from other routers on the network? What service is required?

A. RIP for IP

10. CORRECT ANSWER: A

RIP for IP is the service that provides compatibility to other routers for updating tables automatically. This implementation requires that the other routers run RIP as well.

Dynamic Routing

Manually editing route tables to notify routers of the existence of networks to which they are not physically connected can be an enormously difficult task on large networks. Setting tables manually opens your infrastructure to errors and complexities such as relying on the router for dead gateway detection. These problems led to the development of routing protocols, used specifically by routers to dynamically update one another's tables. Two of the most common protocols used by dynamic routers are RIP and OSPF. These protocols notify other routers of their reachable destinations as well as other information such as links being disconnected or becoming too congested to efficiently pass traffic.

The standard rule of thumb when considering the use of either protocol is that RIP works well for small- to medium-sized networks, and OSPF works well for medium to large networks. Because OSPF is not supported without a third-party add-on, it is not discussed as a Microsoft solution.

Routing Internet Protocol

To better understand RIP on routers, first consider static routing, where routing tables have to be built manually. To pass packets from one network to another, each router has to be told where to send packets destined for a specific network (route table entry) or where to send packets without a specific destination (default gateway).

By default, routers know about the networks to which they are physically attached because their IP addresses on each of those networks give them the necessary information. Unfortunately, they can't detect those that are remote. This shortcoming led to the development of routing protocols, which enable routers to communicate with one another. The protocols enable one router to dynamically send and receive information about the networks to any other router physically connected to the wire.

The RIP procedure for communicating between routers is through broadcasts over *User Datagram Protocol* (UDP) port 520. RIP routers broadcast their route tables and listen for updates over this port. In this way, eventually all routers that are physically connected have up-to-date route tables and know where to send data for any network in the environment.

Routers broadcast both the networks to which they are attached and the distance of remote networks from their location. The distance to another network is called a hop, cost, or metric, and each router keeps track of this value within the route table. Each router along the path to a destination network represents a hop. For this reason, RIP is considered a distance-vector routing protocol. As such, RIP can determine the route with the least number of hops necessary to get a packet to its final destination.

As RIP was being developed, it was decided that routers would need to keep track of a maximum of 15 hops between networks. Therefore, any network address that has a hop count of 16 is considered unreachable. If a router's route table has two different hop counts for a particular network, the router sends the data to the route that has the least number of hops.

Because RIP routers broadcast the networks they know about and how far away they are from those networks, certain precautions must be made in case any of these connections fail. After a router determines that a connection has failed, it must find a better route to that network from other route tables. This process could create circular and upward-spiraling loops between routers, and the hop count could continue to increase ad infinitum.

If a redundant connection to that network exists with a higher hop count, eventually each router's tables increase to the point that the redundant route is chosen over the connection that died. But if no redundant route is available, the hop count could continue to increase indefinitely. To reduce this risk, several algorithms have been written to successfully react to connection failures. Administrators also have the ability to alter the hop count between routers in order to encourage the use of some network routers over others that may be used purely for redundancy. Broadcasts between routers always occur every 30 seconds, whether the route table has changed or not.

Because RIP is the oldest routing protocol and is widely used throughout the industry, several well-known problems exist when trying to implement this protocol in larger networks. These protocol deficiencies result in RIP being useful only in small- to medium-sized networks. RIP falls short in the following categories:

- Because RIP keeps track of every route table entry, including multiple paths to a particular network, routing tables can become large rather quickly. This condition can result in the broadcasting of multiple RIP packets, which sends a complete route table to other routers.
- Because RIP can allow hop counts only up to 15, with 16 representing an unreachable network, the size of networks on which RIP can be successfully implemented is necessarily restricted. Any large enterprise may need to achieve hop counts beyond this value.
- Broadcasts are sent by default every 30 seconds, resulting in time delays of networks going down up to 30 seconds per hop. This also causes—depending on the number of routers—a significant amount of WAN traffic in sending routes.

But these problems should not discourage the administrator of a small- to medium-sized network from using the RIP protocol. As long as you understand its benefits and limitations, you should be able to use it quite successfully.

11. You are configuring a Windows NT network to interface with an existing static and dynamic combo network. What is the first step that you should take to prepare the system in a multihomed configuration?

C. Add a second network card

11. CORRECT ANSWER: C

The first step in configuring a multihomed system, regardless of function, is adding the second network adapter. TCP/IP cannot be configured until such time. And until TCP/IP is configured, the routing methods do not matter.

Building a Multihomed Router

Windows NT enables an administrator to convert a machine into either a static or dynamic IP router. Static routers work well for extending a small network segment, and dynamic routers using RIP work well on small- to medium-sized networks. A multihomed computer would probably not work well on large networks, however, based on RIP's limitations and the significant overhead associated with maintaining large route tables. Other considerations aside, however, building a Windows NT router is fairly simple and easy to do.

But before continuing, a definition of the term *multihomed computer,* or *multihomed router,* is in order. A multihomed router is simply a computer with more than one network card that has been configured to route packets from one network segment to another. On a multihomed router the operating system performs the routing; in contrast, a hardware router is a device that is specifically manufactured and designed exclusively for routing. In simpler terms, you can run any Windows application, including Freecell, on a multihomed router, but you can't run applications on a hardware router.

The first step in building a Windows NT router is to install two or more network cards in the machine. Anyone who has ever tried to do this will tell you that this job can often sound much easier than it is. Each network card has to have its own IRQ and I/O address to use on the machine. These must be independent of other hardware cards you may be using in your machine, including video cards, sound cards, modems, hard-disk controller cards, and so on. Basically, the machine needs to be stripped of any bells and whistles and other functions so that enough resources are available. Any resource conflicts result in significant headaches as your network cards don't appear and protocol drivers fail to load.

The typical machine built for Windows NT seminars and classes uses a Windows NT router with three network cards and little else. After the machine successfully identifies the network cards, be careful when installing additional third-party utilities. Sometimes they decide to steal the I/O addresses that your network cards are using. The bottom line is that after this machine is built, try to leave it alone. Stabilizing your machine will be the toughest part of the job. After that, everything else is easy.

After you install your network cards, be sure to assign separate IP addresses to each card. Follow this procedure:

1. In the Network section of Control Panel under the Protocol tab, select TCP/IP and choose Properties. Notice that where the network card is identified, the drop-down box reveals all the network cards you have installed, enabling you to choose a different IP address scheme for each network card.

2. After you give each network card its own IP address, indicating which network it is on, the machine can respond to packets coming from the networks to which it is attached. However, the machine is still not a router.

3. To turn the machine into a router, go back to TCP/IP properties and choose the Routing tab. Select the Enable IP Forwarding check box. After you select this box and have chosen OK to exit this configuration and the network configuration, you are asked to reboot your machine.

4. Reboot the machine. Now the machine is officially a router that can pass packets from one network to another.

The administrator then needs to decide whether the router will be static or dynamic. After IP forwarding is enabled, the router is static. If a static router is desired, no more configuration is necessary. If the administrator wants to have a dynamic router instead, the RIP protocol needs to be installed.

The RIP protocol can be installed in the Services tab through the Network icon. After RIP is installed, this router listens for other RIP broadcasts and broadcasts its own route table entries.

Although Windows NT supports the capability to create a static or dynamic router, the most important consideration for an administrator is probably whether to upgrade a machine for occasional routing of packets or to purchase a hardware router. If the administrator plans to spend more than $1,000 for a machine to route packets on a network, he or she may be better off spending it on hardware optimized for that purpose. Think of Windows NT routing versus hardware routing in much the same way as you would think about Windows NT RAID versus hardware RAID. Hardware implementation is usually a little more expensive, but it is optimized for that specific task; on the other hand, Windows NT implementations work well and are cheaper, but are not designed for constant pounding by a large network.

CHAPTER SUMMARY

This chapter presented detailed information about how Windows NT functions in a multiple-network environment. As you have seen, Windows NT can function on multiple networks as a workstation, a router, and more. The key points to remember are how addressing, naming, and access are performed in a multihomed environment. Furthermore, it is crucial to understand the types of routers and how Windows NT can integrate into an existing networked environment.

CHAPTER REVIEW

REVIEW QUESTIONS

Note: The additional Chapter Review section that ends each chapter is unique to this member of the *New Riders TestPrep, Second Edition* series. We've included it to more fully and fairly cover the unique aspects of TCP/IP in relation to its mastery in preparation for MCSE examination.

1. **You need to verify that you can communicate via TCP/IP to a Windows NT Server on a remote subnet separated by a Windows NT system acting as a router. Which utility should you use?**

   A. netstat.exe

   B. arp.exe

   C. route.exe

   D. ping.exe

   E. nbtstat.exe

2. **A given network contains eight Windows NT Servers all configured as static routers. Which utility can be used to identify the path that a packet takes as it passes through the routers?**

   A. ipconfig.exe

   B. netstat.exe

   C. tracert.exe

   D. Network Monitor

   E. Route.exe

3. **Which utility can be used to add to the routing table on a Windows NT Server computer?**

   A. route.exe

   B. netstat.exe

   C. nbtstat.exe

   D. ipconfig.exe

   E. arp.exe

4. **To configure a multihomed Windows NT Server as a TCP/IP static router, what two steps must you complete?**

   A. Enable IP forwarding

   B. Configure each network adapter with an IP address so that each IP address is from a different address class

   C. Configure each network adapter with an IP address so that each IP address is from a different subnet

   D. Configure each network adapter with a unique subnet mask

5. **You are adding a test lab that will be used for software product development. Since routers are very expensive and you have no need for an additional one after this project, you determine that you will use Windows NT with two network cards for this function. Your test lab will need to communicate with the outside network. However, you want it to interact with your current routers. The current routers forward Ethernet Frames, route IPX, and are configured for BOOTP and RIP.**

You want to configure the IP routing tables on this server with the least amount of continuing effort. What should you do?

A. Install RIP for IP

B. Install the DHCP Relay Agent

C. Use `route.exe` to configure the routing tables

D. Use `netstat.exe` to configure the routing tables

6. **You are installing a Windows NT TCP/IP server with three network adapters. You also plan and require this server to act as a router to route TCP/IP. For points with your new boss, you would like to have the router dynamically update its routing tables, provide IP addresses to all clients located on all subnets, and send trap messages across the network to a Windows NT workstation computer.**

One of your coworkers suggests that you install TCP/IP and configure one IP address for each of the servers' network adapters, enable IP forwarding, and install RIP for IP plus DHCP with scopes for all subnets.

Your coworker's proposed solution produces which results?

A. The proposed solution produces the required result and only two of the optional desired results.

B. The proposed solution produces the required result but does not produce any of the optional desired results.

C. The proposed solution produces the required result and all of the optional desired results.

D. The proposed solution does not produce the required result.

ANSWER KEY

1. D	3. A	5. A
2. C	4. A-C	6. A

REVIEW ANSWERS

1. You need to verify that you can communicate via TCP/IP to a Windows NT Server on a remote subnet separated by a Windows NT system acting as a router. Which utility should you use?

D. ping.exe

1. CORRECT ANSWER: D

The PING utility is used to verify communications. Commonly, PING is used with TRACERT to verify connectivity. PING verifies an end point, while TRACERT processes the points in between.

2. A given network contains eight Windows NT Servers all configured as static routers. Which utility can be used to identify the path that a packet takes as it passes through the routers?

C. tracert.exe

2. CORRECT ANSWER: C

Tracert.exe can be used to verify the path that a packet takes across a network. TRACERT will return the IP address of each router along the way to a remote point. If a host name is assigned, it will also be returned to the client running TRACERT.

3. Which utility can be used to add to the routing table on a Windows NT Server computer?

A. route.exe

3. CORRECT ANSWER: A

The ROUTE utility is the primary interface for dealing with a static routing table. It can be used to add, remove, and print entries. The NETSTAT utility can be used only to display the table.

4. To configure a multihomed Windows NT Server as a TCP/IP static router, what two steps must you complete?

A. Enable IP forwarding

C. Configure each network adapter with an IP address so that each IP address is from a different subnet

4. CORRECT ANSWERS: A-C

To configure a system as a router, you must enable IP forwarding and configure each network adapter with an IP address so that each IP address is from a different subnet.

5. **You are adding a test lab that will be used for software product development. Since routers are very expensive and you have no need for an additional one after this project, you determine that you will use Windows NT with two network cards for this function. Your test lab will need to communicate with the outside network. However, you want it to interact with your current routers. The current routers forward Ethernet Frames, route IPX, and are configured for BOOTP and RIP. You want to configure the IP routing tables on this server with the least amount of continuing effort. What should you do?**

   A. Install RIP for IP

5. CORRECT ANSWER: A

Because IP tables are the only thing that you need to configure as per the question, simply install RIP for IP. If you also wanted to route IPX, you would have to add the RIP IPX component as well. However, assuming that only IP traffic is used, this will fulfill the requirement of minimal administrative efforts.

6. **You are installing a Windows NT TCP/IP server with three network adapters. You also plan and require this server to act as a router to route TCP/IP. For points with your new boss, you would like to have the router dynamically update its routing tables, provide IP addresses to all clients located on all subnets, and send trap messages across the network to a Windows NT workstation computer. One of your coworkers suggests that you install TCP/IP and configure one IP address for each of the servers' network adapters, enable IP forwarding, and install RIP for IP plus DHCP with scopes for all subnets.**

   Your coworker's proposed solution produces which results?

   A. The proposed solution produces the required result and only two of the optional desired results.

6. CORRECT ANSWER: A

The proposed solution produces the required result and only two of the optional desired results. The configuration must also include SNMP (configured to send traps to a specified workstation) in order to meet all optional requirements. The Windows NT workstation must be configured with an SNMP manager to properly receive a trap message.

CHAPTER 7

Heterogeneous Operating Systems and Printing

Most users in the PC world have little or no familiarity with UNIX, or other operating systems for that matter. If you stop to examine the history behind TCP/IP and the development of most utilities, you can observe strong roots in the UNIX environment. Because the origins commonly define syntax, the formatting for many of the commands presented in this chapter are the same as their UNIX counterparts.

The key concepts to watch in this chapter are which utilities perform which operations, the differences between the utilities, and when it is appropriate to use them.

This chapter features those utilities that are delivered as part of the TCP/IP suite as it pertains to Windows NT. The key points to remember in this chapter are the functionality of each utility and, when prompted with a requirement, the knowledge of which utility to use.

OBJECTIVES

This chapter helps you prepare for the exam by covering the following objectives:

Given a scenario, identify which utility to use to connect to a TCP/IP-based UNIX host for use on a TCP/IP-based UNIX host.

- Microsoft's implementation of TCP/IP includes a number of utilities that are common to the UNIX world. These utilities include mechanisms for remote file transfer, remote control, printing, and so forth. The first half of this chapter focuses primarily on the utilities and their abilities.

Configure a Windows NT Server computer to support TCP/IP printing.

- Windows NT Server supports and integrates with UNIX and other platforms by providing two-directional TCP/IP printing. The second part of this chapter goes into detail regarding this feature.

PRACTICE QUESTIONS

GIVEN A SCENARIO, IDENTIFY WHICH UTILITY TO USE TO CONNECT TO A TCP/IP-BASED UNIX HOST FOR USE ON A TCP/IP-BASED UNIX HOST

1. **Remote execution utilities transmit passwords as which of the following? Select the best answer.**
   A. Encrypted text
   B. Plain text
   C. LAN Manager-compatible text
   D. RS232 strings
2. **Which three of the following are execution utilities available with Windows NT?**
   A. REXEC
   B. Telnet
   C. FTP
   D. RSH
3. **REXEC can specify a host by which two methods?**
   A. Host name
   B. ARP address
   C. MAC address
   D. IP address
4. **Which parameter is used with REXEC to specify a different username on the remote host?**
   A. `–n`
   B. `–l`
   C. `–u`
   D. `–name`
5. **Which parameter is used with REXEC to specify that the input should be null?**
   A. `–n`
   B. `–l`
   C. `–u`
   D. `–name`
6. **For which of the following applications would REXEC *not* be appropriate? Select the best answer.**
   A. Obtaining a directory listing with the command `ls`
   B. Checking which processes are running with the command `ps`
   C. Starting a text editor with the command `vi`
   D. Checking the amount of free space on a drive with the command `df`
7. **Which method does the REXEC command use to authenticate the user?**
   A. Username
   B. Password
   C. Username and password
   D. `.rhosts` file

8. **The biggest difference between RSH and REXEC is in which area?**
   A. Availability to system resources
   B. System overhead
   C. Permissions
   D. Authentication
9. **If no username is given, what username does RSH use to establish a connection to the remote host?**
   A. Root
   B. Anonymous
   C. Current username
   D. Guest
10. **Which method does the RSH command use to authenticate the user?**
    A. Username
    B. Password
    C. Username and password
    D. `.rhosts` file
11. **Which two files can be used on a UNIX system to grant access to all users or some users for remote authentication?**
    A. `/passwd`
    B. `/dialup`
    C. `.rhosts`
    D. `hosts.equiv`
12. **In the UNIX world, which of the following is comparable to a service in the NT world?**
    A. Command
    B. Daemon
    C. Setting
    D. Environment
13. **Which Telnet option is used to connect to a remote host?**
    A. Connect/Remote
    B. Get
    C. Establish
    D. Call
14. **Which of the following items are required for a Telnet session?**
    A. Port
    B. Service
    C. Terminal type
    D. Host name
15. **Ports supported by Telnet applications include all except which of the following? Select the best answer.**
    A. vt100
    B. daytime
    C. echo
    D. quotd
16. **What is the default port used by Telnet?**
    A. 20
    B. 21
    C. 23
    D. 25
    E. 80
17. **Which method does the `telnet` command use to authenticate the user?**

A. Username

B. Password

C. Username and password

D. `.rhosts` file

18. Which of the following utilities does Windows NT *not* support for data file transfer? Select the best answer.

A. Telnet

B. RCP

C. FTP

D. TFTP

19. Which method does the `RCP` command use to authenticate the user?

A. Username

B. Password

C. Username and password

D. `.rhosts` file

20. What is the parameter used with RCP to transfer hidden files?

A. `–b`

B. `–r`

C. `–a`

D. `–h`

21. What is the parameter used with RCP to copy subdirectories and files beneath a specified directory?

A. `–b`

B. `–r`

C. `–a`

D. `–h`

22. What is the parameter used with RCP to convert EOL characters to a carriage return?

A. `–b`

B. `–r`

C. `–a`

D. `–h`

23. What is the parameter used with RCP to specify binary transfer mode?

A. `–b`

B. `–r`

C. `–a`

D. `–h`

24. What does FTP stand for?

A. Fast Transfer Protocol

B. File Transfer Protocol

C. Fixed Transfer Protocol

D. Flash Timing Protocol

25. To establish an FTP session, which of the following criteria must be met? Select all that apply.

A. Both systems must be running TCP/IP.

B. NetBEUI must be used to broadcast service availability.

C. The remote system must be running an FTP host service.

D. The client system must be running FTP client software.

E. A username and password (or anonymous) must be on the remote.

26. **Which parameter is used with FTP (in command-line mode) to suppress the display of remote server responses?**

    A. `-i`

    B. `-v`

    C. `-n`

    D. `-d`

27. **Which parameter is used with FTP (in command-line mode) to enable debugging?**

    A. `-i`

    B. `-v`

    C. `-n`

    D. `-d`

28. **Which parameter is used with FTP (in command-line mode) to suppress the auto-login?**

    A. `-i`

    B. `-v`

    C. `-n`

    D. `-d`

29. **Which parameter is used with FTP (in command-line mode) to turn off interactive prompting?**

    A. `-i`

    B. `-v`

    C. `-n`

    D. `-d`

30. **How many modes are available with FTP?**

    A. 1

    B. 2

    C. 3

    D. 4

31. **Which FTP command changes directories on the local system?**

    A. `cd`

    B. `lcd`

    C. `open`

    D. `get`

    E. `put`

32. **Which FTP command starts a file transfer from the remote host?**

    A. `cd`

    B. `lcd`

    C. `open`

    D. `get`

    E. `put`

33. **Which FTP command starts a file transfer from the local host?**

    A. `cd`

    B. `lcd`

    C. `open`

    D. `get`

    E. `put`

34. **Which FTP command specifies a remote system to connect to?**

    A. `cd`

    B. `lcd`

C. `open`

D. `get`

E. `put`

35. Which of the following represent the differences between FTP and TFTP? Select all that apply.

A. FTP is connection oriented.

B. TFTP is connection oriented.

C. FTP is connectionless oriented.

D. TFTP is connectionless oriented.

36. How many modes are available with TFTP?

A. 1

B. 2

C. 3

D. 4

37. Which type of support for TFTP is available from third parties, but is not included in Windows NT?

A. As a client.

B. As a server.

C. As a server or a client.

D. Windows NT includes full TFTP support.

38. Which document type will a Web browser read?

A. HTTP

B. HTML

C. JAVA

D. XLS

39. In what way does a Web browser connect to a site?

A. IP Address

B. URL

C. Path

D. All of the above

E. None of the above

ANSWER KEY

1. B	11. C-D	21. B	31. B
2. A-B-D	12. B	22. C	32. D
3. A-D	13. A	23. A	33. E
4. B	14. A-C-D	24. B	34. C
5. A	15. A	25. A-C-D-E	35. A-D
6. C	16. C	26. B	36. A
7. C	17. C	27. D	37. B
8. D	18. A	28. C	38. B
9. C	19. D	29. A	39. B
10. D	20. D	30. B	

ANSWERS & EXPLANATIONS

GIVEN A SCENARIO, IDENTIFY WHICH UTILITY TO USE TO CONNECT TO A TCP/IP-BASED UNIX HOST FOR USE ON A TCP/IP-BASED UNIX HOST

1. Remote execution utilities transmit passwords as which of the following? Select the best answer.

B. Plain text

1. CORRECT ANSWER: B

Remote execution utilities transmit passwords as plain text, creating a security weakness. The weakness is that anyone can use a "sniffer" to read packets as they are transmitted. The password at that time is completely exposed.

2. Which three of the following are execution utilities available with Windows NT?

A. REXEC

B. Telnet

D. RSH

2. CORRECT ANSWERS: A-B-D

REXEC, RSH, and Telnet are remote execution utilities. Note that although FTP is also supported, it is a file transfer utility, not a remote execution utilities program.

```
Utilities Used to Connect to a TCP/IP-Based UNIX
Host
```

Windows NT includes TCP/IP utilities that provide many options for connecting to foreign systems using the TCP/IP protocol. At times during which connection to remote host systems using Microsoft networking is impossible, these utilities provide a variety of network services.

These utilities allow Microsoft clients to perform remote execution, data transfer, printing services, and much more.

Remote Execution Utilities

Windows NT includes three remote execution utilities (RSH, REXEC, and Telnet) that enable a user to execute commands on a UNIX host system. These utilities provide varying degrees of security. Note that varying subsets of these utilities are available with Windows NT Server and Workstation, whereas the Windows NT Server Resource Kit includes all of these utilities.

▼ **NOTE**

Any of these utilities that require passwords transmit the password as plain text. Unlike the Windows NT logon sequence, the logon information is not encrypted before being transmitted. Any unscrupulous user with access to network monitoring software could intercept the username and password for the remote host. If you use the same username and password on the remote host and on your Windows NT system, your Windows NT account could be compromised.

3. REXEC can specify a host by which two methods?

A. Host name

D. IP address

3. CORRECT ANSWERS: A-D

REXEC can specify a host by its IP address or host name. Because this command is based on using a host name rather than a NetBIOS name as the NET USE and NET VIEW commands, it has the flexibility to use an alias or not.

4. Which parameter is used with REXEC to specify a different username on the remote host?

B. `—l`

4. CORRECT ANSWER: B

`REXEC —l {username}` is the syntax used to specify a different username on the remote host. Remember that depending on the host, a username may be case sensitive.

5. Which parameter is used with REXEC to specify that the input should be null?

A. `—n`

5. CORRECT ANSWER: A

`REXEC —n` is the syntax used to specify that the input should be redirected to `NULL`. This option provides a special situation in which "nothing" or a "zero output" can be used. For instance, if you were writing a batch file and did not want a user to see any information, this option would allow you to hide materials from appearing on the screen.

6. For which of the following applications would REXEC not be appropriate? Select the best answer.

C. Starting a text editor with the command `vi`

6. CORRECT ANSWER: C

REXEC should be used for commands that do not require interactive input. This makes the `vi` text editor a bad choice. `vi` would probably work best with Telnet.

7. Which method does the REXEC command use to authenticate the user?

C. Username and Password

7. CORRECT ANSWER: C

REXEC authenticates a user by username and password. The key point regarding REXEC is that it is a secure remote launcher. Unlike Telnet, in which a session is actually opened, REXEC simply starts a process. This is useful in scripting batch files because REXEC can start a process server side without having the client operator perform additional commands.

The REXEC Utility

REXEC enables a user to start a process on a remote host system, using a username and password for authentication. If the host authenticates the user, REXEC starts the specified process and terminates. Command-line options are as follows:

```
D:\>rexec /?
Runs commands on remote hosts running the REXEC
➥service. REXEC
authenticates the user name on the remote host
➥before executing the
specified command.

REXEC host [-l username] [-n] command

  host              Specifies the remote host on
➥which to run command.
  -l username      Specifies the user name on the
➥remote host.
  -n                Redirects the input of REXEC to
➥NULL.
  command          Specifies the command to run.
```

You can specify the remote host as an IP address or as a host name. After REXEC connects to the specified host, it prompts for a password. If the host authenticates the user, the specified command is executed, and the REXEC utility exits. REXEC can be used for command-line programs—interactive programs such as text editors would not be usable with REXEC.

This utility provides a reasonable degree of security because the remote host authenticates the user. The downside is that the username and password are not encrypted prior to transmission.

8. The biggest difference between RSH and REXEC is in which area?

D. Authentication

8. CORRECT ANSWER: D

RSH works like REXEC but is not as stringent on authentication. RSH bases its security against information found in the `.rhosts` file rather than against the UNIX database. Using RSH, a user name is optional based upon the configuration of they system that runs the host service (daemon).

9. If no username is given, what username does RSH use to establish a connection to the remote host?

C. Current username

9. CORRECT ANSWER: C

If no username is specified, RSH uses the current username. This can be overwritten such that no name is specified. Depending on the configuration of the system that offers the RSH service (daemon), removing the user name may be desirable to help create a generic execution that is independent of users.

10. Which method does the RSH command use to authenticate the user?

D. `.rhosts` file

10. CORRECT ANSWER: D

The `.rhosts` file is used to authenticate users with RSH. Unlike the REXEC, which authenticates against the UNIX account database, RSH is independent.

11. Which two files can be used on a UNIX system to grant access to all users or some users for remote authentication?

C. `.rhosts`

D. `hosts.equiv`

11. CORRECT ANSWERS: C-D

The `.rhosts` and `hosts.equiv` files can be used on UNIX systems for authentication of remote users (if security is to be used). The `hosts.equiv` is typically used to prevent the prompting for a password. When used, a name and IP address are placed into this file, thus limiting the connection to a trusted machine.

12. In the UNIX world, which of the following is comparable to a service in the NT world?

B. Daemon

12. CORRECT ANSWER: B

A daemon is to the UNIX world what a service is to the NT world. In order for a client utility such as RSH to operate, the host UNIX system must have the RSH host daemon running.

The RSH Utility

RSH provides much the same function as REXEC, but user authentication is handled differently. In contrast to REXEC, RSH does not require you to specify a username. The only validation performed by RSH is to verify that the username is in a hidden file on the UNIX system (the `.rhosts` file). If the remote host is configured to allow any user to use RSH, a username is not necessary.

▼ **NOTE**

On UNIX systems, the `.rhosts` and the `hosts.equiv` files are used for authentication. Because these files can be used to grant access to either all users on a computer or some users on a computer, be careful with their use.

However, because it is extremely unlikely for a system to be configured in this way, the RSH utility provides the logged-on username if no username is provided. This can be overridden if desired. RSH has the following command-line options:

```
C:\>rsh /?
rsh: remote terminal session not supported

Runs commands on remote hosts running the RSH
➥service.

RSH host [-l username] [-n] command

  host              Specifies the remote host on
➥which to run command.
  -l username       Specifies the user name to use on
➥the remote host. If
                     omitted, the logged on user name
➥is used.
  -n                 Redirects the input of RSH to
➥NULL.
  command           Specifies the command to run.
```

After you start RSH, it connects to the remote system's RSH daemon (UNIX-speak for a service). The RSH daemon ensures that the username is in the `.rhosts` file on the remote host, and if authentication succeeds, the specified command is executed.

Like REXEC, RSH provides a certain degree of security insofar as the remote host validates the access.

13. Which Telnet option is used to connect to a remote host?

A. Connect/Remote

13. CORRECT ANSWER: A

The Connect/Remote system option of Telnet is used to connect to a remote host. By default, Telnet connects to port 23. However, if initiated from the command line, a port can be specified such that alternates can be used. This allows other services such as Mail (port 25) to be verified and also provides additional security to those systems that want to mask their Telnet service.

14. Which of the following items are required for a Telnet session?

A. Port

C. Terminal type

D. Host name

14. CORRECT ANSWERS: A-C-D

Terminal type, port, and host name or IP address are required information for a Telnet session. The host name can be interchanged with the IP address. If not specified, the port defaults to 23. To change the port, the connection must be initiated from command line. Most systems will emulate a VT-100/ANSI terminal. Depending on the type and age of the system, the terminal type may need to be adjusted.

15. Ports supported by Telnet applications include all except which of the following? Select the best answer.

A. vt100

15. CORRECT ANSWER: A

vt100 is a supported terminal type, not a port. When referring to a port, use the appropriate number corresponding to the service that you would like to connect. The common and default ports can be found in the `services.` file.

16. What is the default port used by Telnet?

C. 23

16. CORRECT ANSWER: C

Port 23 is the default port. You can use other ports when communicating to other services. For example, if you opened a Telnet session to port 25, you could communicate directly to an SMTP gateway. Ports 20 and 21 are used for FTP, and 80 is used for HTTP sessions.

17. Which method does the `telnet` command use to authenticate the user?

C. Username and password

17. CORRECT ANSWER: C

Telnet authenticates users by username and password. Like REXEC, Telnet verifies a user against the UNIX database. Passwords are sent as clear text.

18. Which of the following utilities does Windows NT *not* support for data file transfer? Select the best answer.

A. Telnet

18. CORRECT ANSWER: A

Telnet is a remote execution utility; it isn't used for data file transfer. To transfer files, consider using FTP (File Transfer Protocol), TFTP (Trivial FTP), or RCP (Remote Copy).

The Telnet Utility

Telnet is defined in RFC 854 as a remote terminal emulation protocol. It provides terminal emulation for DEC VT100, DEC VT52, and TTY terminals. Telnet uses the connection-oriented services of the TCP/IP protocol for communications.

The remote host system must be running a Telnet daemon. After you start Telnet, you can connect to a remote host using the Connect/Remote system option. You are prompted for the information required for a Telnet session:

- **Host name**—The IP address or host name of the remote host
- **Port**—One of the ports supported by the Telnet application—Telnet, daytime, echo, quotd, or chargen
- **Terminal type**— vt100, ANSI (TTY), or VT52

As with REXEC and RSH, Telnet provides some security, insofar as access to the remote system requires a username and password.

▼ **NOTE**

Telnet does not encrypt any information whatsoever. The password and username are sent as clear text, as is your entire terminal session. If you are using Telnet to perform remote administration on a UNIX system, your root password could be intercepted by an unscrupulous user.

Data Transfer Utilities

The Microsoft TCP/IP suite includes several utilities that enable you to transfer files between Windows NT systems and remote hosts. As with remote execution utilities, you must use care when dealing with usernames and passwords.

19. Which method does the RCP command use to authenticate the user?

D. `.rhosts` file

19. CORRECT ANSWER: D

RCP authenticates users by the `.rhosts` file much in the same method as RSH (Remote Shell) RCP performs authentication against the `.rhosts` file.

20. What is the parameter used with RCP to transfer hidden files?

D. —h

20. CORRECT ANSWER: D

`RCP —h` is the syntax used to transfer hidden files. Because these files are hidden, the default is to not transfer them. For security reasons, this condition may be desirable.

21. What is the parameter used with RCP to copy subdirectories and files beneath a specified directory?

B. —r

21. CORRECT ANSWER: B

`RCP —r` is the syntax used to recursively copy subdirectories and files. This option can be thought of in terms of using the `/s` option with `XCOPY`. When applicable, this command can eliminate the redundant creation of directories followed by copying files.

22. What is the parameter used with RCP to convert EOL characters to a carriage return?

C. —a

22. CORRECT ANSWER: C

`RCP —a` is the syntax used to convert files to ASCII format. That is not to say that the format is not ASCII, but rather a standard. For example, PC systems use CR-LF (Carriage returns and LineFeeds). When looking in Debug (DOS Utility) at such a file, this (Carriage return and Line Feed) appears as two characters (0D 0A). However, UNIX systems require only a single character to designate EOL (End of Line). The a option performs an on-the-fly conversion.

23. What is the parameter used with RCP to specify binary transfer mode?

A. —b

23. CORRECT ANSWER: A

`RCP —b` is the syntax used to specify binary transfer mode. When transferring data, text files can be moved in binary, but you lose certain conversion options. Binary is best used with program files and other non-text data.

RCP

The RCP command copies files from a Windows NT system to a remote host and handles authentication in much the same way as RSH does. To communicate with the RCP daemon on the remote system, the username provided must be in the remote host's .rhosts file. The following command-line options are available:

```
C:\>rcp ?

Copies files to and from computer running the RCP
➥service.

RCP [-a ¦ -b] [-h] [-r] [host][.user:]source
➥[host][.user:] path\destination

  -a                      Specifies ASCII transfer mode.
➥This mode converts
                          the EOL characters to a
➥carriage return for UNIX
                          and a carriage
                          return/line feed for personal
➥computers. This is
                          the default transfer mode.
  -b                      Specifies binary image
➥transfer mode.
  -h                      Transfers hidden files.
  -r                      Copies the contents of all
➥subdirectories;
                          destination must be a
➥directory.
  host                    Specifies the local or remote
➥host. If host is
                          specified as an IP address,
➥you must specify the
                          user.
  .user:                  Specifies a user name to use,
➥rather than the
                          current user name.
  source                  Specifies the files to copy.
  path\destination      Specifies the path relative to
➥the logon directory
                          on the remote host. Use the
➥escape characters
                          (\ , ", or ') in remote
➥paths to use wildcard
                          characters on the remote
➥host.
```

As with RSH, RCP provides security by matching the username provided with a username in the `.rhosts` file. Unlike RSH, RCP does not prompt for a password.

24. What does FTP stand for?

B. File Transfer Protocol

24. CORRECT ANSWER: B

FTP stands for File Transfer Protocol. This protocol is used to connect to a system that is running a server service or daemon on ports 20 and 21. Using FTP, you can connect over TCP (connection based) to a remote system and transfer files in either direction. FTP services are built into most Web browsers.

25. To establish an FTP session, which of the following criteria must be met? Select all that apply.

A. Both systems must be running TCP/IP.

C. The remote system must be running an FTP host service.

D. The client system must be running FTP client software.

E. A username and password (or anonymous) must be on the remote.

25. CORRECT ANSWERS: A-C-D-E

NetBEUI is not used with FTP, whereas all other choices are correct. Because FTP is part of the TCP/IP protocol suite, it uses the TCP/IP stack to perform communications. This happens independently of any installed requestors such as Microsoft Client for Networks. Obviously, a host must be listening to inbound requests before they will be serviced—thus the host's service. Finally, when connecting, a user is prompted for his username and password. This can be an account on the UNIX system or "anonymous" if so configured. Usually, the system asks for the user's email address for the anonymous password; however it is not verified. Web browsers automatically place "anonymous" in for any connection. To bypass this, use **`username@site`**. For example: **`FTP://erik@ftp.microsoft.com`**.

26. Which parameter is used with FTP (in command-line mode) to suppress the display of remote server responses?

B. –v

26. CORRECT ANSWER: B

The –v parameter suppresses the display of remote server responses. In certain conditions, it is not desirable to display remote responses. Reasons could be anything from security to a lack of bandwidth.

27. Which parameter is used with FTP (in command-line mode) to enable debugging?

D. `—d`

27. CORRECT ANSWER: D

The `—d` parameter enables debugging. This command is useful when trying to create a scripted file transfer or determine where a failure has occurred. When debugging is enabled, each command sent to the remote host is printed, preceded by an arrow.

28. Which parameter is used with FTP (in command-line mode) to suppress the auto-login?

C. `—n`

28. CORRECT ANSWER: C

The `—n` parameter suppresses auto-login. Under certain conditions, such as with scripting, it may be desirable to disable the prompting for name and password. In this way, a user name and password can be specified on one line.

29. Which parameter is used with FTP (in command-line mode) to turn off interactive prompting?

A. `—i`

29. CORRECT ANSWER: A

The `—i` parameter turns off interactive prompting during multiple file transfers. Suppose you need to transfer numerous files and leave the computer unattended—perhaps you are performing a file update. This option keeps a user from having to interact with a computer during the transfer process. With this option specified, a user can go on to other activities.

30. How many modes are available with FTP?

B. 2

30. CORRECT ANSWER: B

FTP supports two modes: command line and command interpreter. The command line can be executed in one line by specifying all commands at once. Using a response file designated by the -s option, each command will execute. This is great for automation—however, when you are uncertain of the files that you will be transferring, the FTP command interpreter works better.

31. Which FTP command changes directories on the local system?

B. `lcd`

31. CORRECT ANSWER: B

The `lcd` command changes directories on the local host. as in DOS, the command to change a directory is CD. To designate that this command applies locally rather than remotely, the command is `lcd`. This command is generally used to locate a file that is to be transferred or to set a location to receive a file.

32. Which FTP command starts a file transfer from the remote host?

D. `get`

32. CORRECT ANSWER: D

The `get` command starts a file transfer from a remote host (Download). If transferring multiple files such as with a wildcard (*), then use MGET.

33. Which FTP command starts a file transfer from the local host?

E. put

33. CORRECT ANSWER: E

The `put` command starts a file transfer from the local host (Upload). If transferring multiple files such as with a wildcard (*), then use `MPUT`.

34. Which FTP command specifies a remote system to connect to?

C. `open`

34. CORRECT ANSWER: C

The `open` command specifies a remote host to connect to. In most cases, the host name is usually specified via the command line. For example **`FTP FTP.MICROSOFT.COM`**. However, that command is equivalent to running FTP, then typing **`Open FTP.MICROSOFT.COM`**.

35. Which of the following represent the differences between FTP and TFTP?

A. FTP is connection oriented.

D. TFTP is connectionless oriented.

35. CORRECT ANSWERS: A-D

FTP is connection oriented, whereas TFTP is connectionless. That is to say that FTP uses TCP while TFTP uses UDP. This is observable by looking at the protocol specification located in the services file.

FTP

File Transfer Protocol, or FTP, provides a simple but robust mechanism for copying files to or from remote hosts using the connection-oriented services of TCP/IP. FTP is a component of the TCP/IP protocol, and is defined in RFC 959. To use FTP to send or receive files, the following requirements must be met:

- The client computer must have FTP client software, such as the FTP client included with Windows NT.
- The user must have a username and password on the remote system. In some cases, a username of *anonymous* with no password or your email address suffices.

- The remote system must be running an FTP daemon or service (depending upon whether it is UNIX or NT).
- Your system and the remote system must be running the TCP/IP protocol.

You can use FTP in either a command-line mode or in a command-interpreter mode. The following options are available from the command line:

```
C:\>ftp ?
Transfers files to and from a computer running an
➥FTP server service
(sometimes called a daemon). Ftp can be used
➥interactively.

FTP [-v] [-d][-i] [-n] [-g] [-s:filename] [-a] [-
➥w:windowsize] [host]

  -v              Suppresses display of remote
➥server responses.
  -n              Suppresses auto-login upon
➥initial connection.
  -i              Turns off interactive prompting
➥during multiple file
                  transfers.
  -d              Enables debugging.
  -g              Disables filename globbing (see
➥GLOB command).
  -s:filename    Specifies a text file containing FTP
➥commands; the
                  commands will automatically run
➥after FTP starts.
  -a              Use any local interface when
➥binding data connection.
  -w:buffersize  Overrides the default transfer
➥buffer size of 4096.
  host            Specifies the host name or IP
➥address of the remote
                  host to connect to.
```

If you use FTP in a command-interpreter mode, some of the more frequently used options are as follows:

- **open**—Specifies the remote system to which you connect.
- **close**—Disconnects from a remote system.
- **ls**—Obtains a directory listing on a remote system, much like the `dir` command in DOS. Note that the `ls –l` command provides file size and time stamps.

- **cd**—Changes directories on the remote system. This command functions in much the same way as the DOS cd command.
- **lcd**—Changes directories on the local system. This command also functions in much the same way as the DOS cd command.
- **binary**—Instructs FTP to treat all files transferred as binary.
- **ascii**—Instructs FTP to treat all files transferred as text. You must choose a transfer type because certain files cannot be read correctly as binary, whereas ASCII is universally accepted.
- **get**—Copies a file from the remote host to your local computer.
- **put**—Copies a file from your local computer to the remote host.
- **debug**—Turns on debugging commands that can be useful in diagnosing problems.

Because remote host systems are typically based on UNIX, you will encounter a number of nuances relating to UNIX, such as the following:

- The UNIX operating system uses the forward slash in path references, not the backward slash. The Windows NT filename `\WINNT40\README.TXT` would be `/WINNT40/README.TXT` in the UNIX format.
- UNIX is case sensitive at all times—the command `get MyFile` and the command `get MYFILE` are not the same. Usernames and passwords are also case sensitive.
- UNIX treats wildcard characters, such as the asterisk and the question mark, differently. The `glob` command within FTP controls the way that wildcard characters in local filenames are treated.

You can also install a Windows NT FTP server, which can provide FTP file transfer services to other systems. This approach allows the server to serve clients in the manner that has been traditional on UNIX machines. The FTP service is a component of Internet Information Server (IIS).

36. How many modes are available with TFTP?

A. 1

36. CORRECT ANSWER: A

In the Windows NT implementation of TCP/IP, TFTP has only the command-line mode. However, third-party clients are available that offer GUI mode. One limitation with Windows NT is that no TFTP server service is available. Again, third-party resources must be used. Commonly, TFTP is used to update firmware on devices such as routers.

37. Which type of support for TFTP is available from third parties, but is not included in Windows NT?

B. As a server

37. CORRECT ANSWER: B

Windows NT does not include support for TFTP server services. Only the TFTP client is offered. Many implementations of a server service simply run as applications rather than traditionally installed services.

TFTP

TFTP and FTP provide similar functions. Unlike FTP, however, TFTP uses the connectionless communication features of TCP/IP. Consequently, you can equate TFTP to FTP in the same way that you can equate UDP to TCP. FTP uses a TCP port to connect, whereas TFTP uses a UDP port. Both TCP and FTP require connections to be established, whereas UDP and TFTP work without requiring an established connection.

The features available in FTP are complex; those in TFTP are simpler. Unlike FTP, TFTP can be used only in a command-line mode—no command-interpreter mode is available. For command-line mode, the following options are available:

```
C:\>tftp /?

Transfers files to and from a remote computer
➥running the TFTP service.
```

```
TFTP [-i] host [GET ¦ PUT] source [destination]

  -i                Specifies binary image transfer
➥mode (also called
                    octet). In binary image mode the
➥file is moved
                    literally, byte by byte. Use
➥this mode when
                    transferring binary files.
  host              Specifies the local or remote
➥host.
  GET               Transfers the file destination on
➥the remote host to
                    the file source on the local
➥host.
  PUT               Transfers the file source on the
➥local host to
                    the file destination on the
➥remote host.
  source            Specifies the file to transfer.
  destination       Specifies where to transfer the
➥file.
```

Windows NT does not include a TFTP server, but third-party TFTP servers are available.

Why use TFTP instead of FTP? Some platforms—notably devices that require firmware updates—don't support FTP. Routers typically require the use of TFTP to update firmware information, such as microkernels.

▼ NOTE

Many network devices, such as routers and concentrators, use an operating system stored in firmware. As such, upgrades are usually handled using TFTP—the process is known as a firmware update.

38. Which document type will a Web browser read?

B. HTML

38. CORRECT ANSWER: B

Hypertext Markup Language is a document format that all Web browsers can read. By default, Windows NT includes Internet Explorer, Microsoft's Web browser. The other major browser is Netscape Navigator. HTTP is the protocol that information is transferred with. Much like FTP, Java is a Web language. And finally, XLS is Excel's format—thrown in to add confusion.

39. In what way does a Web browser connect to a site?

B. URL

39. CORRECT ANSWER: B

This question might appear to be misleading; however, a URL specifies the protocol type (HTTP://), the name of the system, and the path. An IP address alone does not completely determine a Web page. Also, a path does not necessarily determine host or protocol. In many Microsoft questions, you may find several answers that seem to fit. Most questions require only a single answer, so select the best of the possible answers.

HTML and HTTP

The explosive growth of the Internet in recent years is largely due to its flexibility. One of the Internet's building blocks is the Hypertext Transfer Protocol (HTTP). It defines a way of transferring hypertext data across TCP/IP networks. The hypertext data is formatted in Hypertext Markup Language (HTML). An HTML document can have a link to any other HTML document. This feature enables Web page designers to include text, audio files, graphics, and video in the same page.

HTTP and HTML are comprehensive standards, and a full discussion is outside the scope of this book. However, a limited discussion of Web browsers is in order here. You can use Web-browsing software to download and view HTML documents using the HTTP protocol, as well as documents using FTP, Gopher, or other protocols.

Unlike the other file transfer utilities mentioned in these sections, HTTP does not use a username or password by default. Information on the World Wide Web is typically destined for access by any user, and therefore usually does not require authentication, although that function can be enabled.

Many Web browsers are available; however, they all function in much the same way. All read HTTP documents. All address sites by URL (Uniform Resource Locator). The URL format is *`Protocol://host/path`*. *`Protocol`* is commonly HTTP or FTP, although others are supported. *`Host`* is typically a site name such as **`WWW.MICROSOFT.COM`**. And *`path`* is the location of the page that you are viewing relative to the host system.

PRACTICE QUESTIONS

CONFIGURE A WINDOWS NT SERVER COMPUTER TO SUPPORT TCP/IP PRINTING

Windows NT can be considered adaptive when it comes to printing in a TCP/IP based environment. The key reason for its adaptivity is the basis that its resources as well as its clients are focused on work with either UNIX or NT shared printers. For example, Windows NT can redirect client requests to a printer hosted on a UNIX system or take requests from a UNIX system for one of its own printers.

1. A user at a Windows NT computer running the TCP/IP protocol wants to send a print job to an LPR printer on a remote host system. Which methods enable the user to send the print job to the remote host?

A. Using the LPD command-line utility from the Windows NT system, and specifying the host name, printer name, and filename

B. Using the LPR command-line utility from the Windows NT system, and specifying the host name, printer name, and filename

C. Creating an LPR printer in Control Panel, Printers, and specifying the host name and printer name required for the creation of an LPR port

D. Creating an LPR printer in Control Panel, Printers, and specifying the host name and printer name required for the creation of an LPD server on the Windows NT computer

2. Which procedure enables a remote UNIX-based computer to send a print job to a Windows NT printer in the fewest steps?

A. Creating an LPR printer on the Windows NT computer, sharing the printer, and running the `LPR` command from the remote host system specifying the required information

B. Creating the LPD printer on the Windows NT computer and running the `LPR` command from the remote host system specifying the required information

C. Running the `LPR` command on the remote system—Windows NT automatically routes the print job to the printer with no further configuration on the Windows NT computer

D. Running the `LPD` command from the remote host because the `LPD` command spawns a copy of the `LPDSVC` command on the Windows NT computer whether or not TCP/IP printing support is installed

3. Which of the following configurations allows a Windows NT computer to act as a print gateway to an LPR printer on a remote host?

A. Creating an LPR printer on the Windows NT computer, sharing the printer, and connecting to the newly created printer from any other computer on the network

B. Creating an LPR printer on the Windows NT computer and installing an LPR printer on every other computer on the network because Windows NT computers cannot act as print gateways to LPR printers

C. Creating an LPR printer on the Windows NT computer and installing the LPDSVC service on every other computer on the network

D. None of the above: Windows NT automatically routes print jobs to any printer, including LPR, without any configuration

4. **Which parameters are required when using the `LPR` command on a Windows NT computer to send a print job to a remote host?**

   A. The remote host name

   B. Username and password for the remote system

   C. The remote printer name

   D. The name of the file to be printed

   E. The remote system's SMB server name

5. **By creating an LPR printer on a Windows NT computer and sharing the newly created printer, which of the following statements describes the added functions?**

   A. Remote host systems can print to the LPR printer, and Windows NT client computers can print to the LPR printer, but only by using the `LPR` command.

   B. Remote host systems can print to the LPR printer, and Windows NT computers can print to the LPR printer using Windows NT printing, but other Windows NT computers cannot print to the LPR printer.

   C. Remote host systems can print to the LPR printer, Windows NT computers can print to the LPR printer using Windows NT printing, and other Windows NT computers can print to the LPR printer.

   D. Remote host systems cannot print to the LPR printer, but Windows NT computers can print to the LPR printer using Windows NT printing, and other Windows NT computers can print to the LPR printer.

ANSWER KEY

1. B-C
2. B
3. A
4. A-C-D
5. C

ANSWERS & EXPLANATIONS

CONFIGURE A WINDOWS NT SERVER COMPUTER TO SUPPORT TCP/IP PRINTING

1. A user at a Windows NT computer running the TCP/IP protocol wants to send a print job to an LPR printer on a remote host system. Which methods enable the user to send the print job to the remote host?

B. Using the LPR command-line utility from the Windows NT system, specifying the host name, printer name, and filename

C. Creating an LPR printer in Control Panel, Printers, specifying the host name and printer name required for the creation of an LPR port

1. CORRECT ANSWERS: B-C

Several methods are available for setting up UNIX printers. You can use the LPR command-line utility from the Windows NT system, specifying the host name, printer name and filename; or you can create an LPR printer in Control Panel, Printers, specifying the host name and printer name required for the creation of an LPR port. This is not the limit of setting of such devices. Many third-party installation programs also perform these actions at other levels, producing the same results.

Windows NT Client Printing to a Remote Host System

You can use two methods to print to a remote host from a Windows NT client: using the LPR command from the Windows NT client computer, or creating an LPR printer on a Windows NT client computer.

Using the LPR Command-Line Utility

One of the utilities included with Microsoft TCP/IP Printing is LPR. This program allows a Windows NT computer to send a print job to a remote host printer. The remote host system must be running the LPD daemon, and you must know the name of the remote host and the printer. This utility has the following command-line options:

```
Sends a print job to a network printerUsage: lpr -S
➥server -P printer [-C class] [-J job] [-o option]
➥[-x] [-d] filename
```

```
Options:
     -S server   Name or IP address of the host
➥providing lpd service
     -P printer  Name of the print queue
     -C class    Job classification for use on the
➥burst page
     -J job      Job name to print on the burst
➥page
     -o option   Indicates the type of file (by
➥default assumes a text
                 file). Use "-o l" for binary (for
➥example, postscript)
                 files
     -x          Compatibility with SunOS 4.1.x
➥and prior versions
     -d          Sends data file first
```

2. Which procedure enables a remote UNIX-based computer to send a print job to a Windows NT printer in the fewest steps?

B. Creating the LPD printer on the Windows NT computer and running the LPR command from the remote host system specifying the required information.

2. CORRECT ANSWER: B

When integrating networks, taking the shortest path can often reduce the setup time required to complete a large merger. In the case of allowing UNIX workstations to print to Windows NT, the shortest path is to create the LPD printer on the Windows NT computer and run the LPR command from the remote host system, specifying the required information. Because setting up the printer is performed only once, the other configuration options that are performed on the UNIX side can be scripted to further reduce implementation time.

3. Which of the following configurations allows a Windows NT computer to act as a print gateway to an LPR printer on a remote host?

A. Creating an LPR printer on the Windows NT computer, sharing the printer, and connecting to the newly created printer from any other computer on the network.

3. CORRECT ANSWER: A

A printer gateway allows the Windows NT server to share an LPR device. Having a printer configured in a gateway reduces the configurations that are required to be performed on clients. Clients simply access the device as they would any other printer.

Creating an LPR Printer on a Windows NT Computer

Creating an LPR printer on the Windows NT client computer provides a higher degree of transparency. If the printer is shared, the Windows NT client can act as a print gateway for other Windows NT computers.

To create an LPR printer under Windows NT after MS TCP/IP Printing has been installed, simply follow this procedure:

1. Select Settings, Printers, and then click Add Printer. Select My Computer to add a new printer port.
2. At this point, select Add Port and then select LPR port.
3. You are prompted to provide the host name (or IP address) of the remote host system, as well as the printer name.
4. If you choose to share the printer, any client computer that can print to your Windows NT computer can also print to the LPR printer on the remote host system.

4. Which parameters are required when using the LPR command on a Windows NT computer to send a print job to a remote host?

A. The remote host name

C. The remote printer name

D. The name of the file to be printed

4. CORRECT ANSWERS: A-C-D

When using the LPR command, you must designate the host system or IP address of the host system to which you are sending, include the name of the printer (because there may be multiple printers on the system), and the name of the file that you are printing. Note that the document that you are printing must be in a supported format or in standard text (ASCII) form.

5. By creating an LPR printer on a Windows NT computer and sharing the newly created printer, which of the following statements describes the added functions?

C. Remote host systems can print to the LPR printer, Windows NT computers can print to the LPR printer using Windows NT printing, and other Windows NT computers can print to the LPR printer.

5. CORRECT ANSWER: C

The basic idea is that if TCP/IP printing is installed, then virtually any client can print to it.

Remote Host Client Printing to a Windows NT Server

Remote hosts can print to a Windows NT printer because Windows NT can provide an LPD service. The LPD service (lpdsvc) provides the same service that an LPD daemon provides on a UNIX host. Because LPD is implemented as a service, it is controlled through Control Panel, Services. This service automatically installs when you opt to install TCP/IP print services.

Remote host systems use different commands for printing. One command that works on most systems is the LPR command. A sample command line that would work on most systems is as follows:

```
lpr "s NTSYSTEM "p NTPRINTER filename
```

For the LPR command on the remote system, specify the DNS name (or IP address) of your Windows NT system, along with the printer name. Windows NT internally directs the print job to the specified printer.

FURTHER REVIEW

WHAT IS A HETEROGENEOUS ENVIRONMENT?

Most computer systems in today's large corporations are comprised of a vast array of differing operating systems and hardware. Over the years, systems that had planned obsolescence had been upgraded, whereas other operating systems were added as an alternate solution in parallel (for example, upgrading CPM and adding DOS). This led to differing versions of UNIX, DOS, Windows, OS/2, MAC OS, and so forth. Considering that each platform offered different capabilities and met certain company requirements, none of the different systems could easily be removed. As a part of a solution, TCP/IP as a protocol had custom-tailored utilities that were ported to each operation system while maintaining a similar command structure and compatibility (between platform implementations).

Key points to remember are which utilities perform which function and when to use them. Also, to avoid confusion, take note of which utilities function with NetBIOS versus host names.

CHAPTER SUMMARY

This chapter discussed the various utilities that are featured as part of the Windows NT operating system environment. When working in the TCP/IP suite, you have many inherent functions for operations, such as remote execution, file transfer, printing, sharing, and reviewing information. Noting Windows NT's capabilities for integration, Microsoft's TCP/IP suite provides a platform-independent solution that seamlessly integrates with UNIX operating systems.

CHAPTER REVIEW

REVIEW QUESTIONS

Note: The additional Chapter Review section that ends each chapter is unique to this member of the *New Riders TestPrep, Second Edition* series. We've included it to more fully and fairly cover the unique aspects of TCP/IP in relation to its mastery in preparation for MCSE examination.

1. **Which utility can you use to transfer a file to a remote host by using the connection-oriented services of TCP/IP?**

   A. TFTP

   B. HTML

   C. FTP

   D. Telnet

2. **Which remote execution utility encrypts usernames and passwords before transmission?**

   A. REXEC

   B. RSH

   C. Telnet

   D. No remote execution utility encrypts usernames and passwords.

3. **Which of the following statements about REXEC are *incorrect*?**

   A. REXEC can start processes on Windows NT computers.

   B. REXEC does not require a username or password.

   C. REXEC can establish terminal sessions on a remote host.

   D. REXEC does not encrypt passwords and usernames during authentication.

4. **Given a remote host system running TCP/IP and having an SMB server service (Standard Windows NT Server service), which of the following provides the most transparent network connectivity for file transfer?**

   A. Using an NFS client on a Windows NT computer

   B. Using Microsoft networking functions on a Windows NT computer

   C. Using FTP to copy files from the remote host to your local computer

   D. Using Telnet to establish a remote terminal session with the remote host

5. **Which of the following statements about Telnet are *incorrect*?**

   A. Telnet can be used to remotely administer Windows NT computers.

   B. Telnet encrypts usernames and passwords for enhanced security.

   C. Telnet can be used to provide terminal emulation when connecting to remote host systems.

   D. Telnet can be used to view HTML documents with graphical images.

6. **A user on a Windows NT computer wants to run an interactive text editor on a remote host computer. Which utilities would be suitable for use?**

   A. Telnet

   B. FTP

   C. REXEC

   D. RSH

   E. HTTP

7. **Your network includes a number of NT Servers, workstations, and TCP/IP host systems. To establish a secure terminal session to a host system from a Windows NT client, which of the following utilities is adequate?**

   A. Telnet

   B. FTP

   C. TFTP

   D. You need a third-party utility.

8. **You have a client computer using TCP/IP on a local subnet, and you want to transfer a file to a remote system overseas. Which of the following utilities provides the most reliable file transfer?**

   A. Telnet

   B. TFTP

   C. TCP

   D. FTP

9. **In a network that has a mixture of Windows NT and remote host systems, you want to administer remote host systems from a Windows NT computer by running remote system jobs. Which of the following utilities allows you to execute a job on a remote system without requiring a logon password?**

   A. TFTP

   B. REXEC

   C. RSH

   D. Telnet

10. **Which of the following statements about FTP are *incorrect*?**

    A. FTP encrypts usernames and passwords.

    B. FTP does not encrypt usernames and passwords, but uses MD5 and CHAP to encrypt data transfer.

    C. FTP does not perform any encryption whatsoever.

    D. FTP is connection oriented.

11. **You are configuring an Internet site for your company. You are required to supply a full set of featured functions in a protected manner. Effectively, you provide a Web server to the Internet through a firewall. Which of the following protocols is usually *not* available to a client on the other side of the firewall?**

    A. HTTP

    B. FTP

    C. TFTP

    D. Telnet

12. **You are configuring a Web page host server. This server will send data over a 56KB frame relay line. With three users, the data line is completely saturated.**

Noting that HTML documents are transferred using the HTTP protocol, and that TCP/IP supports broadcast, your boss recommends that the Web pages be set to broadcast all graphics and as nonsecured. Of the following statements, which accurately describes the flaw in your boss's thinking with respect to the HTTP protocol?

A. HTTP uses the nonconnection-oriented communication features of TCP/IP for data transfer.

B. HTTP requires a username and password for all HTML documents.

C. The HTTP protocol uses the connection-oriented communication features of TCP/IP for data transfer.

D. HTTP can be used only for text files.

ANSWER KEY

1. C
2. D
3. A-B-C
4. B
5. A-B-D
6. A-D
7. D
8. D
9. C
10. A-B
11. D
12. C

REVIEW ANSWERS

1. **Which utility can you use to transfer a file to a remote host by using the connection-oriented services of TCP/IP?**

   C. FTP

1. CORRECT ANSWER: C

Of all choices listed, FTP and TFTP are the only two transfer protocols. Of these two protocols, FTP operates over TCP (connection based) and TFTP over UDP (connectionless).

2. **Which remote execution utility encrypts usernames and passwords before transmission?**

   D. No remote execution utility encrypts usernames and passwords.

2. CORRECT ANSWER: D

None of the Windows NT TCP/IP utilities offer encryption. At best, some of the UNIX implementations have a form of encoding known as UUCP; however, this is not truly encryption as much as it is a packaging format for sending data.

3. **Which of the following statements about REXEC are incorrect?**

   A. REXEC can start processes on Windows NT computers.

   B. REXEC does not require a username or password.

   C. REXEC can establish terminal sessions on a remote host.

3. CORRECT ANSWERS: A-B-C

The true statement is that REXEC does not encrypt passwords or usernames during authentication. This utility is used to non-interactively execute a command on a remote system running the REXEC server service.

4. **Given a remote host system running TCP/IP and having an SMB server service (Standard Windows NT Server service), which of the following provides the most transparent network connectivity for file transfer?**

   B. Using Microsoft networking functions on a Windows NT computer

4. CORRECT ANSWER: B

The method that Microsoft Networking uses to communicate is known as SMB (System Message Blocks). Data is simply formatted in SMB, then transferred via communication protocols (TCP/IP, IPX, NetBEUI, and so on) between two Microsoft systems.

5. Which of the following statements about Telnet are *incorrect*?

A. Telnet can be used to remotely administer Windows NT computers.

B. Telnet encrypts usernames and passwords for enhanced security.

D. Telnet can be used to view HTML documents with graphical images.

5. CORRECT ANSWERS: A-B-D

The only statement here that is true about Telnet is that it is used to provide terminal emulation. Because Windows NT does not have a Telnet server service, it does not support a client connection. Also, as a standard UNIX compatibility utility, Telnet does not offer encryption of any kind. Finally, Telnet cannot be used with HTML documents because it is text-based only.

6. A user on a Windows NT computer wants to run an interactive text editor on a remote host computer. Which utilities would be suitable for use?

A. Telnet

D. RSH

6. CORRECT ANSWERS: A-D

They key to answering this question is the need for interactive remote execution. REXEC is used simply to issue a command, but not interactively, while FTP is used to transfer files. The primary choice for remote interactive activities is usually Telnet; however, RSH can also be applied.

7. Your network includes a number of NT Servers, workstations, and TCP/IP host systems. To establish a secure terminal session to a host system from a Windows NT client, which of the following utilities is adequate?

D. You need a third-party utility.

7. CORRECT ANSWER: D

Because the question asks about communications to a Windows NT server rather than remote operations from, you must use a third-party utility such as PC Anywhere, Timbuktu, MS Terminal Server (coming soon), and so on.

8. You have a client computer using TCP/IP on a local subnet, and you want to transfer a file to a remote system overseas. Which of the following utilities provides the most reliable file transfer?

D. FTP

8. CORRECT ANSWER: D

Because FTP uses a connection-based protocol, all communications are acknowledged and confirmed as valid. This is the best choice for file transfer. On the other hand, the fastest is TFTP; however, if one block of bad data is received, the entire file must be resent.

9. In a network that has a mixture of Windows NT and remote host systems, you want to administer remote host systems from a Windows NT computer by running remote system jobs. Which of the following utilities allows you to execute a job on a remote system without requiring a logon password?

C. RSH

9. CORRECT ANSWER: C

When configured, RSH does not require a logon password in order to perform remote operations. This is useful to maintain a secure network environment. Security is assigned based on the `.rhosts` file.

10. Which of the following statements about FTP are *incorrect*?

A. FTP encrypts usernames and passwords.

B. FTP does not encrypt usernames and passwords, but uses MD5 and CHAP to encrypt data transfer.

10. CORRECT ANSWERS: A-B

Standard TCP/IP utilities perform no encryption whatsoever. Regardless, any data may be transferred. That is, if you encrypt a file, it can be transferred as binary, but it must use a third-party program to decrypt it.

11. You are configuring an Internet site for your company. You are required to supply a full set of featured functions in a protected manner. Effectively, you provide a Web server to the Internet through a firewall. Which of the following protocols is usually *not* available to a client on the other side of the firewall?

D. Telnet

11. CORRECT ANSWER: D

A firewall is used to prevent many things from happening, including remote execution. The firewall essentially blocks any program that requests a port that could compromise security. If Web publishing is enabled, it is common that ports such as 20, 21, 25, 80, and so forth, are left open. Some firewalls will allow Telnet sessions, but must have the port open, and maintain the IP address of the client making the request.

12. You are configuring a Web page host server. This server will send data over a 56KB frame relay line. With three users, the data line is completely saturated. Noting that HTML documents are transferred using the HTTP protocol, and that TCP/IP supports broadcast, your boss recommends that the Web pages be set to broadcast all graphics and as nonsecured. Of the following statements, which accurately describes the flaw in your boss's thinking with respect to the HTTP protocol?

C. The HTTP protocol uses the connection-oriented communication features of TCP/IP for data transfer.

12. CORRECT ANSWER: C

This question demonstrates that protocols are connectionless or connection based. The basic fact is that certain types of data such as HTTP transfers are made as TCP connections. It is not a matter of reselecting UDP so much as it is a design of the protocol to operate only over TCP.

CHAPTER 8

Connectivity

Although it would seem that the on-ramp to the information superhighway is the home computer, in fact the computer is more the vehicle, whereas the on-ramp is the phone line used to connect to the ISP. Believe it or not, this connection typically featured in the Microsoft operating system world as dial-up networking (aka RAS) uses TCP/IP as its link into the Internet. That is to say that such a system with dial-up networking can be used to connect a network to the Internet.

Regardless of whether we are connecting one system or many via a dial-up network, Windows NT includes both the client and server components of RAS. This chapter discusses the configuration and use of Windows NT in a remote connectivity environment. The key concepts to note in this chapter are how information is assigned, what security features are available, and how Windows NT is configured in such an environment.

OBJECTIVE

This chapter helps you prepare for the exam by covering the following objective:

Configure a RAS server and dial-up networking for use on a TCP/IP network.

- Configuring Windows NT for RAS services and its clients for dial-up networking allows clients the ability to extend their remote connectivity. The primary focus of this chapter deals explicitly with this function.

PRACTICE QUESTIONS

CONFIGURE A RAS SERVER AND DIAL-UP NETWORKING FOR USE ON A TCP/IP NETWORK

1. **A RAS Server can be which of the following? Select all that apply.**
   A. Windows NT Server
   B. Windows NT Workstation
   C. Windows 95
   D. Windows 3.11

2. **When users are dialing in to a Microsoft RAS, what line protocol is always used?**
   A. SLIP
   B. PPP
   C. TCP/IP
   D. NetBEUI

3. **Which of the following is an extension to PPP that enables clients to connect to remote servers over the Internet?**
   A. SLIP
   B. POP
   C. PPTP
   D. PPP+

4. **Windows NT Workstation 4.0 supports which two line protocols?**
   A. SLIP
   B. PPP
   C. PPTP
   D. TCP/IP

5. **Which of the following is an industry standard that supports only TCP/IP connections made over serial lines?**
   A. SLIP
   B. PPP
   C. PPTP
   D. TCP/IP

6. **Which of the following protocols works with SLIP?**
   A. TCP/IP
   B. NetBEUI
   C. IPX/SPX
   D. PPTP

7. **How does Windows NT Workstation support SLIP functionality?**
   A. As a server.
   B. As a client.
   C. As a client and a server.
   D. Windows NT Workstation does not support SLIP.

8. **Which of the following protocols work with PPP? Select all that apply.**
   A. TCP/IP
   B. NetBEUI
   C. IPX/SPX
   D. PPTP

9. **Which of the following line protocols supports DHCP addresses?**
   A. SLIP
   B. PPP
   C. IPX/SPX
   D. TCP/IP

10. **Which of the following protocols creates virtual private networks over the Internet?**
   A. SLIP
   B. PPP
   C. POP
   D. PPTP

11. **Which of the following are limitations of SLIP for Dial-Up Networking (DUN) clients?**
   A. DUN doesn't support use as a SLIP client.
   B. SLIP doesn't support NWLink or NetBEUI.
   C. SLIP doesn't support DHCP.
   D. SLIP doesn't support encrypted authentication.

12. **What are the two major concerns when configuring an internal modem or adding a port for an external modem?**
   A. IRQ Settings
   B. Valid Memory Ranges
   C. Port Selection
   D. DMA Channel

13. **Which of the following are configurable components of a port?**
   A. Baud Rate Settings
   B. Flow Control Type
   C. Number of Stop Bits
   D. Type of Modem

14. **Which of the following are configurable components of a modem?**
   A. Baud Rate
   B. Speaker Settings
   C. COM Port
   D. Line Protocol Type

15. **Which of the following are possible solutions for remote communications?**
   A. X.25
   B. ISDN
   C. X.400
   D. FTP
   E. XNS

16. **Which of the following security features are included with Windows NT?**
   A. Dial Back to Predefined Number
   B. Dial Back Where Caller Sets Number
   C. No Call Back
   D. Enable/Disable According to User Manager
   E. TCP/IP Thumbprint via IP Address
   F. MultiLink Call Back
   G. Automatic Security Protocol Matching

17. **Which of the following items cannot be configured when adding a dial-up connection? Select the best answer.**

A. Phone Number

B. Protocol Specifications

C. Before and After Dialing Scripts

D. Initial Web Site to Connect To (Home Page)

E. User Name and Password

18. How are authentication and encryption settings set?

A. For each workstation

B. For each domain

C. For each phonebook entry

D. For each user

19. The Dialing Properties dialog box is accessed from which Control Panel applet?

A. System

B. Services

C. RAS

D. Telephony

20. How many RAS sessions can Windows NT Workstation serve at a time?

A. 1

B. 2

C. 5

D. 255

21. RAS can be configured in which three of the following ways?

A. Dial out only

B. Receive calls only

C. Dial out and receive calls

D. Manual

22. Which of the following configuration settings is the default for Workstation RAS?

A. Dial out only

B. Receive calls only

C. Dial out and receive calls

D. Manual

23. What kinds of management or information tools are available from the RAS server that are directly related to the RAS service?

A. Remote Access Administator

B. Dial-Up Networking Monitor

C. Status Tab

D. Summary Tab

E. RAS ADMIN Notifier

ANSWER KEY

1. A-B-C
2. B
3. C
4. A-B
5. A
6. A
7. B
8. A-B-C
9. B
10. D
11. B-C-D
12. A-C
13. A-B-C
14. A-B-C
15. A-B
16. A-B-C-D
17. D
18. C
19. D
20. A
21. A-B-C
22. A
23. A-B-C-D

ANSWERS & EXPLANATIONS

CONFIGURE A RAS SERVER AND DIAL-UP NETWORKING FOR USE ON A TCP/IP NETWORK

1. A RAS Server can be which of the following? Select all that apply.

A. Windows NT Server

B. Windows NT Workstation

C. Windows 95

1. CORRECT ANSWERS: A-B-C

A RAS Server can be an NT Server, an NT Workstation, or a Windows 95 machine. You will notice that all current Microsoft Operating systems support RAS. With this said, do you think Windows NT 5.0 will support it? How about Windows 98? Of course, it will! Note that both Windows 95 and 98 refer to the RAS Server as Dial-Up Server.

RAS Servers and Dial-Up Networking

Essentially, RAS allows users to connect to your network and act as if they are directly connected to it. There are two main components to RAS: the server (Remote Access Service) and the client (Dial-Up Networking). The RAS Server can be Windows NT Server, Windows NT Workstation, or Windows 95 (either with Service Pack 1 or OEM Service Release 2) and enables users to connect to the network from a remote location. The Microsoft RAS Server always uses the Point-to-Point Protocol (PPP) as the line protocol when users are dialing in to the network.

In addition to connecting to a Microsoft RAS Server, Windows Dial-Up Networking can connect with other forms of RAS (other dial-in servers such as UNIX terminal servers) by using either Serial Line Internet Protocol (SLIP) or PPP. All that is required is a communications device.

2. When users are dialing in to a Microsoft RAS, what line protocol is always used?

B. PPP

2. CORRECT ANSWER: B

PPP will always be used when clients are dialing in to a Microsoft RAS Server. PPP is the best choice for connecting to a RAS server because it has the best overall flexibility to interact for telecommunications over others such as SLIP.

3. Which of the following is an extension to PPP that enables clients to connect to remote servers over the Internet?

C. PPTP

3. CORRECT ANSWER: C

The Point-to-Point Tunneling Protocol (PPTP) is an extension to PPP that enables clients to connect to remote servers over the Internet. PPTP is secured and sometimes referred to as Virtual Private Networking or VPN.

4. Windows NT Workstation 4.0 supports which two line protocols?

A. SLIP

B. PPP

4. CORRECT ANSWERS: A-B

Windows NT Workstation 4.0 supports two different line protocols: SLIP and PPP. In most cases, PPP is the preferred or required line protocol choice. PPP is a newer version of SLIP that supports multiple protocols and DHCP.

5. Which of the following is an industry standard that supports only TCP/IP connections made over serial lines?

A. SLIP

5. CORRECT ANSWER: A

SLIP is an industry standard that supports TCP/IP connections made over serial lines. No other protocols are supported with SLIP and IP addresses must be preassigned. SLIP has no place with VPN or variations beyond basic TCP/IP.

6. Which of the following protocols works with SLIP?

A. TCP/IP

6. CORRECT ANSWER: A

SLIP supports only TCP/IP. With respect to PPP, it is somewhat outdated and inflexible. PPP works with DHCP, whereas SLIP does not. PPP works with IPX, NetBEUI, and so on, whereas SLIP is limited to TCP/IP.

7. How does Windows NT Workstation support SLIP functionality?

B. As a client.

7. CORRECT ANSWER: B

Windows NT Workstation supports only SLIP client functionality. In other words, you may communicate to a foreign system with SLIP, but you cannot use it to connect to a Windows NT system.

8. Which of the following protocols work with PPP? Select all that apply.

A. TCP/IP

B. NetBEUI

C. IPX/SPX

8. CORRECT ANSWERS: A-B-C

PPP supports TCP/IP, NetBEUI, and IPX/SPX, among others. You may find third-party clients such as IBM's 8235 DIALS client, which include DLC (used for communications with mainframes, AS400s, and HP JET direct devices), for example.

9. Which of the following line protocols supports DHCP addresses?

B. PPP

9. CORRECT ANSWER: B

TCP/IP and IPX/SPX are not line protocols. SLIP does not support DHCP addressing—only static addressing. PPP supports DHCP addressing.

10. Which of the following protocols creates virtual private networks over the Internet?

D. PPTP

10. CORRECT ANSWER: D

You can use PPTP to create virtual private networks (VPN) over the Internet. This protocol is useful for remote users because they need only dial to the local ISP, rather than dial long distance to connect to a network.

11. Which of the following are limitations of SLIP for Dial-Up Networking (DUN) clients?

B. SLIP doesn't support NWLink or NetBEUI.

C. SLIP doesn't support DHCP.

D. SLIP doesn't support encrypted authentication.

11. CORRECT ANSWERS: B-C-D

Windows NT Workstation 4.0 supports use as a SLIP client, but not as a SLIP Server. SLIP is a technology that was designed as a quick-fix solution to remote communications support. However, this solution was never expected to be adapted as it has. As such, most communications should be held on PPP connections. However, to support those legacy systems, Windows NT provides a SLIP client.

PPP Versus SLIP

When clients connect to a server using a modem, they must do so through something other than the frames that normally traverse a network (such as IEEE802.3). Some other transport method is needed. In the case of dial-up servers (or terminal servers), two popular line protocols are available. SLIP, the older of the two, is used frequently in UNIX implementations and is geared directly toward TCP/IP communications. Windows NT can use the services of a SLIP Server, but does not provide a SLIP Server. Microsoft's RAS Server uses PPP because SLIP requires a static IP address and does not provide a facility for secured logon (passwords are sent as clear text).

PPP was developed as a replacement for SLIP and provides several advantages over the earlier protocol. PPP can automatically provide the client computer with an IP address and other configuration. It provides a secure logon and can transport protocols other than TCP/IP (such as AppleTalk, IPX, and NetBEUI).

Two important extensions to PPP are the Multilink Protocol (MP) and Point-to-Point Tunneling Protocol (PPTP). Windows NT supports both extensions.

MP allows a client station to connect to a remote server by using more than one physical connection. This capability provides better throughput over standard modems. You will, however, need multiple phone lines and modems to enable this protocol. MP can be an easy interim solution if you need to temporarily connect to offices and don't have the time or the budget to set up a leased line or other similar connection.

PPTP facilitates secure connections across the Internet. Using PPTP, users can connect to any Internet Service Provider (ISP) and use the ISP's network as a gateway to connect to the office network. During the session initialization, the client and server negotiate a 40-bit session key. This key is then used to encrypt all packets that are sent back and forth over the Internet. The packets are encapsulated into PPP packets as the data.

PPP Problems

As was mentioned earlier, Windows NT acts as a PPP Server. Consequently, the client station and the server undergo a negotiation during the initial phase of the call.

During the negotiation, the client and server decide on the protocol to be used and the parameters for the protocol. If there are problems attempting to connect, you may want to set up PPP logging to actually observe the negotiation between the server and client.

PPP logging is set up on the server by changing the Logging option under the following:

```
HKEY_LOCAL_MACHINE\SYSTEM\CurrentControlSet\Services
➥\RASMAN\PPP\Parameters
```

The log file is in the `system32\RAS` directory and, as with the modem log, can be viewed by using any text editor.

Some of the most common problems that you may encounter with PPP follow:

- You must ensure that the protocol that you are requesting from the RAS client is available on the RAS Server. If no common protocol is available, the connection will fail.
- If you are using NetBEUI, ensure that the name you are using on the RAS client is not in use on the network that you are attempting to connect to.
- If you are attempting to connect by using TCP/IP, then the RAS Server must be configured to provide you with an address.

12. What are the two major concerns when configuring an internal modem or adding a port for an external modem?

A. IRQ Settings

C. Port Selection

12. CORRECT ANSWERS: A-C

The two major concerns of any serial device are typically the IRQ and COM port settings. The IRQ should not be the same as one that is used by a mouse—this tends to hang a system. As for the COM port assignment, any will do so long as the resource is available.

13. Which of the following are configurable components of a port?

A. Baud Rate Settings

B. Flow Control Type

C. Number of Stop Bits

13. CORRECT ANSWERS: A-B-C

The only item listed that is not a configurable component of a port is the type of modem. In order to establish a connection, both sides must use the same speed, flow control, and stop bits. When you see a phone number followed by a series of numbers and letters such as N-8-1, this means no parity, eight data bits, and one stop bit. Again, both sides must match in order to communicate properly.

Modems

Modems have been around for years and provide a cheap and relatively reliable method of communications over the Public Switched Telephone Network (PSTN). Installing a modem in a computer is a straightforward process.

The two main types of modems are internal and external. Internal modems cost a little less than external modems do, but you have to open the computer to install them; in addition, internal modems require a free interrupt (IRQ). If you elect to go with an external modem, you should check that you have a communications (COM) port available and that it will be able to handle the speed of the modem.

Ports

Regardless of whether you have an internal or external modem, you need to install the modem as a communications port. Normally, doing so is no problem; however, sometimes (notably with internal modems) you must change the settings for the port. Changing port settings can also cause problems with an external modem. If you cannot talk to the modem, you should also check the port settings.

To check the port settings in NT, open the Control Panel (Start, Settings, Control Panel) and double-click on the Ports icon. This will bring up the Ports dialog box.

Select the port that you want to inspect and click Settings. Another dialog box (port settings) shows the settings for the port.

Five settings are available. These are general settings, however, and deal only with applications that don't set these parameters. The following list briefly describes the settings:

- **Baud Rate**—This setting controls the rate at which the data flows. Serial communications move your data one bit at a time. In addition, for every byte that is sent there are (normally) four bits of overhead. To find the transfer rate in bytes, divide this number by 12.
- **Data Bits**—Not all systems use eight bits to store one character. Some systems use only seven. This setting enables the computer to adjust the number of bits used in the transfer.

- **Parity**—Parity is used to verify that information that is being transferred is getting across the line successfully. The parity can be Even, Odd, Mark, or Space, or you can use No Parity (which is the normal setting).
- **Stop Bits**—In some systems, these are used to mark the end of the transmission.
- **Flow Control**—This option can be set to Xon/Xoff, Hardware, or None. Flow control, as the name implies, controls the movement of the data between the modem and your computer. Hardware flow control uses Request to Send (RTS) and Clear to Send (CTS). The system sends a signal through the RTS wire in the cable, telling the modem it wants to send. When the modem has finished transmitting the contents of its buffer and has space, it signals the computer that it can send the data by using the CTS wire. Xon/Xoff is a software form of flow control in which the modem sends Xon (ASCII character 17) when it is ready for data from the computer, and Xoff (ASCII character 19) when it has too much data. (This type of flow control does not work well with binary transfers because the Xon and Xoff characters can be part of a file.)

In most cases, you can ignore these settings. They are set and reset by the application that you use. However, if you click the Advanced button, you can find some settings that you need to be aware of.

The options that you can set in here will affect all applications that use the communications port. The following list provides an overview of the options that you can set.

▼ NOTE

If you make changes in the Advanced dialog box, the system will no longer be a standard system. Many applications can be affected if you make changes here.

- **COM Port Number**—Here you can select the port that you want to configure.
- **Base I/O Port Address**—When information is received from a hardware (physical) device, the BIOS places that information in RAM. This setting changes the place in RAM where you will place the information. Unless your hardware requires a different address, do not change this setting.
- **Interrupt Request Line (IRQ)**—After the BIOS places the information in RAM, it uses a hardware interrupt to alert the CPU to the presence of the data. Interrupts are a prime source for conflicts and one of the main causes of system failures. Thus, unless your hardware requires you to do so, do not change this option.
- **FIFO Enabled**—This setting enables the on-chip buffering available in 16550 UARTs. Note that on some of the older revisions of the 16550, there were problems with random data loss when using FIFO. If you are experiencing unexplained problems, try disabling FIFO. Enabling FIFO might provide a slight increase in throughput. Note that FIFO is a system in which the first data in is the first data out.

When you attempt to troubleshoot a serial problem, you should always check that these settings are correct. Making sure that the port options are correct allows you to communicate with the modem.

14. Which of the following are configurable components of a modem?

A. Baud Rate

B. Speaker Settings

C. COM Port

14. CORRECT ANSWERS: A-B-C

The Baud rate, speaker settings, and COM port are all configurable components of a modem. Line Protocol Type is a matter of the dialer that you use for remote connectivity. The specification of controllable items is very extensive; however, you must be careful not to confuse which items are configured as a factor of which component. The following sections describe this extensive list of configurable items.

Configuring Modems

The most common method of connecting to an office network or to the Internet is to connect by using a modem.

Installing a Modem

Installing a modem is simple in Windows NT. After the hardware is connected, go to the Control Panel and double-click the Modems icon. If no modem is installed, the modem installer starts automatically. This wizard steps you through the installation of the modem. If you have a modem already, then click Add.

If the installer is unable to detect the modem, you probably have one of two problems: Either the modem cannot be detected and you must install it manually, or the system cannot see the modem, in which case you should check the port. If you need to install the modem manually, place a check in the Don't Detect My Modem, I Will Select It from a List check box. You can select the modem from the following screen.

After you have the modem installed, you can check modem properties by using the Modems icon in the Control Panel. When you open the icon, you will see a dialog box that lists the available modems.

From here, you can check and set the properties for the modems that are installed in the computer. Several options are of interest. Select Modem, Properties to display the General properties for the modem.

The General tab contains only a few settings that you need to set. The following list describes the properties on the General tab and explains the elements you should check for.

- **Port**—Displays the port on which the modem was installed.
- **Speaker Volume**—Determines the volume of the speaker during the connection phase.

- **Maximum Speed**—Sets the fastest rate at which the system will attempt to communicate with the modem.
- **Only Connect at This Speed**—Instructs the modem that it must connect to the remote site at the same speed you set for communications with the modem.

The other tab in the Modem Properties dialog box is the Connections tab, which deals with the way that the modem connects. The Connections tab has two sections: Connection Preferences and Call Preferences. The Connection Preferences are the communications settings (which were discussed in the Ports section). These settings override the port settings. The three items from the Call Preferences section are described next.

- **Wait for Tone Before Dialing**—Normally, this item should be selected, unless the telephone system that you are connected to does not support tone operations.
- **Cancel the Call If Not Connected Within**—This option sets the maximum length of time that it takes for the call to be established.
- **Disconnect a Call If Idle for More Than**—This option enables you to set the maximum length of time that a call can sit idle. Windows NT 4 provides an autodial service that automatically calls back a server if you are disconnected and then attempt to use a network service. This feature reduces the amount of time a user will tie up a line and can prevent massive long-distance charges.

The final thing to check when configuring modems and troubleshooting is the Advanced Connection information. These settings can adversely affect communications.

You will want to verify several of the Advanced options. The following list describes the options and the things that you should look for.

- **Use Error Control**—Turns on or off some common settings that affect the way the system deals with the modem. The specific options follow.
  - **Required to Connect**—Forces the modem to establish that an error-correcting protocol (such as MNP class 5) be used before the connection is made. This option should not be used by default. If the modem on the other end of the connection does not support the same class of error detection, the connection will fail.
  - **Compress Data**—Tells the modem to use data compression. Microsoft RAS will automatically implement software compression between the client and workstation if both are Microsoft servers. This option should be turned on only if you will be talking to a non-Microsoft server; otherwise, the modem will try to compress data that is already compressed.
  - **Use Cellular Protocol**—Tells the system that the modem is cellular based.
- **User Flow Control**—Overrides the flow control setting for the port. Both types of flow control are available (hardware and software). In most cases, you should choose to use hardware flow control. Using flow control enables you to set the speed of the transmission between the computer and the modem. The choices are Xon/Xoff and hardware.
- **Modulation Type**—Enables users to set the type of frequency modulation for the modem to that of the phone system they are using. The modulation is either standard or Bell, and deals with the sound frequency that is used for the send and receive channels for the communicating hosts.

- **Extra Settings**—Enables you to enter extra modem initialization strings that you want to send to the modem whenever you place a call.
- **Record a Log File**—The log file is a record of the communications that take place between the modem and the computer during the connection phase of the communications.

Dialing Properties

From the Modem Properties dialog box, you can also click on the Dialing Properties button, which enables you to configure the system so that it knows where you are dialing from. This information is used in conjunction with Dial-Up Networking to allow the system to determine whether your call is long distance, if it (the call) should use a calling card, how to disable the call waiting feature, and so on.

Several items are available in the Dialing Properties dialog box, and if this information is not set correctly, the client computer may attempt to connect to a local server as a long-distance call (or vice versa). The following list describes the Dialing Properties entries.

- **I Am Dialing From**—This entry is the name of the location. To create a new entry, click the New button and enter a name in this box. The user needs to know which entry to use when dialing.
- **The Area Code Is**—The computer uses this information to determine whether to dial the call as a long-distance call or a local call.
- **I Am In**—Sets the country code for dialing purposes so the system is able to connect to international numbers.
- **To Access an Outside Line, First Dial**—Sets the access code for dialing out from a location. There is an entry for local calls and one for long distance.

- **Dial Using Calling Card**—Enables you to have the computer enter the calling-card information to make the connection with the remote host. Click the Change button to review or change your calling-card information.
- **This Location Has Call Waiting**—The call waiting tone can cause a connection to be dropped. You can tell the computer to disable call waiting for the location that you are dialing from.
- **The Phone System at This Location Uses**—Specifies whether the system that you are calling from uses tone or pulse dialing.

If you encounter any connection problems, you should always verify the information in the Dialing Properties dialog box.

15. Which of the following are possible solutions for remote communications?

A. X.25

B. ISDN

15. CORRECT ANSWERS: A-B

A number of technologies are available for remote access. The determining factors typically are availability, cost, and speed. In the case of this question, X.25 and ISDN are the only two that qualify as a remote communications solution. Others might include PPTP via the Internet, analog telephone lines, and so on.

Other Communications Technologies

As stated earlier, there are other ways in which you can connect to the Windows NT server. There are two principal ways that you will be able to connect: by using the Integrated Services Digital Network (ISDN), or X.25 (which is a wide area networking standard).

ISDN

ISDN is one of the most common choices for connecting remote sites or for individuals or small organizations to connect to the Internet. Indeed, ISDN is becoming a very common method of communication.

A standard phone line can handle transmission speeds of up to 9,600 bits per second (compression makes up the rest of the transmission speed in most modems such as those that transfer data at 33.6Kbps). ISDN transmits at speeds of 64Kbps or 128Kbps, depending on whether it is one- or two-channel.

ISDN is a point-to-point communications technology, and special equipment must be installed at both the server and the remote site. You must install an ISDN card (which acts as a network card) in place of a modem in both computers. As you will have guessed by now, ISDN connections are more expensive than modems. However, if your site has a requirement for higher speed, the cost will most likely be justified. Be aware, however, that in some parts of the world, ISDN is a metered service—the more you use, the more you pay.

X.25

The X.25 protocol is not an actual device, but rather a standard for connections. It is a packet-switching communication protocol that was designed for WAN connectivity.

RAS supports X.25 connections by using Packet Assemblers/Disassemblers (PADs) and X.25 smart cards. These are installed as network cards, just as ISDN is.

16. Which of the following security features are included with Windows NT?

A. Dial Back to Predefined Number

B. Dial Back Where Caller Sets Number

C. No Call Back

D. Enable/Disable According to User Manager

16. CORRECT ANSWERS: A-B-C-D

Windows NT security features include items A through D. A TCP/IP Thumbprint according to an IP address is more along the lines of what a firewall or Virtual Private Networking would provide. However, the terminology is wrong. Multilink Call Back does not function. Also, if security does not match, there is not an option to match.

Dial-In Permissions

As with all other aspects of Windows NT, security is built into the RAS server. At a minimum, a user will require an account in Windows NT, and that account will need to have dial-in permissions set.

You can grant users dial-in permission by using the User Manager (or User Manager for Domains) or through the Remote Access Admin program. If you are having problems connecting to the RAS Server, permissions is one of the first things you should check. Follow these steps to set or check dial-in permissions:

1. Open the User Manager for Domains utility (Start, Programs, Administrative Tools, User Manager for Domains).
2. Select the account that you are using and choose User, Properties. You will see the User Properties sheet.
3. Click the Dialin button to open the Dialin Information permissions dialog box.
4. Check the Grant Dialin Permission to User box to allow the user to dial in.

You can also check the permissions from the Remote Access Admin utility by following these steps:

1. Start the Remote Access Admin (Start, Programs, Administrative tools, RAS Admin).
2. From the menu, choose Users, Permissions.
3. In the Permissions dialog box, select the user and ensure that Dialin permission is granted.

Callback Security

You probably noticed a setting for Call Back in both of the preceding methods. *Call Back* means that the server returns the user's call. This feature can be set to one of three options:

- **No Call Back**—This option is the default and means that the Call Back feature is disabled.
- **Set by Caller**—This option enables the user to set the number that should be used when the server calls back.

This option is useful if you have many users who will be traveling and want to centralize long distance calls.

- **Preset To**—This option enhances the security of the network by forcing the user to be at a set phone number. If set, the user can place a call only from that one location.

Call Back Security with Multilink

Currently, Windows NT does not support Call Back security in a Multilink setup. If you attempt to do so, the initial connections are made, but then the server hangs up. The server has only one number for the client and therefore calls back to only one port.

Common RAS Security Problems

Authentication can be a problem in two areas. The first is obvious: The client can attempt to connect by using the incorrect username and password. This situation can easily occur if the user is dialing from a home system. The RAS client may be set to attempt the connection by using the current username and password.

The other authentication problem occurs if the security settings on the server and the client do not match. You can get around this problem by using the Allow Any Authentication setting or possibly by using the After Dial terminal window.

17. Which of the following items *cannot* be configured when adding a dial-up connection? Select the best answer.

D. Initial Web Site to Connect To (Home Page).

17. CORRECT ANSWER: D

The only feature from the list that is *not* included as a part of dial-up networking is the Initial Web Site to Connect To. This setting is made as a function of your Web browser, not the dialer. However, you can create a script that opens a Web browser to a given site. Note that this functionality is not directly related to the Dial-Up networking configuration.

18. How are authentication and encryption settings set?

C. For each phonebook entry

18. CORRECT ANSWER: C

Authentication and encryption settings are set individually for each phonebook entry. Authentication and encryption apply only to those services that support it. If you are to connect to a Windows NT system, this option should most likely be enabled. However, if connecting to a UNIX-based system, this option should most likely be disabled. There are some third-party devices that are marketed as remote access servers that vary on encryption support. Devices such as Shiva's Lan Rover/Access Switch, Cisco's AS5200/5300, and so forth, fall into this category.

19. The Dialing Properties dialog box is accessed from which Control Panel applet?

D. Telephony

19. CORRECT ANSWER: D

Telephony is the Control Panel applet that gives access to Dialing Properties. When switching locations such as area code or prefixes to dial for an outside line, or disabling call waiting, users should make changes here. Then when a dial-up network connection is accessed, the dial-out phone number dials all numbers to perform all actions required. Although you could manually type these numbers on-the-fly into the number that you dial, these changes are not saved.

Dial-Up Networking

Dial-Up Networking is the component that is used to connect to the RAS Server. Before you can configure Dial-Up Networking, you must install a modem or other means of communication.

By using Dial-Up Networking, you create a phonebook entry for each location that you will call. Follow these steps to create an entry:

1. Open the My Computer icon and then open Dial-Up Networking. (If you do not have an entry, a wizard steps you through creating a phonebook entry.)
2. Click the New button to create an entry. You can also select an entry in the list, click More, and choose Edit the Entry.

If you choose New, the New Entry Wizard appears. You can choose to enter the information manually, as explained in this section.

3. The New (or Edit) Phonebook Entry dialog box opens. By default, it opens to the Basic tab; enter or verify the following information:

   - **Entry Name**—The name of the entry.
   - **Comment**—Any comment you want to make about the entry.
   - **Phone Number**—The phone number for the entry, which you should verify. You can enter multiple phone numbers by selecting the Alternates button.
   - **Use Telephony-Dialing Properties**—Tells the system to use the properties that you set for your location when dialing the number.
   - **Dial Using**—Tells the system which modem you want to use when dialing.
   - **Use Another Port If Busy**—Tells the system to use another modem if the modem specified is busy.

4. Select the Server tab and enter or verify the following information:

   - **Dial-Up Server Type**—Tells the system what type of server you are trying to connect to. You can use three types of servers: PPP such as Windows NT, SLIP, and Windows NT 3.1 RAS. If the correct type is not selected, your computer attempts to use the wrong line protocol.
   - **Network Protocols**—Tells the computer which protocols you want to use: TCP/IP, IPX, and/or NetBEUI.
   - **Enable Software Compression**—If you are working with a Windows NT server, you can select this option to turn on the software compression feature.

- **Enable PPP LCP Extensions**—Tells the system that the PPP Server can set up the client station and verify the username and password.

5. If you are using TCP/IP for this connection, you should also set or verify the TCP/IP settings. The TCP/IP Setting screen appears; the selections depend on the type of server you selected. The following list describes the TCP/IP setting options.

   - **Server Assigned IP Address**—Tells the computer that the server will assign the IP address for this station by using a DHCP-like service or reserved range of addresses.
   - **Specify an IP Address**—Enables you to give the station an IP address.
   - **Server Assigned Name Server Addresses**—Tells the system that the server will assign the IP addresses for DNS and Windows Internet Naming Service (WINS) servers.
   - **Specify Name Server Addresses**—Enables you to set the addresses for DNS and WINS servers. This setting enables you to see whether the server is giving you correct addresses.
   - **Use IP Header Compression**—Using IP header compression reduces the overhead that is transmitted over the modem.
   - **Use Default Gateway on the Remote Network**—If you are connected to a network and dialed into a service provider, this setting tells NT to send information that is bound for a remote network to the gateway on the dial-in server.

6. Set the script options on the Script tab.

   - **After Dialing (Login)**—Three settings are available here; make sure the correct one is used. For NT-to-NT communications, you can select None. For other connections, you may have to make custom configurations.

- **Before Dialing**—If you click this button, you will see the same basic options that were presented in the After Dialing dialog box.

7. Check or enter the security information on the Security tab. This should be set to the same level as the security on the server, or the connection will probably fail.
    - **Authentication and Encryption Policy**—Here you can set the level of security that you want to use. This setting should be set to match the setting on the server.
    - **Require Data Encryption**—If you are using Microsoft-encrypted authentication, you have the option to encrypt all data that is being sent over the connection. This should be set the same as the server.
    - **User Current Name and Password**—Allows Windows to send the current username and password as your logon information. If you are not using the same name and password on the client as you do on the network, do not check this box. You are prompted for the username and password to log on as when you attempt to connect.
    - **Unsave Password**—If you told the system to save the logon password for a connection, you can clear it by clicking this button. You should unsave the password in the case of a logon problem.
8. Enter or verify the information for X.25 connections.

There are many different options that you can configure, and therefore the potential for errors is great. Client errors tend to be either validation problems or errors in the network protocols. Remember that you may need to verify the configuration of the server.

20. How many RAS sessions can Windows NT Workstation serve at a time?

A. 1

20. CORRECT ANSWER: A

Windows NT Workstation is limited to one RAS session at a time. This limitation is to help indicate the differences between Server and Workstation. Think of this limitation in the same context as you would to consider the number of users that can connect via the regular network.

21. RAS can be configured in which three of the following ways?

A. Dial out only

B. Receive calls only

C. Dial out and receive calls

21. CORRECT ANSWERS: A-B-C

While configured for dial out, you are setting the server to act as a client. When set to receive calls, it is set as a server. Finally, when set for both, the system acts as both client and server. Client functionality allows the system to dial into another network in the same manner that clients dial into it. Each modem on a system can be configured individually for each function.

22. Which of the following configuration settings is the default for Workstation RAS?

A. Dial out only

22. CORRECT ANSWER: A

Dial out only is the default RAS setting. This setting is taken for security reasons. By default, you would not want to potentially open an area into your network by enabling dial-in also unless it was intended.

23. What kinds of management or information tools are available from the RAS server that are directly related to the RAS service?

A. A Remote Access Administrator

B. Dial-Up Networking Monitor

C. Status Tab

D. Summary Tab

23. CORRECT ANSWERS: A-B-C-D

Of the entire list, only the RAS Admin Notifier does not provide management capabilities or information. In fact, it does not exist!

Configuring the RAS Server

Both Windows NT Server and Workstation can be configured to function as RAS servers. Windows NT Server is limited to 255 connections, whereas Workstation supports only one. The RAS configuration is done when you install RAS or when you verify it after installation by going to the Network Settings dialog box and double-clicking on Remote Access Service from the Services tab.

The Remote Access Setup dialog box enables you to configure each port and set the overall network preferences. The following four buttons relate to port settings:

- **Add**—Enables you to add another port to the RAS Server. This could be a modem, X.25 PAD, or a PPTP Virtual Private Network.
- **Remove**—Removes the port from RAS.
- **Configure**—Opens a dialog box that enables you to configure how this port is to be used. You should inspect this setting if no users are able to dial in.
- **Clone**—Enables you to copy a port. Windows NT Server has been tested with up to 256 ports.

▼ **NOTE**

Windows NT Workstation and Windows 95 (with Service Pack 1 or the OSR2 release) allow only one client to dial in, whereas Windows NT has been tested for up to 256 simultaneous connections.

After the ports are configured, you must configure the network settings. These affect what users can see, how the users are authenticated, and what protocols the users can use when they dial in to the network. When you click the Network button, you see a Network Configuration dialog box.

This dialog box has three main sections. The dial-out protocols specify the protocols you can use to dial into another server. The dial-in protocols set the protocols with which users can connect to you. The third section specifies encryption settings. The level of security that you choose must also be set on the client computer. If the client and the server do not use the same level of security, the server will not be able to validate the client.

Each server-side protocol has a configuration button. The following sections explain these configurations. Before you can use a protocol with RAS, it has to be installed on the server.

Configuring TCP/IP on the RAS Server

If you run a mixed network that includes UNIX-like hosts, then you should enable the TCP/IP protocol on the RAS Server. Doing so also enables your clients to use an Internet connection on your network. The TCP/IP configuration dialog box includes the capability to restrict network access to the RAS server.

The other options deal with the assignment of TCP/IP address to the clients that are dialing in. By default, the RAS server uses the services of a Dynamic Host Configuration Protocol (DHCP) server to assign the addresses. If your DHCP server has a long lease period, you may want to assign the numbers from a pool of addresses that are given on the server. If you allow the client to request an address, you must configure the client stations for all other parameters.

If your clients are having problems connecting, assign a range of addresses to the RAS server. This approach eliminates any problems that are related to the DHCP server and still allows you to prevent clients from requesting specific IP addresses.

Monitoring the RAS Connection

After you make the RAS connection, you can monitor the connection. There is a tool for the client side and for the server side. The following sections look at the Remote Access Admin tool and the Dial-Up Networking Monitor, and examine how they can be used to see what is happening with the connection.

The Remote Access Admin Tool

From the server, you can use the Remote Access Admin tool to monitor the ports. From the Start menu, choose Programs, Administrative tools, RAS Admin to display the Admin tool.

Double-click the server that you want to inspect. A list of the communications ports appears. For every port that is available on the server, you should see the name of the currently connected user and the time when the connection was made.

From here, you can disconnect users, send a message to a single user, or send a message to all the users who are connected to the server. You can also check the Port Status. This area displays all the connection information for the port.

The Dial-Up Networking Monitor

The Dial-Up Networking Monitor application on the client side enables you to check the status of the communications. The monitor has three tabs.

The Status Tab

The Status tab provides basic information about the connection. From here, you have the option to hang up the connection or to view details about the connection.

The Details tab provides detailed information about the names of the clients (using the service) on the network.

The Summary Tab

The Summary tab summarizes all the connections that the client currently has open. This information is most useful when you have multiple connections.

The Preferences Tab

The Preferences tab enables you to control the settings for Dial-Up Networking. The options that you can set on this tab break down into two main areas. You can control when a sound is played and how the Dial-Up Networking monitor will look.

FURTHER REVIEW

CONFIGURE A RAS SERVER AND DIAL-UP NETWORKING FOR USE ON A TCP/IP NETWORK

What Is RAS?

Simply put, RAS (Remote Access Service) is an add-on service that combines networking protocols with telecommunications. RAS is both a service and a client and is a key feature of the Windows NT Operating System. Through RAS, a modem is emulated as network adapters such that network protocols such as IPX, NetBEUI, and IPX are communicated through a device as if it were a network board.

Installing the RAS Server

Follow these steps to install RAS:

1. Open the Network Setting dialog box (Start, Settings, Control Panel, Network).
2. From the Services tab, choose Add.
3. Choose Remote Access Service and then click OK.
4. When prompted, enter the path to the Windows NT source files.
5. RAS asks you for the device that it should use at that point. (This includes ISDN and X.25.)
6. When the Remote Access Setup dialog box opens, click Continue.
7. From the Network settings dialog box, click Close.
8. When prompted, shut down and restart your system.

CHAPTER SUMMARY

A key point regarding TCP/IP is its capability to function with virtually any network adapter, including those that are emulated. The chapter focused on Windows NT and its built-in functionality for operating as a network via remote connectivity such as Dial-Up Networking. Windows NT embeds adapters for direct access by the operating system or any of its subcomponents. By allowing emulated network adapters, ISDN may be applied such that full network functionality is available in dial-up systems.

CHAPTER REVIEW

REVIEW QUESTIONS

Note: The additional Chapter Review section that ends each chapter is unique to this member of the *New Riders TestPrep, Second Edition* series. We've included it to more fully and fairly cover the unique aspects of TCP/IP in relation to its mastery in preparation for MCSE examination.

1. **Where can you enable a log that will record all the communications between the modem and the system?**
    A. In the Telephony API Advanced options
    B. In the RAS Administration tool under Advanced options
    C. In the Modem Advanced Properties
    D. In the Port Settings Advanced dialog box

2. **Can the Telephony API be set to turn off call waiting?**
    A. Yes
    B. No
    C. Only by the anonymous account
    D. Only by the IUSR_computername account

3. **What types of security does the RAS Server accept?**
    A. Clear text
    B. Kerberos
    C. Shiva
    D. Microsoft

4. **How do you create a shortcut to a phonebook entry?**
    A. From the RAS administrator
    B. From the Dial-Up Networking icon
    C. From the RAS Administrator
    D. By using drag and drop

5. **What do you have to change in order to use a different DNS for a phonebook entry?**
    A. Change the Dial-Up TCP/IP Networking properties.
    B. Change the TCP/IP properties.
    C. Change the settings in RAS Administrator.
    D. Dial-Up Networking will always use the default.

6. **If your dial-in server requires you to log on and the logon cannot be scripted, what can you do?**
    A. Use NT logon.
    B. Bring up a terminal window.
    C. Use Client Services for Netware.
    D. You will not be able to dial in.

7. **How can the Dial-Up Networking Monitor be displayed? Select all that apply.**
    A. As an icon on the taskbar (beside the clock)

B. As a regular icon on the taskbar

C. As a window

D. As an animated GIF

8. What does Autodial do for you?

A. Allows you to dial users from the User Manager

B. Allows you to connect to your ISP using Windows Messaging

C. Reconnects network resources when accessed

D. Automatically dials at a given time

9. Which events can cause the Dial-Up Networking Monitor to make a sound?

A. Connection

B. Errors

C. Program starts

D. Program terminations

10. From where can you grant a user dial-in permissions? Select all that apply.

A. From the command prompt

B. From the User Manager

C. From the RAS Administrator

D. From Server Manager

11. You have been tasked by your company to provide Remote access. One member of your team suggests using the Internet so that users with dial-up connections to ISP can connect to it and then to the company. For speed, these users can take advantage of using multiple lines because the company has a T1 connection. Your boss says a buzzword: PPTP. What is the purpose of PPTP?

A. New form of the PPP protocol

B. Allows tuned connections

C. Allows secured connections across the Internet

D. Allows the user to dial in using more than one line

12. You are attempting to configure a test machine for access to your network. You have completed all required installation procedures for PPTP, and have begun testing. When monitoring throughput, your coworker does not see your client. How does PPTP show up in the Remote Access Admin?

A. RPN

B. VPN

C. SPN

D. DPN

ANSWER KEY

1. C
2. A
3. A-D
4. B
5. A
6. B
7. A-B-C
8. C
9. A-B
10. B-C
11. C
12. B

REVIEW ANSWERS

1. Where can you enable a log that will record all the communications between the modem and the system?

C. In the Modem Advanced Properties

1. CORRECT ANSWER: C

The advanced modem properties enable a user to record communications between a modem and a computer. This functionality is useful for troubleshooting faults, and events that cause a line to drop and so forth. However, the advance properties is not intended as a security device to trace user activities.

2. Can the Telephony API be set to turn off call waiting?

A. Yes

2. CORRECT ANSWER: A

The Telephone API can be set to dial any prefix or suffix that you specify. Assuming that you have the ability through your phone company to turn off call waiting, this can be accomplished. These settings are made in the control panel.

3. What types of security does the RAS Server accept?

A. Clear text

D. Microsoft

3. CORRECT ANSWERS: A-D

The RAS service is limited to Clear Text and Microsoft's Encryption, which is available through any Microsoft Client. The clear text allows compatibility with dial-up with other operating systems such as OS/2 and UNIX.

4. How do you create a shortcut to a phonebook entry?

B. From the Dial-Up Networking icon

4. CORRECT ANSWER: B

While looking in the Dial-Up networking folder, if you use the mouse to right-click on any entry, you can create a shortcut. This shortcut is placed on the desktop by default.

5. What do you have to change in order to use a different DNS for a phonebook entry?

A. Change the Dial-Up TCP/IP Networking properties

5. CORRECT ANSWER: A

The dial-up networking properties are on a per-entry basis. For any entry, review the dial-up networking properties to make modifications.

6. If your dial-in server requires you to log on and the logon cannot be scripted, what can you do?

B. Bring up a terminal window.

6. CORRECT ANSWER: B

When a script cannot automate a process and the dial-up networking is not fully functional with the Microsoft Logon, you must use a terminal window. This window provides access to a text screen in which you can manually perform logon functions.

7. How can the Dial-Up Networking Monitor be displayed? Select all that apply.

A. As an icon on the taskbar (beside the clock)

B. As a regular icon on the taskbar

C. As a window

7. CORRECT ANSWERS: A-B-C

The Dial-Up Networking Monitor is used to manage current RAS connections. Essentially, it can appear on the Taskbar, as an icon next to the clock or as a window. The icon on the Taskbar is simply an option, whereas an open window is used to display connections.

8. What does Autodial do for you?

C. Reconnects network resources when accessed

8. CORRECT ANSWER: C

As a toll saver, Windows NT has the capability to disconnect from a network and then reconnect on demand by using the RAS Autodial feature.

9. Which events can cause the Dial-Up Networking Monitor to make a sound?

A. Connection

B. Errors

9. CORRECT ANSWERS: A-B

When a connection is initialized or when an error occurs, the Dial-Up Networking can create a sound. This sound alerts the system's user of a critical event that is transpiring.

10. From where can you grant a user dial-in permissions? Select all that apply.

B. From the User Manager

C. From the RAS Administrator

10. CORRECT ANSWERS: B-C

Both the RAS Manager and the User Manager can be used to set user permission for dial-in. If a user is not granted rights, he can still connect, but will be disconnected upon entering his credentials.

11. You have been tasked by your company to provide Remote access. One member of your team suggests using the Internet so that users with dial-up connections to ISP can connect to it and then to the company. For speed, these users can take advantage of using multiple lines because the company has a T1 connection. Your boss says a buzzword: PPTP. What is the purpose of PPTP?

C. Allows secured connections across the Internet

11. CORRECT ANSWER: C

PPTP is Microsoft's support protocol for a Virtual Private Network connection created securely over the Internet. Before PPTP will work with many implementations, the firewalls and proxy servers (with inbound packet filters) may require additional configuration.

12. You are attempting to configure a test machine for access to your network. You have completed all required installation procedures for PPTP, and have begun testing. When monitoring throughput, your coworker does not see your client. How does PPTP show up in the Remote Access Admin?

B. VPN

12. CORRECT ANSWER: B

Any links via PPTP appear in the Remote Access Administrator as VPN (Virtual Private Network). The key is that the connection is VPN, whereas the protocol is PPTP (which operates over TCP/IP).

CHAPTER 9

Monitoring and Optimization

Perhaps the most important duty of maintaining a network is monitoring and optimization. When a network is installed, typically it is designed with certain capacities and applications in mind. As time progresses and different needs arise, the usage of the network changes. After a short period of time, these networks can lose footing as to their functionality and manageability.

This chapter emphasizes the monitoring of a network, how adjustments should be made, and those tools that are available to assist in the process. While reading this section, be sure to note how TCP/IP standardizes management by allowing common access point to certain data-gathering mechanisms such that management is platform independent.

Objectives

This chapter helps you prepare for the exam by covering the following objectives:

Given a scenario, identify which tool to use to monitor TCP/IP traffic.

- Monitoring TCP/IP traffic is an important part of a network's upkeep. Depending on the situation, different tools will apply.

Configure SNMP.

- SNMP is a key component for external management applications. SNMP's configuration dictates all aspects of control including which systems are informed of errors, security, and so on.

PRACTICE QUESTIONS

GIVEN A SCENARIO, IDENTIFY WHICH TOOL TO USE TO MONITOR TCP/IP TRAFFIC AND CONFIGURE SNMP

1. You're using an NT server. You want to gather TCP/IP protocol statistics and save them to a log file. You will eventually use this log file to export the data so that it can be read in a spreadsheet. Which utility should you use?

A. nbtstat.exe

B. netstat.exe

C. Performance Monitor

D. Network Monitor

2. To gather TCP/IP frames that are received by your Windows NT Server computer and save the data in a file, which utility should you use?

A. netstat.exe

B. Network Monitor

C. Performance Monitor

D. nbtstat.exe

3. You are having problems communicating with a remote system. You decide that you are going to use ARP to verify that you are able to connect to it at a lower level. When you view the ARP table, what hardware address should appear associated with the remote host?

A. Your hardware address

B. The hardware address of the remote host

C. The first interface of the router (default gateway)

D. The second (remote) interface of the router (default gateway)

4. You are unable to communicate with a system that is named according to an alias with your DNS. Upon booting up, your system reports that DHCP was unable to obtain an address. The scope on your DHCP server is activated and contains plenty of addresses and the global configuration contains the proper DNS entry. What utilities should be used to resolve this problem?

A. Windows NT Event Viewer

B. IPCONFIG

C. NETSTAT

D. NBTSTAT

E. NSLOOKUP

5. You are attempting to determine and isolate a connectivity problem to a remote host. Local operations are fine. What utilities should you use to do this?

A. PING

B. ROUTE

C. TRACERT

D. ARP

6. When you are using SNMP in a TCP/IP network across a router with UNIX hosts, Windows NT Servers, and LAN Manager stations, how can SNMP resolve a host name? Choose all that apply.

A. `HOSTS` file

B. `LMHOSTS` file

C. DNS

D. DHCP

E. WINS

7. Why would you install the SNMP Service? Choose all that apply.

A. You want to monitor TCP/IP with Performance Monitor.

B. You want to remotely manage a proxy agent.

C. You want to monitor a Windows NT–based system with a third-party application.

D. You want to set up your computer as an SNMP agent.

8. Which of the following statements regarding the activity of SNMP and its actions is *false*?

A. Reports traps to multiple hosts

B. Responds to requests from multiple hosts

C. Sets up counters in Performance Monitor for SNMP

D. Uses host names and IP addresses to identify source and destination

9. You are attempting to configure the best, quickest path through your network. Your network is equipped with six Windows NT Server computers all configured as static routers. Which utility should you use to identify the path that a packet takes as it passes through the routers?

A. Route.exe

B. Network Monitor

C. tracert.exe

D. netstat.exe

E. ipconfig.exe

10. Through the use of SNMP, you can find out remote management information about which of the following items? Choose all that apply.

A. Hub

B. Router

C. Bridge

D. Windows NT Server

E. Windows 3.1

11. The commands that you are able to implement on the management system side when making requests to the agents consist of which of the following?

A. `get`, `set`, `go`

B. `walk`, `get`, `get-next`

C. `get`, `get-next`, `go`

D. `set`, `get-next`, `get`

12. The message sent by an SNMP agent to warn an SNMP management system of an error or specific event is known as which of the following?

A. Net

B. Trap

C. `get`

D. Warning event

13. Which of the following is the active component of the SNMP system that performs the trap?

A. Management system

B. Agent

C. Alert

D. Monitor

14. Which SNMP operation is instituted by the agent instead of the management system?

A. Walk

B. `set`

C. Trap

D. `get`

15. Part of SNMP has specific objects related to the type of item that the management system is able to make queries against. This part of SNMP is stored on the agent. What is this part of SNMP called?

A. MIIB

B. Management Information Base

C. MHB

D. Management Internet Information Base

16. When setting up an SNMP management system on a Windows NT host machine, what MIBs are supported by default under Windows NT 4.0?

A. Internet MIB I, LAN Manager MIB II, WINS MIB, DHCP MIB

B. Internet MIB II, LAN Manager MIB I, WINS MIB, DHCP MIB

C. Internet MIB II, LAN Manager MIB II, WINS MIB, DHCP MIB

D. Internet MIB II, LAN Manager MIB II, WINS MIB I, DHCP MIB

17. When using an SNMP management system to query an agent, you can find out which of the following when querying the WINS MIB?

A. The number of WINS servers available on your network

B. The number of successful queries made on the WINS proxy server

C. The number of unsuccessful queries processed by the WINS server

D. The number of unsuccessful queries processed by DNS

18. What is the object identifier for a MIB II?

A. iso.org.dod.internet.management.mib2

B. iso.org.dod.internet.management.mibii

C. 1.3.6.2.2

D. 2.2.6.3.1

19. What can you use to extend the MIB architecture to enable developers to create their own MIB libraries?

A. Extension agents

B. Extender agents

C. Additional dynamic link libraries

D. Relay agents

20. A community is a group of hosts running SNMP, to which they all belong and respond to requests from a management system to agents. What is the default community name for all communities?

A. Punic

B. Comm

C. Community

D. Public

21. For SNMP agents and management systems to communicate with each other, they both need to be set up with which of the following names?

A. Public

B. Unity

C. Group

D. Community

22. When setting up security in SNMP, what is the most secure option you can select without limiting the potential for additional communities?

A. Have a community name other than public, select Only Accept SNMP Packets from These Hosts, and set a trap to alert invalid inquiries.

B. Have a community name of public, select Only Accept SNMP Packets from These Hosts, and set a trap to alert invalid inquiries.

C. Have a community name of public and select Accept SNMP Packets from These Hosts.

D. Have a community name other than public, select Not Only Accept SNMP Packets from These Hosts, and set a trap to ignore invalid inquiries.

23. If you are having problems with SNMP, where in Windows NT should you look?

A. Event Viewer in Windows NT Administrative Tools

B. Performance Monitor

C. The SNMP log

D. The System log

24. Which agent services are enabled by default when setting up the Windows NT SNMP agent?

A. Internet

B. Physical

C. End-to-end

D. Application

25. Which utility in the Windows NT Resource Kit enables you to check whether the SNMP Service is configured correctly and working with the SNMP management system?

A. SNMPCHECK

B. SNMPSTAT

C. SNMPUTIL

D. SNMPMANG

ANSWER KEY

1. C	8. C	15. B	22. A
2. B	9. C	16. C	23. A
3. C	10. A-B-C-D	17. C	24. A-C-D
4. A	11. D	18. B	25. C
5. A-B-C	12. B	19. A	
6. A-B-C-E	13. B	20. D	
7. A-C-D	14. C	21. D	

ANSWERS & EXPLANATIONS

GIVEN A SCENARIO, IDENTIFY WHICH TOOL TO USE TO MONITOR TCP/IP TRAFFIC AND CONFIGURE SNMP

1. You're using an NT server. You want to gather TCP/IP protocol statistics and save them to a log file. You will eventually use this log file to export the data so that it can be read in a spreadsheet. Which utility should you use?

C. Performance Monitor

1. CORRECT ANSWER: C

Performance Monitor is used to gather and monitor statistics. This utility has the capability to log and export statistics for use in a spreadsheet. The next best answer would have been Network Monitor; however, the data read by this utility is not statistical, rather it grants a user the ability to view information directly from a packet.

2. To gather TCP/IP frames that are received by your Windows NT Server computer, and save the data in a file, which utility should you use?

B. Network Monitor

2. CORRECT ANSWER: B

Network Monitor is used in the same regard as a network sniffer. It has the capability to read data directly from the network line regardless of its destination. Also, this data can be stored for later review.

Monitoring and Optimization Utilities

Monitoring and optimization require tools that are capable of performing certain tasks in order to be successful. Windows NT is shipped with a number of utilities that are available for this purpose. Although additional products can be added from third-party or resource kits, you should primarily focus on those that pertain to the core product only.

Optimization changes are made primarily through the Registry Editor (`Regedt32.exe` and `Regedit`), whereas two other tools are used primarily for monitoring TCP/IP traffic:

- Performance Monitor
- Network Monitor

There are a number of other utilities that do not perform actual monitoring but can be used to gather configuration and statistical information. You must know what these utilities offer when compared to Performance Monitor and Network Monitor, and when you would use each one. These utilities are discussed in the later section "Other Utilities."

Performance Monitor

The Performance Monitor is NT's all-around tool for monitoring a system using statistical measurements called *counters*. It has the capability to collect data on both hardware and software components, called *objects*, and its primary purpose is to establish a baseline from which everything can be judged. It offers the capability to check/monitor/identify the following:

- The demand for resources
- Bottlenecks in performance
- The behavior of individual processes
- The performance of remote systems
- The generation of alerts to exception conditions
- The exportation of data for analysis

Components of a system are represented as *objects*. Every object has *attributes*. And each attribute has *counters*. If, for example, more than one device such as a NIC or hard disk exists, each object is then broken down by instance. As one of your main concerns, you should be familiar with the ones for the Paging File object—`%Usage` and `%Usage Peak`, which will determine whether a paging file is reaching its maximum size.

▼ NOTE

To get numerical statistics, use the Report (columnar) view. To see how counters change over a period of time, use the Log feature. To spot abnormalities that occur in data over a period of time, use the Chart view.

Establishing Alerts with Performance Monitor

To monitor a number of servers and be alerted if a counter exceeds a specified number, create one Performance Monitor alert for each server on your workstation. Enter your username in the Net Name on the Alert Options dialog box (below the Send Network Message check box) and you will be alerted when the alert conditions arise. Only one name can be placed here; that name can be of a user or group, but cannot be multiple users or groups.

When monitoring over long periods of time, a log file should be used. This offers the advantage of a track record that can be compared on a day-to-day basis. The main issue with the chart is an inability to follow trends after the information begins to refresh.

If you are monitoring a number of performance counters and that monitoring is slowing down other operations on your workstation, the best remedy is to increase the monitoring interval or perform the monitoring from a separate station on the network. The majority of the counters that you will be working with will include Network Interface, ICMP, IP, TCP, UDP, DHCP, WINS, and NBT Connections. For most administrators, the average and maximums of each counter are the most critical pieces of data. The maximums usually are best calculated over time (history) or in terms of a device's capacity.

To tune or optimize Windows NT, you will need to be able to look at the performance of the server on many different levels.

▼ NOTE

There are two important pieces of knowledge to remember: You must install the Network Monitor Agent to be able to see several of the network performance counters, and you must install SNMP service in order to gather TCP/IP statistics.

Network Monitor

Network Monitor is a Windows tool that enables you to see network traffic that is sent or received by a Windows NT computer. Network Monitor is included with Windows NT 4.0, but must be installed to be active.

To install Network Monitor, select Control Panel, Network, and then add the Network Monitor Tools and Agent from the Services tab. The version of Network Monitor that comes with Windows NT 4.0 is a simple version: It captures traffic only for the local machines (incoming and outgoing traffic).

Microsoft's System Management Server, a network management product, comes with a more complete version of Network Monitor that enables you to capture packets on the local machine for the entire local network segment. Both versions (the NT and SMS versions) allow you to capture the packets that are flowing into and out of your computer. The full version that comes with SMS will also allow you extra functionality such as the ability to capture all packets on the local network or on remote networks, to edit those packets, and to derive statistics about protocols and users on the network.

There are two pieces to the Network Monitor: the Agent that captures the data, and the Monitor Tool, which can be used to view the data. You also can filter out traffic that isn't important to the troubleshooting process.

The Network Monitor can be used to diagnose more complex connectivity issues by allowing you to see the actual packets that are flowing on the network, verifying which steps are being used to resolve names or which port numbers are being used to connect. These are considered more complex connectivity issues because several machines may be involved on several networks. Handling these issues is much more difficult than determining connectivity between two systems.

▼ NOTE

Filters allow you to limit what you are viewing and to keep the data from being overwhelming. The most commonly used filters are `INCLUDE` and `EXCLUDE`, which capture or avoid capturing (respectively) specific data. The Network Monitor included with Windows NT Server can monitor only the specific system on which it is installed, unlike the Network Monitor in SMS, which can monitor other systems on the network.

3. You are having problems communicating with a remote system. You decide that you are going to use ARP to verify that you are able to connect to it at a lower level. When you view the ARP table, what hardware address should appear associated with the remote host?

C. The first interface of the router

3. CORRECT ANSWER: C

When sending to a remote client, messages are in fact sent to the local router. Therefore, the MAC address of the router would be used to represent any remote system.

Other Utilities

You can use a number of tools to help troubleshoot and isolate the source of TCP/IP problems. Each tool gives you a different view of the process used to resolve an IP address to a hardware address, and then route the IP packet to the appropriate destination. As a general rule of thumb, however, the following items apply to the tools listed in this section:

- If TCP/IP cannot communicate from a Microsoft host to a remote host system, the utilities discussed in this chapter will not work correctly.
- If the systems are on different subnets and cannot communicate, remember that TCP/IP requires routing to communicate between subnets.
- If the systems were previously able to communicate but can no longer do so, suspect either your router(s) or changes in software configuration.
- Utilities that require usernames and passwords on the remote host need user accounts on the remote system. If you have an account on a Windows NT system, the remote host system does not know or care. Trust relationships are not the same as achieving connectivity.
- On Windows NT computers, never forget to consult the Event Viewer. Messages that are out of the ordinary often provide valuable clues about the cause of a problem.

ARP

After the name has been resolved to an IP address, your computer must resolve the IP address to a MAC address. This is handled by the Address Resolution Protocol (ARP).

ARP, as a utility, can be used to see the entries in the address resolution table, which maps network card addresses (MAC addresses) to IP addresses. You can check whether the IP addresses you believe should be in the table are there and whether they are mapped to the correct computers. You do not usually know the MAC addresses of the hosts on your network. However, if you cannot contact a host, or if a connection is made to an unexpected host, you can check this table with the arp command to begin isolating which host is actually assigned an IP address.

The ARP utility enables you to view the addresses that have been resolved with the following syntax options:

```
C:\>arp /?Displays and modifies the IP-to-Physical
➥address
translation tables used by address resolution
➥protocol (ARP).

ARP -s inet_addr eth_addr [if_addr]
ARP -d inet_addr [if_addr]
ARP -a [inet_addr] [-N if_addr]


 -at             Displays current ARP entries by
                 interrogating the current protocol
                 data. If inet_addr is specified, the
                 IP and Physical addresses for only
                 the specified computer are dis-
                 played. If more than one network
                 interface uses ARP, entries for
                 each ARP table are displayed.
 -g              Same as -a.
 inet_addr       Specifies an internet address.
 -N if_addr      Displays the ARP entries for the
                 network interface specified by
                 if_addr.
 -d              Deletes the host specified by
                 inet_addr.
 -s              Adds the host and associates the
                 Internet address inet_addr with
                 the Physical address eth_addr.
                 The Physical address is given as
                 6 hexadecimal bytes separated by
                 hyphens. The entry is permanent.
 eth_addr        Specifies a physical address.
 if_addr         If present, this specifies the
                 Internet address of the interface
                 that has the address translation
                 table that should be modified. If
                 not present, the first applicable
                 interface will be used.
```

4. You are unable to communicate with a system that is named according to an alias with your DNS. Upon booting up, your system reports that DHCP was unable to obtain an address. The scope on your DHCP server is activated and contains plenty of addresses and the global configuration contains the proper DNS entry. What utilities should be used to resolve this problem?

A. Windows NT Event Viewer

4. CORRECT ANSWER: A

When a client is unable to retrieve a DHCP address, typically this is a problem either with the network card not properly loading or another service/driver such as a TCP/IP component. In this case, because no IP information has been gathered, IPCONFIG will not have any information that is of value, NETSTAT will not be able to generate any protocol-specific figures (TCP/IP cannot act without an address), and NBTSTAT will not list any name (no connection could be established). Finally, NSLOOKUP is used to perform queries against a router and would not assist in this problem because without an address, name resolution would not matter.

Event Log

The Event log in Windows NT is used to track events and errors. The System Event log in NT is where all critical system messages are stored—not just those related to TCP/IP.

IPCONFIG

One of the key areas that causes problems with TCP/IP is configuration. Windows NT provides the IPCONFIG utility to allow you to view and verify the configuration of a workstation. The following listing provides a summary of the usage of IPCONFIG.

```
C:\>ipconfig /?Windows NT IP Configurationusage:
➥ipconfig
[/? ¦ /all ¦ /release [adapter] ¦ /renew [adapter]]
     /?          Display this help message.
     /all        Display full configuration
                 ➥information.
     /release    Release the IP address for the
                 ➥specified adapter.
     /renew      Renew the IP address for the
                 ➥specified adapter.
```

The default is to display only the IP address, subnet mask, and default gateway for each adapter bound to TCP/IP.

If no adapter name is specified for `release` and `renew`, the IP address leases for all adapters bound to TCP/IP will be released or renewed.

NBTSTAT

NBTSTAT is a command-line utility that enables you to check the resolution of NetBIOS names to TCP/IP addresses. With NBTSTAT, you can check the status of current NetBIOS sessions. You also can add entries to the NetBIOS name cache from the LMHOSTS file or check your registered NetBIOS name and the NetBIOS scope assigned to your computer, if any.

▼ NOTE

Whereas NETSTAT deals with all the connections that your system has with other computers, NBTSTAT deals with only the NetBIOS connections.

NBTSTAT also allows you to verify that name resolution is taking place by providing a method of viewing the name cache. A number of parameters can be used with the utility, as shown in the following code list.

```
C:\>nbtstat /?
Displays protocol statistics and current TCP/IP
➥connections using NBT
(NetBIOS over TCP/IP).
NBTSTAT [-a RemoteName] [-A IP address] [-c] [-n]
        [-r] [-R] [-s] [-S] [interval] ]
  -a   (adapter status) Lists the remote machine's
                        name table given its name
  -A   (Adapter status) Lists the remote machine's
                        name table given its IP
                        address.
  -c   (cache)          Lists the remote name cache
                        including the IP addresses
  -n   (names)          Lists local NetBIOS names.
  -r   (resolved)       Lists names resolved by
                        broadcast and via WINS
  -R   (Reload)         Purges and reloads the
                        remote cache name table
  -S   (Sessions)       Lists sessions table with
                        the destination IP addresses
  -s   (sessions)       Lists sessions table con-
                        verting destination IP
                        addresses to host names via
                        the hosts file.

  RemoteName   Remote host machine name.
  IP address   Dotted decimal representation of the
               IP address.
```

```
interval    Redisplays selected statistics,
            pausing interval seconds between each
            display. Press Ctrl+C to stop redis-
            playing statistics.
```

NETSTAT

NETSTAT is a command-line utility that enables you to check the status of current IP connections. Executing NETSTAT without switches displays protocol statistics and current TCP/IP connections.

After you have determined that your base-level communications are working, you will need to verify the services on your system. This involves looking at the services that are listening for incoming traffic and/or verifying that you are creating a session with a remote station. The `NETSTAT` command will allow you to do this.

A number of parameters can be used with the utility, as shown in the following code list.

```
C:\>netstat /?

Displays protocol statistics and current TCP/IP
network connections.

NETSTAT [-a] [-e] [-n] [-s] [-p proto] [-r]
[interval]
 -a          Displays all connections and listening
             ports. (Server-side connections are nor-
             mally not shown.)
 -e          Displays Ethernet statistics. This may
             be combined with the -s option.
 -n          Displays addresses and port numbers in
             numerical form.
 -p proto    Shows connections for the protocol spec-
             ified by proto; proto may be tcp or udp.
             If used with the -s option to display
             per-protocol statistics, proto may be
             tcp, udp, or ip.
 -r          Displays the contents of the routing
             table.
 -s          Displays per-protocol statistics. By
             default, statistics are shown for TCP,
             UDP and IP; the -p option may be used
             to specify a subset of the default.
```

```
interval    Redisplays selected statistics, pausing
            interval seconds between each display.
            Press CTRL+C to stop redisplaying sta-
            tistics. If omitted, netstat will print
            the current configuration information
            once.
```

NSLOOKUP

NSLOOKUP is a command-line utility that enables you to verify entries on a DNS server. You can use NSLOOKUP in two modes: interactive and noninteractive. In interactive mode, you start a session with the DNS server, in which you can make several requests. In noninteractive mode, you specify a command that makes a single query of the DNS server. If you want to make another query, you must type another non-interactive command.

▼ NOTE

One of the key issues in using TCP/IP is the capability to resolve a host name to an IP address—an action usually performed by a DNS server.

A number of parameters can be used with the utility, as shown in the following code list:

```
Usage:  nslookup [-opt ...]
 # interactive mode using default server
nslookup [-opt ...] - server
# interactive mode using 'server'
nslookup [-opt ...] host
# just look up 'host' using default server
nslookup [-opt ...] host server
# just look up 'host' using 'server'
```

5. You are attempting to determine and isolate a connectivity problem to a remote host. Local operations are fine. What utilities should you use to do this?

A. PING

B. ROUTE

C. TRACERT

5. CORRECT ANSWERS: A-B-C

The first step in tracing this kind of issue is to determine whether the remote host can be reached through a utility such as PING. If PING is able to respond, then end-to-end connectivity can be established. If PING does not respond, however, the next step would be to run TRACERT to try to resolve where the problem is occurring. If the fault can be traced down to a Windows NT router, then the `ROUTE` command should be used to view and adjust the routing table.

PING

The `PING` command is one of the most useful commands in the TCP/IP protocol. It sends a series of packets to another system, which in turn sends back a response. This utility can be extremely useful in troubleshooting problems with remote hosts.

The PING utility is used as a command-line program, and accepts the following parameters:

```
Usage: ping [-t] [-a] [-n count] [-l size] [-f] [-i
           ➥TTL] [-v TOS]
           [-r count] [-s count] [[-j host-list] ¦
           ➥[-k host-list]]
           [-w timeout] destination-list
Options:
  -t             Pings the specified host until
                 ➥interrupted
  -a             Resolves addresses to host names
  -n count       Number of echo requests to send.
  -l size        Sends buffer size
  -f             Sets Don't Fragment flag in packet
  -i TTL         Time to Live
  -v TOS         Type of Service
  -r count       Records route for count hops
  -s count       Time stamp for count hops
  -j host-list   Loose source route along host-list
  -k host-list   Strict source route along host-
                 ➥list
  -w timeout     Time-out in milliseconds to wait
                 ➥for each reply
```

The `PING` command indicates whether the host can be reached, and how long it took for the host to send a return packet. On a local area network, the time is indicated as less than 10 milliseconds; across wide area network links, this value can be much greater.

Use PING to resolve connectivity problems. First, verify that your workstation has a properly installed TCP/IP configuration by pinging the loopback address 127.0.0.1. Assuming that this works, your TCP/IP file and driver installation should be okay. Next, PING your local IP address. Assuming this works, you will have verified basic address configuration settings. Do not be misled into thinking that there still may be no problems with the subnet mask. Next, verify that the default gateway is reachable. If your workstation is able to reach this point and in fact you are using PING with the proper address, a problem is more likely due to routers or subnet configurations. Finally, test the remote system by using PING with it. If this fails, you should use TRACERT to trace where the failure is occurring. Note that if you are using a proxy system, PING may not be supported and may appear unreachable even though it actually is reachable.

ROUTE

ROUTE is a command-line utility that enables you to see and add entries to the local routing table. It is sometimes necessary to check how a system will route packets on the network. Normally, your system will simply send all packets to the default gateway, but in cases where you are having problems communicating with a group of computers, the ROUTE command might provide an answer.

A number of parameters can be used with the ROUTE utility, as shown in the following code list.

```
C:\>route
Manipulates network routing tables.
ROUTE [-f] [command [destination] [MASK netmask]
➥[gateway]
[METRIC metric]]
  -f           Clears the routing tables of all
               gateway entries. If this is used in
               conjunction with one of the commands,
               the tables are cleared prior to
               running the command.
  -p           When used with the ADD command, makes
               a route persistent across boots of
               the system. By default, routes are
               not preserved when the system is
               restarted. When used with the PRINT
               command, displays the list of regis-
               tered persistent routes. Ignored for
               all other commands, which always
               affect the appropriate persistent
               routes.

  command      Specifies one of four commands
                 PRINT   Prints a route
                 ADD     Adds a route
                 DELETE  Deletes a route
                 CHANGE  Modifies an existing route
```

`destination`	`Specifies the host.`
`MASK`	`If the MASK keyword is present, the next parameter is interpreted as the netmask parameter.`
`netmask`	`If provided, specifies a subnet mask value to be associated with this route entry. If not specified, it defaults to 255.255.255.255.`
`gateway`	`Specifies gateway`
`METRIC`	`Specifies the metric/cost for the destination`

All symbolic names used for destination are looked up in the network database file `NETWORKS`. The symbolic names for gateway are looked up in the host name database file `HOSTS`.

If the command is `print` or `delete`, wildcards can be used for the destination and gateway, or the gateway argument may be omitted.

6. When you are using SNMP in a TCP/IP network across a router with UNIX hosts, Windows NT Servers and LAN Manager stations, how can SNMP resolve a host name? Choose all that apply.

A. **`HOSTS`** file

B. **`LMHOSTS`** file

C. DNS

E. WINS

6. CORRECT ANSWERS: A-B-C-E

SNMP would not use DHCP to resolve a host name; all other choices are correct—in fact, they are all services or features for name resolution.

7. Why would you install the SNMP Service? Choose all that apply.

A. You want to monitor TCP/IP with Performance Monitor.

C. You want to monitor a Windows NT–based system with a third-party application.

D. You want to set up your computer as an SNMP agent.

7. CORRECT ANSWERS: A-C-D

The SNMP Service should be used if you want to monitor TCP/IP with Performance Monitor, monitor a Windows NT–based system with a third-party application, or set up your computer as an SNMP agent. The basic idea of SNMP is that if you desire to monitor an object, installing SNMP for an item will allow you to do so.

8. Which of the following statements regarding the activity of SNMP and its actions is *false*?

C. Sets up counters in Performance Monitor for SNMP

8. CORRECT ANSWER: C

SNMP does not set up counters in Performance Monitor; all other statements are true. In fact, installing SNMP enables performance monitor to observe additional counters which are not available without SNMP (and TCP/IP, of course).

SNMP (Overview)

The SNMP protocol enables TCP/IP to export information to troubleshooting tools such as Performance Monitor or to other third-party tools. By itself, SNMP does not report any troubleshooting information. If you are using tools that depend on SNMP, however, you cannot see all the information available from these tools until you install SNMP. To install SNMP, select Control Panel, Network, and then add SNMP from the Services tab.

The SNMP service is an additional component of Windows NT TCP/IP software. SNMP includes the four supported MIBs; each is a dynamic-link library and can be loaded and unloaded as needed. SNMP provides SNMP agent services to any TCP/IP host running SNMP management software. It also performs the following tasks:

- Reports specific happenings, such as traps, to the management systems
- Responds to requests for information from multiple hosts
- Can be set up on any system running Windows NT and TCP/IP
- Sets up special counters in Performance Monitor that can be used to monitor the TCP/IP performance related to SNMP
- Uses host names and IP addresses to recognize which hosts it receives, and requests information

The SNMP service can be installed for the following reasons:

- You want to monitor TCP/IP with Performance Monitor.
- You want to monitor a Windows NT–based system with a third-party application.
- You want to set up your computer as an SNMP agent.

9. You are attempting to configure the best, quickest path through your network. Your network is equipped with six Windows NT Server computers all configured as static routers. Which utility should you use to identify the path that a packet takes as it passes through the routers?

C. tracert.exe

9. CORRECT ANSWER: C

TRACERT (trace route) is a standard TCP/IP utility that is used to track the course of a packet as it progresses though a network. Although this command can be used to troubleshoot a connection fault, it also is useful in determining a network path. None of the other answers have any bearing on the type of functionality. You could load Network Monitor and trace a packet, but it would hardly be worth the effort when other utilities do this with far greater efficiency. You could look at the routing table with the `ROUTE` command, but would still require testing. Neither NETSTAT nor IPCONFIG has any functionality to assist in this type of troubleshooting. Finally, PING could be used to determine path timings, but it is not useful for showing a path to a target.

TRACERT

TRACERT is a command-line utility that enables you to verify the route to a remote host. Execute `tracert` *`hostname`*, where *`hostname`* is the computer name or IP address of the computer whose route you want to trace. TRACERT will return the different IP addresses through which the packet was routed to reach the final destination. The results also include the number of hops needed to reach the destination. Execute TRACERT without any options to see a help file that describes all the TRACERT switches.

The TRACERT utility determines the intermediary steps involved in communicating with another IP host. It provides a road map of all the routing an IP packet takes to get from host A to host B.

A number of parameters can be used with the utility, as shown in the following code list.

```
Usage: tracert [-d] [-h maximum_hops] [-j host-list]
➥[-w timeout]
target_name
Options:
  -d                  Does not resolve addresses to
                      ➥host names
  -h maximum_hops     Maximum number of hops to
                      ➥search for target
  -j host-list        Loose source route along host-
                      ➥list
  -w timeout          Wait time-out milliseconds for
                      ➥each reply
```

As does the `PING` command, `TRACERT` returns the amount of time required for each routing hop.

10. Through the use of SNMP, you can find out remote management information about which of the following items? Choose all that apply.

A. Hub

B. Router

C. Bridge

D. Windows NT Server

10. CORRECT ANSWERS: A-B-C-D

You cannot find remote management information on Windows NT Workstation; all other choices are correct. Windows NT Workstation is not a monitorable object as it does not have an SNMP agent. However, Windows NT workstation can be used to monitor SNMP activities.

SNMP

Simple Network Management Protocol (SNMP) is part of the TCP/IP protocol suite. It corresponds to the Application layer in the Internet Protocol suite.

SNMP enables network administrators to remotely troubleshoot and monitor hubs, routers, printers, switches, remote access devices, and virtually any object that uses TCP/IP. Much of SNMP is defined within RFCs 1157 and 1212, although other RFCs are relevant. SNMP can be found, along with other RFCs, on various Web sites, including **http://ds.internic.net**. You can also do a search on SNMP or RFC and find more specific information related to a specific part of SNMP—for example, on just ethernet and SNMP.

SNMP enables you to obtain information about remote devices without having to be at the device itself. SNMP can be a very useful tool if understood and used properly. You can find a wide variety of information about these devices, depending on the device itself, of course. Some examples include the following:

- IP address of a router
- Number of open files
- Amount of hard drive space available
- Version number of a Windows NT host

Before you set up SNMP, you need the IP address or host names of the systems that will be the initiators or those that will respond to the requests. Microsoft's SNMP Service uses the regular Windows NT host name resolution, such as HOSTS, DNS, WINS, and LMHOSTS. Therefore, if you are using one of these resolution methods, add the correct host name to IP address resolution for the computers that you are setting up with SNMP.

The types of systems on which you can find data include the following:

- Mainframes
- Gateways and routers
- Hubs and bridges
- Windows NT Servers
- LAN Manager servers
- SNMP agents

SNMP uses a distributed architecture design to facilitate its properties. That is, various parts of SNMP are spread throughout the network to complete the task of collecting and processing data to provide remote management.

Because SNMP is a distributed system, you can spread out the management of it in different locations so as not to overtax any one PC and for multiple management functionality.

An SNMP Service by Microsoft enables a machine running Windows NT to transfer its current condition (send a fault alert) to a computer running an SNMP management system. However, sending fault messages is performed only on the agent side, not the management tools. Various third-party management utilities are available, including the following:

- IBM NetView
- Sun Net Manager
- Hewlett-Packard OpenView

EXAM TIP

The management utilities are not included on the Microsoft exam.

SNMP Agents and Management

SNMP has two main parts: the agent system and the management system.

- The management station is the centralized location from which you can manage SNMP.
- The agent station is the piece of equipment from which you are trying to extract data.

11. The commands that you are able to implement on the management system side when making requests to the agents consist of which of the following?

D. `set`, `get-next`, `get`

11. CORRECT ANSWER: D

Agent commands consist of `set`, `get-next`, and `get`. These are simple commands that all Management systems are able to issue to agents. The most common commands are `get` and `get-next`. In certain cases, the `set` command is issued to define a parameter to a read/write object.

12. The message sent by an SNMP agent to warn an SNMP management system of an error or specific event is known as which of the following?

B. Trap

12. CORRECT ANSWER: B

A trap is a message sent to warn of an error. In order for this process to work correctly, the IP address of a management system should be specified during SNMP setup so that the trap is set as a directed message.

The SNMP Management System

The management system is the key component for obtaining information from the client. You need at least one management system to even be able to use the SNMP Service. The management system is responsible for requesting the information. There is a certain number of questions it can ask each device, depending upon the type of device. The management system is a computer running one of the various software components mentioned earlier (HP Openview, Tivoli, and so on).

In addition, certain commands can be given specifically at the management system. These are generic commands, not specific to any type of management system:

- **`get`**—Requests a specific value. For example, it can query how many active sessions are open.
- **`get-next`**—Requests the next object's value. For example, you can query a client's ARP cache and then ask for each subsequent value.
- **`set`**—Changes the value on an object that has the properties of read/write. For security reasons, this command is not often used; in addition, most objects have a read-only attribute.

Usually, you have only one management system running the SNMP Service per group of hosts. This group is known as a *community*. Sometimes, however, you may want multiple management systems. Some of these reasons are addressed in the following list:

- You may want multiple management systems to send different queries to the same agents.
- There might be different management sites for one community.
- As the network grows and becomes more complex, you may need to help differentiate certain aspects of your community.

13. Which of the following is the active component of the SNMP system that performs the trap?

B. Agent

13. CORRECT ANSWER: B

The agent is the active component of SNMP that performs the trap. The trap is generated when a fault is detected or if a threshold is passed. Trap messages are part of standard SNMP protocol and do not require additional components, with the exception of a location to which to send a message.

14. Which SNMP operation is instituted by the agent instead of the management system?

C. Trap

14. CORRECT ANSWER: C

In the event that an error occurs or a threshold is exceeded, a trap message will be generated by the agent at a device. The trap message is typically sent as a directed message to a designated management system.

The SNMP Agent

You have seen so far what the SNMP management side is responsible for and can specifically do. For the most part, the management side is the active component for getting information. The SNMP *agent*, on the other hand, is responsible for complying with the requests and responding to the SNMP manager accordingly. Generally, the agent is a router, server, or hub. The agent is usually a passive component responding only to a direct query.

In one particular instance, however, the agent is the initiator, acting on its own without a direct query. This special case is called a *trap*. A trap is set up from the management side on the agent. But the management does not need to go to the agent to find out whether the trap information has been tripped. The agent sends an alert to the management system when the event has occurred. Except in this instance, the agent is passive.

A trap is similar to a father and son fishing with a net on a stream. The dad sets up the net on the stream. The holes in the net are just the right size for catching a certain type and size of fish. The dad then goes downstream to set up more, leaving his son to tend to the net. When the fish comes along, it gets caught in the net and the son runs to tell his father.

The stream is the traffic going through the router. The net is the trap set by the management system. The son is the agent responding to the trap and running to tell his father, the management, that a fish has been caught, without the father having to go back and check on his trap. The special fish that is caught might be an alert that a particular server's hard drive is full or that there is a duplicate IP address. Although this analogy is rough, it helps illustrate the basic idea. What happens, however, if a spare tire comes down the stream and gets caught in the trap? Sometimes invalid packets can set off the trap without it being what you are looking for. These are rare events, and the traps are very specific in what they are looking for.

15. Part of SNMP has specific objects related to the type of item that the management system is able to make queries against. This part of SNMP is stored on the agent. What is this part of SNMP called?

B. Management Information Base

15. CORRECT ANSWER: B

The Management Information Base, or MIB, is what queries are made against. Depending on the device, some devices will have the agent gather statistics and perform storage functions. However, other devices inherently store this information, which can be read directly from the device.

16. When setting up an SNMP management system on a Windows NT host machine, what MIBs are supported by default under Windows NT 4.0?

C. Internet MIB II, LAN Manager MIB II, WINS MIB, DHCP MIB

16. CORRECT ANSWER: C

By default, Windows NT includes support for Internet MIB II, LAN Manager MIB II, WINS MIB, and DHCP MIB. Notice that these are the base services that can be monitored for network functionality. If, for example, you were attempting to monitor data according to a share, you would have to use a specialized tool such as Server Manager. Otherwise, data is concentrated on the statistical information and faults governed by TCP/IP.

Management Information Base (MIB)

The data that the management system requests from an agent is contained in a *Management Information Base (MIB)*, which is a list of questions that the management system can ask. The list of questions depends on what type of device it is asking. The MIB is the database of information that can be queried against. The specific queries that can be asked (or queried against) depend on what type of system it is. The MIB defines what type of objects can be used and what type of information is available about the network device.

A variety of MIB databases can be established. The MIB is stored on the SNMP agent and is similar to the Windows NT Registry in its hierarchical structure. These MIBs are available to both the agents and management system as a reference from which both can retrieve information.

The Microsoft SNMP Service supports the following MIB databases:

- Internet MIB II
- LAN Manager MIB II
- DHCP MIB
- WINS MIB

These databases are discussed in the following sections.

Internet MIB II

Internet MIB II defines 171 objects for fault troubleshooting on the network and configuration analysis. It is defined in RFC 1212, which adds to and overwrites the previous version, Internet MIB I.

LAN Manager MIB II

LAN Manager MIB II defines about 90 objects associated with Microsoft Networking, such as the following:

- Shares
- Users
- Logons
- Sessions
- Statistics

Most of LAN Manager MIB II's objects are set to read-only mode due to the limited security function of SNMP.

DHCP MIB

The DHCP MIB identifies objects that can monitor the DHCP server's actions. It is set up automatically when a DHCP server service is installed and is called DHCPMIB.DLL. It has 14 objects that can be used for monitoring the DHCP server activity, including items such as the following:

- The number of active leases
- The number of failures
- The number of DHCP discover requests received

17. When using an SNMP management system to query an agent, you can find out which of the following when querying the WINS MIB?

C. The number of unsuccessful queries processed by the WINS server

17. CORRECT ANSWER: C

The WINS MIB reports the number of unsuccessful queries processed by the WINS server. This is actually the same information that is available through the WINS manager.

WINS MIB

WINS MIB (WINSMIB.DLL) is a Microsoft-specific MIB relating directly to the WINS server service. It is automatically installed when WINS is set up. It monitors WINS server activity and has approximately 70 objects. It checks such items as the number of resolution requests, success and failure, and the date and time of last database replication.

18. What is the object identifier for a MIB II?

B. iso.org.dod.internet.management.mibii

18. CORRECT ANSWER: B

You will note while examining the structure of the identifier that it reads like a full distinguished Internet name. Because the structure is hierarchical, you will note that this lends flexibility to defining unique names anywhere on a network, including the Internet.

19. What can you use to extend the MIB architecture to enable developers to create their own MIB libraries?

A. Extension agents

19. CORRECT ANSWER: A

Extension agents allow developers to create their own MIB libraries. These agents can be thought of in the same functionality as APIs. Using a standardized format, developers can customize as required data that they need from a device.

MIB Structure

The name space for MIB objects is hierarchical. It is structured in this manner so that each manageable object can be assigned a globally unique name. Certain organizations have the authority to assign the name space for parts of the tree design.

The MIB structure is similar to TCP/IP addresses. You get only one address from the InterNIC and then subnet it according to your needs. You do not have to contact InterNIC to inquire about each address assignment. The same applies here. Organizations can assign names without consulting an Internet authority for every specific assignment. For example, the name space assigned to Microsoft's LAN Manager is 1.3.6.1.4.1.77. More recently, the Microsoft corporation has been assigned 1.3.6.1.4.1.311; any new MIB would then be identified under that branch.

The object identifier in the hierarchy is written as a sequence of labels beginning at the root and ending at the object. It flows down the chart, starting with the International Standards Organization (ISO) and ending with the object MIB II. Labels are separated by periods. The following is an example of this labeling technique.

Object Name	*Object Number*
Object Identifier for MIB II	
Iso.org.dod.internet. management.mibii	1.3.6.2.2.1
Object Identifier for LAN Manager MIB II	
iso.org.dod.internet.private. enterprise.lanmanager	1.3.6.1.4.77

▼ **NOTE**

The name space used here for the object identifiers is completely separate from that used with UNIX domain names.

Microsoft SNMP Service

The SNMP Service is an additional component of Windows NT TCP/IP software. It includes the four supported MIBs; each is a dynamic link library and can be loaded and unloaded as needed. It provides SNMP agent services to any TCP/IP host running SNMP management software. It also performs the following tasks:

- Reports special happenings, such as traps, to multiple hosts
- Responds to requests for information from multiple hosts
- Can be set up on any system running Windows NT and TCP/IP
- Sets up special counters in Performance Monitor that can be used to monitor the TCP/IP performance related to SNMP
- Uses host names and IP addresses to recognize which hosts it receives; requests information

SNMP MIB Architecture

The MIB architecture can be extended to enable developers to create their own MIB libraries, called *extension agents.* Extension agents expand the list of objects that a MIB can report on, making the list not only more expansive but also specifically related to network setup and devices.

Although the Microsoft SNMP Service doesn't include management software, it does have a Microsoft Win32 SNMP Manager Application Programming Interface (API) that works with the Windows Sockets. The API can then be used by developers to create third-party SNMP management utilities.

SNMP uses User Datagram Protocol (UDP port 161) to send and receive messages and IP to route messages.

20. A community is a group of hosts running SNMP, to which they all belong and respond to requests from a management system to agents. What is the default community name for all communities?

D. Public

20. CORRECT ANSWER: D

The public community is the default. Depending on the scope of objects managed and security requirements, it often works best to change the community to represent a managed group. For example, change Network equipment from public to Networkops.

21. For SNMP agents and management systems to communicate with each other, they both need to be set up with which one of the following names?

D. Community

21. CORRECT ANSWER: D

Agents and management systems must have the same community name to communicate with each other.

SNMP Communities

A community is simply a defined group of hosts running the SNMP Service. These usually consist of at least one management system and multiple agents. The idea is to logically organize systems into organizational units for better network management.

Communities are called by a *community name*. This name is case sensitive. The default community name is public and generally all hosts belong to it. Also by default, all SNMP agents respond to any request using the community public name. By using unique community names, however, you can provide limited security and segregation of hosts.

Agents do not accept requests nor respond to hosts that are not from their configured community. Agents can be members of multiple communities at the same time, but they must be explicitly configured as such. This feature enables them to respond to different SNMP managers from various communities.

22. When setting up security in SNMP, what is the most secure option you can select without limiting the potential for additional communities?

A. Have a community name other than public, select Only Accept SNMP Packets from These Hosts, and set a trap to alert invalid inquiries.

22. CORRECT ANSWER: A

The most secure option is to have a community name other than public, select Only Accept SNMP Packets from These Hosts, and set a trap to alert invalid inquiries. If these options are not changed, virtually anyone with an SNMP management program can review network conditions.

Security

There really is no established security with SNMP. The data is not encrypted, and there is no setup to stop someone from accessing the network, discovering the community names and addresses used, and sending fake requests to agents.

A major reason most MIBs are read-only is to prevent unauthorized changes. The best security you can have is to use unique community names. Choose Send Authentication Trap and specify a trap destination; you can also stipulate Only Accept SNMP Packets from These Hosts.

You might also set up traps that let you know whether the agents receive requests from communities or addresses not specified. This way, you can track down unauthorized SNMP activity.

Installing and Configuring SNMP

The SNMP Service can be installed for the following reasons:

- You want to monitor TCP/IP with Performance Monitor.
- You want to monitor a Windows NT–based system with a third-party application.
- You want to set up your computer as an SNMP agent.

The following steps install the SNMP Service, assuming you already have TCP/IP installed and set up. These steps also assume you have administrative privileges to install and utilize SNMP.

1. Click on Start, Settings, Control Panel.
2. Double-click on Network to bring up the Network Properties dialog box.
3. On the Network Settings dialog box, click Add.
4. Click the Services tab and click Add. The Select Network Service dialog box appears.
5. Click SNMP Service and then click OK.

6. Specify the location of the Windows NT distribution files.
7. After the files are copied, the SNMP Service Configuration dialog box appears. The parameters that need to be configured are shown in Table 9.1.

TABLE 9.1 SNMP CONFIGURATION OPTIONS

Parameter	*Definition*
`Community Name`	The community name to which traps are sent. Remember, it is public by default. There must be a management system in that community to receive and request information.
`Trap Destination`	The IP addresses of hosts to which you want the SNMP Service to send traps. Note that you can use IP addresses, host names (as long as they are resolved properly), and IPX addresses.

8. Now click OK to close the SNMP Properties dialog box. Then choose Close to exit the Network properties dialog box. When prompted, restart your computer.

SNMP Security Parameters

There are several options you can set that affect the security of the SNMP agent. By default, the agent will respond to any manager using the community name public. Because this name can be inside or outside of your organization, you should at the very least change the community name.

Table 9.2 describes the options that are available.

TABLE 9.2 SECURITY OPTIONS FOR THE SNMP AGENT

Parameter	*Description*
`Send Authentication Trap`	Sends information back to the trap initiator, responding that the trap failed. This failure could occur because of an incorrect community name or because the host is not specified for service.

Parameter	*Description*
`Accepted Community Names`	When a manager sends a query, a community name is included (this is a list of community names that the agent will respond to).
`Accept SNMP Packets from Any Host`	Responds to any query from any management system in any community.
`Only Accept SNMP Packets from These Hosts`	Responds to only the hosts listed.

23. If you are having problems with SNMP, where in Windows NT should you look?

A. Event Viewer in Windows NT Administrative Tools

23. CORRECT ANSWER: A

The event viewer can be used to determine the cause of a variety of problems. Any service or driver that fails to load will display a red stop sign in the log. Among the various information recorded in the log, SNMP problems will be included.

24. Which agent services are enabled by default when setting up the Windows NT SNMP agent?

A. Internet

C. End-to-end

D. Application

24. CORRECT ANSWERS: A-C-D

Internet, End-to-end, and Application agent services are enabled by default. Note that these agents correspond to the top three layers of the DOD networking model.

SNMP Agent

In some cases, you will configure other aspects of the SNMP agent. These set the type of devices that you will monitor and who is responsible for the system.

The options available on the SNMP configuration screen are as follows:

- The contact name of the person you want to be alerted about conditions on this station—generally, this person is the user of the computer.
- The location is a descriptive field for the computer to help keep track of the system sending the alert.
- The last part of the screen identifies the types of connections/devices this agent will monitor. These include the following:

- **Physical**—You are managing physical devices such as repeaters or hubs.
- **Applications**—Set if the Windows NT computer uses an application that uses TCP/IP. You should place a checkmark in this box every time; just by using SNMP you should have TCP/IP set up.
- **Datalink/Subnetwork**—For managing a bridge.
- **Internet**—When Enable IP Forwarding is turned on, this monitors the Windows NT computer's acting as an IP gateway, or router.
- **End-to-end**—Causes the Windows NT computer to act as an IP host. You should check this box every time because you are most likely an IP host.

Any errors with SNMP will be recorded in the System log. The log records any SNMP activity. Use Event Viewer to look at the errors and to find the problem and possible solutions.

25. Which utility in the Windows NT Resource Kit enables you to check whether the SNMP Service is configured correctly and working with the SNMP management system?

C. SNMPUTIL

25. CORRECT ANSWER: C

SNMPUTIL is included in the Windows NT Resource Kit. Using this utility, you can query an SNMP agent to determine whether it is configured correctly. Depending on the management interface, the MIB information can create difficulties that can be hard to isolate. This utility helps pinpoint problem areas through elimination.

Using the SNMP Utility

The SNMP utility does not come with Windows NT. It is included in the Windows NT Resource Kit and called SNMPUTIL.EXE. Basically, it is a command-line management system utility. It checks that the SNMP Service has been set up and is working correctly. You can also use it to make command calls. You cannot perform full SNMP management from this utility but, as you will see, you would not want to, due to the complex syntax.

The following is the general syntax structure:

```
snmputil command agent community
➥object_identifier_(OID)
```

The following are the commands you can use:

- **`walk`**—Moves through the MIB branch identified by what you have placed in the `object_identifer`
- **`get`**—Returns the value of the item specified by the `object_identifier`
- **`getnext`**—Returns the value of the next object after the one specified by the `get` command

To find out the time the WINS server service began, for example, providing WINS is installed and the SNMP agent is running, you query the WINS MIB with the following command:

```
c:\>snmputil getnext localhost public
➥.1.3.6.1.4.1.311.1.1.1.1
```

In this example, the first part refers to the Microsoft branch: .1.3.6.1.4.1.311 (or iso.org.dod.internet.private.enterprise. microsoft). The last part of the example refers to the specific MIB and object you are querying; .1.1.1.1 (or .software.Wins. Par.ParWinsStartTime). A returned value might appear as follows:

```
Value = OCTET STRING - 01:17:22 on 11:23:1997.<0xa>
```

What SNMP Is Really Doing

The following example tracks a sample of SNMP traffic between a manager and an agent. Remember that in real life you will use management software (such as HP's Openview) that will enable you to see the MIBs and query without knowing all the numbers.

1. The SNMP management system makes a request of an agent using the agent's IP address or host name.

   A. Request sent by the application to UDP port 161.

   B. Host name resolved to an IP address, if host name was used, using host name resolution methods:

localhost, HOSTS file, DNS, WINS, broadcast, LMHOSTS file.

2. SNMP packet gets set up with the listed information inside, and routes the packet on the agent's UDP port 161:

   A. The command for the objects: `get`, `get-next`, `set`

   B. The community name and any other specified data

3. An SNMP agent gets the packet and puts it into its buffer.

   A The community name is checked for validity. If it is not correct or is corrupted, the packet is rejected.

   B. If the community name checks out, the agent checks whether the originating host name or IP address is correct as well. If not, the packet is thrown out.

   C. The inquiry is then passed to the correct DLL as described in the preceding section on MIBs.

   D. The object identifier gets mapped to the specific API and that call gets made.

   E. The DLL sends the data to the agent.

4. The SNMP packet is given to the SNMP manager with the requested information.

FURTHER REVIEW

GIVEN A SCENARIO, IDENTIFY WHICH TOOL TO USE TO MONITOR TCP/IP TRAFFIC AND CONFIGURE SNMP

What Are Monitoring and Optimization?

As you may have guessed, *monitoring* is a process of constantly reviewing statistics and data regarding a network for the purpose of its optimization. The key to monitoring is setting a standard or baseline, then noting when data reveals that the network is not functioning properly. When errors are noted, corrective actions can take place. Additionally, the standards can be used to analyze trends so that future growth and new deployments can be planned. Of course, in this chapter, these actions are referred to as *optimization.*

CHAPTER SUMMARY

The health and serviceability of any network can be judged by its management. While working in TCP/IP, you will note that a number of components, both software and hardware, contain information gathering/reporting functions that allow an administrator to determine where a potential problem will arise. The primary technology behind TCP/IP management is SNMP. Through its capabilities, a network can be monitored and optimized to perform at its best.

CHAPTER REVIEW

REVIEW QUESTIONS

Note: The additional Chapter Review section that ends each chapter is unique to this member of the *New Riders TestPrep, Second Edition* series. We've included it to more fully and fairly cover the unique aspects of TCP/IP in relation to its mastery in preparation for the MCSE examination.

1. **You are using Performance Monitor, but very few TCP/IP statistics are available. How can you increase the number of TCP/IP objects and counters to monitor?**

   A. Install a promiscuous mode adapter card.

   B. Configure the correct default gateway in Performance Monitor.

   C. Bind TCP/IP to the Monitor service.

   D. Install the SNMP service.

2. **TCP/IP is not working. You recall that when Windows NT first booted, the message `A Dependency Service Failed to Start` appeared. What is a possible cause of the problem?**

   A. The SNMP service is not installed.

   B. The network card is not configured correctly.

   C. The secondary WINS server is down.

   D. The PDC of your domain is down.

3. **On an NT computer, where does TCP/IP display its error messages?**

   A. In the TCP/IP log file

   B. In the SNMP log file

   C. In the System log

   D. In the `TCP.ERR` file

4. **Referring to question #3, what tool is used to view these errors?**

   A. Network Monitor

   B. Performance Monitor

   C. Event Viewer

   D. ARP

5. **To see the majority of networking performance counters in Performance Monitor, what must be installed?**

   A. NetBEUI

   B. Network Monitor Agent

   C. Network Monitor Server

   D. TCP/IP

6. **Which protocol handles the IP address-to-MAC address resolution?**

   A. WINS

   B. ARP

   C. DHCP

   D. NBTSTAT

7. **Executing NETSTAT with what parameter will display connections and listening ports, even those ports not currently involved in a connection?**

   A. `-A`

   B. `-s`

C. `-p`

D. `-?`

8. Optimization changes are made primarily through which of the following?

A. Performance Monitor

B. Network Monitor

C. ARP

D. `REGEDT32.EXE`

9. What are the statistical measurements used by Performance Monitor called?

A. Counters

B. Baselines

C. Benchmarks

D. Objects

10. In addition to gathering information, which utility can also be used to release an IP address?

A. Performance Monitor

B. IPCONFIG

C. PING

D. ARP

ANSWER KEY

1. D
2. B
3. C
4. C
5. B
6. B
7. A
8. D
9. A
10. B

REVIEW ANSWERS

1. You are using Performance Monitor, but very few TCP/IP statistics are available. How can you increase the number of TCP/IP objects and counters to monitor?

D. Install the SNMP service.

1. CORRECT ANSWER: D

The SNMP server will install additional counters to monitor. Although you may review these counters with Performance Monitor, a network management console can also be used.

2. TCP/IP is not working. You recall that when Windows NT first booted, the message `A Dependency Service Failed to Start` appeared. What is a possible cause of the problem?

B. The network card is not configured correctly.

2. CORRECT ANSWER: B

A dependency service is one that is required before services above it can load. In this case, if a network adapter can load, then TCP/IP can't be bound to it, and therefore no DHCP information can be requested, and no network services can be accessed.

3. On an NT computer, where does TCP/IP display its error messages?

C. In the System Log

3. CORRECT ANSWER: C

Windows NT will display its error messages in the system log. Additionally, further information may be found in the security and application logs.

4. Referring to question #3, what tool is used to view these errors?

C. Event Viewer

4. CORRECT ANSWER: C

When troubleshooting a system, the first and most practical place to look is the Event Viewer. Services that fail to load or warnings that are listed are often indicators of problems that users are experiencing.

5. To see the majority of networking performance counters in Performance Monitor, what must be installed?

B. Network Monitor Agent

5. CORRECT ANSWER: B

The network monitoring agent opens a number of counters to an administrator. NetBEUI and TCP/IP are both requirements of their respective networks and should be disregarded in this respect. As for the Network Monitoring server, this implies a separate interface rather than additions for Performance Monitor.

6. Which protocol handles the IP address-to-MAC address resolution?

B. ARP

6. CORRECT ANSWER: B

ARP is address resolution protocol. This protocol sends a message to a given IP address to determine its hardware (MAC) address. Another utility, known as RARP, performs this identical operation in reverse—MAC address to IP address.

7. Executing NETSTAT with what parameter will display all connections and listening ports, even those ports not currently involved in a connection?

A. -A

7. CORRECT ANSWER: A

When using NETSTAT with the -A parameter, *all* connections and ports will be listed. Displayed with each connection is the protocol (TCP or UDP) and the state of the connection.

8. Optimization changes are made primarily through which of the following?

D. REGEDT32.EXE

8. CORRECT ANSWER: D

Although a number of changes can occur through utilities such as the Control Panel and various management programs, REGEDT32.EXE is the primary tool for making custom changes to the Registry, which produces optimized results.

9. What are the statistical measurements used by Performance Monitor called?

A. Counters

9. CORRECT ANSWER: A

Performance Monitor can be used to measure throughput and capacities. Each measured item is considered an object. When multiple objects of the same type are present, each object is referenced as instances. Of these, counters are used to measure the aspect of how the object performs.

10. In addition to gathering information, which utility can also be used to release an IP address?

B. IPCONFIG

10. CORRECT ANSWER: B

Under Windows NT and Windows for Workgroups, IPCONFIG can be used to gather IP information, and renew/release DHCP settings. Under Windows 98 and 95, the WINIPCFG utility performs this same function.

CHAPTER 10

Troubleshooting

Perhaps the truest form of testing your knowledge and understanding of TCP/IP is your ability to troubleshoot faults as they occur. Because of the structure of TCP/IP, you will observe that many of the problems and solutions that apply to Windows NT will also apply to other operating systems.

Do not fool yourself into thinking that this is an easy chapter. In fact, you will find that while taking the Microsoft exam, approximately 50% of *all* questions relate to this chapter—some directly, some not. You should note the tools that can be used to locate a problem and the solution required. You should notice that most of the problems either relate to resolution (names to IP addresses, IP address to Mac address), or to the lack of resolution following a procedure.

OBJECTIVES

This chapter helps you prepare for the exam by covering the following objectives:

Diagnose and resolve IP addressing problems.

- TCP/IP is traditionally a manually configured protocol. The main problems that most administrators come across in such cases are related to addressing issues. This chapter will demonstrate how to find these problems and how they should be resolved.

Use Microsoft TCP/IP utilities to diagnose configuration problems.

- Windows NT provides a number of utilities that can be used for informational purposes as well as diagnostics.

Identify which Microsoft TCP/IP utility to use to diagnose IP configuration problems.

- TCP/IP has the potential for a number of configuration errors. Understanding this, Microsoft provides a number of utilities to diagnose IP configuration issues.

continues

OBJECTIVES (continued)

Diagnose and resolve name resolution problems.

- Name resolution is a complex set of tasks that has a high potential for error. Determining the points of failure and resolving them are key to managing a successful and functional network.

PRACTICE QUESTIONS

DIAGNOSE AND RESOLVE IP ADDRESSING PROBLEMS

1. **What are the three main parameters that specify how TCP/IP is configured?**
   A. The IP address
   B. The TCP address
   C. The subnet mask
   D. The default gateway
2. **The three parameters discussed in question #1 are configured through which tab of the Network Properties dialog box?**
   A. Services
   B. Adapters
   C. Protocols
   D. Address
3. **Which of the following specifies the network address and host address of the computer?**
   A. The IP address
   B. The TCP address
   C. The subnet mask
   D. The default gateway
4. **Which of the following is the address of the router?**
   A. The IP address
   B. The TCP address
   C. The subnet mask
   D. The default gateway
5. **The subnet mask specifies what two components of the IP address?**
   A. The network address
   B. The default gateway
   C. The host address
   D. The IP address
6. **What can cause a problem with communication with a client by name but not by IP address?**
   A. The IP address
   B. Static files such as an `LMHOSTS` file or a DNS database
   C. Subnet mask
   D. The default gateway
7. **What can greatly reduce TCP/IP configuration problems?**
   A. WINS Server
   B. WINS Proxy
   C. DHCP Server
   D. PDC
8. **What is the term used to describe addresses available on a DHCP server?**
   A. Pools
   B. Scopes
   C. Ranges
   D. Notes

9. The most important part of a multiple DHCP configuration is to make sure you don't have which of the following in the different scopes? Select the best answer.

A. Duplicate addresses

B. Duplicate pools

C. Duplicate subnets

D. Duplicate default gateways

10. Which of the following best describes the scopes on each DHCP server, in the absence of configuration problems with DHCP addresses, if you use multiple DHCP servers in your environment?

A. Unique to that subnet only

B. For different subnets

C. For no more than two subnets

D. For no subnets

ANSWER KEY

1. A-C-D
2. C
3. A
4. D
5. A-C
6. B
7. C
8. B
9. A
10. B

ANSWERS & EXPLANATIONS

DIAGNOSE AND RESOLVE IP ADDRESSING PROBLEMS

1. What are the three main parameters that specify how TCP/IP is configured?

A. The IP address

C. The subnet mask

D. The default gateway

1. CORRECT ANSWERS: A-C-D

The three main parameters that specify how TCP/IP is configured are the IP address, the subnet mask, and the default gateway. Although your answer may not have included a default gateway, it is required if you are communicating beyond your network. For example, if your department has its own network, you will not be able to communicate with any other network without this value set.

2. The three parameters discussed in question #1 are configured through which tab of the Network Properties dialog box?

C. Protocols

2. CORRECT ANSWER: C

These parameters are configured through the Protocols tab of the Network Properties dialog box. It is important to recognize where configurations are made and the proper settings. If, for example, you were installing an application designed for an earlier version of Windows NT, you might find that you have to augment the documentation to perform a proper installation.

Diagnosing and Resolving IP Addressing Problems

Three main parameters specify how TCP/IP is configured: the IP address, the subnet mask, and the default gateway, which is the address of the router. These parameters are configured through the Protocols tab of the Network Properties dialog box. Although you may receive an IP address from a Dynamic Host Configuration Protocol (DHCP) server, for the moment this discussion focuses on parameters that are manually configured. DHCP-related issues are discussed later in the section "DHCP Client Configuration Problems."

If these three TCP/IP parameters are not configured correctly, you cannot connect with TCP/IP. An incorrect configuration can result from typos; if you type the wrong IP address, subnet mask, or default gateway, you may not connect properly—or you may not be able to connect at all. To illustrate, if you dial the wrong number when making a telephone call, you can't reach the party you're calling. If you read the wrong phone number out of the phone book, you won't ever make a correct call, even if you redial the same number.

Regardless of whether the TCP/IP configuration parameters are wrong because of a typo or a mistaken number, the incorrect parameters affect communications. Different types of problems occur when any one of these parameters has a configuration error.

IP Address Configuration Problems

An incorrect TCP/IP address will almost always cause problems. However, if you configure an IP address that is on the correct subnet, but uses the wrong host ID and is not a duplicate, the client may be able to communicate just fine. On the other hand, if the correct IP address has been entered in a static file or database that resolves host names to IP addresses, such as an LMHOSTS file or a domain name server (DNS) database file, some communication problems can occur. Typically, therefore, an incorrect IP address does cause problems.

Each TCP/IP parameter reacts differently if configured incorrectly. The following sections examine the effects that each TCP/IP parameter can have on IP communications.

3. Which of the following specifies the network address and host address of the computer?

A. The IP address

3. CORRECT ANSWER: A

The IP address specifies the network address and host address of the computer. You should be able to recall that the IP address is the combination of the network and host IDs. The dividing point of which portion of the address is network and which is host is determined by applying the subnet mask.

4. Which of the following is the address of the router?

D. The default gateway

4. CORRECT ANSWER: D

The default gateway is also the common designation of the router's local IP address. Often you will find that terminology differs depending on its application. To most who are not familiar with TCP/IP, the default gateway would be interpreted as a conversion process of source that is used to communicate between two noncompatible systems. In this case, because IP can communicate only with addresses that are local, the router (called a gateway) is used to communicate between two networks with no ability to communicate otherwise.

IP Address

A TCP/IP address has two, or sometimes three, components that uniquely identify the computer to which the address is assigned. At the very least, the IP address specifies the network address and host address of the computer. Also, if you are *subnetting* (using part of the host address to specify a subnet address), a third part of the address specifies the subnet address of the host.

You're likely to encounter the following problems with IP addresses:

- If the incorrect host (for example, 143.168.3.9) sends a message to a local client (for example, 133.168.3.20), the TCP/IP configuration of the sending host indicates that this is a remote address because it doesn't match the network address of the host initiating the communication. The packet won't ever reach the local client, because the address 133.168.3.20 is interpreted as a remote address.
- If a local client (133.168.3.6) sends a message to the incorrect host (143.168.3.9), the message never reaches its intended destination. The message is either routed (if the local client sends the message to the IP address as written) or it stays on the local subnet (if the local client sends it to what should have been the address: 133.168.3.9).

- If the message is routed, the incorrect client does not receive the message because it is on the same segment of the network as the local client.
- If the message is not routed, the message still does not reach the incorrect client because the IP address for the destination host (133.168.3.9) does not match the address as configured on the incorrect client (143.168.3.9).

Figure 10.1 gives an example of an incorrect IP address. In this case, a class A address is used (33.x.x.x). The subnet mask (255.255.0.0) indicates that the second octet is also being used to create subnets. In this case, even though the client has the same network address as the other clients on the same subnet, the client has a different subnet number because the address was typed incorrectly. The incorrect address specifies the wrong subnet ID. The client 33.5.8.4 is on subnet 5, whereas the other clients on the subnet have the address 33.4.x.x. If the client 33.5.8.4 tries to contact other clients on the same subnet, the message is routed because the subnet ID doesn't match the subnet number of the source host. If the client 33.5.8.4 tries to send a message to a remote host, the message is routed; however, the message isn't returned to the client, because the router doesn't handle subnet 5, only subnet 4.

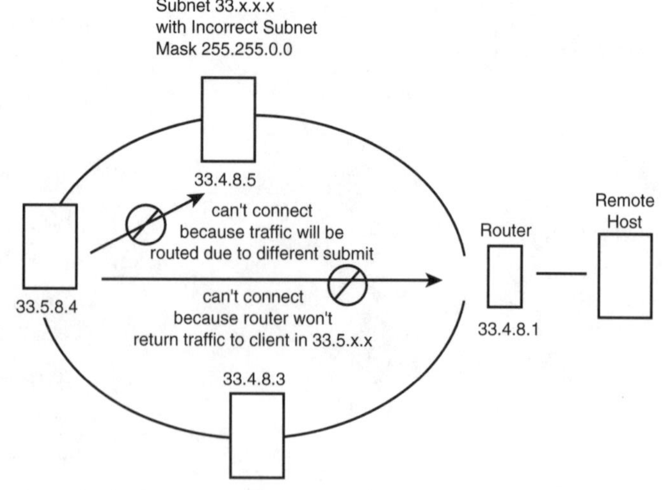

FIGURE 10.1
An incorrect subnet address.

If a local client tries to send a message to 33.5.8.4, the message doesn't reach the client. If the local client uses the address as configured, the message is routed, which isn't the correct solution, because the destination host is local. If the local client sends the message to what should have been the IP address, 33.5.8.4 doesn't receive the message, because the IP address isn't configured correctly.

The final component of an IP address that can cause communication problems is the host address. An incorrect host address may not always cause a problem, however. In Figure 10.2, a local client has the wrong IP address, but only the host address portion of the address is wrong. The network address and subnet match the rest of the clients on the subnet. In this case, if a client sends a message to the client with the incorrect address, the message still reaches the client. However, if someone tries to contact the client with what should have been the address, he doesn't contact the client. In fact, he could contact another host that ended up with the address that was supposed to be given to the original host. If the original host ends up with the same IP address as another host through the configuration error, the first client to boot works, but the second client to boot may note the address conflict and not load the TCP/IP stack at all. In this case, the second client to boot isn't able to make any TCP/IP communications.

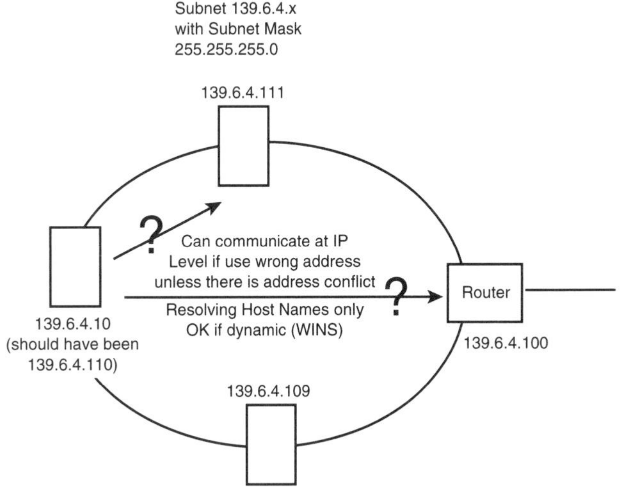

FIGURE 10.2
Incorrect host address.

Another problem occurs when the correct address was registered in static files, such as an LMHOSTS file or a DNS database, but an incorrect address is entered elsewhere. In this case, no one can communicate with this client by name because the name resolution for this host always returns the correct address, which can't be used to contact the host, because the address has been typed incorrectly. Basically, the problems you encounter with an incorrect host address are intermittent. However, if the host was configured to be a WINS client, the host name is registered along with the incorrect address. Another WINS client trying to connect with this computer receives an accurate mapping for the host name.

5. The subnet mask specifies what two components of the IP address?

A. The network address

C. The host address

5. CORRECT ANSWERS: A-C

The subnet mask identifies which portion of the IP address is the network id and which portion is the host id. Moveover, the subnet tells a system how many bits are used in the network id and host id. This allows a network to be logically divided into smaller or larger segments.

Subnet Mask

The subnet mask states which portion of the IP address specifies the network address and which portion of the address specifies the host address. The subnet mask also can be used to take part of what would have been the host address and use it to further divide the network into subnets. If the subnet mask is not configured correctly, your clients may not be able to communicate at all, or you may see partial communication problems.

Figure 10.3 shows a subnet on a TCP/IP network. The network uses a class B network address of 138.13.x.x. However, the third octet is used in this case for subnetting, so all the clients in the figure should be on subnet 4, as indicated by the common addresses 138.13.4.x. Unfortunately, the subnet mask entered for one client is 255.255.0.0. When this client tries to communicate with other hosts on the same subnet, it should be able to contact them because the subnet mask indicates they are on the same subnet, which is correct.

If the client tries to contact a host on another subnet such as 138.13.3.x, however, the client fails. In this case, the subnet mask still interprets the destination host to be on the same subnet, and the message is never routed. Because the destination host is on another subnet, the message never reaches its intended destination. The subnet mask is used to determine routing for outgoing communications, so the client with the incorrect subnet mask can receive incoming messages. However, when the client tries to return communications, the message isn't routed if the source host is on the same network but on a different subnet. Consequently, the client really can establish communications in a single direction with nonrouted clients. Contact with hosts outside the local network still works because those contacts are routed.

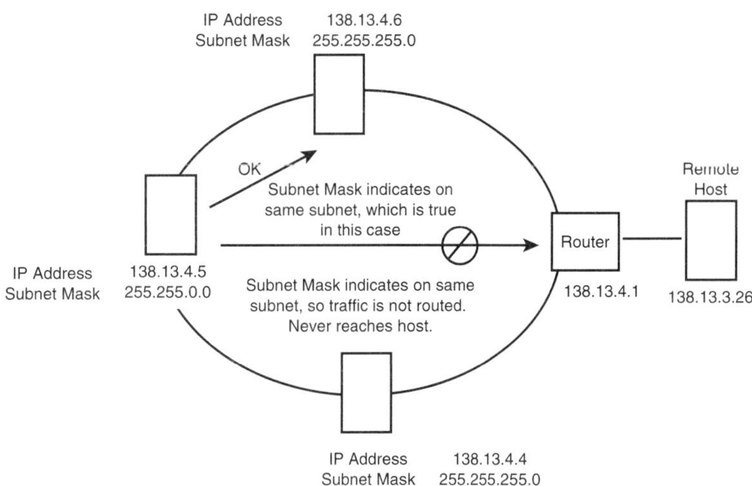

FIGURE 10.3
Incorrect subnet mask—missing third octet.

Figure 10.4 shows a subnet mask that masks too many bits. In this case, the subnet mask is 255.255.255.0. However, the network designers had intended the subnet mask to be 255.255.240.0, with four bits of the third octet used for the subnet and four bits as part of the host address. If the incorrect client tries to send a message to a local host and the third octet is the same, the message is not routed and thus reaches the local client.

However, if the local client has an address that differs in the last four bits of the third octet, the message is routed and never reaches its destination. If the incorrect client tries to send a message to another client on another subnet, the message is routed because the third octet is different. The whole problem can be summed up by the incorrect subnet mask in the third octet.

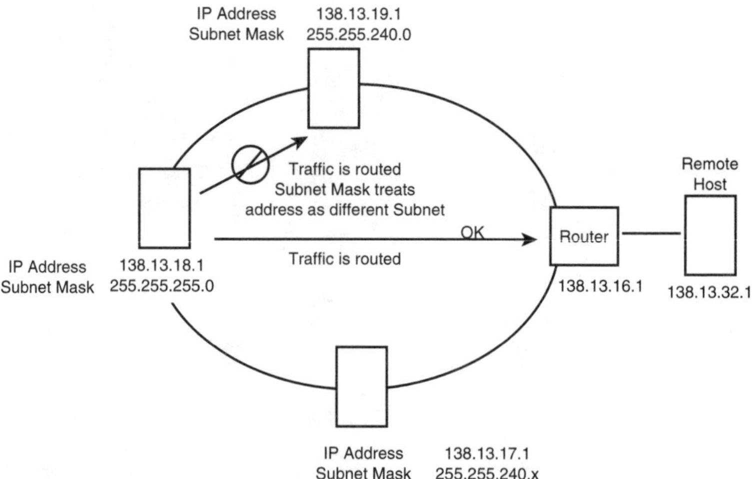

FIGURE 10.4
Incorrect subnet mask—incorrect third octet.

▼ NOTE

Problems with the subnet mask might appear as intermittent connections. Sometimes the connection works; sometimes it doesn't. The problems show up when the IP address of the destination host causes a packet to be routed when it shouldn't be, or to remain local when it should be routed.

6. What can cause a problem with communication with a client by name but not by IP address?

B. Static files such as an LMHOSTS file or a DNS database

6. CORRECT ANSWER: B

The problem is a matter of name resolution. Because host names and IP addresses are interchangeable, the problem is not communications. You should be able to conclude that the name is not getting translated to the proper address. The best thing to do in a situation like this is to use PING with the host name and verify that the proper address is displayed.

Default Gateway

The default gateway address is the address of the router—the gateway to the world beyond the local subnet. If the default gateway address is wrong, the client with the wrong default gateway address can contact local hosts but is not able to communicate at all beyond the local subnet. It is also possible for the incorrect client to receive a message. However, as soon as the incorrect client attempts to respond to the incoming message, the default gateway address doesn't work and the message doesn't reach the host that sent the original message. In many cases, the default gateway will not show up in an `IPCONFIG /ALL` response if the gateway has not been entered correctly.

7. What can greatly reduce TCP/IP configuration problems?

C. DHCP Server

7. CORRECT ANSWER: C

Using a DHCP server can greatly reduce the likelihood of TCP/IP configuration problems. A number of problems occur when configuring workstations manually. Perhaps the biggest problem is duplicate IP addresses. This prevents any IP communication. Also, user error can create issues that can potentially be difficult to determine. The most common type of error is a typo.

8. What is the term used to describe addresses available on a DHCP server?

B. Scopes

8. CORRECT ANSWER: B

Scopes are ranges of available addresses on a DHCP server. When configuring scopes, remember that options can be applied globally, by scope, or by client reservation. The more specific the DHCP-delivered settings, the higher the precedence. If any settings exist on a system after DHCP is installed, those will override any DHCP information potentially causing problems.

9. The most important part of a multiple DHCP configuration is to make sure you don't have which of the following in the different scopes? Select the best answer.

A. Duplicate addresses

9. CORRECT ANSWER: A

The most important part of the configuration is to make sure you don't have duplicate addresses in the different scopes. Remember that when configuring multiple DHCP servers, no communications will exist between them. As an effect, overlaps are not automatically determined.

10. Which of the following best describes the scopes on each DHCP server in the absence of configuration problems with DHCP addresses, if you use multiple DHCP servers in your environment?

B. For different subnets

10. CORRECT ANSWER: B

Even when no configuration problems occur with DHCP addresses, DHCP clients can get a duplicate IP address from a DHCP server. If you have multiple DHCP servers in your environment, you should have scopes on each DHCP server for different subnets.

DHCP Client Configuration Problems

All the TCP/IP parameters mentioned previously can cause communication problems if they are not configured correctly. Using a DHCP server can greatly reduce these configuration problems. If the DHCP scope is set up properly, without any typos or other configuration errors, DHCP clients shouldn't have any configuration problems. Although you can't completely eliminate human error, using DHCP should reduce the points of potential errors to just the DHCP servers, rather than every client on the network.

Even when no configuration problems occur with DHCP addresses, DHCP clients can get a duplicate IP address from a DHCP server. If you have multiple DHCP servers in your environment, you should have scopes on each DHCP server for different subnets. Usually, you have scopes with a larger number of addresses for the local subnet where the DHCP server is located and smaller scopes for other subnets. Creating multiple scopes on one server provides backup for giving clients IP addresses. If the server on the local scope is busy or down, the client can still receive an address from a remote DHCP server. When the router forwards this DHCP request to another subnet, the router includes the address of the subnet the request came from so that the remote DHCP server knows from which scope of addresses to lease an address to the remote client. Using this type of redundancy, however, can cause problems if you don't configure the scopes on all the DHCP servers correctly.

The most important part of the configuration is to make sure you don't have duplicate addresses in the different scopes. On one server, for example, you could have a scope in the range 134.57.2.100 to 134.57.2.170. On the remote DHCP server, you could have a scope of 134.57.2.171 to 134.57.2.200.

By setting up the scopes without overlap, you should not have any problems with clients receiving duplicate IP addresses. DHCP servers do not communicate with one another, so one server does not know anything about the addresses the other server has leased. Therefore, you must ensure that the servers never give out duplicate information by making sure the scopes for one subnet on all the different DHCP servers have unique IP addresses.

Another common problem with having multiple scopes on one server is entering the configuration parameters correctly. For example, if you enter the default gateway as 134.57.3.1 (instead of 134.57.2.1) for the scope 134.57.2.100 to 134.57.2.170, the clients receiving these addresses will not be able to communicate beyond the local subnet because they have the wrong router address. With one scope on a DHCP server, you are usually quite sure of what all the configuration parameters should be. With multiple scopes on one server, however, you can easily get confused about which scope you are editing and what the parameters should be for that scope. To avoid this type of problem, check each scope's parameters very carefully to make sure the parameters match the address of the scope, not the subnet where the DHCP server is located.

Also, if the client doesn't receive an address because the server is down or doesn't respond in a timely manner, the client is not able to communicate with any other system. Without an IP address, the IP stack does not initialize, and the client can't communicate at all with TCP/IP.

PRACTICE QUESTIONS

USE MICROSOFT TCP/IP UTILITIES TO DIAGNOSE CONFIGURATION PROBLEMS

1. **How can you see the address of the DHCP server from which a client received its IP address?**
   - A. By using Advanced Properties of TCP/IP
   - B. By using `IPCONFIG /ALL`
   - C. By using DHCPINFO
   - D. By pinging DHCP
2. **If you configure the TCP/IP address and other TCP/IP parameters manually, you can always verify the configuration through which of the following? Select the best answer.**
   - A. Network Properties dialog box
   - B. Server Services dialog box
   - C. DHCPINFO command-line utility
   - D. Advanced Properties tab of TCP/IP Info
3. **If the client receives an address from a DHCP server, what is the only information available in the Network Properties dialog box?**
   - A. The IP address
   - B. The subnet address
   - C. That the client is receiving its address from DHCP
   - D. The default gateway
4. **Because the configuration information for a DHCP client is received dynamically, you must use which utility to read the current configuration to verify the settings?**
   - A. PING
   - B. TRACERT
   - C. ARP
   - D. IPCONFIG
5. **The command-line utility IPCONFIG can be used to see which two of the following items?**
   - A. Configuration of the local host
   - B. Whether the parameters come from manual configuration or from a DHCP server
   - C. PING request status
   - D. Protocol statistics

ANSWER KEY

1. B
2. A
3. C
4. D
5. A-B

ANSWERS & EXPLANATIONS

USE MICROSOFT TCP/IP UTILITIES TO DIAGNOSE CONFIGURATION PROBLEMS

1. How can you see the address of the DHCP server from which a client received its IP address?

B. By using `IPCONFIG /ALL`

1. CORRECT ANSWER: B

`IPCONFIG /ALL` is the command-line utility used to obtain this information. This command is compatible with Windows for Workgroups and Windows NT. On Windows 95 and 98 systems, the WINIPCFG GUI utility should be used. This utility is available in the NT resource for Windows NT as well.

2. If you configure the TCP/IP address and other TCP/IP parameters manually, you can always verify the configuration through which of the following? Select the best answer.

A. Network Properties dialog box

2. CORRECT ANSWER: A

With the exception of DHCP, you should review the Network Properties dialog box to review configuration settings. In this case, to review TCP/IP you should look at the Protocols tab and examine each option individually. DHCP-delivered information can be found by typing **`IPCONFIG /ALL`** or under Windows 95/98 WINIPCFG.

3. If the client receives an address from a DHCP server, what is the only information available in the Network Properties dialog box?

C. That the client is receiving its address from DHCP

3. CORRECT ANSWER: C

If the client receives an address from a DHCP server, the only information available in the Network Properties dialog box is that the client is receiving its address from DHCP. That is to say that if you look at the properties of TCP/IP, all that the Network Properties dialog box should show is `Obtain Address Automatically`. However, if you have elected to override any of the DHCP-delivered information, then this information may appear.

4. Because the configuration information for a DHCP client is received dynamically, you must use which utility to read the current configuration to verify the settings?

D. IPCONFIG

4. CORRECT ANSWER: D

DHCP-delivered information will not appear in the TCP/IP protocol settings. The only information that will appear there is the setting to configure DHCP information automatically.

To determine what information has been assigned, use the IPCONFIG utility with the /ALL option.

5. The command-line utility IPCONFIG can be used to see which two of the following items?

A. Configuration of the local host

B. Whether the parameters come from manual configuration or from a DHCP server

5. CORRECT ANSWERS: A-B

Regardless of how IP information is assigned, the IPCONFIG utility can be used to display the current settings. Typically, you should use the /ALL option to see all settings.

Microsoft Configuration Utilities

If you configure the TCP/IP address and other TCP/IP parameters manually, you can always verify the configuration through the Network Properties dialog box. However, if the client receives an address from a DHCP server, the only information available in the Network Properties dialog box is that the client is receiving the address from DHCP. Because the configuration information for a DHCP client is received dynamically, you must use a utility that can read the current configuration to verify the settings.

You can use the command-line utility IPCONFIG to see how the local host is configured, regardless of whether the parameters come from manual configuration or from a DHCP server. Running IPCONFIG from a command prompt displays the basic configuration parameters: the IP address, the subnet mask, and the default gateway. You can see additional information by using IPCONFIG with the /ALL switch.

Executing `IPCONFIG /ALL` in a command prompt not only shows the standard parameters but also displays information such as the WINS server address and the DNS server address.

▼ NOTE

A Windows NT version of IPCONFIG, called *IP Configuration*, is included with the Windows NT Resource Kit and is installed under the Internet Utils program group. IP Configuration reports the same information as the IPCONFIG command-line utility. IP Configuration can also be used to release and renew DHCP addresses, as described in the following section.

Using IPCONFIG to Resolve DHCP Address Problems

When a DHCP client gets an IP address that is not configured correctly or if the client doesn't get an IP address at all, you can use IPCONFIG to resolve these problems. If the client gets incorrect IP parameters, it should be apparent from the results of `IPCONFIG /ALL`. You should be able to see that some of the parameters don't match the IP address or that some parameters are completely blank. For example, you could have the wrong default gateway (in which case the entry would not appear), or the client might not be configured to be a WINS client.

When a DHCP client fails to receive an address, the results of `IPCONFIG /ALL` are different. In this case, the client has an IP address of 0.0.0.0—an invalid address—and the DHCP server is 255.255.255.255—a broadcast address.

To fix this problem, you can release the incorrect address with `IPCONFIG /release` and then try to obtain a new IP address with `IPCONFIG /renew`. The `IPCONFIG /renew` command sends out a new request for a DHCP address. If a DHCP server is available, the server responds with the lease of an IP address.

In many cases, the DHCP client will acquire the same address after releasing and renewing. That the client receives the same address indicates that the same DHCP server responded to the renewal request and gave out the address that had just been released back into the pool of available addresses. If you need to renew an address because the parameters of the scope are incorrect, you must fix the parameters in the DHCP configuration before releasing and renewing the address. Otherwise, the client could receive the same address again with the same incorrect parameters.

▼ **NOTE**

Occasionally, a DHCP client will not acquire an address regardless of how many times you release and renew the address. One way to try to fix the problem is to manually assign the client a static IP address. After the client is configured with this address, which you can verify by using IPCONFIG, switch back to DHCP.

Microsoft IP Configuration Troubleshooting Utilities

A number of tools come with TCP/IP when the protocol is installed on a Windows NT computer. After you have resolved any problems caused by the Windows NT network configuration, you can focus on using the TCP/IP tools to solve IP problems. Some tools can be used to verify the configuration parameters. PING is discussed in detail in the later section "Identify Which Microsoft TCP/IP Utility to Use to Diagnose IP Configuration Problems." Other tools can be used to test the connectivity capabilities of TCP/IP as configured. NBSTAT and Hostname are discussed in the later section "Diagnose and Resolve Name Resolution Problems."

PRACTICE QUESTIONS

IDENTIFY WHICH MICROSOFT TCP/IP UTILITY TO USE TO DIAGNOSE IP CONFIGURATION PROBLEMS

1. **Which command-line tool is included with every Microsoft TCP/IP client?**
   A. DHCP
   B. WINS
   C. PING
   D. WINIPCFG
2. **The first step in troubleshooting many problems is to verify which of the following?**
   A. The subnet mask is valid.
   B. TCP/IP is installed correctly on the client.
   C. The WINS server is running.
   D. The BDC is operable.
3. **What is the loopback address?**
   A. 127.0.0.1
   B. 255.0.0.0
   C. 255.255.0.0
   D. 255.255.255.0
4. **When you ping the loopback address, a packet is sent where?**
   A. On the network
   B. Down through the layers of the IP architecture and then up the layers again
   C. Across the wire
   D. Through the loopback dongle
5. **When using the loopback address, if TCP/IP is installed correctly, when should you receive a response?**
   A. Immediately
   B. Only if the address fails
   C. After the next host comes online
   D. Within two minutes
6. **After you have verified that TCP/IP is installed correctly, what is the next step in verifying the TCP/IP configuration?**
   A. Ping the broadcast address.
   B. Ping the Microsoft Web site.
   C. Ping a distant router.
   D. Ping the address of the local host.
7. **If the default gateway ping fails, possible sources for the error include which of the following? Select all that apply.**
   A. The router has failed or is down.
   B. The client has lost a physical connection with the router or with the network.
   C. The client has the wrong router address.
   D. The wrong subnet mask is configured.

8. If you can communicate with hosts on the same subnet but cannot establish communications with hosts beyond the subnet, where might the problem lie?

A. The router or the way its address is configured

B. The subnet mask

C. The IP address

D. The WINS Server

ANSWER KEY

1. C
2. B
3. A
4. B
5. A
6. D
7. A-B-C-D
8. A

ANSWERS & EXPLANATIONS

IDENTIFY WHICH MICROSOFT TCP/IP UTILITY TO USE TO DIAGNOSE IP CONFIGURATION PROBLEMS

1. **Which command-line tool is included with every Microsoft TCP/IP client?**

   C. PING

1. CORRECT ANSWER: C

PING is a command-line tool included with every Microsoft TCP/IP client. It is used to confirm that a TCP/IP static is properly configured and to verify that a destination is reachable.

2. **The first step in troubleshooting many problems is to verify which of the following?**

   B. TCP/IP is installed correctly on the client.

2. CORRECT ANSWER: B

Begin by using the IPCONFIG or WINIPCFG (WIN95/98) to verify that settings are proper. Then use the PING utility to test the stack for both your configured IP address and the loopback address (127.0.0.1). If successful, ping the default gateway. Proceed from there to determine the root source of a problem.

Using PING to Test an IP Configuration

PING is a command-line tool included with every Microsoft TCP/IP client (any DOS or Windows client with the TCP/IP protocol installed). You can use PING to send a test packet to the specified address; if things are working properly, the packet is returned. Figure 10.5 shows the results of a successful `ping` command. Note that four successful responses are returned. Unsuccessful pings can result in different messages, depending on the type of problem Ping encounters while trying to send and receive the test packet.

Although PING is a simple tool to use (from the command prompt simply type **`ping`** with the IP address or host name you want to ping), choosing what to ping is the key to using it for successful troubleshooting. The remainder of this section covers which IP addresses or hosts you should ping to troubleshoot a variety of TCP/IP connectivity problems.

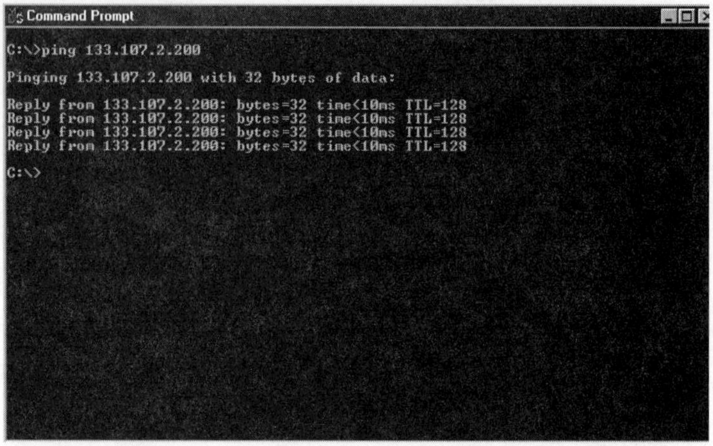

```
Command Prompt

C:\>ping 133.107.2.200

Pinging 133.107.2.200 with 32 bytes of data:

Reply from 133.107.2.200: bytes=32 time<10ms TTL=128
Reply from 133.107.2.200: bytes=32 time<10ms TTL=128
Reply from 133.107.2.200: bytes=32 time<10ms TTL=128
Reply from 133.107.2.200: bytes=32 time<10ms TTL=128

C:\>
```

FIGURE 10.5
The results of a successful `ping` command.

3. What is the loopback address?

A. 127.0.0.1

3. CORRECT ANSWER: A

The loopback address is 127.0.0.1. This is a special reserved address used to verify that the TCP/IP stack is in fact working. When pinging addresses, 127.0.0.1 should respond regardless of whether it has been given a proper IP address as long as the stack has not been shut down and all TCP/IP support files load.

4. When you ping the loopback address, a packet is sent where?

B. Down through the layers of the IP architecture and then up the layers again

4. CORRECT ANSWER: B

The process of pinging the loopback address will verify the TCP/IP stack is functioning. This is useful when attempting to determine whether a problem exists at the driver level of the local system. After a system has been verified locally, you can attempt communications with other systems.

5. When using the loopback address, if TCP/IP is installed correctly, when should you receive a response?

A. Immediately

5. CORRECT ANSWER: A

Assuming that TCP/IP is installed correctly, you will get an immediate response to confirm. However, a failure would indicate that a problem is occurring with TCP/IP somewhere local to the system itself. In that case, you should review any messages that appear in the event viewer, check the TCP/IP Configuration page of the Network dialog box, and if all else fails, remove, and then reinstall TCP/IP.

Troubleshooting IP Protocol Installation by Pinging the Loopback Address

The first step of troubleshooting many problems is to verify that TCP/IP installed correctly on the client. You can look at the configuration through the Network Properties dialog box or with IPCONFIG, but to actually test the working status of the protocol stack you should try to ping the loopback address. The loopback address is 127.0.0.1. When you ping this address, a packet is not sent on the network. The `ping` command simply sends a packet down through the layers of the IP architecture and then up the layers again. If TCP/IP is installed correctly, you should receive an immediate successful response. If the IP is not installed correctly, the response fails.

To correct problems of this type, you should verify the NT network configuration and the protocol installation. You should check the following items:

- Make sure TCP/IP is listed on the installed protocols.
- Make surc the network adapter card is configured correctly.
- Make sure TCP/IP shows up in the bindings for the adapter card and that the bindings are not disabled for TCP/IP.
- Check the System log for any errors indicating that the network services didn't start.

If you try the preceding suggestions, or even reboot the system, and have no success, you may have to remove TCP/IP and install it again. Sometimes NT gets hung up somewhere and thinks things are really installed when they are not. Removing the protocol and then installing it again can often resolve this halfway state.

6. After you have verified that TCP/IP is installed correctly, what is the next step in verifying the TCP/IP configuration?

D. Ping the address of the local host.

6. CORRECT ANSWER: D

The object behind the steps of what to do next is to determine in a logical path where errors are taking place. The first step is to ping the loopback address, in this example, the local host. Assuming a positive response is received, next ping the router.

Troubleshooting Client Address Configuration by Pinging the Local Address

Another step in verifying the TCP/IP configuration, after you have verified that TCP/IP is installed correctly, is to ping the address of the local host. Simply ping the IP address that you think is configured for the client. You should receive an immediate successful reply if the client address is configured as specified in the `ping` command. You can also ping the name of the local host; problems with name resolution are discussed later in this chapter's section "Name Resolution Problems." For the moment, you are concerned with raw TCP/IP connectivity—the capability to communicate with another IP host by using its IP address.

Correcting a failure at this level involves checking the way the client address was configured. Was the address typed in correctly? Did the client receive the IP address from the DHCP server that you expected? Also, does the client have a connection on the network? Pinging the local host address does not cause a packet to be sent on the network, so if you have lost network connectivity, this Ping won't indicate a network failure.

7. If the default gateway ping fails, possible sources for the error include which of the following? Select all that apply.

A. The router has failed or is down.

B. The client has lost a physical connection with the router or with the network.

C. The client has the wrong router address.

D. The wrong subnet mask is configured.

7. CORRECT ANSWERS: A-B-C-D

If the default gateway ping fails, there are several possible sources for the error: The router has failed or is down, the client has lost a physical connection with the router or with the network, the IP address on the router may be configured incorrectly, the client has the wrong router address, or the wrong subnet mask is configured. Other errors are also possible such as having an invalid IP address, a bad or corrupted TCP/IP installation, and so forth.

Troubleshooting Router Problems by Pinging the Default Gateway

If you can communicate with hosts on the same subnet but cannot establish communications with hosts beyond the subnet, the problem may be with the router or the way its address is configured.

To communicate beyond the subnet, a router must be enabled with an address that matches the subnet address for the clients on the local subnet. The router also has other ports configured with different addresses so it can send packets out to the network at large. Pinging the default gateway address tests the address you have configured for the router and also tests the router itself.

If the default gateway ping fails, there are several possible sources for the error:

- The router has failed or is down. In this case, you cannot make connections outside the subnet until the router is brought up again. However, you should be able to communicate with hosts on the same subnet.
- The client has lost a physical connection with the router or with the network. You can test a network connection at a hardware level and also through the software by trying to establish a session with a server with another protocol, such as NetBEUI. If you have only TCP/IP on your network, you can temporarily install NetBEUI on the client and on another computer on the same subnet. Test connectivity by connecting to a file share on the other computer. Remember, the computer should be on the same subnet because NetBEUI packets don't usually route.
- The IP address on the router may be configured incorrectly. The router address must match the client's default gateway address so that packets can move outside the subnet.
- The client has the wrong router address. Of course, if you ping the correct router address and it works, you also should make sure the default gateway address configured on the client matches the address you successfully pinged.
- The wrong subnet mask is configured. If the subnet mask is wrong, packets destined for a remote subnet may not be routed.

You should also ping each IP address used by the different ports on your router. The local interface for your subnet may be working, but other interfaces on the router, which actually connect the router to the other subnets on the network, could have some type of problem.

8. If you can communicate with hosts on the same subnet but cannot establish communications with hosts beyond the subnet, where might the problem lie?

A. The router or the way its address is configured

8. CORRECT ANSWER: A

Because communications work at a local level, the problem is most likely with the router. The only thing on the workstation to verify is that it has the proper subnet mask. Otherwise, the system may think a remote host is local when in fact it is not. Use the TRACERT utility to find which router the packet fails.

Pinging a Remote Host

As a final test in using PING, you can ping the IP address of a remote host, a computer on another subnet, or even the IP address of a Web server or FTP server on the Internet. If you can successfully ping a remote host, your problem doesn't lie with the IP configuration; you are probably having trouble resolving host names.

If pinging the remote host fails, your problems may be with the router, the subnet mask, or the local IP configuration. However, if you have followed the earlier steps of pinging the loopback, local host address, and the default gateway address, you have already eliminated many of the problems that could cause this ping to fail.

When a remote host ping fails after you have tried the other ping options, the failure may be due to other routers beyond the default gateway used for your subnet. If you know the physical layout of your network, you can ping other router addresses along the path to the remote host to see where the trouble lies. Remember to ping the addresses on both sides of the router—the address that receives the packet and the address that forwards the packet on. You can also use the ROUTE command to view the routing table of an NT router to determine whether a fault internal to the route is occurring.

Another possibility is that a physical path to the remote host no longer exists because of a router crash, a disruption in the physical network, or a crash on the remote host.

Many troubleshooters prefer to simply try this last step when using PING to troubleshoot IP configuration and connectivity. If you can successfully ping a remote host, then the other layers of TCP/IP must be working correctly. For a packet to reach a remote host, IP must be installed correctly, the local client address must be configured properly, and the packet must be routed. If a Ping to the remote host works, then you can look to other sources (usually name resolution) for your connection problems. If the Ping fails, you can try each preceding step until you find the layer where the problem is located. Then you can resolve the problem at that layer. You can either start by pinging the loopback address and working up through the architecture, or you can ping the remote host. Of course, if pinging the remote host works, you can stop. If not, you can work back through the architecture until you find a layer at which PING succeeds. The problem must therefore be at the next layer.

PRACTICE QUESTIONS

DIAGNOSE AND RESOLVE NAME RESOLUTION PROBLEMS

The first three questions refer to the following HOSTS file:

```
127.0.0.1        localhost
192.200.2.4      karen      Kristin
➥#Evan
192.200.2.5      Spencer    Sales
192.200.2.6      #Lorraine Buis
192.200.2.7      Sales
```

1. **Kristin, in Finance, is having trouble connecting to the host called Lorraine. When Kristin pings 192.200.2.6, the result is successful, but when she pings Lorraine, the error message says the host is not found. What is causing this problem?**

   A. Invalid IP address

   B. Duplicate entry

   C. Comment character in the wrong position

   D. Improper spelling of host name

2. **Evan, in Accounting, needs to get into 192.200.2.7. He can ping the IP address, but if he tries to ping Sales, the results tell him that 192.200.2.5 is responding. What is causing this problem?**

   A. Invalid IP address

   B. Duplicate entry

   C. Comment character in the wrong position

   D. Improper spelling of host name

3. **Spencer, in Sales, needs to connect to the host Karen and has the preceding host file on his NT 3.51 machine. He can ping the IP address successfully, but if he attempts to ping Karen, the host is not found. What is causing this problem?**

   A. Invalid IP address

   B. Duplicate entry

   C. Comment character in the wrong position

   D. Improper spelling of host name

4. **Which utility is useful for troubleshooting NetBIOS name resolution problems?**

   A. NBTSTAT

   B. Netstat

   C. PING

   D. Hostname

5. **Which utility is useful for finding the local host name?**

   A. NBTSTAT

   B. Netstat

   C. PING

   D. Hostname

6. **Which utility is an all-purpose tool for troubleshooting TCP/IP problems?**

   A. NBTSTAT

   B. Netstat

   C. PING

   D. Hostname

7. **Which of the following files is used for NetBIOS name resolution?**

   A. `HOSTS`

   B. `LMHOSTS`

   C. `ARP`

   D. `FQDN`

8. **`HOSTS` file entries are limited to how many characters?**

   A. 8

   B. 255

   C. 500

   D. Unlimited

9. **What is the maximum number of entries in the `HOSTS` file?**

   A. 8

   B. 255

   C. 500

   D. Unlimited

10. **Which of the following files is case sensitive on NT 3.5 systems?**

    A. `HOSTS`

    B. `LMHOSTS`

    C. `ARP`

    D. `FQDN`

ANSWER KEY

1. C
2. B
3. D
4. A
5. D
6. C
7. B
8. B
9. D
10. A

ANSWERS & EXPLANATIONS

DIAGNOSE AND RESOLVE NAME RESOLUTION PROBLEMS

1. **Kristin, in Finance, is having trouble connecting to the host called Lorraine. When Kristin pings 192.200.2.6, the result is successful, but when she pings Lorraine, the error message says the host is not found. What is causing this problem?**

   C. Comment character in the wrong position

1. CORRECT ANSWER: C

The comment character is preceding the host name and thus preventing the name from being recognized.

2. **Evan, in Accounting, needs to get into 192.200.2.7. He can ping the IP address, but if he tries to ping Sales, the results tell him that 192.200.2.5 is responding. What is causing this problem?**

   B. Duplicate entry

2. CORRECT ANSWER: B

The Sales entry is duplicated on two lines and thus the second entry is never activated.

3. **Spencer, in Sales, needs to connect to the host Karen and has the preceding host file on his NT 3.51 machine. He can ping the IP address successfully, but if he attempts to ping Karen, the host is not found. What is causing this problem?**

   D. Improper spelling of host name

3. CORRECT ANSWER: D

Prior to NT 4.0, the `HOSTS` file was case sensitive. This file has the entry `karen`, but Spencer is trying to reach `Karen`—two different entries.

Diagnosing and Resolving Name Resolution Problems

Name resolution problems are easily identified as such with the PING utility. If you can ping a host by using its IP address, but cannot ping it by its host name, then you have a resolution problem. If you cannot ping the host at all, then the problem lies elsewhere.

Problems that can occur with name resolution and their solutions fit into the following five categories:

1. **The entry is misspelled**—Examine the HOSTS or LMHOSTS file to verify that the host name is correctly spelled. If you are using the HOSTS file on a system prior to NT 4.0, capitalization is important because the file is case sensitive; LMHOSTS is not case sensitive (regardless of NT version number).
2. **Comment characters prevent the entry from being read**—Verify that a pound sign is neither at the beginning of the line nor anywhere on the line prior to the host name.
3. **The file has duplicate entries**—Because the files are read in linear fashion, with any duplication only the first entry is read and all others are ignored. Verify that all host names are unique.
4. **A host other than the one you want is contacted**—Verify that the IP address entered in the file(s) is valid and corresponds to the host name.
5. **The wrong file is used**—HOSTS and LMHOSTS are not as interchangeable as you might think. HOSTS maps IP addresses to host names, whereas LMHOSTS maps NetBIOS names to IP addresses.

In addition to the PING utility, the all-purpose TCP/IP troubleshooting tool, two other useful name resolution utilities are as follows:

- NBTSTAT
- Hostname

4. Which utility is useful for troubleshooting NetBIOS name resolution problems?

A. NBTSTAT

4. CORRECT ANSWER: A

Hostname is a good utility especially in scripting since it will inform you of your local system's name. On the other hand, while dealing with NetBIOS names, the NBTSTAT utility can be used to determine what names have been resolved and are available in the local cache.

NBTSTAT

The NBTSTAT utility (NetBIOS over TCP/IP) displays protocol statistics and current TCP/IP connections. It is useful for troubleshooting NetBIOS name resolution problems, and various parameters and options can be used with it:

- `-a` **(adapter status)**—Lists the remote machine's host name table given its NetBIOS name
- `-A` **(Adapter status)**—Lists the remote machine's name table given its IP address
- `-c` **(cache)**—Lists the remote name cache including the IP addresses
- `-n` **(names)**—Lists local NetBIOS names
- `-r` **(resolved)**—Lists names resolved by broadcast and via WINS
- `-R` **(Reload)**—Purges and reloads the remote cache name table
- `-S` **(Sessions)**—Lists sessions table with the destination IP addresses
- `-s` **(sessions)**—Lists sessions table converting destination IP addresses to host names via the `LMHOSTS` file

5. Which utility is useful for finding the local host name?

D. Hostname

5. CORRECT ANSWER: D

The Hostname utility is useful in scripting and for verifying the local registered name. This utility is available in Windows NT only and not 95 or 98. This utility helps clarify names if the NetBIOS name differs from its host counterpart.

Hostname

The hostname.exe utility, located in `\systemroot\System32`, returns the name of the local host. You cannot use this utility to change the name. The host name is changed from the Network Control Panel applet.

If you have configured TCP/IP correctly and the protocol is installed and working, then the problem with connectivity is probably associated with errors in resolving host names. When you test connectivity with TCP/IP addresses, you are testing a lower level of connectivity than users generally use. When users want to connect to a network resource, such as mapping a drive to a server or connecting to a Web site, they usually refer to that server or Web site by its name rather than by its TCP/IP address. In fact, users do not usually know the IP address of a particular server.

The name used to establish a connection must be resolved down to an IP address so that the networking software can make a connection. After you've tested the IP connectivity, the next logical step is to check the resolution of a name down to its IP address. If a name cannot be resolved to its IP address or if it is resolved to the wrong address, users will not be able to connect to the network resource with that name, even if you can connect to it by using an IP address.

Two types of computer names are used when communicating on the network. A *NetBIOS* name is assigned to a Microsoft computer, such as a Windows NT server or a Windows 95 client. A *host* name is assigned to non-Microsoft computers, such as a UNIX server. (Host names can also be assigned to a Windows NT server running Internet Information Server. For example, the name `www.microsoft.com` refers to a Web server on the Microsoft Web site. This server is running on Windows NT.) In general, when using Microsoft networking, such as connecting to a server for file sharing, print sharing, or applications, you refer to that computer by its NetBIOS name. When executing a TCP/IP-specific command, such as FTP, or using a Web browser, you refer to that computer by its host name.

A NetBIOS name can be resolved to a TCP/IP address in several ways. Figure 10.6 shows how NetBIOS names are resolved. The TCP/IP client initiating a session first looks in its local name cache. If the client cannot find the name in a local cache, the client queries a WINS server if configured to be a WINS client. If the WINS server cannot resolve the name, the client tries a broadcast that reaches only as far as the local subnet.

(Routers, by default, are not configured to forward broadcasts.) If the client cannot find the name through a broadcast, it looks for any LMHOSTS or HOSTS files if it has been configured to do so. Finally, if the client cannot resolve a name in any other way, it queries a DNS server, if it is configured to be a DNS client. However, if the client specifies a name longer than 15 characters (the maximum length of a NetBIOS name), the client first queries DNS before trying a HOSTS file or WINS server.

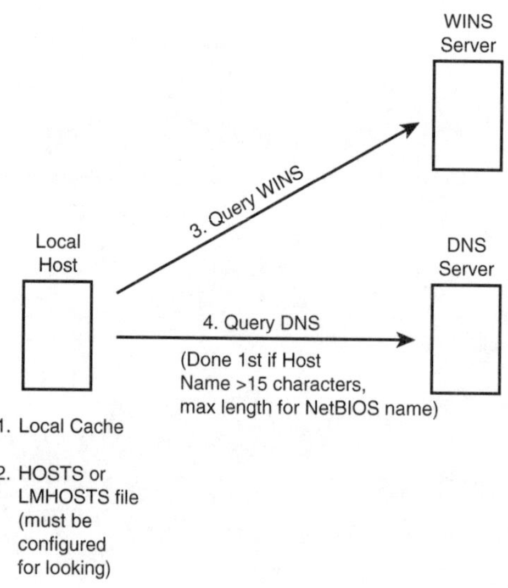

FIGURE 10.6
Resolving NetBIOS names.

Host names are resolved in a similar manner. The client, however, checks sources that are used solely to resolve host names before trying sources that are used to resolve NetBIOS names. In resolving host names, the client first tries the local host name, then the HOSTS file, and then the DNS server, if it is configured to be a DNS client. These two sources resolve only host names. If the client cannot resolve the name, it checks the WINS server, if configured as a WINS client; tries a broadcast; and then looks in the LMHOSTS file. The last three methods to resolve a name are used to resolve NetBIOS names, but a host name might be listed in these sources.

6. Which utility is an all-purpose tool for troubleshooting TCP/IP problems?

C. PING

6. CORRECT ANSWER: C

PING is the most commonly used tool for resolving TCP/IP-related issues. It can be used to verify connectivity, response time, name resolution, proper IP installation, and more.

Just as you can use PING to verify the TCP/IP configuration, you can also use PING to verify host name resolution. If you can successfully ping a host name, then you have verified TCP/IP communication from the Network Interface layer of the TCP/IP architecture to the Transport layer. When you ping a host name, a successful reply shows the IP address of the host. This test shows that the name has been successfully resolved to an IP address and that you can communicate with that host.

7. Which of the following files is used for NetBIOS name resolution?

B. LMHOSTS

7. CORRECT ANSWER: B

`LMHOSTS` is the static file used for NetBIOS name resolution. The `LMHOSTS` file can be edited with any text editor; however, it should be saved without an extension. In most environments, it is recommended that WINS be used in place of the `LMHOSTS` file.

Testing NetBIOS Name Resolution by Establishing a Session

The ultimate test of connectivity is to establish a session with another host. If you can establish a session through mapping a drive or by executing a `Net Use` command (which is the command-line equivalent of mapping a drive), you have made a NetBIOS connection. If you can FTP, Telnet, or establish a Web session with another host, you have made a Sockets connection. NetBIOS and Sockets connections are the two main types of connections made by a TCP/IP client.

After the drive has been mapped with `Net Use`, you can switch to the new drive letter, view files and directories, and do many other things that are specified in the permissions of the share mapped to the drive letter. To get more information about the syntax of the `Net Use` command, type **`net help use`** in a command prompt.

A common problem in making NetBIOS connections is that the wrong NetBIOS name is used. Verify that the destination host has the same name that you are using to make the connection.

Another potential problem with the name configuration occurs when NetBIOS scope IDs are used. Only NetBIOS hosts with the same scope ID can communicate with one another. The scope ID is configured through the advanced TCP/IP parameters. Incorrect share permissions can prevent you from establishing a NetBIOS session. When you try to connect a drive to a share where you have No Access, you receive an `Access Denied` message. This message indicates that you can connect to the server, but your rights did not allow you to make a connection to this specific share. This type of failure has nothing to do with TCP/IP connectivity. Remember that if the administrator adds your account to a group that has access and you want to try again, you must log out and log in again to receive a new access token with the updated permissions.

To resolve NetBIOS connectivity problems, you must know what sources are used to resolve NetBIOS names. The first place a client looks to resolve a NetBIOS name is the local cache. You can view the contents of the NetBIOS cache with the `NBTSTAT` command. You should verify that no incorrect entry is in the cache that maps the NetBIOS name to an incorrect IP address. If you find an incorrect entry, however, you can remove the entry and then try to make another connection.

The next place to attempt NetBIOS name resolution is in a query to a WINS server. The client must be configured to be a WINS client. You can verify the address of the WINS server through the Advanced properties of TCP/IP or by using `IPCONFIG /ALL`. You can view the contents of the WINS database by using WINS Manager on the WINS server (or any computer where the management tools are installed). Verify that the host name is in the database and, if so, make sure it is mapped to the correct IP address.

If the WINS server is configured to do a DNS lookup, you have another way to get NetBIOS resolution. The WINS server queries DNS if the WINS server cannot resolve the name from its own database. You can view the contents of the DNS database files by using DNS Manager on the DNS server or by using the Nslookup utility from any client.

The client next tries a broadcast to resolve NetBIOS names, although you cannot configure what the client finds through the broadcast. The next place the client looks for NetBIOS name resolution is the `LMHOSTS` file. You can configure the contents of this file. The client must be configured for LMHOSTS lookup in the advanced TCP/IP configuration. Also, the `LMHOSTS` file must be located in the correct directory path. On an NT computer, the `LMHOSTS` file must be in the path `<winnt root>\system32\drivers\etc`.

Next, verify the entries in the `LMHOSTS` file. The correct host name and IP address must be entered in this file. If you have multiple entries in the file for a host name, only the first entry is used. If you added another entry for a host in the file, you must delete it so that it will not be used.

Domain names are another source of potential problems with `LMHOSTS` files in a non-WINS environment. The domain name must be registered with the IP address of the Primary Domain Controller (PDC) and `#DOM` (a switch that registers the server as a domain controller) on the same line. This entry is necessary to log on to the domain as well as to see the domain in a browse list.

Another problem with `LMHOSTS` files doesn't prevent connectivity, but it can greatly delay it. If you have `#INCLUDE` statements at the top of the `LMHOSTS` file, the files specified by `#INCLUDE` are included first before any other entries lower in the `LMHOSTS` file are searched. You can speed connections to hosts entered in the `LMHOSTS` file by moving the `#INCLUDE` entries to the bottom of the `LMHOSTS` file.

8. HOSTS file entries are limited to how many characters?

B. 255

8. CORRECT ANSWER: B

HOSTS file lines are limited to 255 characters. It is in fact hazardous to have any more than 255 characters per line because it is unpredictable what will happen to additional characters. Some operating systems will ignore them, while others will treat them as if they were on a new line.

9. What is the maximum number of entries in the HOSTS file?

D. Unlimited

9. CORRECT ANSWER: D

The HOSTS file can have an unlimited number of lines. However, when this file becomes large in size, there is a risk of slowing down the system because it will have to parse the entire HOSTS file. Also, maintaining a file of any more than a few entries can be quite a chore.

10. Which of the following files is case sensitive on NT 3.5 systems?

A. HOSTS

10. CORRECT ANSWER: A

The HOSTS file, prior to NT 4.0, was case sensitive and remains so on non-NT systems. You will find that many Internet hosts will be resolved regardless of the case. Considering that a full distinguished name is unlikely to have a counterpart of the opposite case, this is a benefit that simplifies network control.

FURTHER REVIEW

HOW SHOULD TROUBLESHOOTING BE PERFORMED?

There are many methods of troubleshooting a problem. The best method is typically a process of elimination. That is to say that when you deal with a problem, you should divide the problem into sections in order to determine the problem's source. For example, if you were troubleshooting a connectivity problem, you could eliminate your system from the network if it could communicate with other machines, including those on remote networks. Eventually, this elimination process will isolate the error. The key methodology is to always choose one plan, and not switch midstream. Without a logical order to follow, too much is left to chance. In order to understand the problems that you are experiencing, you should take note that you are using the right tool, and have foreknowledge of the result that you are expecting.

Testing TCP Name Resolution by Establishing a Session

Typical TCP/IP connections from a Microsoft client, such as FTP or Telnet, use Windows Sockets. To test connectivity at this level, try establishing an FTP or Telnet session or try to connect to a Web server. When you successfully connect to a Web server, you see the site's Web page and you can navigate through the page. When the connection fails, you receive a message on your Internet browser that the connection failed.

To resolve problems with a Windows Sockets connection, you must understand how a client resolves TCP host names. The first place a client looks to resolve a host name is the local host name. You can see what TCP/IP thinks is the local host name by executing the `Hostname` command. Verify that the local host is what you expect it to be. You can modify the host name in the DNS tab of the TCP/IP properties.

The next place the client looks is in a `HOSTS` file. This file must be located in the path `<winntroot>\system32\drivers\etc`. Verify that any entry in the file for the host is correct, with the correct host name and IP address. If multiple entries for the same host name are in the file, only the first name is used. The `HOSTS` file can also have links to `HOSTS` files on other servers. If links are specified in the local `HOSTS` file, you should make sure entries in the other `HOSTS` files are also correct. You may have an unlimited number of entries in the `HOSTS` file, but each entry can be no more than 255 characters long.

The final place a client can use host name resolution is a DNS server. The client must be configured to use DNS on the DNS tab in the TCP/IP Properties dialog box. The DNS server must have a zone file corresponding to the domain name specified in the host name, or it must be able to query another DNS server that can resolve the name.

Other Symptoms of TCP/IP Configuration Problems

The material in the following sections discusses other symptoms that can indicate problems with TCP/IP connectivity or its configuration. This material is not part of the exam; nevertheless, this information is useful for troubleshooting in the real world. You can refer to this section for additional troubleshooting help with your network.

The Default Gateway Does Not Belong to Configured Interfaces

When you configure TCP/IP manually, you might receive the message `The default gateway does not belong to configured interfaces`. You get this message when the address of the default gateway cannot logically belong to the same subnet as the host IP address. This condition can happen because the subnet mask is wrong, the default gateway address is wrong, or the local host address is wrong.

The TCP/IP Host Does Not Respond

If a remote TCP/IP host does not respond, you can check the status of the connection with the `NETSTAT -a` command. This command shows all the connections established with TCP. Successful connections should have zero bytes in the send and receive queues. If bytes are in the queues, then the problem is with the connection. If the connection appears to be hung but no bytes are in the queues, there's probably a delay in the connection.

The Client Connects to the Wrong Host

You've checked everything in the IP configuration on the host and the client, yet the client connects to the wrong host. (This situation can happen when you establish a session using an IP address rather than a host name, such as when using Telnet.) This symptom can occur when duplicate IP addresses are on the network. You have to find the computer with the duplicate address and modify its address so that it is unique. With duplicate addresses, connections are inconsistent—clients sometimes connect to one host, sometimes to another.

Error 53 Is Returned When Trying to Make a NetBIOS Session

You are trying to establish a NetBIOS session, such as mapping a drive by using the `Net Use` command, but Error 53 is returned. This error happens because the computer name cannot be found on the network. In other words, TCP/IP can't find a computer name to resolve to an IP address. You can use the normal NetBIOS host resolution troubleshooting to resolve this problem. If the host names are correct, it's possible you are using NetBIOS scopes. If NetBIOS scopes are configured (nonblank), only hosts with the same scope ID can communicate with one another.

An FTP Server Does Not Seem to Work

FTP must be installed correctly before any clients can make connections to the server. Just as you can ping the loopback address to test a TCP/IP installation, you can also FTP the loopback address on the FTP server to test the FTP installation.

CHAPTER SUMMARY

Your understanding of TCP/IP is key to your success at problem resolution. In some cases, you will recognize an error as it occurs, but the vast majority of errors are caused by not following directions or by configuring incorrect settings. As you have seen in this chapter, there are quite a number of things that can potentially go wrong. Fortunately for us as professionals, this is more the exception than the rule.

This chapter brings together all your TCP/IP knowledge and applies it accordingly. Unlike many other topics you may have encountered in your testing career, TCP/IP requires a full understanding for you to be competent. If you have had difficulties with a particular subject in this chapter, it is strongly suggested that you review the other chapters in this book that are related to that subject.

CHAPTER REVIEW

REVIEW QUESTIONS

Note: The additional Chapter Review section that ends each chapter is unique to this member of the *New Riders TestPrep, Second Edition* series. We've included it to more fully and fairly cover the unique aspects of TCP/IP in relation to its mastery in preparation for MCSE examination.

1. **Which of the following steps should you perform to verify that your router is configured correctly?**

   A. Ping a remote host.

   B. Ping 127.0.0.1.

   C. Execute the `ROUTE` command.

   D. Execute `IPCONFIG /ALL`.

2. **Your IP address is 136.193.5.1 and your subnet mask is 255.255.240.0. You are trying to ping a host with the command `ping 136.193.2.23`, but the ping doesn't work. What could cause the ping to fail?**

   A. The default gateway is not configured correctly.

   B. The subnet mask interprets the IP address as being on another subnet and the packet is routed.

   C. The subnet mask interprets the address as being on the local subnet and the packet is not routed.

   D. You must ping the local host first.

3. **The network is configured with two subnets divided by a Cisco 2500 Series router. The router has two Ethernet interfaces: Interface E0 with 134.57.32.1 and Interface E1 as 134.57.64.1. All computers use a subnet mask of 255.255.224.0. Your NT Workstation cannot connect to a remote server on Network 0, but all other workstations on Network 1 can. You are located on Network 1. When you run IPCONFIG on your workstation, you receive the following output:**

IP Address	134.57.80.16
Subnet Mask	255.255.240.0
Default Gateway	134.57.32.1

   What is most likely the cause of the problem?

   A. The IP address on workstation is invalid.

   B. The default gateway on the workstation is invalid.

   C. The subnet mask on the workstation is invalid.

   D. The default gateway on the server is invalid.

   E. The IP address on the server is invalid.

4. **TCP/IP is not working. You recall that when Windows NT first booted, the message `A Dependency Service Failed to Start` appeared. What is a possible cause of the problem?**

A. The SNMP service is not installed.

B. The network card is not configured correctly.

C. The secondary WINS server is down.

D. The PDC of your domain is down.

5. **You can ping a remote host's IP address, but you cannot connect to a share on that host. What is a possible cause of this problem?**

A. The share must be configured to enable anonymous connections.

B. The Host Name Resolution Protocol must be installed.

C. The `LMHOSTS` file does not have an entry for this server.

D. The client has not been configured to use DHCP.

6. **You made a mistake in configuring an IP address and typed the client's address as 96.82.49.208 rather than 196.82.49.208. What is the most likely result of this configuration error?**

A. The client can communicate only with hosts having the network address 96.x.x.x.

B. The client cannot communicate with hosts beyond the local subnet.

C. The client cannot communicate with hosts on the local subnet.

D. The client cannot communicate with any hosts.

7. **You are using NWLink and TCP/IP. How can you reduce the time that is needed to establish a TCP/IP session with another host?**

A. Move TCP/IP to the top of the bindings for the workstation service.

B. Configure the default gateway address to point to a faster router.

C. Decrease the TTL for WINS registrations.

D. Use SNMP to tune the TCP/IP cache size.

8. **A DHCP client has failed to lease an IP address. What is the best way to have the client try again to get a lease?**

A. Issue a `REQUEST` command to the DHCP server.

B. Reserve an address for the client on the DHCP server.

C. Use `IPCONFIG /release`, then `IPCONFIG /renew`.

D. Reboot the client.

9. **What is the effect if you do not configure a router address on a TCP/IP client?**

A. You cannot communicate with any other TCP/IP hosts.

B. You can communicate only with hosts connected to the default gateway.

C. You can communicate only with hosts on the local subnet.

D. TCP/IP doesn't initialize.

10. You have several entries for a host name in an `LMHOSTS` file. Which entry is used to resolve the host name to an IP address?

A. The entry with the most current time stamp

B. The first entry in the file

C. The last entry in the file

D. The entry with the largest IP address

11. A DHCP client has been configured to use the wrong DNS server. How can you correct the problem?

A. Change the scope options on DHCP and then renew the lease on the client.

B. Use `IPCONFIG /update:DNS` to make the change.

C. Enter the address of the DNS server on the DNS tab of the TCP/IP configuration properties.

D. Add an entry for the DHCP client on the other DNS server.

12. A TCP/IP client had a drive mapped to an NT Server. You have just changed the IP address of the server and rebooted. Now the client can't connect to the new server, even though the server is configured to be a WINS client. What is the most likely cause of this problem?

A. The WINS server hasn't copied the new registration to all its clients.

B. The client has the old IP address cached.

C. The `LMHOSTS` file on the NT Server needs to be updated.

D. The DNS server needs to be updated.

13. On an NT computer, where does TCP/IP display its error messages?

A. In the TCP/IP log file

B. In the SNMP log file

C. In the system log

D. In the `TCP.ERR` file

14. How can you test the installation of an FTP server?

A. Ping the FTP loopback address.

B. Ping another FTP server.

C. FTP another server.

D. FTP the loopback address.

15. What is the default subnet mask for a class C network?

A. 127.0.0.1

B. 255.0.0.0

C. 255.255.0.0

D. 255.255.255.0

16. What is the default subnet mask for a class A network?

A. 127.0.0.1

B. 255.0.0.0

C. 255.255.0.0

D. 255.255.255.0

17. What is the default subnet mask for a class B network?

A. 127.0.0.1

B. 255.0.0.0

C. 255.255.0.0

D. 255.255.255.0

18. You are running a TCP/IP-based application on several workstations. You do not want to determine each workstation address as it may potentially change due to DHCP. Also, because employees change the host name frequently, you do not want to use it. You decide on using a loopback address for uniformity. Which is the loopback address?

A. 0.0.0.1

B. 127.0.0.0

C. 127.0.0.1

D. 255.255.255.255

19. You are working at a Windows NT Workstation that is exclusively functioning with a `HOSTS` file that reads as follows:

134.57.132.9 #Production's FTP server	**prods**
134.57.18.54 #Web server	**www**
134.57.116.7 #Marketing	**retail sales**
134.57.116.2 #Sales FTP server	**sales**

When you FTP 134.57.116.2, you connect to a Windows NT server on a remote subnet, but when you try FTP to sales, it fails. What is most likely the problem?

A. The `HOSTS` file on your workstation does not contain a FQDN for the server.

B. The host name assigned to the server is not sales.

C. The `HOSTS` file on the server does not contain a FQDN for your workstation.

D. The `HOSTS` file on your workstation is not returning the correct IP address for the server.

20. You have an NT Workstation on subnet A and your NT Server is on subnet B. You receive `Network Name Not Found` error when typing the command `net use f: \\bright.firefly.com\luminate`. The IPCONFIG utility shows you the following output:

Host Name:	**burntout.firefly.com**
DNS Server	
Node Type:	**Hybrid**
NetBIOS Scope ID	
IP Routing Enabled:	**No**
WINS Proxy Enabled	**No**
NetBIOS Resolution Uses DNS:	**No**
Description:	**PCI Ethernet Adapter**
Physical Address:	**B2-19-69F-A6-14-73**
DHCP Enabled	**Yes**
IP Address	**134.57.14.5**
Subnet mask	**255.255.240.0**
Default Gateway	**134.57.13.1**
DHCP Server	**134.57.18.15**
Primary WINS Server	**134.57.18.15**
Secondary WINS Server	**134.57.18.16**
Lease Obtained:	**Sunday, Aug 9, 1998 12:12:23 PM**
Lease Expires:	**Wednesday, Aug 12, 1998 12:12:23 PM**

What is most likely the cause of the problem?

A. You have specified a host name in the path.

B. The workstation is not configured to resolve the specified host name.

C. The WINS proxy is not enabled.

D. An invalid NetBIOS scope ID is specified.

ANSWER KEY

1. A	6. D	11. A	16. B
2. C	7. A	12. B	17. C
3. B	8. C	13. C	18. C
4. B	9. C	14. D	19. D
5. C	10. B	15. D	20. A

REVIEW ANSWERS

1. Which of the following steps should you perform to verify that your router is configured correctly?

A. Ping a remote host.

1. CORRECT ANSWER: A

If the router is configured correctly, it should be able to forward a ping message to a remote host and allow the host to respond in the reverse order. A failure would indicate a problem. If multiple routers are involved, use traceroute to resolve any issues.

2. Your IP address is 136.193.5.1 and your subnet mask is 255.255.240.0. You are trying to ping a host with the command `ping 136.193.2.23`, but the ping doesn't work. What could cause the ping to fail?

C. The subnet mask interprets the address as being on the local subnet and the packet is not routed.

2. CORRECT ANSWER: C

If you calculate 255.255.240.0 for the class B network, you would find that both addresses are in fact on the same network.

3. The network is configured with two subnets divided by a Cisco 2500 Series router. The router has two Ethernet interfaces: Interface E0 with 134.57.32.1 and Interface E1 as 134.57.64.1. All computers use a subnet mask of 255.255.224.0. Your NT Workstation cannot connect to a remote server on Network 0, but all other workstations on Network 1 can. You are located on Network 1. When you run IPCONFIG on your workstation, you receive the following output:

IP Address	134.57.80.16
Subnet Mask	255.255.240.0
Default Gateway	134.57.32.1

What is most likely the cause of the problem?

B. The default gateway on the workstation is invalid.

3. CORRECT ANSWER: B

Your workstation is attempting to point at the default gateway of the remote network. The default gateway must always be a local address. Considering the subnet mask, the default gateway is remote.

4. TCP/IP is not working. You recall that when Windows NT first booted, the message `A Dependency Service Failed to Start` appeared. What is a possible cause of the problem?

B. The network card is not configured correctly.

4. CORRECT ANSWER: B

With the focus on choosing the best possible answer, the problem is most likely due to a network card that is not operating correctly. Although in some instances you may find that this is a problem that occurs with a correct installation of DHCP at the client, this was not one of the possible answers.

5. You can ping a remote host's IP address, but you cannot connect to a share on that host. What is a possible cause of this problem?

C. The `LMHOSTS` file does not have an entry for this server.

5. CORRECT ANSWER: C

The problem is clearly related to name resolution or a problem with the share itself. Because you can ping the remote system, communications are functioning fine. At this point, you must try to determine where name resolution fails—`HOSTS`, `LMHOSTS`, DNS, WINS, and so on.

6. You made a mistake in configuring an IP address and typed the client's address as 96.82.49.208 rather than 196.82.49.208. What is the most likely result of this configuration error?

D. The client cannot communicate with any hosts.

6. CORRECT ANSWER: D

Because communications must always take place with local addresses, if a remote address is used, traffic will be generated, but ignored.

7. You are using NWLink and TCP/IP. How can you reduce the time that is needed to establish a TCP/IP session with another host?

A. Move TCP/IP to the top of the bindings for the workstation service.

7. CORRECT ANSWER: A

The binding order also dictates the default protocol to use. When connections are being established, Windows will attempt to communicate in the order in which the protocols have been bound.

8. A DHCP client has failed to lease an IP address. What is the best way to have the client try again to get a lease?

C. Use `IPCONFIG /release`, then `IPCONFIG /renew`.

8. CORRECT ANSWER: C

On Windows NT systems, the `IPCONFIG` command should be used to renew and release IP addresses. However, on Windows 95 and 98 systems, the WINIPCFG GUI should be used in its place.

9. What is the effect if you do not configure a router address on a TCP/IP client?

C. You can communicate only with hosts on the local subnet.

9. CORRECT ANSWER: C

Without a default gateway, communications are limited to the local network. The default gateway setting is used to send information to a remote network. However, if other protocols such as NetBEUI or IPX are present, non-TCP/IP communications are possible.

10. You have several entries for a host name in an LMHOSTS file. Which entry is used to resolve the host name to an IP address?

B. The first entry in the file

10. CORRECT ANSWER: B

Regardless of the number of times that any entry appears in either the LMHOSTS or HOSTS file, the first entry is always used. Systems that contain spaces in the name and that share a common name with other systems, such as MIS and MIS EMAIL, tend to experience this type of issue.

11. A DHCP client has been configured to use the wrong DNS server. How can you correct the problem?

A. Change the scope options on DHCP and then renew the lease on the client.

11. CORRECT ANSWER: A

Because you are working with a DHCP client, you will have to make the modifications at the DHCP server, then have the client renew the changes. Depending on the client, you may have to perform a release first. The issue is due to the fact that a client will communicate only with a DHCP server whose lease time is less than 50% depleted.

12. A TCP/IP client had a drive mapped to an NT Server. You have just changed the IP address of the server and rebooted. Now the client can't connect to the new server, even though the server is configured to be a WINS client. What is the most likely cause of this problem?

B. The client has the old IP address cached.

12. CORRECT ANSWER: B

Using the NBTSTAT utility (-c option), you should be able to verify the address that the client was using to communicate with the server. If the address is incorrect, use the -R to purge and restart the NetBIOS cache.

13. On an NT computer, where does TCP/IP display its error messages?

C. In the system log

13. CORRECT ANSWER: C

As a system component, TCP/IP errors are displayed in the system log of the event viewer. Often, programs that require TCP/IP also show other errors here, and in the application and security logs.

14. How can you test the installation of an FTP server?

D. FTP the loopback address.

14. CORRECT ANSWER: D

To test an FTP server, you can open a FTP session to it either by its own IP address, its host name, or the loopback address. The client will run the full range of the stack and data will be passed to and from the server. A better test, however, would be to use a remote client—perhaps one opposite your firewall if necessary.

15. What is the default subnet mask for a class C network?

D. 255.255.255.0

15. CORRECT ANSWER: D

The default subnet mask for a class C network is 255.255.255.0. With this mask, you are notified that the first three octets (which are 11111111 three times) are used for the Network ID, whereas the 0 indicates a maximum of 254 clients.

16. What is the default subnet mask for a class A network?

B. 255.0.0.0

16. CORRECT ANSWER: B

The default subnet mask for a class A network is 255.0.0.0. With this mask, you are notified that the first octet (which is 11111111) is used for the Network ID, while the three zeros indicates the host IDs that can be assigned to your clients. Typically, this mask is seen on the Internet only because companies and organizations with class A networks will all subdivide them.

17. What is the default subnet mask for a class B network?

C. 255.255.0.0

17. CORRECT ANSWER: C

The default subnet mask for a class B network is 255.255.0.0. With this mask, you are notified that the first two octets (which are 11111111 twice) are used for the Network ID, whereas the zeros indicate a maximum of approximately 65,000 clients.

18. You are running a TCP/IP-based application on several workstations. You do not want to determine each workstation address as it may potentially change due to DHCP. Also, because employees change the host name frequently, you do not want to use it. You decide on using a loopback address for uniformity. Which is the loopback address?

C. 127.0.0.1

18. CORRECT ANSWER: C

Begin this question by skipping to the point: What is the loopback address? You should be able to recall that 127.0.0.1 is *the* loopback address. Note that practically anything that ends with 255 will always be a broadcast, whereas anything that ends with a 0 will always be for the local network (subnet mask permitting).

19. You are working at a Windows NT Workstation that is exclusively functioning with a `HOSTS` file that reads as follows:

134.57.132.9	prods	#Production's FTP server
134.57.18.54	www	#Web server
134.57.116.7	retail sales	#Marketing
134.57.116.2	sales	#Sales FTP server

When you FTP 134.57.116.2, you connect to a Windows NT server on a remote subnet, but when you try FTP to sales, it fails. What is most likely the problem?

D. The `HOSTS` file on your workstation is not returning the correct IP address for the server.

19. CORRECT ANSWER: D

This is a simple problem. The word `sales` appears in the `HOSTS` file twice. During name resolution, the first entry is getting selected.

20. You have an NT Workstation on subnet A and your NT Server is on subnet B. You receive `Network Name Not Found` error when typing the command `net use f: \\bright.firefly.com\luminate`. The IPCONFIG utility shows you the following output:

Host Name:	burntout.firefly.com
DNS Server	
Node Type:	Hybrid
NetBIOS Scope ID	
IP Routing Enabled:	No
WINS Proxy Enabled	No
NetBIOS Resolution Uses DNS:	No
Description:	PCI Ethernet Adapter
Physical Address:	B2-19-69F-A6-14-73
DHCP Enabled	Yes
IP Address	134.57.14.5
Subnet mask	255.255.240.0
Default Gateway	134.57.13.1
DHCP Server	134.57.18.15
Primary WINS Server	134.57.18.15
Secondary WINS Server	134.57.18.16
Lease Obtained:	Sunday, Aug 9, 1998 12:12:23 PM
Lease Expires:	Wednesday, Aug 12, 1998 12:12:23 PM

What is most likely the cause of the problem?

A. You have specified a host name in the path.

20. CORRECT ANSWER: A

NetBIOS names are not compatible with host names. It's just that simple. Even if the NetBIOS name is Bright, using a fully distinguished name such as `Bright.firefly.com` changes everything.

EXAM QUESTIONS

Practice Exam 1

1. **You are in the process of analyzing a problem that requires you to collect and store TCP/IP packets. Which of the following utilities is best suited for this purpose?**

   A. NBTSTAT

   B. Performance Monitor

   C. NETSTAT

   D. Network Monitor

   E. DHCP Management Console

2. **You need to determine whether IP information has been assigned to your Windows NT. Which utility should you use?**

   A. NBTSTAT

   B. NETSTAT

   C. IPCONFIG

   D. WINIPCFG

   E. PING

3. **A network consists of eight NT servers. You are planning to move servers to different segments of your network. What utility should be used at each server to determine which server generates the most traffic?**

   A. NBTSTAT.EXE

   B. NETSTAT.EXE

   C. Performance Monitor

   D. Network Monitor

   E. ARP.EXE

4. **You are working with a network that is 172.16.0.0 and would like to have the maximum number of hosts per subnet. This assumes support for eight subnets. What subnet mask should you use?**

   A. 255.255.192.0

   B. 255.255.224.0

   C. 255.255.240.0

   D. 255.255.248.0

   E. 255.255.255.0

5. **You are working with a network that is 172.16.0.0 and would like to support 600 hosts per subnet. What subnet mask should you use?**

   A. 255.255.192.0

   B. 255.255.224.0

   C. 255.255.240.0

   D. 255.255.248.0

   E. 255.255.252.0

6. **You are working with a network that has the network ID 10.9.0.0 and contains 73 networks. In the next year, you will be adding an additional 27 branch offices to your company. For simplified management, you want to keep the most possible hosts per subnet. Which subnet mask should you use?**

   A. 255.224.0.0

   B. 255.240.0.0

   C. 255.248.0.0

   D. 255.252.0.0

   E. 255.254.0.0

7. **You are working with a network that has the network ID 172.16.0.0, and you require 25 subnets for your company and an additional 30 for the company that will merge with you within a month. Each network will contain approximately 600 nodes. What subnet mask should you assign?**

   A. 255.255.192.0

   B. 255.255.224.0

   C. 255.255.240.0

   D. 255.255.248.0

   E. 255.255.252.0

8. **You are working with a network that has the network ID 192.168.10.0 and require nine subnets for your company and the maximum number of hosts. What subnet mask should you use?**

   A. 255.255.255.192

   B. 255.255.255.224

   C. 255.255.255.240

   D. 255.255.255.248

   E. 255.255.255.252

9. **You are working with a class C network. You are required to configure it for five subnets, each of which will support 25 nodes. What subnet should you use?**

   A. 255.255.255.0

   B. 255.255.255.224

   C. 255.255.255.240

   D. 255.255.255.248

   E. 255.255.255.252

10. **You are working with three networks that have the network IDs 192.168.5.0, 192.168.6.0, and 192.168.7.0. What subnet mask can you use to combine these addresses into one?**

    A. 255.255.252.0

    B. 255.255.254.0

    C. 255.255.255.240

    D. 255.255.255.252

    E. 255.255.255.254

11. **You are working with a network that has the network ID 192.168.10.0. What subnet should you use that supports four subnets and a maximum number of hosts?**

    A. 255.255.255.192

    B. 255.255.255.224

    C. 255.255.255.240

    D. 255.255.255.248

    E. 255.255.255.252

12. You are working with a network that has the network ID 192.168.10.0. What subnet should you use that supports up to 12 hosts and a maximum number of subnets?

A. 255.255.255.192

B. 255.255.255.224

C. 255.255.255.240

D. 255.255.255.248

E. 255.255.255.252

13. You are working with a network that has the network ID 192.168.10.0. What subnet should you use that supports up to 25 hosts and a maximum number of subnets?

A. 255.255.255.192

B. 255.255.255.224

C. 255.255.255.240

D. 255.255.255.248

E. 255.255.255.252

14. Which of the following utilities is used to view captured packets on your Windows NT server?

A. NBTSTAT

B. NETSTAT

C. Network Monitor

D. Performance Monitor

E. IPCONFIG

15. You are in the process of dividing your class B network into several segments. One of the segments will be connected to the Internet. You want all of your systems to be able to communicate to the Internet. How should you define your subnet mask?

A. Use the default subnet mask.

B. Use one that includes the IP address of the router.

C. Use a custom subnet mask.

D. Use a subnet mask of 0.0.0.0.

E. Do not use a subnet mask.

16. You are planning a network implantation. How many host IDs are required when you determine a subnet mask? Select two answers.

A. One per subnet

B. One per WAN connection

C. One per router

D. One per network

E. One per network adapter in a host device

17. You are planning a network implementation. How many network IDs are required when you determine a subnet mask? Select two answers.

A. One per subnet

B. One per WAN connection

C. One per router

D. One per device

E. One per network adapter in a host device

18. You are planning a network implementation. Which two considerations must you make to define the subnet? Select two answers.

A. Number of subnets to the network

B. Location of DNS servers

C. Default gateways

D. Network traffic

E. Number of host IDs

19. Your system cannot communicate with a remote network. It can communicate with any system including the default gateway on your local network, but no further. Everyone else's system works fine. Which of the following are possible problems? Select two answers.

A. The route is not defined at the router.

B. Your subnet mask is invalid.

C. Your default gateway is invalid.

D. The subnet mask at the router is wrong.

E. No mappings have been defined in the `LMHOSTS` file.

20. A user can ping her own local address but no other systems. The `net view` command returns an empty list. What is a likely problem?

A. The user has a duplicate IP address.

B. WINS has not been enabled.

C. The subnet mask is incorrect.

D. The default gateway is wrong.

E. The network adapter is faulty.

21. While browsing Network Neighborhood, you are able to establish a session with a remote system, but not to any of those that are local. What should you suspect is the problem?

A. Your default gateway is incorrect.

B. Your subnet mask is incorrect.

C. The default gateway on the local server is incorrect.

D. The subnet mask on the remote server is incorrect.

E. You have an invalid IP address.

22. While browsing Network Neighborhood, you are not able to establish a session with a local system, although all other workstations can. You run Network Monitor and find that while trying to connect to the local server, your system makes an ARP request of the router. What should you suspect is the problem?

A. Your default gateway is incorrect.

B. Your subnet mask is incorrect.

C. The default gateway on the local server is incorrect.

D. The subnet mask on the remote server is incorrect.

E. You have an invalid IP address.

23. While browsing Network Neighborhood, you are not able to establish a session with a remote server, although all other workstations can. Aside from the remainder of the WAN that you never use to communicate, your LAN consists of two segments divided by a single Cisco 2500 series router. The first Ethernet interface on the router is configured with an IP address of 172.16.32.1, and the second interface is 172.16.64.1. Every device on the network is using a subnet mask of 255.255.240.0.

When you run IPCONFIG, your IP address is shown as 172.16.80.10, using 172.16.64.1 as the default gateway. What should you suspect is the problem?

A. Your default gateway is incorrect.

B. Your subnet mask is incorrect.

C. IP address is invalid on the remote server.

D. The remote server is using the wrong default gateway.

E. You have an invalid IP address.

24. **While troubleshooting an NT Server on network 172.16.10.0, you find that remote users cannot establish connections. By running IPCONFIG /ALL, you find the following information:**

Host Name	firefly
DNS Servers	
Node Type	Hybrid
NetBIOS Scope ID	
IP Routing Enabled	no
WINS Proxy Enabled	no
NetBIOS Resolution Uses DNS	no
Physical Address	02-10-BF-DB-E2-257
DHCP Enabled	no
IP Address:	172.16.10.10
Subnet Mask	255.255.0.0
Default Gateway	172.16.10.1
Primary WINS Server	172.16.10.3

What item would seem to be the cause of the problem?

A. The NetBIOS scope ID is not set.

B. The NetBIOS node type is incorrect.

C. The IP address is invalid.

D. The subnet mask is invalid.

E. The default gateway is invalid.

25. **You are installing DHCP on your network and want all clients to receive the identical settings for the DNS servers. You have 22 network segments. How should DHCP be configured to deliver the DNS information?**

A. Using a global option

B. Using a local option

C. Using a scope option

D. Using a client option

E. Using a network option

26. **Your routers do not support BOOTP forwarding. You would like to use the DHCP relay agent. What information is required?**

A. The name of the DHCP server

B. The IP address of the DHCP server

C. The network ID for the DHCP server

D. The address of the router that connects the DHCP server

E. All of the above

27. **You are configuring DHCP client reservations for your servers. What information is required? Select two answers.**

A. Lease period

B. IP address

C. Hardware address

D. Subnet mask

E. Default gateway

28. Your network consists of 22 segments serviced by two DHCP servers. If one DHCP server fails, the other server must function in its place. How should this be done?

A. Create a global DHCP scope on each server.

B. Create two global DCHP scopes on each server.

C. Create 11 scopes on each DHCP server.

D. Create 22 scopes on each DHCP server.

E. Create 44 scopes on each DHCP server.

29. You are configuring a sales office for laptop users. You need to configure them to receive TCP/IP configuration information only for the short time that they are in the office. What should you use to do this?

A. DHCP.

B. DNS.

C. WINS.

D. BOOTP.

E. Configure the workstations statically.

30. Using DHCP to assign addresses, what do you do to configure your servers to receive the same IP address each time?

A. Use the client reservation feature.

B. You can't; the information must be static.

C. Use the Exclude feature and label the exclusion description as the server name.

D. Use a scope that is limited to servers only.

E. Set the server lease period to Never Expire.

31. Your network of 205 hosts is divided into department segments: Sales, Engineering, and Accounting. All Sales users have laptops that they take with them into the field. You want these users to have addresses for nine hours, while all others should have theirs for five days. What should you do?

A. Create a DCHP scope for each segment with a nine-hour lease duration. Then define client reservations for each workstation that sets the lease period to five days.

B. Create three DHCP scopes. Set the scope accordingly for each subnet to which it is assigned.

C. Create one DHCP that defines 18 hours (2 × 9). Because every client renews at half its lease period, laptop users will have nine hours, and all other clients will be able to renew their information for the next five days, until the weekend.

D. DCHP does not support the requirements of the question.

E. Only one scope should be created, of which the maximum of five days should be specified. There should be enough addresses, regardless.

32. Your network is configured with a number of mobile users that interface your network from different subnets.
You want to configure them so that they automatically receive IP addresses for the WINS server. Which of the following provides this capability?

A. DNS

B. WINS

C. DHCP

D. SNMP

E. BOOTP

33. Your network consists of three NT servers—one on network A, one on network B, and the third acting as a router. The NT Server on network A hosts DHCP. The client on network B needs to get DHCP assigments. What is required to do this?

A. DHCP Relay Agent.

B. WIN Relay Agent.

C. RIP for IP.

D. A Route command to forward all broadcasts.

E. You must move the DHCP server to the router.

34. Using DHCP, you want to provide 125 clients with addresses and configure 10 servers with the same information each time the users boot up. Your network is designed with the following structure:

Routers 1–5

Clients 5–100 and 150–254

Server 101–149

What is the correct way to set this configuration in DHCP?

A. Create three scopes for each type of client.

B. Create four scopes—two for the clients, one for the routers, and one for the servers.

C. Create one scope that excludes gateway addresses and has reservations for servers.

D. Create one scope that reserves both gateways and server addresses.

E. Create two scopes. One scope should begin at 5, exclude the server range, but include client reservations for each server. A second scope should be created for the server range.

35. You are planning DHCP services for three subnets: A, B, and C. You are using NT routers. You plan to have the server on subnet A. Which of the following are good locations for the relay agents? Select two answers.

A. On subnets B and C.

B. On subnet A.

C. At the DHCP server.

D. At the router.

E. Relay agents are not needed.

36. Your network consists of 350 clients, 18 servers, two DHCP systems, two WINS servers, and one DNS. Many clients are receiving duplicate addresses. What is the most likely problem?

A. The two WINS servers are not communicating their databases.

B. All DHCP addresses have been used.

C. The two DHCP servers have overlapping ranges.

D. The DNS reports two systems with the same IP address.

E. You must use the relay agent to support more than 254 node objects per network.

37. **This question is based on the following scenario.**

Scenario:
Your TCP/IP network consists of eight Windows NT servers, 23 NT workstations, 206 Windows 95/98 Systems, and 15 UNIX hosts. All 206 users play musical chairs and do not remain on any particular subnet. All NT and UNIX systems are stationary. A single DHCP server has been configured with multiple scopes to support all subnets. All Microsoft systems use DHCP.

Required Results:
All systems must be able to communicate with every other system via host name.

All systems must be able to get an IP address lease from the DHCP server.

Optional Results:
The UNIX systems should be able to communicate with NT servers running FTP services via host name.

All systems should be able to communicate with the UNIX systems for Telnet and FTP services by host name.

Proposed Solution:
Exclude all UNIX hosts' IP addresses at the DHCP server. Set a DHCP to deliver clients with the WINS and DNS servers. Configure a DNS server with reverse lookup to WINS. Install WINS and configure it with static mappings for the UNIX systems. Set all routers to forward DHCP requests.

Evaluation of Proposed Solution:
What results will the proposed solution produce?

A. The proposed solution fulfills all the required and optional results.

B. The proposed solution fulfills the required results but only one of the optional results.

C. The proposed solution fulfills the required results but none of the optional results.

D. The proposed solution does not fulfill the required or optional results.

E. Only the optional results are fulfilled.

38. **This question is based on the following scenario.**

Scenario:
Your TCP/IP network consists of eight Windows NT servers, 23 NT workstations, 206 Windows 95/98 systems, and 15 UNIX hosts. All 206 users play musical chairs and do not remain on any particular subnet. All NT and UNIX systems are stationary. A single DHCP server has been configured with support for all subnets. All Microsoft systems use DHCP.

Required Results:
All Windows systems must be able to communicate with every other system via host name.

All Windows systems must be able to get an IP address lease from the DHCP server.

Optional Results:
The UNIX systems should be able to communicate with NT servers running FTP services via host name.

All systems should be able to communicate with the UNIX systems for Telnet and FTP services by host name.

Proposed Solution:
Exclude all UNIX hosts' IP addresses at the DHCP server. Set a DHCP to deliver clients with the WINS servers. Install WINS and configure it with static mappings for the UNIX systems. Set all routers to forward DHCP requests.

Evaluation of Proposed Solution:
What results will the proposed solution produce?

A. The proposed solution fulfills all the required and optional results.

B. The proposed solution fulfills the required results but only one of the optional results.

C. The proposed solution fulfills the required results but none of the optional results.

D. The proposed solution does not fulfill the required or optional results.

E. Only the optional results are fulfilled.

39. This question is based on the following scenario.

Scenario:
Your TCP/IP network consists of eight Windows NT servers, 23 NT workstations, 206 Windows 95/98 Systems, and 15 UNIX hosts. All 206 users play musical chairs and do not remain on any particular subnet. All NT and UNIX systems are stationary. A single DHCP server has been configured with support for all subnets. All Microsoft systems use DHCP.

Required Results:
All Windows systems must be able to communicate with every other system via host name.

All Windows systems must be able to get an IP address lease from the DHCP server.

Optional Results:
The UNIX systems should be able to communicate to NT servers running FTP services via host name.

All systems should be able to communicate with the UNIX systems for Telnet and FTP services by host name.

Proposed Solution:
Exclude all UNIX hosts' IP addresses at the DHCP server. Set a DHCP to deliver clients with the WINS servers. Install WINS. Set all routers to forward DHCP requests. Configure each Windows system with a `HOSTS` file containing all UNIX hosts.

Evaluation of Proposed Solution:
What results will the proposed solution produce?

A. The proposed solution fulfills all the required and optional results.

B. The proposed solution fulfills the required results but only one of the optional results.

C. The proposed solution fulfills the required results but none of the optional results.

D. The proposed solution does not fulfill the required or optional results.

E. Only the optional results are fulfilled.

40. This question is based on the following scenario.

Scenario:
Your TCP/IP network consists of eight Windows NT servers, 23 NT workstations, 206 Windows 95/98 systems, and 15 UNIX hosts. All 206 users play musical chairs and do not remain on any particular subnet. All NT and UNIX systems are stationary. A single DHCP server has been configured with support for all subnets. All Microsoft systems use DHCP.

Required Results:
All Windows systems must be able to communicate with every other system via host name.

All Windows systems must be able to get an IP address lease from the DHCP server.

Optional Results:
The UNIX systems should be able to communicate with NT servers running FTP services via host name.

All systems should be able to communicate with the UNIX systems for Telnet and FTP services by host name.

Proposed Solution:
Set a DHCP to deliver clients with the WINS servers. Install WINS. Set all routers to forward DHCP requests.

Evaluation of Proposed Solution:
What results will the proposed solution produce?

A. The proposed solution fulfills all the required and optional results.

B. The proposed solution fulfills the required results but only one of the optional results.

C. The proposed solution fulfills the required results but none of the optional results.

D. The proposed solution does not fulfill the required or optional results.

E. Only the optional results are fulfilled.

41. This question is based on the following scenario.

Scenario:
You desire to configure all clients on your eight-subnet network for DHCP. Two DHCP servers have been installed.

Required Result:
If one server fails the other must take over its responsibilities.

Optional Results:
Each server must get the same IP address each time it is started.

WINS and DNS information is to be delivered by DHCP.

Proposed Solution:
Install DHCP's relay agent on each subnet. Define a scope with the IP range for each subnet on DHCP server 1. Perform the exact same operation on DHCP server 2.

Evaluation of Proposed Solution:
What results will the proposed solution produce?

A. The proposed solution fulfills all the required and optional results.

B. The proposed solution fulfills the required result and only one of the optional results.

C. The proposed solution fulfills the required result but none of the optional results.

D. The proposed solution does not fulfill the required or optional results.

E. Only the optional results are fulfilled.

42. You just configured your DHCP server to deliver WINS information. Which node type will check resolution with the server before broadcasting?

A. B-NODE

B. P-NODE

C. M-NODE

D. H-NODE

E. Z-NODE

43. A user named Al uses the command `NET USE F: \\BRIGHT.FIREFLY.COM\SHARE` but is unable to map a drive on the system on the remote network. Al has verified that he can establish communications with the `PING` command. What is the problem?

A. BRIGHT.FIREFLY.COM is not a NetBIOS name.

B. No such name exists in the DNS server.

C. The workstation is not set to use the DNS.

D. The workstation is not set to use WINS.

E. The workstation has a corrupt `LMHOSTS` file.

44. Your TCP/IP network consists of four segments, each with an NT domain controller. You would like all your Windows-based clients to automatically register their names. Which service should you use?

A. DHCP

B. WINS

C. DNS

D. SNMP

E. SMTP

45. You have 10 subnets with two domain controllers per subnet. What should you put in the `LMHOSTS` file of each client PC? Select two answers.

A. An entry for each router

B. The default gateway

C. An entry for each domain controller

D. An entry for each PDC in other domains

E. An entry for each BDC in other domains

46. You are looking for a dynamic solution to host name resolution. Which of the following best represents that solution?

A. Use DNS and WINS where DNS is using WINS for name lookups.

B. Use standard DNS and set dynamic on.

C. Build a centralized `HOSTS` file.

D. Use WINS only.

E. Use DNS and DHCP, where DNS is using DHCP for name lookups.

47. You have a network comprised of many subnets. No WINS services have been installed on the network. What should you do to ensure network authentication?

A. Modify the `HOSTS` file so that each domain controller is listed, followed by `#DOM`.

B. Modify the routers to bridge all traffic.

C. Modify your `LMHOSTS` file so that each domain controller is listed, followed by `#PRE #DOM`.

D. Set the default gateway to the IP address of the PDC.

E. Do nothing.

48. Your network has four segments, each with a domain controller. You need to guarantee that BDCs can communicate with the PDC. WINS is not installed, but each domain controller acts as the master browser for each respective subnet. Which of the following is required?

A. Create an LMHOSTS file that lists the PDC with #PRE and #DOM flags and place it on each BDC.

B. Modify the routers to bridge all traffic.

C. Modify your LMHOSTS file so that each domain controller is listed, followed by #PRE #DOM.

D. Install the DNS service on the PDC and each BDC; specify that for host name resolution.

E. Set the default gateway to the IP address of the PDC.

49. Your network has four segments, each with a domain controller. WINS is not installed, but each domain controller acts as the master browser for each respective subnet. You want each domain controller to perform authentication services and to update itself with the PDC. Which of the following is required? Select two answers.

A. Create an LMHOSTS file on each domain controller that lists the other domain controllers.

B. Modify the LMHOSTS file on each client computer so that each domain controller is listed, followed by #PRE-#DOM.

C. Install the DNS service on the PDC and each BDC; specify that for host name resolution.

D. Set the default gateway to the IP address of the PDC.

E. Do nothing.

50. While you are trying to connect to a remote Windows NT server using `net use j: \\firefly\bright`, you get an error stating that the computer or sharename could not be found. You are able to ping the system by IP address (172.16.32.12) to communicate, but not with `net use`. Your system is running Windows NT workstation as a WINS client and contains an LMHOSTS file with the following entries:

```
172.16.32.12   FIREFLY
172.16.33.8    LIGHTHOUSE
172.16.33.9    HORSEFLY
```

What appears to be the problem?

A. The Workstation is configured to resolve NetBIOS names in a P-NODE configuration.

B. The computer name is incorrect in the LMHOSTS file.

C. The workstation is configured for DNS.

D The host name and IP address in the LMHOSTS file are reversed.

E. The HOSTS file is incorrectly configured.

51. You are troubleshooting your HOSTS file. Every time you attempt to connect to any servers via host name, you receive an error message. Your HOSTS file appears as follows:

127.0.0.1	#localhost #$Loop & Test
172.16.30.2	#CDServer MainDTS # CDR$ & Server
172.16.42.1	#router RouterXOver # Engr $ router
172.16.42.96	#ENGNET NET42 # Engineering & Group

What should you do to correct the problems?

A. Remove the # characters after the IP address.

B. Remove the $ characters.

C. Remove the & characters.

D. Delete the HOSTS file.

E. Reorder the IP addresses to follow the text portion of each line.

52. To ensure authentication, you want to place an entry for the PDC in your company NPS into the LMHOSTS file. (The name of both the company and domain is NPS.) Which of the following would be correct if the PDC is named NETPRO and its IP address is 172.16.10.5?

A. `172.16.10.5 NPS NETPRO #PRE #DOM`

B. `172.16.10.5 NETPRO #PRE #DOM`

C. `172.16.10.5 NPS #PRE #DOM`

D. `172.16.10.5 NETPRO #PRE #DOM:NPS`

E. `172.16.10.5 NPS #PRE #DOM:NETPRO`

53. Your network consists of UNIX, Windows NT Servers, Windows NT Workstations, and Windows 98 clients with four DNS servers. You want all DNS servers to look up any entries not in their databases from WINS. How should this be done?

A. Set all DNS servers to use WINS reverse lookup.

B. Set the primary DNS server to use WINS reverse lookup.

C. Set TCP/IP on all DNS servers to use WINS for name resolution.

D. Set TCP/IP on the primary DNS to use WINS for name resolution.

E. Set WINS for reverse lookup and list all DNS servers.

54. You are setting up an Internet solution. Internally, your system is known as NetFLY, but after installing IIS, you decide that you want users to refer to the system by service (WWW and FTP). That way, if you expand later, there will be no problems. How should this be done?

A. Add a DNS MX Record.

B. Add a DNS CNAME Record.

C. Change the computer name to WWW and the host name to FTP.

D. Modify WINS with an additional static entry.

E. Use two systems.

55. You are attempting to configure your NT server as the print server for a TCP/IP-based printer. You want all users to be able to use this printer. How should you perform this configuration?

A. Redirect traffic to a logical printer port by using the LPR command.

B. Redirect traffic to a logical printer port by using the LPQ command.

C. Redirect traffic to a logical printer port by using the NET PRINT command.

D. Install TCP/IP printing services on the NT server.

E. Both A and C.

56. A UNIX system is configured as an LPD server. Microsoft Client wants to send documents directly to that printer. How should this be done?

A. By using the LPR command

B. By using the LPQ command

C. By using the NET PRINT command

D. By installing TCP/IP printing services

E. Both A and C

57. What configuration changes should you make so that your UNIX systems can print to a device on a Windows NT Server computer using the LPR command?

A. Share the printer on the NT Server.

B. Assign an IP address to the printer.

C. Install TCP/IP printing services on each UNIX system.

D. Install TCP/IP printing services on the NT server.

E. Run the LPR server daemon on the NT Server.

58. You want to share a printer on your Windows NT Server with UNIX clients. What do you do?

A. Make the appropriate IP setting on the printer.

B. Create a share on the Windows system.

C. Install the LPR service.

D. Install TCP/IP Printing Service.

E. Use the TCP/IP to UNIX gateway.

59. Your main production printer is UNIX based on a system that runs the LPD service. You want all your Microsoft clients to print to it via the Windows NT Server. How should this be performed? Select two answers.

A. On the NT Server, redirect a port to the UNIX system.

B. On the NT Server, redirect a port to the printer.

C. Use the LPR command on all workstations.

D. Install TCP/IP printing at the NT Server.

E. Add a printer to the Windows NT Server that uses an LPR port to send documents to the UNIX print device.

60. You are the administrator of a network containing UNIX, Macintosh, and Microsoft-based clients. You want all clients to be able to share files with one another and store them on the Windows NT Server. What service should you use?

A. WWW

B. DHCP

C. FTP

D. DNS

E. NET Share

61. UNIX systems must be able to connect to a server on a remote network via the UNC name. The FTP 172.16.20.5 command fails. What is the problem?

A. Permissions to FTP have not been assigned.

B. The server does not have a default gateway.

C. The server is not configured for WINS.

D. The workstation does not have a default gateway.

E. Your server is not configured in DNS.

62. **You are troubleshooting FTP problems that you have on your system. Because you do not have a DNS, your workstation has been configured with the following `HOSTS` file:**

```
172.16.10.5   Marketing  #Creative People
172.16.15.5   Accounting #Bean Counters
172.16.15.10  Prod Engr  #Product Engineering
172.16.20.10  Engr       #Engineering and design
```

When you open an FTP session to 172.16.20.10, the connection is fine. However, when you attempt to connect to the host name `ENGR`, it fails. What is the problem?

A. You are required to use a DNS to resolve names.

B. You need to add `#PRE #DOM` to the `ENGR` line.

C. The `HOSTS` file is returning the wrong IP address.

D. You can't use a host name with the FTP service.

E. The `HOSTS` file on the FTP server does not contain your IP address.

63. **You want to connect to a remote Windows NT FTP server. You resolve its IP address via your `HOSTS` file on your UNIX workstation. The file appears as follows:**

```
172.16.10.5         Bright.FireFly.Com
➥#Bright Ideas Server
172.16.10.10        Burnt.FireFly.Com
➥#Not So Bright Server
172.16.10.15        Dead.FireFly.Com
➥#Bad Business Server
```

You can open FTP to 172.16.10.10. However, if you attempt to run `ftp burnt.firefly.com`, you get a "bad IP address" response. What is the most likely problem?

A. A NetBIOS name has been used with FTP.

B. FTP does not support names—only IP addresses.

C. The `HOSTS` file is incorrect as to the name associated with the IP address.

D. The name used with the FTP command is wrong.

E. The FTP service is down.

64. **You are able to open an FTP session to BRIGHT.FIREFLY.COM. However, when you use Windows NT Explorer, you are unable to access anything. What is the most likely problem?**

A. Your workstation has the wrong subnet mask.

B. The server has the wrong default gateway.

C. Your workstation has the wrong default gateway.

D. The server is not set to use WINS.

E. Your workstation is not set to use WINS.

65. **You are able to ping a server. However, when you attempt to FTP to the server FTP.FIREFLY.COM, you get a "bad IP address" response. What possible problem should you suspect? Select two answers.**

A. The ARP cache does not have a mapping for FTP.FIREFLY.COM.

B. There is no entry in the DNS database for FTP.FIREFLY.COM

C. The NetBIOS name cache does not contain an entry for FTP.FIREFLY.COM.

D. Your workstation has an invalid IP address.

E. Your workstation has the wrong address for the DNS server.

66. You want to view all documents that have been sent to a UNIX print server. Which utility should you use?

A. FTP

B. LPQ

C. LPR

D. RSH

E. TELNET

67. Which of the following utilities can be used for remote execution on a UNIX server?

A. FTP

B. LPR

C. LPQ

D. RCP

E. Telnet

68. Which of the following utilities can be used to copy binary data files to a UNIX system?

A. TFTP

B. Telnet

C. LPR

D. LPQ

E. RSH

69. Which of the following utilities can be used to print a text file to a UNIX-based print server?

A. FTP

B. LPR

C. LPQ

D. LPD

E. RCP

70. You have a Windows NT Server running the FTP service. When you attempt to connect, it fails. However, you are able to transfer files via NT Explorer. What problem should you suspect?

A. Your workstation has the wrong default gateway.

B. Your workstation is not set to use a DNS.

C. The server has the wrong default gateway.

D. The server is not set to use DNS.

E. The server is not set to use WINS.

71. You are attempting to configure your two NT static routers to support three networks. They are chained such that router 1 links networks A and B, and router 2 links B and C. The network is configured as follows:

Network A: 172.16.32.0 Mask 255.255.224.0

Network B: 172.16.64.0 Mask 255.255.224.0

Network C: 172.16.96.0 Mask 255.255.224.0

The routers are configured as follows:

Router 1: A Interface 172.16.32.1

B Interface 172.16.64.1

Router 2: B Interface 172.16.64.2

C Interface 172.16.96.1

You want to set router 1 to forward data from network A to network C. Which of the following commands should you issue?

A. `Route ADD 172.16.64.2 mask ➥255.255.224.0 172.16.96.0`

B. `Route ADD 172.16.96.0 mask ➥255.255.224.0 172.16.64.2`

C. `Route ADD 172.16.96.0 172.16.64.2`

D. `Route ADD 172.16.96.0 mask ➥255.255.224.0 172.16.64.1`

E. `Route ADD 172.16.96.0 172.16.64.1`

ANSWERS & EXPLANATIONS

1. **D.** Network Monitor is a utility that can be used to analyze network traffic, essentially providing the same features as a network sniffer. In order to use this application, the server must include a network adapter that supports promiscuous mode.

2. **C.** IPCONFIG is the main utility that is used to view IP configuration information. On Windows 95/98, you would use the WINIPCFG command instead.

3. **D.** Network Monitor provides the required solution. Performance Monitor is good for quantity information but not for this type of threshold because it yields instantaneous data less than the cumulative abilities of Network Monitor. NETSTAT should be used to view network connections, whereas NBTSTAT should be used with NetBIOS names. ARP is used to review IP address resolution.

4. **C.** Considering that you are working with a class B network and must have eight subnets, you know that you must have at least four bits reserved for the network ID—that is, (2^4) - 2, or 14 subnets. The 12 leftover bits can be used for host IDs.

5. **E.** To achieve 600 hosts per subnet, you must reserve 10 bits—that is to say, (2^{10}) - 2, or 1,022 hosts. The other six bits in the class B network can be assigned to the host IDs.

6. **E.** Because you require 100 subnets in your class A network, reserve seven bits for the host ID—that is, (2^7) - 2, or 126 subnets.

7. **E.** The requirements are 55 subnets and 600 hosts. Therefore, to have 55 subnets, you must use six additional bits. That will yield (2^6) - 2, or 62 networks. Because you used six bits for the network, that leaves 10 bits for the host—(2^{10}) - 2, or 1,022 hosts.

8. **C.** For this class C network, you require four bits to define (2^4) - 2, or 14 networks. That will leave four bits, or 14 hosts per network.

9. **B.** For five networks, you must reserve three bits—(2^3) - 2, or six subnets. By calculating the five remaining bits for the number of hosts, you find (2^5) - 2, or 30 hosts.

10. **A.** To combine these addresses into one network, you must use supernetting. To combine three hosts, you are required to borrow two bits from the network mask. That will change the third octet from 255 to 252.

11. **B.** For four networks, you must reserve three bits—(2^3) - 2, or 6 subnets. By calculating the five remaining bits for the number of hosts, you find (2^5) - 2, or 30 hosts.

12. **C.** For 12 hosts, you must reserve four bits—or (2^4) - 2, or 14 hosts. That will leave four bits, or 14 subnets, available.

13. **B.** For 25 hosts, you must reserve five bits—or (2^5) - 2, or 30 hosts. That will leave three bits, or six subnets, available.

14. **C.** Network Monitor can be used in the same capacity as a sniffer. As such, it has the ability to capture packets and display their contents.

15. **C.** You need to use a custom mask. Regardless of the mask that is set on the router connecting your network to the Internet, you need to have a subnet mask that internally defines your segments. As far as the Internet is concerned, it will see your network as one.

16. **C-E.** Each device on a network must have an IP address. That includes the router, printers, and so on.

17. **A-B.** Each subnet and WAN connection must have a network ID defined. In reality, a WAN connection is a special subnet of networking equipment such as routers.

18. **A-E.** The number of subnets combined with the number of required hosts per network define the network subnet mask.

19. **B-C.** This problem is obviously specific to your computer if no one else has the problem. In this case, your subnet may be incorrect (which makes your system think the remote systems are local), or you are attempting to send to the wrong default gateway.

20. **C.** The subnet mask is most likely incorrect. You know that IP address is valid because you can ping it. Therefore, it must be valid. WINS does not matter at this stage, and you would not have any IP response with a bad network adapter. Finally, because local communications do not work, the default gateway would not matter.

21. **B.** If your workstation is configured with a subnet mask that is incorrect, depending on the IP address of the local system you are trying to communicate with, your system will send the message to the default gateway rather than to the system. Moreover, your system may observe remote systems as local and may not be able to communicate with them, either.

22. **B.** If your workstation is configured with a subnet mask that is incorrect, depending on the IP address of the local system you are trying to communicate with, your system will send the message to the default gateway rather than to the system. That is why the system made the ARP request to the default gateway. Moreover, your system may observe remote systems as local and may not be able to communicate with them, either.

23. **E.** The IP address is wrong. When using a subnet mask of 255.255.240.0, for example, the valid ranges are 16–31, 32–47, 48–63, 64–79, 80–95, and so on. If you were using a subnet mask of 255.255.240.0, this would work; however, it does not in this case. As you can see when using 240, you are using an additional four bits for the network ID, which provides (2^4) - 2, or 14 networks. If you divide the 256 possible addresses by 2^4, you will find that the counter is 16 nodes per network as explained here. Since the third octet of your IP address is 80, it is then logically configured as if it were on a different network than the gateway.

24. **D.** The key to resolving this problem is to note that the question makes mention of three octets describing the network ID, but the subnet mask only defines two. Presumably, the server is trying to send to each workstation directly rather than to the default gateway.

25. **A.** Although a scope option would work, it is not efficient to perform this action for all 22 networks. This opens the possibility of incorrect assignments. To assign this setting to all scopes, use a global option.

26. **B.** The IP address of the DHCP server must be used when configuring a relay agent. This is a direct message, no longer a broadcast as implied by some of the other answers.

27. **B-C.** For each reserved IP address, you must associate it to a hardware address to which it will be assigned.

28. **D.** DHCP servers do not communicate with one another. Each one must be configured as if it were the only server, but must not include any overlapping addresses. One scope per segment is required.

29. **A.** DHCP is the service used to deliver TCP/IP information. Lease times can be longer or shorter depending on configuration settings.

30. **A.** The DHCP feature that assigns an address to a server is the client reservation feature.

31. **B.** The correct method for setting up this configuration is to define each scope with its own lease period. Although answer C is true, it does not answer the question that is posed. Answer E is also true, but it fails to meet the requirements of the question and does not account for future expansion.

32. **C.** TCP/IP configuration information, including the addresses of WINS and DNS servers, is always delivered by Windows NT Server via DHCP.

33. **A.** The DHCP relay agent can be used to forward requests from the B network to the A network. The solution is not to forward all broadcast traffic because that would defeat the purpose of routing. Although answer E is a possible solution, it is not the best choice.

34. **C.** You must exclude those addresses that you do not want to assign and reserve those that must be held for specific systems.

35. **A-D.** Unless it's stated that the router supports RFC1542 or BOOTP, you must add this support (to forward DHCP requests). Because you're using a Windows NT router, you can add this forwarding functionality via the relay agent. On the other hand, placing the relay agents on subnets B and C will achieve the same effect.

36. **C.** Because DHCP servers do not communicate with one another, you must configure them manually to prevent overlapping ranges.

37. **B.** For host name resolution, you are required to use a DNS. With the DNS configured to use WINS and static mappings, the host name requirement is met. However, no configuration changes are mentioned for UNIX; this support is somewhat of a gray area. UNIX may not support DHCP, depending on the release (version), and no DNS changes are created by this solution for these (UNIX) systems.

38. **B.** Configuring the WINS and DHCP servers meets the core requirements; however, without a DNS, the UNIX systems will not be able to resolve addresses.

39. **B**. Configuring the WINS and DHCP servers meets the core requirements; however, without a DNS or `HOSTS` file at the UNIX system, clients will be unable to resolve addresses for the Windows-based systems.

40. **D.** Because the UNIX system must interface with other systems, it (the UNIX system) requires a `HOSTS` file or DNS. Configuring the WINS and DHCP servers meets the core requirements; however, without a DNS or `HOSTS` file at the UNIX system, the UNIX computers will be unable to resolve addresses for the Windows-based systems. Because the network is designed of multiple segments, broadcasting will not work for name resolution.

41. **D.** Because DHCP servers will not communicate with one another, they will not give or receive notification of addresses that have been assigned. Therefore, duplicate addresses that occur will cause network failures.

42. **D.** The H-NODE 0x8 setting will check name resolution with a WINS server before broadcasting.

43. **A.** The `net use` command uses NetBIOS names. Therefore, placing a host name in that location will not work. A giveaway is that the name is more than 15 characters.

44. **B.** The WINS service acts as a centralized database for looking up NetBIOS names. When all clients are configured to work with it, name registration is performed automatically.

45. **C-D.** The purpose behind placing your domain controllers in the `HOSTS` file is to ensure that you are able to get security authentication validated. This is extremely useful when you are changing your password because you must communicate with the primary domain controller for this function. Also, if a user from another domain attempts to use your system, that user will have no problems because his PDC is included, as well.

46. **A.** The process of creating a dynamic DNS is actually a reverse lookup through a WINS server. This works as long as the host and NetBIOS names are identical.

47. **C.** The `#PRE` flag designates that an entry should be loaded upon startup, whereas the `#DOM` flags notify a client that the entry specifies a domain. A better solution would be to install WINS; however, that option is not offered.

48. **A.** The best solution would be to install WINS; however, because that option is not offered, in this case, the next best thing to do is create an `LMHOSTS` file that contains the PDC and its IP address, followed by `#PRE #DOM`.

49. **A-B.** The solution is to inform the workstation of the presence of each domain controller. When validations are being processed, they can simply be looked up locally, ensuring that they can be found. The same applies to the domain controllers; however, the catch is that in this scenario, you are concerned only with other controllers and not yourself.

50. **B.** The problem here is elimination. Communications operates fine to the NT Server system via ping and IP address. Because this is a NetBIOS name, not a host name, the problem is very unlikely to be with the DNS or WINS. And if the workstation were acting as a P-NODE system, it would still look at the `LMHOSTS` file first. The problem, therefore, must be with the `LMHOSTS` file, although it appears to be correct. The system that you are connecting to may be of a different IP address, and another machine could respond to the ping. The best bet is to remove the `LMHOSTS` file and use WINS if at all possible.

51. **A.** The problem is that every host name is treated as a comment. Deleting the `#` character will fix this problem.

52. **D.** The correct syntax is to place the IP address first, followed by the system name, the identifier tag `#PRE #DOM`, and the domain name.

53. **A.** When a zone is configured with WINS resolution and all DNS systems are equal, all should be set for WINS reverse lookup. However, if this is a non-Microsoft DNS, you need to reference a Microsoft DNS.

54. **B.** The best solution would be to add a common name alias record for each service type. This solution allows you to remain on a single system, but because you are using a host-based service, you would not want to use WINS.

55. **D.** The TCP/IP printing service allows an administrator to redirect print jobs to a TCP/IP print device. After this has been performed, users simply point to the Windows NT print share.

56. **A.** The LPR utility is a workstation-specific solution. Although you could install TCP/IP printing services, this is good only for NT clients, and no others. After a print job has been issued, it can be viewed in the queue with the `LPQ` command.

57. **D.** The TCP/IP printing service is used by Windows NT to emulate the LPD print server service. This service will handle requests generated by the LPR utility.

58. **D.** This question focuses on UNIX integration with Windows NT. Essentially, the NT Server needs a service or daemon process to handle the request for these clients. `LPR` is used at the UNIX side, but is a command, not a service. Sharing the printer is required for your Microsoft Client, but not UNIX. You must assign the printer network configuration regardless of the network—something must be able to communicate with it (the printer). Finally, there is no gateway as suggested in choice E.

59. **D-E.** Installing the TCP/IP print service enables an NT server to recognize a TCP/IP print device while allowing the use of a redirected TCP/IP port. After this has been done, Microsoft clients can communicate with the NT server via native NetBIOS use and can access any shared resource.

60. **C.** FTP is independent of the operating system. It is designed as a file transfer mechanism between TCP/IP systems.

61. **D.** Because you are working with IP addresses, name resolution is not an issue. Therefore, it is most likely to be a problem in which the workstation does not have a default gateway.

62. **C.** When parsing the `HOSTS` file, the system will return the first host name it comes across. In this case, `ENGR` is in both 172.16.15.10 and 172.16.20.10. Delete `ENGR` from the Product Engineering Server.

63. **D.** The problem in this case is that your UNIX system is case sensitive. Otherwise, you might look at the `HOSTS` file for order-related problems.

64. **D.** The problem has to do with NetBIOS name resolution rather than host name resolution. In this case, the system is registered in the DNS, but not WINS. Therefore, unless the option Use DNS to Resolve NetBIOS Names is checked on the DNS configuration tab of TCP/IP's setup, the system NetBIOS name can't be resolved.

65. **B-E.** The confusing part to a question like this is that it states that you are able to ping a server. However, it does not state whether that was done against the IP address or host name. If you look at the addresses, you must assume the IP address was used with the Ping command rather than the name. Effectively, that would indicate a name-resolution problem. Either the DNS IP address is incorrect, or the entry is not in the DNS database.

66. **B.** The LPQ utility is used to view the queue on a UNIX-based IP print server. The others are used for remote execution, file transfer, and actual printing.

67. **E.** Telnet is a text-based remote execution utility that allows interactive activities.

68. **A.** TFTP is a common file transfer utility for sending files to a UNIX-based system. TFTP will send files using UDP (a connectionless transfer). If any errors occur in the file transfer process, the entire file must be re-sent.

69. **B.** LPR is the line print utility used to print text files to UNIX-based print servers. A Windows client can also perform this operation if a Windows NT Server has TCP/IP printing services installed and set up for a specific printer. This allows a Microsoft client to access such a printer through a NetBIOS name as if it were based off the Windows NT Server.

70. **B.** Name resolution through NT Explorer is for NetBIOS names that use WINS, `LMHOSTS`, or Broadcast. For FTP, name resolution takes place using the `HOSTS` file, DNS, or broadcast. Of the available answers, the problem is that your workstation is not set to use a DNS.

71. **B.** The `route` command takes the format `route add` *`remote-NetID subnet-mask default-gateway`*. In this case, you want to add a route to the router attached to Network A, so you use 172.16.96.0 with a subnet mask of 255.255.224.0 via a default gateway of 172.16.64.2.

Practice Exam 2

EXAM QUESTIONS

1. **You are attempting communications with a Windows-based system on a remote subnet. You can ping all other systems on that subnet by IP address, but not this one. What could the problem be? Select two answers.**

   A. Your Workstation has the wrong default gateway.

   B. The remote system has the wrong default gateway.

   C. Your system is using the wrong subnet mask.

   D. The remote system is using the wrong subnet mask.

   E. The remote system does not use WINS.

2. **You are experiencing problems opening a session with a remote system. You suspect that the system may be down. Which utility would be useful in verifying communications?**

   A. ROUTE.EXE

   B. NBTSTAT.EXE

   C. NETSTAT.EXE

   D. PING.EXE

   E. TELNET.EXE

3. **You are attempting to communicate with a server on the far side of your WAN. You use PING and receive a failure message. You are aware of at least eight routers that exist between you and the remote system. Some of the routers have redundant paths. What utility can you use to find where the packet is failing?**

   A. NBTSTAT.EXE

   B. NETSTAT.EXE

   C. ROUTE.EXE

   D. TRACERT.EXE

   E. Network Monitor

4. **What portions of the DHCP process are initiated by the server?**

   A. Lease acquisition.

   B. Lease renewal.

   C. Lease release.

   D. No processes are initiated by the server.

   E. A, B, and C.

5. **While attempting to establish a remote session to a Windows NT server via Windows Explorer, you receive a failure message. Your system is the only one to receive this message. To resolve this problem, one of the engineers runs Network Monitor and tells you that your system is attempting to run ARP on the remote system's IP address. What is the problem?**

A. The server has the wrong subnet mask.

B. The workstation has the wrong subnet mask.

C. The workstation has the wrong default gateway.

D. The workstation has a bad IP address.

E. The server has a wrong default gateway.

6. This question is based on the following scenario:

Scenario:
Your TCP/IP network is using a Windows NT server with four network adapters as a router.

Required Result:
The NT router must be able to forward IP packets as needed.

Optional Results:
Your server should provide IP information to all clients.

Your server should dynamically adjust its routing tables.

Your server should send trap information to a designated client workstation.

Proposed Solution:
Configure TCP/IP on the server such that each NIC is assigned a specific IP address, then add the PPTP and DHCP relay agent services. Enable IP forwarding.

Evaluation of Proposed Solution:
What results will the proposed solution produce?

A. The proposed solution fulfills all the required and optional results.

B. The proposed solution fulfills the required result but only one of the optional results.

C. The proposed solution fulfills the required result but none of the optional results.

D. The proposed solution does not fulfill any of the required or optional results.

E. Only the optional results are met.

7. You have four NT servers, each with three network interface cards. You want these systems to act as routers for your TCP/IP Network. Considering the complexity of creating static routes, you want to make the routers operate dynamically. What should you do?

A. Install RIP for IP.

B. Enable IP forwarding.

C. Enable DHCP Relay.

D. Enter the command `ROUTE ADD 255.255.255.255 mask 255.255.255.255 0.0.0.0`.

E. Click Enable Dynamic Routing in the Advanced section of the TCP/IP protocol.

8. This question is based on the following scenario:

Scenario:
Your TCP/IP network is using a Windows NT Server with four network adapters as a router.

Required Result:
The NT router must be able to forward IP packets as needed.

Optional Results:
Your server should provide IP information to all clients.

Your server should dynamically adjust its routing tables.

Your server should send trap information to a designated client workstation.

Proposed Solution:
Configure TCP/IP on the server such that each NIC is assigned a specific IP address, then add RIP for IP and DHCP with scopes for each subnet. Install SNMP at the server and a client module at the designated client workstation. Finally, enable IP forwarding.

Evaluation of Proposed Solution:
What results will the proposed solution produce?

A. The proposed solution fulfills all the required and optional results.

B. The proposed solution fulfills the required result but only one of the optional results.

C. The proposed solution fulfills the required result but none of the optional results.

D. The proposed solution does not fulfill any of the required or optional results.

E. Only the optional results are met.

9. **You want to install an existing Windows NT Server as a static router between two LANs. What must you do? Select two answers.**

A. Install an additional network interface card and enable IP forwarding.

B. Define two IP addresses for each network interface card.

C. Define one IP address for each network interface card.

D. Define a different subnet mask per network interface.

E. Reinstall TCP/IP and select Autoconfigure.

10. **You are attempting to configure two routers to the same network for redundancy. When you take one router offline, the other fails to forward information from clients. What is the most likely problem?**

A. You must enable IP forwarding.

B. The client systems require an entry for each default gateway.

C. You must install the DHCP relay agent.

D. You must install WINS/DNS first.

E. The client systems require two IP addresses to operate with multiple routers.

11. **A network is divided by a router into two subnets. The A interface of the router is defined as 172.16.32.1 and the B interface as 172.16.64.1. All nodes on the network use a subnet mask of 255.255.224.0. All systems except yours are operating properly. You are unable to establish a remote session with a system on the A network. You run WINIPCFG**

and find that your IP address is 172.16.81.65 with a subnet mask of 255.255.240.0 and a default gateway of 172.16.32.1. What is the most likely problem?

A. Your IP address is from a different network.

B. Your subnet mask is wrong.

C. The server subnet mask is wrong.

D. Your default gateway is wrong.

E. The server default gateway is wrong.

12. **Your network is linked to the Internet via a RAS server with an ISDN line. You want all your clients to access the Internet via the RAS server. How should you configure the default gateway on the clients?**

A. Use the RAS server's Network Interface Card as the default gateway.

B. Use the RAS server's IP address assigned by the ISP.

C. Use the ISP's default gateway—the same as the RAS server uses.

D. Do not specify a default gateway.

E. The gateway configuration does not have any effect. This access requires a proxy server.

13. **What is the effect of an unlimited lease duration?**

A. DHCP configuration options will never be updated.

B. There is no effect.

C. There will be an increase in network traffic.

D. Addresses cannot be shared dynamically.

14. **This question is based on the following scenario:**

Scenario:
Your TCP/IP network is using a Windows NT server with four network adapters as a router.

Required Result:
The NT router must be able to forward IP packets as needed.

Optional Results:
Your server should provide IP information to all clients.

Your server should dynamically adjust its routing tables.

Your server should send trap information to a designated client workstation.

Proposed Solution:
Configure TCP/IP on the server such that each NIC is assigned a specific IP address, then add RIP for IP and DHCP with scopes for each subnet. Finally, enable IP forwarding.

Evaluation of Proposed Solution:
What results will the proposed solution produce?

A. The proposed solution fulfills all the required and optional results.

B. The proposed solution fulfills the required result but only one of the optional results.

C. The proposed solution fulfills the required result but none of the optional results.

D. The proposed solution does not fulfill any of the required or optional results.

E. Only the optional results are met.

15. Your network contains 12 multihomed NT Server computers. The servers run TCP/IP routing functions. What is the easiest way to configure them?

A. Install RIP for IP.

B. Enable IP forwarding.

C. Enable DHCP Relay.

D. Enter the command `ROUTE ADD 255.255.255.255 mask 255.255.255.255 0.0.0.0`.

E. Click Enable Dynamic Routing in the Advanced section of the TCP/IP protocol.

16. You are troubleshooting your network. What utility will allow you to view packets and analyze traffic?

A. NBTSTAT

B. NETSTAT

C. IPCONFIG

D. Network Monitor

E. Performance Monitor

17. A client is working on a workstation that is linked to your two networks with two network adapters. These networks are also linked by a router that processes information in a secure manner. You would like to add the client system to the WINS database as a static entry. What type of entry should you make?

A. Domain Name

B. Group

C. Internet Group

D. Multihomed

E. Unique

18. How do you configure two WINS servers to replicate their databases?

A. Use the `AT` command to schedule each server to copy its database into the import directory of the other.

B. Use the directory replication service to export the database to each WINS server.

C. Install DHCP and use dynamic assignments.

D. Use the WINS manager to configure each server as a push and pull partner of the other.

E. Run the WINS NT script utility, select Train, and then manually run the replication procedure. When complete, schedule the function to occur once every 12 hours.

19. While working with DHCP and defining a WINS server, what else must you also specify?

A. The default gateway

B. The node type

C. The IP address of the DHCP server

D. The nearest server

E. The DNS server for host name resolution

20. Which of the following services provides centralized NetBIOS name resolution?

A. DHCP

B. WINS

C. SNMP

D. SMTP

E. DNS

21. All of your Windows-based clients operate off a single WINS server. However, they cannot resolve UNIX systems' names. What should you do to fix this problem?

A. Move the WINS database to the head UNIX system.

B. Create an `LMHOSTS` file that contains the required UNIX systems and place it on the WINS server.

C. Add a static mapping for each UNIX system on the WINS server.

D. Change the name resolution method to b-node.

E. This cannot be done.

22. Your network is arranged such that all servers are located on a single network in the computer room. All printers and computers, however, are located in other places (alternate segments) on the network. Which of the following components will allow a system to browse the network regardless of location?

A. DHCP

B. WINS

C. SNMP

D. SMTP

E. DNS

23. You have just completed installing a WINS server to support your 100-client network. What do you need to do next?

A. Install DHCP.

B. Install the WINS Proxy.

C. Configure client systems for WINS.

D. Change the routers to support BOOTP.

E. Create client reservations for each workstation.

24. You would like to use the Import feature of the WINS server. Which file can you import?

A. `HOSTS`

B. `LMHOSTS`

C. `CACHE.DNS`

D. `DHCP.MDB`

E. `SERVICES`

25. You are experiencing browser problems with all systems. Your network is configured in 23 segments. Each segment contains a domain controller. What is the best way to resolve this problem?

A. Add DHCP to the PDC and enable BOOTP on all routers.

B. Install WINS and modify all clients to use it.

C. Add an `LMHOSTS` file for distribution to each client via a logon script. The `LMHOSTS` file should contain a list of all domain controllers.

D. Reboot your system to reannounce itself.

E. Do nothing. Browsing is intermittent due to a delay in updating the browse masters.

26. Your network is divided upon multiple subnets. Odd-numbered subnets use WINS server A, whereas even-numbered subnets use WINS server B. Clients of the A server cannot see those clients that use the B server, and vice versa. What should you do to correct this problem?

A. Configure the A server as a push/pull partner of the B server, and vice versa.

B. Enable IP forwarding.

C. Set the clients to use both WINS servers.

D. Configure DNS to do reverse lookups against the opposite WINS server. Set each client to use DNS for name resolution.

E. Do nothing; the clients are mistaken. It just takes time for the browse lists to update.

27. You are trying to troubleshoot some problems that you are experiencing with a client using the `NET USE` command to establish a session with an NT server. You run some preliminary tests and find that IP is installed and loaded, so then you try to FTP to the server by its IP address with success. What does the problem appear to be?

A. You forgot to set a DNS server on the client.

B. The client is using the wrong gateway to communicate with the remote server.

C. Permissions are limited to the server such that you can't use it.

D. The server is not set to use WINS.

E. The server is using the wrong default gateway.

28. This question is based on the following scenario:

Scenario:

Your network is configured on a 256KB Frame Relay WAN. The primary location contains 1,000 users with 10 NT servers, of which one (WINA) is designated as the WINS server. The secondary location contains 340 users with four NT servers, of which one (WINB) is designated as the WINS server. You want users at each site to be able to browse the other network.

Required Result:

You must replicate the WINB server to the WINA server.

Optional Results:

You want to replicate the WINA server to the WINB.

WINS replication should occur once a day maximum.

Proposed Solution:

Using the WINS Manager, set the WINB server to be a pull partner of WINA and replicate every 24 hours. Set the WINB server to be a push partner of WINA with a count of 3.

Evaluation of Proposed Solution:
What results will the proposed solution produce?

A. The proposed solution fulfills all the required and optional results.

B. The proposed solution fulfills the required result but only one of the optional results.

C. The proposed solution fulfills the required result but none of the optional results.

D. The proposed solution does not fulfill any of the required or optional results.

E. Only the optional results are met.

29. A user informs you that she is able to browse her own network, but not others. When logging into the network, she noticed that the `Net Use` command links her with servers on other networks. What do you think the problem might be? Select two answers.

A. The client is configured with the wrong gateway.

B. The WINS server is offline.

C. The client is not configured to use WINS.

D. `BOOTP` is not configured on the router where the client is located.

E. You need to enable IP forwarding on the client first.

30. This question is based on the following scenario:

Scenario:
Your network is configured on a 256KB Frame Relay WAN. The primary location contains 1,000 users with 10 NT servers of which one (WINA) is designated as the WINS server. The secondary location contains 340 users with four NT servers of which one (WINB) is designated as the WINS server. You want users at each site to be able to browse the other network.

Required Result:
You must replicate the WINB server to the WINA server.

Optional Results:
You want to replicate the WINA server to the WINB.

WINS replication should occur once a day maximum.

Proposed Solution:
Using the WINS Manager, set the WINB server to be a pull partner of WINA and replicate every 24 hours. Set the WINA server to be a push partner of WINB with a count of 3.

Evaluation of Proposed Solution:
What results will the anticipated design produce?

A. The proposed solution fulfills all the required and optional results.

B. The proposed solution fulfills the required result but only one of the optional results.

C. The proposed solution fulfills the required result but none of the optional results.

D. The proposed solution does not fulfill any of the required or optional results.

E. Only the optional results are met.

31. Which of the following services provides centralized host name resolution?

A. DHCP

B. WINS

C. SNMP

D. SMTP

E. DNS

32. You are adding static entries to your WINS database for your UNIX systems. Which type of entry should you be adding?

A. Domain Name

B. Group

C. Internet Group

D. Multihomed

E. Unique

33. You are attempting to configure a name resolution set of services that require a minimal amount of administration for your mix of UNIX and NT Workstation systems. How should you configure this solution?

A. Install WINS and enable WINS Lookup on your Microsoft DNS. Make static entries for your UNIX systems in the WINS server.

B. Define a WINS server in the TCP/IP configuration of the DNS.

C. Install Microsoft's DNS only.

D. Install Microsoft's WINS only.

E. Create a centralized `HOSTS` file that is distributed via login script.

34. Your network operates on four DNS servers for network resources. You are planning to install a fifth server for use of resolving queues bound for the Internet. How should you configure the new DNS?

A. Primary Name Server

B. Secondary Name Server

C. Forwarder for WINS servers

D. Forwarder for existing DNS servers

E. Backup Secondary Name Server

35. Your network is presently configured with a single DNS server. You are worried that if it were to break, you do not have a backup solution. You elect to add an additional server. How should it be configured?

A. Primary Server

B. Secondary Server

C. Cache Only Server

D. Forwarder for WINS servers

E. New Zone and Primary Server

36. You are configuring Exchange 5.5 as your Internet email server. After completing the installation, how do you make it publicly known what your email server is?

A. Send an email message including your server's name to InterNIC.

B. Create an `MX` record in the DNS linked to the Internet.

C. Send an email message including your server's IP address to all companies that send you email.

D. Post this information on your Web server.

E. Add a `CNAME` record in the DNS linked to the Internet that calls the server as `EMAIL` (regardless of its actual name) and include its IP address.

37. This question is based on the following scenario:

Scenario:
Your network is configured on a 256KB Frame Relay WAN. The primary location contains 1,000 users with 10 NT servers of which one (WINA) is designated as the WINS server. The secondary location contains 340 users with four NT servers of which one (WINB) is designated as the WINS server. You want users at each site to be able to browse the other network.

Required Result:
You must replicate the WINB server to the WINA server.

Optional Results:
You want to replicate the WINA server to the WINB.

WINS replication should occur once a day maximum.

Proposed Solution:
Using the WINS Manager, set each WINS server to be a pull/push partner of the other with replication every 24 hours and a count of 40,000.

Evaluation of Proposed Solution:
What results will the proposed solution produce?

A. The proposed solution fulfills all the required and optional results.

B. The proposed solution fulfills the required result but only one of the optional results.

C. The proposed solution fulfills the required result but none of the optional results.

D. The proposed solution does not fulfill any of the required or optional results.

E. Only the optional results are met.

38. You would like to expand your current DNS systems with an additional unit. You do not want any zone transfer traffic. How should you configure the new DNS server?

A. Primary Server

B. Secondary Server

C. Cache Only Server

D. Forwarder for WINS servers

E. New Zone and Primary Server

39. Which service will allow all clients to use the host name to locate your Web server?

A. DHCP

B. DNS

C. SNMP

D. SMTP

E. WINS

40. This question is based on the following scenario:

Scenario:
Your network is configured on a 256KB Frame Relay WAN. The primary location contains 1,000 users with 10 NT servers of which one (WINA) is designated as the WINS server. The secondary location contains 340 users with four NT servers of which one (WINB) is designated as the WINS server. You want users at each site to be able to browse the other network.

Required Result:
You must replicate the WINB server to the WINA server.

Optional Results:
You want to replicate the WINA server to the WINB.

WINS replication should occur once a day maximum.

Proposed Solution:
Using the WINS Manager, set the WINA server to be a pull partner of WINB and replicate every 24 hours. Set the WINB server to be a push partner of WINA with a count of 40,000.

Evaluation of Proposed Solution:
What results will the proposed solution produce?

A. The proposed solution fulfills all the required and optional results.

B. The proposed solution fulfills the required result but only one of the optional results.

C. The proposed solution fulfills the required result but none of the optional results.

D. The proposed solution does not fulfill any of the required or optional results.

E. Only the optional results are met.

41. You are working on a secured government network that will never be connected to the Internet. Which file should you modify on the DNS?

A. `HOSTS`

B. `WINS.MDB`

C. `DNS.MDB`

D. `CACHE.DNS`

E. `HOSTS.DNS`

42. How do you configure a DNS server to use the DNS root servers located on the Internet?

A. Do nothing. The Microsoft DNS includes these root servers in the default `cache.dns` file.

B. In the DNS manager, individually specify each root server.

C. In the DNS manager, specify Use Internet DNS Root Servers.

D. Create a new zone on a primary DNS server.

E. Use WINS and specify DNS options to receive this information dynamically.

43. You are working with a Microsoft DNS and would like to minimize the number of manual entries made to the database. A colleague suggests using WINS. You install it on the same server. What else must you do?

A. Set TCP/IP such that both WINS server addresses are the address of the single WINS server.

B. Install DHCP to configure clients.

C. Enable reverse lookup on the Microsoft DNS.

D. Reboot all clients for changes to take effect.

E. Use Jet Pack to set the WINS database to operate with the DNS.

44. Your clients are assigned all information via DHCP. Recently you replaced your DNS with a new server and made the appropriate changes in the DHCP global option for this assignment. A user says that he cannot resolve any names. Upon looking at the IPCONFIG printout, you find that the user has a valid IP address, but not the DNS setting you made the day before. Address lease time is eight hours on all subnets. Which of the following are possible reasons? Select two answers.

A. A DNS entry was already present in the client TCP/IP configuration.

B. The client is on a subnet that uses a different DHCP scope than you assigned the DNS changes to.

C. The client has not renewed its data with the DHCP server.

D. The system has a different setting in its client reservation.

E. This is not a Windows NT, 98, or 95 client.

45. You are working on a small network on which each system is individually configured with a `HOSTS` file for name resolution:

```
172.16.10.5    Marketing   #Creative People
172.16.15.5    Accounting  #Bean Counters
172.16.15.10   Prod Engr   #Product Engineering
172.16.20.10   Engr        #Engineering and Design
```

When you open an FTP session to ENGR, the connection is fine. However, when you attempt to connect to 172.16.20.10, it fails. What is the problem?

A. You are required to use a DNS to resolve names.

B. You need to add `#PRE #DOM` to the ENGR line.

C. The `HOSTS` file is returning the wrong IP address.

D. You can't use a host name with the FTP service.

E. The `HOSTS` file on the FTP server does not contain your IP address.

46. How can you prevent unauthorized SNMP management systems from controlling data from an NT server that has the SNMP service installed?

A. Define on the server the hosts from which it is authorized to receive packets.

B. Disable sharing of SNMP$.

C. Password-protect the server and community name.

D. Restrict the `MIB` file to administrators only.

E. Windows NT automatically secures SNMP data.

47. Your sales force is spread out across the entire United States. You would like each member of the sales force to dial in to the Internet to access your network remotely. You expect no more than five simultaneous users at maximum. You require encryption, additional security, and minimal costs. What should you do?

A. Install PPTP.

B. Buy a third-party product, such as from Shiva (that is, LAN Rover).

C. Program your own custom firewall.

D. Set your routers to accept only certain IP addresses.

E. This cannot be done.

48. Which information must you provide so that a Windows NT Server can send trap information to a management system?

A. The NetBIOS system name of the management system.

B. The management system's IP address.

C. The community to which the server belongs.

D. Both B and C.

E. Microsoft SNMP dynamically detects all management systems and forwards traps to the management system.

49. You are working at a UNIX network management console and would like to see network statistics for a local Windows NT Server. What should you do on the UNIX system to see this data?

A. Run NETSTAT plus the NT Server's name

B. Run NETSTAT /A:<NTSERVER: NAME>

C. Use the SNMP management console and target the NT server.

D. Load Performance Monitor from the NT CD. Choose the `\UNIX` directory rather than `\I386`.

E. This cannot be done.

50. This question is based on the following scenario:

Scenario:
Your network is configured on a 256KB Frame Relay WAN. The primary location contains 1,000 users with 10 NT servers of which one (WINA) is designated as the WINS server. The secondary location contains 340 users with four NT servers of which one (WINB) is designated as the WINS server. You want users at each site to be able to browse the other network.

Required Result:
You must replicate the WINB server to the WINA server.

Optional Results:
You want to replicate the WINA server to the WINB.

WINS replication should occur once a day maximum.

Proposed Solution:
Using the WINS Manager, set each WINS server to be a pull partner of the other with set replication every 24 hours.

Evaluation of Proposed Solution:
What results will the proposed solution produce?

A. The proposed solution fulfills all the required and optional results.

B. The proposed solution fulfills the required result but only one of the optional results.

C. The proposed solution fulfills the required result but none of the optional results.

D. The proposed solution does not fulfill any of the required or optional results.

E. Only the optional results are met.

51. How can you use Performance Monitor to collect data regarding TCP/IP transmissions on a remote NT server?

A. Install SNMP on the remote server.

B. Run NBTSTAT locally plus the NT server name.

C. Run NETSTAT locally plus the NT server name.

D. Install UNIX locally and then wait for the data to be forwarded automatically.

E. Use Server Manager for domains, and then drag and drop the Performance Monitor icon on the remote server.

52. Which of the following utilities allows you to gather TCP/IP protocol statistics, save them to a log file, and export them to a spreadsheet?

A. NETSTAT.EXE

B. NBTSTAT.EXE

C. SNMP.EXE

D. Performance Monitor

E. Network Monitor

53. Which of the following can be used to view IP and Ethernet statistics summaries? Select two answers.

A. Performance Monitor

B. Network Monitor

C. ROUTE.EXE

D. NBTSTAT.EXE

E. NETSTAT.EXE

54. Which of the following utilities can be used to view a chart of IP statistics?

A. IPCONFIG.EXE

B. Performance Monitor

C. ROUTE.EXE

D. NBTSTAT.EXE

E. NETSTAT.EXE

55. Which of the following utilities can be used to view TCP/IP statistics of a system since it was last booted?

A. IPCONFIG.EXE

B. WINIPCFG.EXE

C. ROUTE.EXE

D. NBTSTAT.EXE

E. NETSTAT.EXE

56. Which of the following utilities will provide you with a list of IP address that have been resolved to hardware addresses?

A. NETSTAT.EXE

B. NBTSTAT.EXE

C. Network Monitor

D. ARP.EXE

E. IPCONFIG.EXE

57. Which of the following utilities can be used to view systems in the NetBIOS name cache?

A. IPCONFIG.EXE

B. WINIPCFG.EXE

C. ROUTE.EXE

D. NBTSTAT.EXE

E. NETSTAT.EXE

58. You are attempting to configure your remote access server to accept requests via PPTP only. How should this be done?

A. Enable Multilink for the Internet connection on the RAS server.

B. Enable call-back security.

C. Enable data encryption, and then select PPTP connections.

D. Enable PPTP filtering.

E. Disable routing.

59. Which of the following utilities can be used to view a multihomed system's routing table? Select two answers.

A. IPCONFIG.EXE

B. WINIPCFG.EXE

C. ROUTE.EXE

D. NBTSTAT.EXE

E. NETSTAT.EXE

60. A user is receiving an error `Network name not found` when she types `NET USE J: \\BRIGHT.FIREFLY.COM\IDEAS.`

You run IPCONFIG /ALL and find the following:

Host Name	bright.firefly.com
DNS Servers	
Node Type	Hybrid
NetBIOS scope ID	
IP Routing Enabled	no
WINS Proxy Enabled	no
NetBIOS Resolution Uses DNS	no
Physical Address	02-10-BF-DB-E2-257
DHCP Enabled	yes
IP Address:	172.16.10.10
Subnet Mask	255.255.0.0
Default Gateway	172.16.10.1
DHCP Server	172.16.10.3
Primary WINS Server	172.16.10.3
Secondary WINS Server	172.16.20.3
Lease Obtained:	Friday, Oct 16, 1998 1:32:13 PM
Lease Expires:	Friday, Oct 16, 1998 9:32:13 PM

Where is the problem occurring?

A. This is a NetBIOS command; you can't use a host name.

B. You have the wrong default gateway.

C. The DNS setting to resolve NetBIOS names has not been checked.

D. The lease has expired.

E. You need to point to the secondary WINS server as your primary.

61. Internal to your company you use static routers. Your ISP has provided you an Ascend Pipeline 50 router to link to the Internet. You are segmented so that you have three subnets: A, B, and C. Two static routers exist, linking subnet A to subnet B by static router ONE, and subnet B to subnet C by static router TWO. The Ascend router is located on subnet C, with an IP address of 172.16.96.2 and 38.5.8.7 on the serial port side. The network is configured as follows:

Subnet A: 172.16.32.0 Mask 255.255.224.0

Subnet B: 172.16.64.0 Mask 255.255.224.0

Subnet C: 172.16.96.0 Mask 255.255.224.0

The routers are configured as follows:

Router ONE:	**A Interface 172.16.32.1**
	B Interface 172.16.64.1
Router TWO:	**B Interface 172.16.64.2**
	C Interface 172.16.96.1

How should you configure the routers to achieve full coverage of your network?

A. Router 1: 172.16.96.0 172.16.64.2
38.0.0.0 172.16.64.2
Router 2: 172.16.32.0 172.16.64.1
38.0.0.0 172.16.96.2

B. Router 1: 172.16.96.0 172.16.64.2
38.0.0.0 172.16.64.1
Router 2: 172.16.32.0 172.16.64.2
38.0.0.0 172.16.96.2

C. Router 1: 172.16.96.0 172.16.64.2
38.0.0.0 172.16.96.2
Router 2: 172.16.32.0 172.16.64.1
38.0.0.0 172.16.96.2

D. Router 1: 172.16.96.0 172.16.64.2
38.0.0.0 255.255.255.255
Router 2: 172.16.32.0 172.16.64.1
38.0.0.0 172.16.96.2

E. Router 1: 172.16.96.0 172.16.32.1
38.0.0.0 172.16.64.2
Router 2: 172.16.32.0 172.16.64.1
38.0.0.0 172.16.96.2

62. What must a router support in order to pass DHCP broadcasts?

A. RFC 1543

B. BOOTP Relay

C. RFC 1544

D. WINS Proxy

E. This can't be done.

63. What is the recommended method of providing backup to the DHCP server?

A. Configure two DHCP servers with the same scope.

B. Configure a BOOTP server.

C. Replicate the database using directory replication.

D. Configure two DHCP servers with different sections of the scope.

64. In what environment is it advisable to have a short DHCP lease duration?

A. In static environments where addresses don't change often

B. When you have fewer hosts than IP addresses

C. In environments where you have hosts moving and many changes to IP addresses

D. When you have more hosts than IP addresses

65. You are able to communicate with all systems locally, but not remotely. What is the first thing you should do?

A. Ping your loopback address.

B. Reboot the system.

C. Ping the default gateway.

D. Ping the remote system.

E. Reload TCP/IP.

66. A network is divided by a router into two subnets. The A interface of the router is defined as 172.16.32.1 and the B interface as 172.16.64.1. All nodes on the network use a subnet mask of 255.255.224.0. All systems except yours are operating properly. You are unable to establish a remote session with a system on the A network. You run WINIPCFG and find that your IP address is 172.16.96.65 with a subnet mask of 255.255.240.0 and a default gateway of 172.16.64.1. You run IPconfig at the server and find that it has an IP address of 172.16.33.9, a subnet mask of 255.255.224.0, and a default gateway of 172.16.64.1. What is the most likely problem?

A. Your IP address is from a different network.

B. Your subnet mask is wrong.

C. The server subnet mask is wrong.

D. Your default gateway is wrong.

E. The server default gateway is wrong.

67. This question is based on the following scenario:

Scenario:
Your TCP/IP network is using a Windows NT server with four network adapters as a router.

Required Result:
The NT router must be able to forward IP packets as needed.

Optional Result:
Your server should provide IP information to all clients.

Your server should dynamically adjust its routing tables.

Your server should send trap information to a designated client workstation.

Proposed Solution:
Configure TCP/IP on the server such that each NIC is assigned a specific IP address, then add the PPTP, DHCP, and SNMP service. The DHCP service will have one scope per subnet, and SNMP will be set to forward traps to a designated client.

Evaluation of Proposed Solution:
What results will the proposed solution produce?

A. The proposed solution fulfills all the required and optional results.

B. The proposed solution fulfills the required result but only one of the optional results.

C. The proposed solution fulfills the required result but none of the optional results.

D. The proposed solution does not fulfill any of the required or optional results.

E. Only the optional results are met.

68. Your network consists of 23 segments spread across four buildings. Which of the following services will allow your clients to browse all subnets without having to search for a master browser for the domain?

A. DHCP

B. WINS

C. SNMP

D. SMTP

E. DNS

69. Which of the following utilities can be used to reset a system's NetBIOS name cache?

A. IPCONFIG.EXE

B. WINIPCFG.EXE

C. ROUTE.EXE

D. NBTSTAT.EXE

E. NETSTAT.EXE

70. Which of the following utilities can be used to view all connections on a Windows NT system?

A. IPCONFIG.EXE

B. WINIPCFG.EXE

C. ROUTE.EXE

D. NBTSTAT.EXE

E. NETSTAT.EXE

71. You have configured the TCP/IP printing service on your Windows NT server. You want UNIX systems to be able to send to a printer on the Windows NT server. Due to the publishing program that is used, clients will sometimes send printer-specific commands. What is the best way to set this configuration?

A. On the UNIX systems, use the LPR command to send all print jobs formatted in text.

B. On the UNIX systems, use the LPR command to send all print jobs formatted as RAW.

C Set the printers on the NT server to use an LPR-compatible print processor.

D. Set the printer with a separator page on the NT Server that contains the control codes for printing the UNIX documents.

E. This cannot be done.

EXAM ANSWERS

1. **B-D.** Because your system can communicate with all others, begin by ruling out your system as the problem. Next, because you are communicating via IP address, this rules out WINS as an answer. This leaves B and D. If the remote system has the wrong gateway, it is possible that you might not get a return response because the remote server can't communicate beyond its own subnet. Also, if the subnet mask on the server is wrong, it may be under the impression that your workstation is local, and not send a reply to the default gateway.

2. **D.** PING is the utility used to verify connectivity. When you run ping, it sends a packet to the remote system to verify that you can reach it. At that point, you would want to verify that whatever service you're trying to reach is active.

3. **D.** TraceRT is a utility that is used to follow the path that a packet takes. This is extremely useful in identifying faults in your network, as well as determining speed issues. For example, if you perform communications to one site on the Internet, you could use TraceRT to see where the packet must be routed to be delivered. You might want to do this when evaluating different Internet providers if you are commonly using a particular site.

4. **D.** No portions of the DHCP process are initiated by the server.

5. **B.** If your workstation is attempting to resolve a remote system's IP address to a hardware address, then it is most likely that your workstation is under the impression that the remote system is local. Otherwise, the ARP request should be for the default gateway.

6. **C.** To dynamically assign IP addresses, you must install DHCP. To send traps, you are required to use SNMP. Otherwise, the router is fine. If, however, dynamic updates were to include additional routers, you would be out of luck.

7. **A.** Router Information Protocol (RIP) is used to automatically configure a route to dynamically configure itself to operate with other routers. This solution is good for small- to mid-sized companies.

8. **A.** The anticipated design fully produces the required results and extras. With only one router, as long as IP forwarding is enabled, the router is dynamic to those networks only. Also, although there was no mention of the client piece as a requirement, it truly is needed. Effectively, this solution covers all bases.

9. **A-C.** To enable routing, you must have at least two network interface adapters. These two interfaces can be of different or like topologies. Each adapter must be assigned an IP address and IP forwarding must be enabled.

10. **B.** Because client systems are sending information to a router, when it goes down, the client has no clue where else to send

data unless listed otherwise. A secondary gateway should be added for this reason.

11. **D.** Your workstation is configured with the default gateway for the other network. If you can't establish a remote session with the A network, then you are working on the B network. The local router should be 172.16.64.1.

12. **A.** Because your clients are local, they must communicate only to a local IP address. They can't set a default gateway that is not on your network. Before this configuration will work, you must set the RAS server to act as a router so that you are using IP forwarding to send information through. To secure your server, you should use the advanced IP options to configure the server to allow access only to certain ports, such as HTTP 80, FTP 20/21, SMTP 25, and so on.

13. **A.** With a lease duration of unlimited, DHCP configuration options will never be updated.

14. **B.** To send traps, you will require SNMP.

15. **A.** With Windows NT, there really are only two ways in which a router can be configured: static or dynamic. In this case, static requires much more work to configure. Installing Router Information Protocol (RIP) reduces efforts significantly.

16. **D.** Network Monitor is useful for viewing packet data. When in Capture mode, you can dynamically view statistics as data is gathered regarding instantaneous traffic during the measurement period. In this capacity, Network Monitor is performing the functions of a device such as a Network General Sniffer.

17. **D.** Because you have multiple network adapters, you should register this system multihomed. In that way, you will not get a duplicate address error if the WINS server picks up on one of the other Network adapters or IP addresses.

18. **D.** The WINS manager contains a special area for configuring push and pull partners. The push occurs after a set number of changes have taken place. The pull occurs after a given period of time has passed.

19. **B.** You must define the node type that the client will become after information is assigned. There are four types of NetBIOS name resolution that may be selected from: b-node, p-node, m-node, and h-node.

20. **B.** WINS provides centralized NetBIOS name resolution. If you were also looking for host name resolution, you could uses DNS as well.

21. **C.** Adding a static mapping for each UNIX system will make it so that if the name is requested for resolution, a client will be able to pull it from the WINS database. The catch is that the name must conform to NetBIOS standards. A better solution would be to configure a DNS or centralized `HOSTS` file; however, that was not an option.

22. **B.** WINS is a centralized repository for NetBIOS object data that can be accessed by WINS clients. This allows systems to browse the network regardless of location on the network.

23. **C.** Before WINS becomes useful, you will be required to configure your clients to support WINS. The configuration can be

done manually or via a DHCP scope change.

24. **B.** The LMHOSTS file contains NetBIOS computer names and IP addresses that can be directly imported into the WINS database.

25. **B.** The best solution is to install WINS and modify your clients to use it. This will greatly reduce the number of points of failure and provide generally faster network access.

26. **A.** The problem is that the two WINS servers are not communicating their databases with each other. The best solution would be configure them as replication partners so each server has a copy of the other's data. Note that the solution presented in C will not fix the problem because you will register with only the first WINS to reply during startup—not both.

27. **D.** This problem is clearly related to NetBIOS name resolution. If the server has not registered itself in a manner that can be resolved by your workstation, then that server would require adjusting—in this case, making it a WINS client. The fact that you could FTP by IP address means the physical and TCP/IP addressing are correct.

28. **B.** Because you are performing two-way replication with a push and pull, you are in fact replicating the database. Although you are performing the pull every 24 hours, you are sending a push with every third change.

29. **B-C.** The problem is accessing the browse list for the domain. Typically, if a system is not configured for WINS, you will locate the domain master browser; however, that is not always true, or as easily done as said. In this case, the WINS server may be offline (down) or the client may not be configured to use WINS.

30. **D.** This solution fails to replicate the WINB server to the WINA server. The WINA to WINB in this solution is covered as both push and pull.

31. **E.** A DNS will allow clients to resolve host names from a centralized database. although this process is slightly slower than other methods, such as using a HOSTS file, it is far more accurate and extensive.

32. **E.** Because each system will have only one name assigned to it regardless of its configuration (not having a NetBIOS name), a unique entry will configure a UNIX system appropriately. The downfall to this solution, however, is that the name must conform to NetBIOS naming standards.

33. **A.** The WINS lookup will allow a client system to make requests and receive a current list of systems. When the UNIX systems perform a DNS lookup, they will have name resolution access to all systems as well. The reason for doing this with WINS is so that you do not have to immediately reconfigure all your clients, while allowing UNIX systems to function.

34. **D.** If you were not aware of the fact that this server is designed to receive requests for Internet name resolution, you would possibly make this a secondary server. However, for its planned capacity, it would best function for caching against Internet Resources.

35. **B.** The function of a secondary server is to back up a primary server in the event of a fault. In this configuration, the primary server's load can be divided and faster name resolution can occur.

36. **B.** The DNS has the capability to create a number of different types of records. As such, mail exchanges are designated as `MX`. Anytime an external mail server wants to send mail to your server, it performs a DNS lookup for the server with the `MX` designation and forwards information to that server.

37. **B.** The solution produces the required results, but with a 40,000 count, eventually, there will be another problem when that number is reached and replication occurs multiple times within 24 hours.

38. **C.** A cache-only server will simply receive requests, forward them on to other DNS servers for resolution, and hold the result in the event that it is requested again. However, it will not perform any zone transfers.

39. **B.** The DNS is used to resolve host names to IP addresses. Because this is a global network service rather than a solution designed solely for a single system, all users of the DNS will receive the change.

40. **C.** This solution fails to replicate the WINA server to the WINB server. With a push setting of 40,000, you will eventually have at least one occurrence where replication happens more than once per day.

41. **D.** The reason that you should modify this file is to set your DNS as a root name server. This file contains a list of those on the Internet. Modify this file instead to reflect your servers and no others.

42. **A.** You are not required to take any action to use the Internet root servers. The default `cache.dns` file contains a list of the Internet root servers. If you desire an update of this list, it should be obtained through InterNIC.

43. **C.** The minimization function is dependent upon the use of WINS and setting WINS lookup on the DNS system. All WINS clients dynamically register themselves rather than require individual entries.

44. **A-D.** The problem is either that the client has the DNS information already in place or that the client has a client reservation that specifies a different address. This would not be a cause of renewing information if leases are only for eight hours, and a day has passed since the changes. Also, because this was a global setting, the scope does not matter. If a client reservation is specifically set for any system, those settings take precedence over all others.

45. **C.** When parsing the `HOSTS` file, the system will return the first host name it comes across. In this case, ENGR is in both 172.16.15.10 and 172.16.20.10. Delete ENGR from the Product Engineering Server. You are opening an FTP session to the Product Engineering Server rather than the Engineering and Design Server.

46. **A.** You need to define whom (management community) the NT server will listen to for SNMP management requests. In this way, if a management console is not on the list, it will be ignored.

47. **A.** The cheapest solution is to use PPTP. Because your users are on dial-up, IP addresses are not deterministic.

48. **D.** The IP address is used for routing, whereas the community name is used to define the set to which the server belongs that is reporting the error. No further information is required.

49. **C.** SNMP agents are platform independent. Any platform with a management console (for example, HP OpenView) can be used to read an agent's data.

50. **A.** This solution meets the requirements to the letter. Each server will receive updates once per day and no more. There is no need to create a push arrangement per this customer's needs.

51. **A.** The bottom line is that you are reading SNMP data from the server. Performance Monitor can be made to read SNMP data. By design, Performance Monitor can monitor remote systems. Installing SNMP on the remote system installs the TCP/IP counters.

52. **D.** Performance Monitor can be used to chart statistics and log them to a file. These logs are useful to review when establishing a baseline and when determining whether load changes have been made to the server. These log files can be exported so that you can import them to a spreadsheet such as Excel.

53. **A-E.** Performance Monitor will display a running total of either IP or Ethernet statistics. In either instance, NETSTAT will display a snapshot of the current summary for this data.

54. **B.** After you have selected the appropriate counters, you can display a progressive chart of data that includes IP statistics.

55. **E.** NETSTAT can be used to view TCP/IP statistics by specifying the `-e` option.

56. **D.** ARP is the address resolution protocol utility. IP addresses are used only for routing packets on a network. However, communications actually occur at the Datalink level, where the hardware address is assigned. Use the –`a` option to display the current list.

57. **D.** `Nbtstat -c` will display the list of systems currently held in the NetBIOS name cache.

58. **D.** The PPTP filter will limit data read by your server to only PPTP requests sent over a valid defined port.

59. **C-E.** Executing either route print or `netstat –r?` will display the routing table.

60. **A.** Unlike TCP/IP-specific utilities, NetBIOS-based utilities cannot be interchanged with FQDN or IP addresses. You need to eliminate the `FIREFLY.COM` part of the command before it will work. Remember that there is a 15-character limit to a NetBIOS name.

61. **A.** The best way to process a question like this is to create a drawing, and then write your own static table and look for a match in the answer. Remember that you must go to a local gateway and not directly to the gateway of a foreign network.

62. **B.** A router must support BOOTP Relay to pass DHCP broadcasts. This is covered by RFC 1542.

63. **D.** Configuring two DHCP servers with different sections of the scope is the recommended method of providing backup to the DHCP server.

64. **C.** A short-lease duration should be used in environments in which you have hosts moving and many changes to IP addresses.

65. **C.** The problem is not local communications, but those that are remote. If you can't communicate remotely, using PING against a remote server would be pointless. Begin by verifying that the default gateway is up and available and that your system is configured to use it, and then proceed to other tests.

66. **B.** Ignoring the fact that the server is obviously wrong, begin by realizing that if everyone else can see the server, the problem is more likely to be with your system. In the case of your subnet mask, you are attempting to communicate with a remote gateway that your system does not see on the same network. This would be the most critical problem. On the other hand, if the server is remote, it cannot share the same default gateway as your system. In this case, it is attempting to send data to your default gateway rather than its own. Although the route has both addresses, each interface will respond only to the correct address. In the case of having the wrong default gateway, the server simply replies to the router as a response to the remote system and does not appear as a problem unless you are working with the server directly at its console.

67. **D.** The requirement was for routing. Did you see anywhere that IP forwarding was enabled? No. In order to route packets, you must have IP forwarding selected. Otherwise, your system will not be functioning as a router, rather just a system on two or more networks.

68. **B.** WINS provides a centralized database of all NetBIOS-based resources that register with it. As such, if all clients are configured to use WINS, then each client will have the capability to browse the entire network through WINS.

69. **D.** `Nbtstat –r` will dump the current NetBIOS cache and load any `#PRE #DOM` entries listed in the `LMHOSTS` file.

70. **E.** `NETSTAT` will display all connections to a given machine. Each connection will include the protocol type of either TCP (connection-based) or UDP (connectionless).

71. **A.** The `LPR` command is reasonably transparent for sending data. As long as all data is formatted as plain text, no problems should occur.

APPENDIX A

Exam Strategies

You must pass rigorous certification exams to become a Microsoft Certified Professional. These closed-book exams provide a valid and reliable measure of your technical proficiency and expertise. Developed in consultation with computer industry professionals who have on-the-job experience with Microsoft products in the workplace, the exams are conducted by two independent organizations. Sylvan Prometric offers the exams at more than 1,400 Authorized Prometric Testing Centers around the world. Virtual University Enterprises (VUE) testing centers offer exams as well.

To schedule an exam, call Sylvan Prometric Testing Centers at 800-755-EXAM (3926) or VUE at 888-837-8616.

This appendix is divided into two main sections. First, it describes the different certification options provided by Microsoft, and how you can achieve those certifications. The second portion highlights the different kinds of examinations and the best ways to prepare for those different exam and question styles.

TYPES OF CERTIFICATION

Currently Microsoft offers seven types of certification, based on specific areas of expertise:

- **Microsoft Certified Professional (MCP).** Qualified to provide installation, configuration, and support for users of at least one Microsoft desktop operating system, such as Windows NT Workstation. Candidates can take elective exams to develop areas of specialization. MCP is the base level of expertise.
- **Microsoft Certified Professional+Internet (MCP+Internet).** Qualified to plan security, install and configure server products, manage server resources, extend service to run CGI scripts or ISAPI scripts, monitor and analyze performance, and troubleshoot problems. Expertise is similar to that of an MCP, but with a focus on the Internet.
- **Microsoft Certified Professional+Site Building (MCP+Site Building).** Qualified to plan, build, maintain, and manage Web sites by using Microsoft technologies and products. The credential is appropriate for people who manage sophisticated, interactive Web sites that include database connectivity, multimedia, and searchable content.
- **Microsoft Certified Systems Engineer (MCSE).** Qualified to effectively plan, implement, maintain, and support information systems with Microsoft Windows NT and other Microsoft advanced systems and workgroup products, such as Microsoft Office and Microsoft BackOffice. MCSE is a second level of expertise.

- **Microsoft Certified Systems Engineer+ Internet (MCSE+Internet).** Qualified in the core MCSE areas, and also qualified to enhance, deploy, and manage sophisticated intranet and Internet solutions that include a browser, proxy server, host servers, database, and messaging and commerce components. An MCSE+Internet–certified professional is able to manage and analyze Web sites.
- **Microsoft Certified Solution Developer (MCSD).** Qualified to design and develop custom business solutions by using Microsoft development tools, technologies, and platforms, including Microsoft Office and Microsoft BackOffice. MCSD is a second level of expertise, with a focus on software development.
- **Microsoft Certified Trainer (MCT).** Instructionally and technically qualified by Microsoft to deliver Microsoft Education Courses at Microsoft-authorized sites. An MCT must be employed by a Microsoft Solution Provider Authorized Technical Education Center or a Microsoft Authorized Academic Training site.

▼ NOTE

For the most up-to-date information about each type of certification, visit the Microsoft Training and Certification Web site at `http://www.microsoft.com/train_cert`. You also can call or email the following sources:

- Microsoft Certified Professional Program: 800-636-7544
- `mcp@msprograms.com`
- Microsoft Online Institute (MOLI): 800-449-9333

CERTIFICATION REQUIREMENTS

The requirements for certification in each of the seven areas are detailed below. An asterisk after an exam indicates that the exam is slated for retirement.

How to Become a Microsoft Certified Professional

Passing any Microsoft exam (with the exception of Networking Essentials) is all you need to do to become certified as an MCP.

How to Become a Microsoft Certified Professional+Internet

You must pass the following exams to become an MCP specializing in Internet technology:

- Internetworking Microsoft TCP/IP on Microsoft Windows NT 4.0, #70-059
- Implementing and Supporting Microsoft Windows NT Server 4.0, #70-067
- Implementing and Supporting Microsoft Internet Information Server 3.0 and Microsoft Index Server 1.1, #70-077

  OR Implementing and Supporting Microsoft Internet Information Server 4.0, #70-087

How to Become a Microsoft Certified Professional+Site Building

You need to pass two of the following exams in order to be certified as an MCP+Site Building:

- Designing and Implementing Web Sites with Microsoft FrontPage 98, #70-055

- Designing and Implementing Commerce Solutions with Microsoft Site Server 3.0, Commerce Edition, #70-057
- Designing and Implementing Web Solutions with Microsoft Visual InterDev 6.0, #70-152

How to Become a Microsoft Certified Systems Engineer

You must pass four operating system exams and two elective exams to become an MCSE. The MCSE certification path is divided into two tracks: the Windows NT 3.51 track and the Windows NT 4.0 track.

The following lists show the core requirements (four operating system exams) for both the Windows NT 3.51 and 4.0 tracks, and the elective courses (two exams) you can take for either track.

The four Windows NT 3.51 Track Core Requirements for MCSE certification are as follows:

- Implementing and Supporting Microsoft Windows NT Server 3.51, #70-043*
- Implementing and Supporting Microsoft Windows NT Workstation 3.51, #70-042*
- Microsoft Windows 3.1, #70-030*

  OR Microsoft Windows for Workgroups 3.11, #70-048*

  OR Implementing and Supporting Microsoft Windows 95, #70-064

  OR Implementing and Supporting Microsoft Windows 98, #70-098
- Networking Essentials, #70-058

The four Windows NT 4.0 Track Core Requirements for MCSE certification are as follows:

- Implementing and Supporting Microsoft Windows NT Server 4.0, #70-067
- Implementing and Supporting Microsoft Windows NT Server 4.0 in the Enterprise, #70-068
- Microsoft Windows 3.1, #70-030*

  OR Microsoft Windows for Workgroups 3.11, #70-048*

  OR Implementing and Supporting Microsoft Windows 95, #70-064

  OR Implementing and Supporting Microsoft Windows NT Workstation 4.0, #70-073

  OR Implementing and Supporting Microsoft Windows 98, #70-098
- Networking Essentials, #70-058

For both the Windows NT 3.51 and the 4.0 tracks, you must pass two of the following elective exams for MCSE certification:

- Implementing and Supporting Microsoft SNA Server 3.0, #70-013

  OR Implementing and Supporting Microsoft SNA Server 4.0, #70-085
- Implementing and Supporting Microsoft Systems Management Server 1.0, #70-014*

  OR Implementing and Supporting Microsoft Systems Management Server 1.2, #70-018

  OR Implementing and Supporting Microsoft Systems Management Server 2.0, #70-086

- Microsoft SQL Server 4.2 Database Implementation, #70-021

  OR Implementing a Database Design on Microsoft SQL Server 6.5, #70-027

  OR Implementing a Database Design on Microsoft SQL Server 7.0, #70-029

- Microsoft SQL Server 4.2 Database Administration for Microsoft Windows NT, #70-022

  OR System Administration for Microsoft SQL Server 6.5 (or 6.0), #70-026

  OR System Administration for Microsoft SQL Server 7.0, #70-028

- Microsoft Mail for PC Networks 3.2-Enterprise, #70-037

- Internetworking with Microsoft TCP/IP on Microsoft Windows NT (3.5-3.51), #70-053

  OR Internetworking with Microsoft TCP/IP on Microsoft Windows NT 4.0, #70-059

- Implementing and Supporting Microsoft Exchange Server 4.0, #70-075*

  OR Implementing and Supporting Microsoft Exchange Server 5.0, #70-076

  OR Implementing and Supporting Microsoft Exchange Server 5.5, #70-081

- Implementing and Supporting Microsoft Internet Information Server 3.0 and Microsoft Index Server 1.1, #70-077

  OR Implementing and Supporting Microsoft Internet Information Server 4.0, #70-087

- Implementing and Supporting Microsoft Proxy Server 1.0, #70-078

  OR Implementing and Supporting Microsoft Proxy Server 2.0, #70-088

- Implementing and Supporting Microsoft Internet Explorer 4.0 by Using the Internet Explorer Resource Kit, #70-079

How to Become a Microsoft Certified Systems Engineer+ Internet

You must pass seven operating system exams and two elective exams to become an MCSE specializing in Internet technology.

The seven MCSE+Internet core exams required for certification are as follows:

- Networking Essentials, #70-058

- Internetworking with Microsoft TCP/IP on Microsoft Windows NT 4.0, #70-059

- Implementing and Supporting Microsoft Windows 95, #70-064

  OR Implementing and Supporting Microsoft Windows NT Workstation 4.0, #70-073

  OR Implementing and Supporting Microsoft Windows 98, #70-098

- Implementing and Supporting Microsoft Windows NT Server 4.0, #70-067

- Implementing and Supporting Microsoft Windows NT Server 4.0 in the Enterprise, #70-068

- Implementing and Supporting Microsoft Internet Information Server 3.0 and Microsoft Index Server 1.1, #70-077

  OR Implementing and Supporting Microsoft Internet Information Server 4.0, #70-087

- Implementing and Supporting Microsoft Internet Explorer 4.0 by Using the Internet Explorer Resource Kit, #70-079

You must also pass two of the following elective exams for MCSE+Internet certification:

- System Administration for Microsoft SQL Server 6.5, #70-026
- Implementing a Database Design on Microsoft SQL Server 6.5, #70-027
- Implementing and Supporting Web Sites Using Microsoft Site Server 3.0, # 70-056
- Implementing and Supporting Microsoft Exchange Server 5.0, #70-076

  OR Implementing and Supporting Microsoft Exchange Server 5.5, #70-081
- Implementing and Supporting Microsoft Proxy Server 1.0, #70-078

  OR Implementing and Supporting Microsoft Proxy Server 2.0, #70-088
- Implementing and Supporting Microsoft SNA Server 4.0, #70-085

How to Become a Microsoft Certified Solution Developer

The MCSD certification is undergoing substantial revision. Listed next are the requirements for the new track (available fourth quarter 1998), as well as the old.

For the new track, you must pass three core exams and one elective exam.

The core exams include the following:

Desktop Applications Development (1 required)

- Designing and Implementing Desktop Applications with Microsoft Visual C++ 6.0, #70-016

  OR Designing and Implementing Desktop Applications with Microsoft Visual Basic 6.0, #70-176

Distributed Applications Development (1 required)

- Designing and Implementing Distributed Applications with Microsoft Visual C++ 6.0, #70-015

  OR Designing and Implementing Distributed Applications with Microsoft Visual Basic 6.0, #70-175

Solution Architecture (required)

- Analyzing Requirements and Defining Solution Architectures, #70-100

Elective Exams

You must also pass one of the following elective exams:

- Designing and Implementing Distributed Applications with Microsoft Visual C++ 6.0, #70-015

  OR Designing and Implementing Desktop Applications with Microsoft Visual C++ 6.0, #70-016

  OR Microsoft SQL Server 4.2 Database Implementation, #70-021*

- Implementing a Database Design on Microsoft SQL Server 6.5, #70-027

  OR Implementing a Database Design on Microsoft SQL Server 7.0, #70-029
- Developing Applications with C++ Using the Microsoft Foundation Class Library, #70-024
- Implementing OLE in Microsoft Foundation Class Applications, #70-025
- Designing and Implementing Web Sites with Microsoft FrontPage 98, #70-055
- Designing and Implementing Commerce Solutions with Microsoft Site Server 3.0, Commerce Edition, #70-057
- Programming with Microsoft Visual Basic 4.0, #70-065

  OR Developing Applications with Microsoft Visual Basic 5.0, #70-165

  OR Designing and Implementing Distributed Applications with Microsoft Visual Basic 6.0, #70-175

  OR Designing and Implementing Desktop Applications with Microsoft Visual Basic 6.0, #70-176
- Microsoft Access for Windows 95 and the Microsoft Access Development Toolkit, #70-069
- Designing and Implementing Solutions with Microsoft Office (Code-named Office 9) and Microsoft Visual Basic for Applications, #70-091
- Designing and Implementing Web Solutions with Microsoft Visual InterDev 6.0, #70-152

Former MCSD Track

For the old track, you must pass two core technology exams and two elective exams for MCSD certification. The following lists show the required technology exams and elective exams needed to become an MCSD.

You must pass the following two core technology exams to qualify for MCSD certification:

- Microsoft Windows Architecture I, #70-160*
- Microsoft Windows Architecture II, #70-161*

You must also pass two of the following elective exams to become an MSCD:

- Designing and Implementing Distributed Applications with Microsoft Visual C++ 6.0, #70-015
- Designing and Implementing Desktop Applications with Microsoft Visual C++ 6.0, #70-016
- Microsoft SQL Server 4.2 Database Implementation, #70-021*

  OR Implementing a Database Design on Microsoft SQL Server 6.5, #70-027

  OR Implementing a Database Design on Microsoft SQL Server 7.0, #70-029
- Developing Applications with C++ Using the Microsoft Foundation Class Library, #70-024
- Implementing OLE in Microsoft Foundation Class Applications, #70-025
- Programming with Microsoft Visual Basic 4.0, #70-065

OR Developing Applications with Microsoft Visual Basic 5.0, #70-165

OR Designing and Implementing Distributed Applications with Microsoft Visual Basic 6.0, #70-175

OR Designing and Implementing Desktop Applications with Microsoft Visual Basic 6.0, #70-176

- Microsoft Access 2.0 for Windows-Application Development, #70-051

  OR Microsoft Access for Windows 95 and the Microsoft Access Development Toolkit, #70-069

- Developing Applications with Microsoft Excel 5.0 Using Visual Basic for Applications, #70-052
- Programming in Microsoft Visual FoxPro 3.0 for Windows, #70-054
- Designing and Implementing Web Sites with Microsoft FrontPage 98, #70-055
- Designing and Implementing Commerce Solutions with Microsoft Site Server 3.0, Commerce Edition, #70-057
- Designing and Implementing Solutions with Microsoft Office (Code-named Office 9) and Microsoft Visual Basic for Applications, #70-091
- Designing and Implementing Web Solutions with Microsoft Visual InterDev 6.0, #70-152

Becoming a Microsoft Certified Trainer

To understand the requirements and process for becoming an MCT, you need to obtain the Microsoft Certified Trainer Guide document from the following site:

`http://www.microsoft.com/train_cert/mct/`

At this site, you can read the document as Web pages or display and download it as a Word file. The MCT Guide explains the four-step process of becoming an MCT. The general steps for the MCT certification are as follows:

1. Complete and mail a Microsoft Certified Trainer application to Microsoft. You must include proof of your skills for presenting instructional material. The options for doing so are described in the MCT Guide.
2. Obtain and study the Microsoft Trainer Kit for the Microsoft Official Curricula (MOC) courses for which you want to be certified. Microsoft Trainer Kits can be ordered by calling 800-688-0496 in North America. Interested parties in other regions should review the MCT Guide for information on how to order a Trainer Kit.
3. Take the Microsoft certification exam for the product about which you want to be certified to teach.
4. Attend the MOC course for the course for which you want to be certified. This is done so you can understand how the course is structured, how labs are completed, and how the course flows.

> **✻ WARNING**
>
> You should consider the preceding steps a general overview of the MCT certification process. The precise steps that you need to take are described in detail on the site mentioned earlier. Do not misinterpret the preceding steps as the exact process you need to undergo.

If you are interested in becoming an MCT, you can receive more information by visiting the Microsoft Certified Training site at `http://www.microsoft.com/train_cert/mct/` or by calling 800-688-0496.

STUDY AND EXAM PREPARATION TIPS

This part of the appendix provides you with some general guidelines for preparing for the exam. It is organized into three sections. The first section, "Study Tips," addresses your pre-exam preparation activities, covering general study tips. This is followed by "Exam Prep Tips," an extended look at the Microsoft Certification exams, including a number of specific tips that apply to the Microsoft exam formats. Finally, "Putting It All Together" discusses changes in Microsoft's testing policies and how they might affect you.

To better understand the nature of preparation for the test, it is important to understand learning as a process. You probably are aware of how you best learn new material. You may find that outlining works best for you, or you may need to see things as a visual learner. Whatever your learning style, test preparation takes place over time. Although it is obvious that you can't start studying for these exams the night before you take them, it is very important to understand that learning is a developmental process. Understanding it as a process helps you focus on what you know and what you have yet to learn.

Thinking about how you learn should help you to recognize that learning takes place when you are able to match new information to old. You have some previous experience with computers and networking, and now you are preparing for this certification exam. Using this book, software, and supplementary materials will not just add incrementally to what you know. As you study, you actually change the organization of your knowledge as you integrate this new information into your existing knowledge base. This will lead you to a more comprehensive understanding of the tasks and concepts outlined in the objectives and of computing in general. Again, this happens as an iterative process rather than a singular event. Keep this model of learning in mind as you prepare for the exam, and you will make better decisions about what to study and how much more studying you need to do.

Study Tips

There are many ways to approach studying, just as there are many different types of material to study. However, the tips that follow should prepare you well for the type of material covered on the certification exams.

Study Strategies

Individuals vary in the ways they learn information. Some basic principles of learning apply to everyone, however; you should adopt some study strategies that take advantage of these principles. One of these principles is that learning can be broken into various depths. Recognition (of terms, for example) exemplifies a more surface level of learning—you rely on a prompt of some sort to elicit recall. Comprehension or understanding (of the concepts behind the terms, for instance) represents a deeper level of learning. The ability to analyze a concept and apply your understanding of it in a new way or novel setting represents an even further depth of learning.

Your learning strategy should enable you to understand the material at a level or two deeper than mere recognition. This will help you to do well on the exam(s). You will know the material so thoroughly that you can easily handle the recognition-level types of questions used in multiple-choice testing. You will also be able to apply your knowledge to solve novel problems.

Macro and Micro Study Strategies

One strategy that can lead to this deeper learning includes preparing an outline that covers all the objectives and subobjectives for the particular exam you are working on. You should delve a bit further into the material and include a level or two of detail beyond the stated objectives and subobjectives for the exam. Then flesh out the outline by coming up with a statement of definition or a summary for each point in the outline.

This outline provides two approaches to studying. First, you can study the outline by focusing on the organization of the material. Work your way through the points and subpoints of your outline with the goal of learning how they relate to one another. For example, be sure you understand how each of the main objective areas is similar to and different from another. Then do the same thing with the subobjectives; be sure you know which subobjectives pertain to each objective area and how they relate to one another.

Next, you can work through the outline, focusing on learning the details. Memorize and understand terms and their definitions, facts, rules and strategies, advantages and disadvantages, and so on. In this pass through the outline, attempt to learn detail rather than the big picture (the organizational information that you worked on in the first pass through the outline).

Research has shown that attempting to assimilate both types of information at the same time seems to interfere with the overall learning process. Separate your studying into these two approaches, and you will perform better on the exam than if you attempt to study the material in a more conventional manner.

Active Study Strategies

In addition, the process of writing down and defining the objectives, subobjectives, terms, facts, and definitions promotes a more active learning strategy than merely reading the material. In human information-processing terms, writing forces you to engage in more active encoding of the information. Simply reading over it constitutes more passive processing.

Next, determine whether you can apply the information you have learned by attempting to create examples and scenarios of your own. Think about how or where you could apply the concepts you are learning. Again, write down this information to process the facts and concepts in a more active fashion.

The hands-on nature of the step-by-step tutorials and exercises at the ends of the chapters provide further active learning opportunities that will reinforce concepts as well.

Common–sense Strategies

Finally, you should follow commonsense practices in studying. Study when you are alert, reduce or eliminate distractions, take breaks when you become fatigued, and so on.

Pre-testing Yourself

Pre-testing allows you to assess how well you are learning. One of the most important aspects of learning is what has been called meta-learning. *Meta-learning* has to do with realizing when you know something well or when you need to study more. In other words, you recognize how well or how poorly you have learned the material you are studying. For most people, this can be difficult to assess objectively on their own. Practice tests are useful in that they reveal more objectively what you have learned and what you have not learned. You should use this information to guide review and further studying. Developmental learning takes place as you cycle through studying, assessing how well you have learned, reviewing, assessing again, until you feel you are ready to take the exam.

You may have noticed the practice exams included in this book. Use them as part of this process.

Exam Prep Tips

Having mastered the subject matter, your final preparatory step is to understand how the exam will be presented. Make no mistake about it—a Microsoft Certified Professional (MCP) exam will challenge both your knowledge and test-taking skills! This section starts with the basics of exam design, reviews a new type of exam format, and concludes with hints that are targeted to each of the exam formats.

The MCP Exams

Every MCP exam is released in one of two basic formats. What's being called exam format here is really little more than a combination of the overall exam structure and the presentation method for exam questions.

Each exam format utilizes the same types of questions. These types or styles of questions include multiple-rating (or scenario-based) questions, traditional multiple-choice questions, and simulation-based questions. It's important to understand the types of questions you will be presented with and the actions required to properly answer them.

Understanding the exam formats is key to good preparation because the format determines the number of questions presented, the difficulty of those questions, and the amount of time allowed to complete the exam.

Exam Formats

There are two basic formats for the MCP exams: the traditional fixed-form exam and the adaptive form. As its name implies, the fixed-form exam presents a fixed set of questions during the exam session. The adaptive format, however, uses only a subset of questions drawn from a larger pool during any given exam session.

Fixed-form

A fixed-form, computerized exam is based on a fixed set of exam questions. The individual questions are presented in random order during a test session. If you take the same exam more than once, you won't necessarily see the exact same questions. This is because two to three final forms are typically assembled for every fixed-form exam Microsoft releases. These are usually labeled Forms A, B, and C.

The final forms of a fixed-form exam are identical in terms of content coverage, number of questions, and allotted time, but the questions themselves are different. You may have noticed, however, that some of the same questions appear on, or rather are shared across, different final forms. When questions are shared across multiple final forms of an exam, the percentage of sharing is generally small. Many final forms share no questions, but some older exams may have a ten to fifteen percent duplication of exam questions on the final exam forms.

Fixed-form exams also have a fixed time limit in which you must complete the exam.

Finally, the score you achieve on a fixed-form exam, which is always reported for MCP exams on a scale of 0 to 1000, is based on the number of questions you answer correctly. The exam passing score is the same for all final forms of a given fixed-form exam.

The typical format for the fixed-form exam is as follows:

- 50–60 questions
- 75–90 minute testing time
- Question review allowed, including the opportunity to change your answers

Adaptive Form

An adaptive form exam has the same appearance as a fixed-form exam, but differs in both how questions are selected for presentation and how many questions actually are presented. Although the statistics of adaptive testing are fairly complex, the process is concerned with determining your level of skill or ability with the exam subject matter. This ability assessment begins by presenting questions of varying levels of difficulty and ascertaining at what difficulty level you can reliably answer them. Finally, the ability assessment determines if that ability level is above or below the level required to pass that exam.

Examinees at different levels of ability will then see quite different sets of questions. Those who demonstrate little expertise with the subject matter will continue to be presented with relatively easy questions. Examinees who demonstrate a higher level of expertise will be presented progressively more difficult questions. Both individuals may answer the same number of questions correctly, but because the exam-taker with the higher level of expertise can correctly answer more difficult questions, he or she will receive a higher score, and is more likely to pass the exam.

The typical design for the adaptive form exam is as follows:

- 20–25 questions
- 90-minute testing time, although this is likely to be reduced to 45–60 minutes in the near future
- Question review not allowed, providing no opportunity to change your answers

Your first adaptive exam will be unlike any other testing experience you have had. In fact, many examinees have difficulty accepting the adaptive testing process because they feel that they are not provided the opportunity to adequately demonstrate their full expertise.

You can take consolation in the fact that adaptive exams are painstakingly put together after months of data gathering and analysis and are just as valid as a fixed-form exam. The rigor introduced through the adaptive testing methodology means that there is nothing arbitrary about what you'll see! It is also a more efficient means of testing, requiring less time to conduct and complete.

As you can see from Figure A.1, there are a number of statistical measures that drive the adaptive examination process. The most immediately relevant to you is the ability estimate. Accompanying this test statistic are the standard error of measurement, the item characteristic curve, and the test information curve.

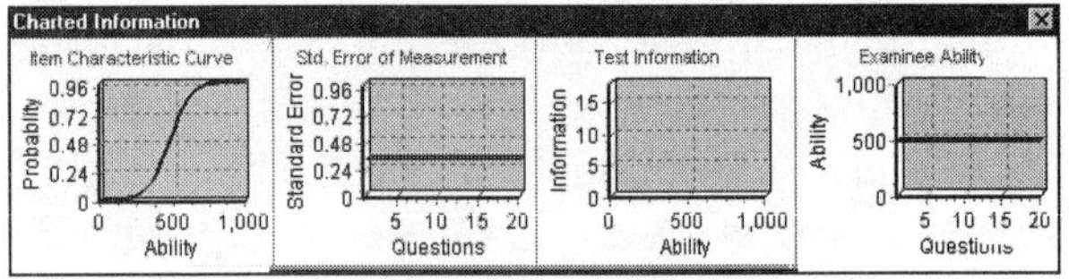

FIGURE A.1
Microsoft's Adaptive Testing Demonstration Program.

The standard error, which is the key factor in determining when an adaptive exam will terminate, reflects the degree of error in the exam ability estimate. The item characteristic curve reflects the probability of a correct response relative to examinee ability. Finally, the test information statistic provides a measure of the information contained in the set of questions the examinee has answered, again relative to the ability level of the individual examinee.

When you begin an adaptive exam, the standard error has already been assigned a target value below which it must drop for the exam to conclude. This target value reflects a particular level of statistical confidence in the process. The examinee ability is initially set to the mean possible exam score: 500 for MCP exams.

As the adaptive exam progresses, questions of varying difficulty are presented. Based on your pattern of responses to these questions, the ability estimate is recalculated. Simultaneously, the standard error estimate is refined from its first estimated value of one toward the target value. When the standard error reaches its target value, the exam terminates. Thus, the more consistently you answer questions of the same degree of difficulty, the more quickly the standard error estimate drops, and the fewer questions you will end up seeing during the exam session. This situation is depicted in Figure A.2.

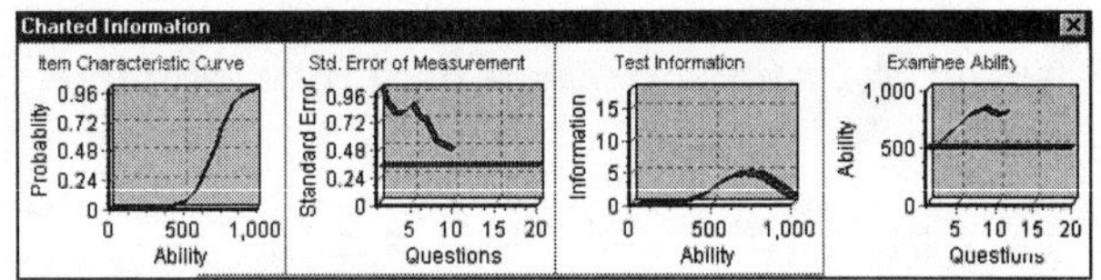

FIGURE A.2
The changing statistics in an adaptive exam.

As you might suspect, one good piece of advice for taking an adaptive exam is to treat every exam question as if it were the most important. The adaptive scoring algorithm is attempting to discover a pattern of responses that reflects some level of proficiency with the subject matter. Incorrect responses almost guarantee that additional questions must be answered (unless, of course, you get every question wrong). This is because the scoring algorithm must adjust to information that is not consistent with the emerging pattern.

New Question Types

A variety of question types can appear on MCP exams. Examples of multiple-choice questions and scenario-based questions appear throughout this book. They appear in the Top Score software as well. Simulation-based questions are new to the MCP exam series.

Simulation Questions

Simulation-based questions reproduce the look and feel of key Microsoft product features for the purpose of testing. The simulation software used in MCP exams has been designed to look and act, as much as possible, just like the actual product. Consequently, answering simulation questions in an MCP exam entails completing one or more tasks just as if you were using the product itself.

The format of a typical Microsoft simulation question is straightforward. It presents a brief scenario or problem statement along with one or more tasks that must be completed to solve the problem. An example of a simulation question for MCP exams is shown in the following section.

A Typical Simulation Question

It sounds obvious, but the first step when you encounter a simulation is to carefully read the question (see Figure A.3). Do not go straight to the simulation application! Assess the problem being presented and identify the conditions that make up the problem scenario. Note the tasks that must be performed or outcomes that must be achieved to answer the question, and review any instructions about how to proceed.

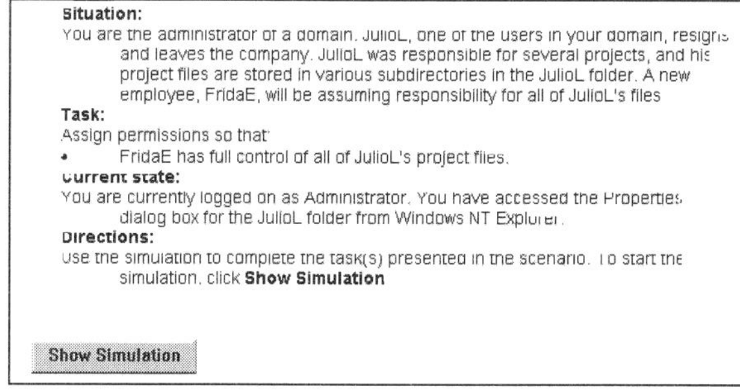

Situation:
You are the administrator of a domain. JulioL, one of the users in your domain, resigns and leaves the company. JulioL was responsible for several projects, and his project files are stored in various subdirectories in the JulioL folder. A new employee, FridaE, will be assuming responsibility for all of JulioL's files

Task:
Assign permissions so that

- FridaE has full control of all of JulioL's project files.

Current state:
You are currently logged on as Administrator. You have accessed the Properties dialog box for the JulioL folder from Windows NT Explorer.

Directions:
Use the simulation to complete the task(s) presented in the scenario. To start the simulation, click **Show Simulation**

Show Simulation

FIGURE A.3
Typical MCP exam simulation question with directions.

The next step is to launch the simulator. Click the Show Simulation button to see a feature of the product, such as the dialog box shown in Figure A.4. The simulation application partially covers the question text on many test center machines. Feel free to reposition the simulation or to move between the question text screen and the simulation using hot keys, point-and-click navigation, or even by clicking the simulation launch button again.

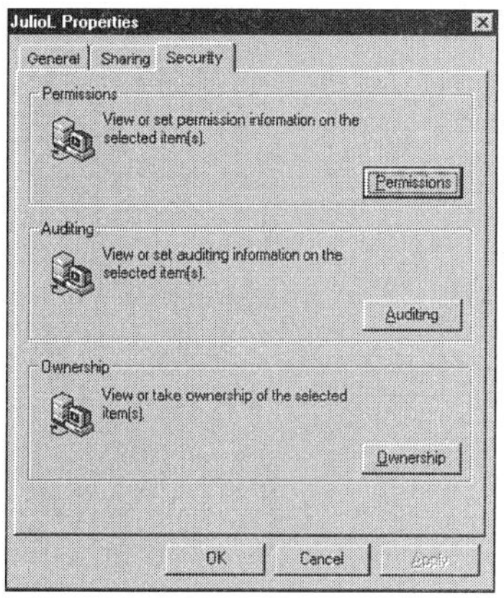

FIGURE A.4
Launching the simulation application.

It is important to understand that your answer to the simulation question is not recorded until you move on to the next exam question. This gives you the added capability to close and reopen the simulation application (using the launch button) on the same question without losing any partial answer you may have made.

The third step is to use the simulator as you would the actual product to solve the problem or perform the defined tasks. Again, the simulation software is designed to function, within reason, just as the product does. But don't expect the simulation to reproduce product behavior perfectly.

Most importantly, do not allow yourself to become flustered if the simulation does not look or act exactly like the product. Figure A.5 shows the solution to the example simulation problem.

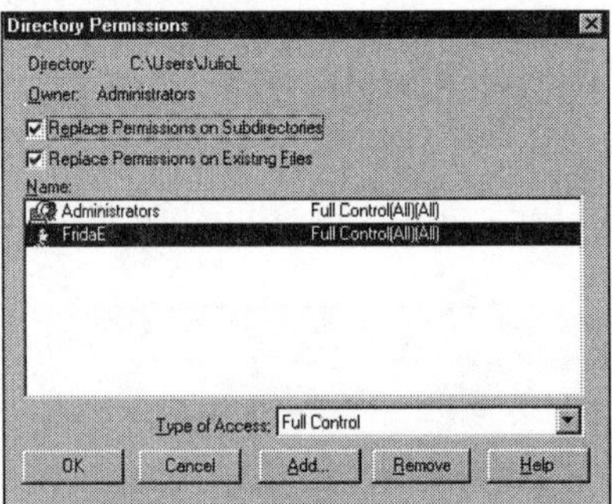

FIGURE A.5
The solution to the simulation example.

There are two final points that will help you tackle simulation questions. First, respond only to what is being asked in the question. Do not solve problems that you are not asked to solve. Second, accept what is being asked of you. You may not entirely agree with conditions in the problem statement, the quality of the desired solution, or the sufficiency of defined tasks to adequately solve the problem. Always remember that you are being tested on your ability to solve the problem as it has been presented.

The solution to the simulation problem shown in Figure A.5 perfectly illustrates both of these points. As you'll recall from the question scenario (refer to Figure aA3), you were asked to assign appropriate permissions to a new user, FridaE. You were not instructed to make any other changes in permissions. Thus, if you had modified or removed Administrators permissions, this item would have been scored as incorrect on an MCP exam.

Putting It All Together

Given all these different pieces of information, the task is now to assemble a set of tips that will help you successfully tackle the different types of MCP exams.

More Pre-exam Preparation Tips

Generic exam preparation advice is always useful. Tips include the following:

- Become familiar with the product. Hands-on experience is one of the keys to success on any MCP exam. Review the exercises and the step-by-step activities in the book.
- Review the current exam preparation guide on the Microsoft MCP Web site. The documentation Microsoft makes publicly available over the Web identifies the skills every exam is intended to test.
- Memorize foundational technical detail as appropriate. Remember that MCP exams are generally heavy on problem solving and application of knowledge rather than just questions that only require rote memorization.
- Take any of the available practice tests. We recommend the ones included in this book and the ones you can create using New Riders' exclusive Top Score Test Simulation software suite, available through your local bookstore or software distributor. Although these are fixed-format exams, they provide practice that is valuable for preparing for an adaptive exam. Because of the interactive nature of adaptive testing, it is not possible to provide examples of the adaptive format in the included practice exams. However,

fixed-format exams do provide the same types of questions as found on adaptive exams and are the most effective way to prepare for either type of exam. As a supplement to the material bound with this book, also try the free practice tests available on the Microsoft MCP Web site.

- Look on the Microsoft MCP Web site for samples and demonstration items. These tend to be particularly valuable for one significant reason: They allow you to become familiar with any new testing technologies before you encounter them on an MCP exam.

During the Exam Session

Similarly, the generic exam-taking advice you've heard for years applies when taking an MCP exam:

- Take a deep breath and try to relax when you first sit down for your exam session. It is very important to control the pressure you may (naturally) feel when taking exams.
- You will be provided scratch paper. Take a moment to write down any factual information and technical detail that you've committed to short-term memory.
- Carefully read all information and instruction screens. These displays have been put together to give you information relevant to the exam you are taking.
- Accept the Non-Disclosure Agreement and preliminary survey as part of the examination process. Complete them accurately and quickly move on.
- Read the exam questions carefully. Reread each question to identify all relevant detail.
- Tackle the questions in the order they are presented. Skipping around won't build your confidence; the clock is always counting down.
- Don't rush, but similarly, don't linger on difficult questions. The questions vary in degree of difficulty. Don't let yourself be flustered by a particularly difficult or verbose question.

Fixed-form Exams

Building from this basic preparation and test-taking advice, you also need to consider the challenges presented by the different exam designs. Because a fixed-form exam is composed of a fixed, finite set of questions, add these tips to your strategy for taking a fixed-form exam:

- Note the time allotted and the number of questions appearing on the exam you are taking. Make a rough calculation of how many minutes you can spend on each question and use this to pace yourself through the exam.
- Take advantage of the fact that you can return to and review skipped or previously answered questions. Mark the questions you can't answer confidently, noting the relative difficulty of each question on the scratch paper provided. When you reach the end of the exam, return to the more difficult questions.
- If there is session time remaining after you have completed all questions (and you aren't too fatigued!), review your answers. Pay particular attention to questions that seem to have a lot of detail or that required graphics.

- As for changing your answers, the rule of thumb here is *don't*! If you read the question carefully and completely, and you felt like you knew the right answer, you probably did. Don't second-guess yourself. If, as you check your answers, one stands out as clearly marked incorrectly, however, you should change it in that instance. If you are at all unsure, go with your first impression.

Adaptive Exams

If you are planning to take an adaptive exam, keep these additional tips in mind:

- Read and answer every question with great care. When reading a question, identify every relevant detail, requirement, or task that must be performed and double-check your answer to be sure you have addressed every one of them.
- If you cannot answer a question, use the process of elimination to reduce the set of potential answers, then take your best guess. Stupid mistakes invariably mean additional questions will be presented.
- Forget about reviewing questions and changing your answers. After you leave a question, whether you've answered it or not, you cannot return to it. Do not skip a question, either; if you do, it's counted as incorrect!

Simulation Questions

You may encounter simulation questions on either the fixed-form or adaptive form exam. If you do, keep these tips in mind:

- Avoid changing any simulation settings that don't pertain directly to the problem solution. Solve the problem you are being asked to solve, and nothing more.
- Assume default settings when related information has not been provided. If something has not been mentioned or defined, it is a non-critical detail that does not factor in to the correct solution.
- Be sure your entries are syntactically correct, paying particular attention to your spelling. Enter relevant information just as the product would require it.
- Close all simulation application windows after completing the simulation tasks. The testing system software is designed to trap errors that could result when using the simulation application, but trust yourself over the testing software.
- If simulations are part of a fixed-form exam, you can return to skipped or previously answered questions and review your answers. However, if you choose to change your answer to a simulation question, or even attempt to review the settings you've made in the simulation application, your previous response to that simulation question will be deleted. If simulations are part of an adaptive exam, you cannot return to previous questions.

FINAL CONSIDERATIONS

There are a number of changes in the MCP program that will impact how frequently you can repeat an exam and what you will see when you do.

- Microsoft has instituted a new exam retake policy. This new rule is "two and two, then one and two." That is, you can attempt any exam two times with no restrictions on the time between attempts. But after the second attempt, you must wait two weeks before you can attempt that exam again. After that, you will be required to wait two weeks between any subsequent attempts. Plan to pass the exam in two attempts, or plan to increase your time horizon for receiving an MCP credential.
- New questions are being seeded into the MCP exams. After performance data has been gathered on new questions, they will replace older questions on all exam forms. This means that the questions appearing on exams are regularly changing.
- Many of the current MCP exams will be republished in adaptive format in the coming months. Prepare yourself for this significant change in testing format; it is entirely likely that this will become the new preferred MCP exam format.

These changes mean that the brute-force strategies for passing MCP exams may soon completely lose their viability. So if you don't pass an exam on the first or second attempt, it is entirely possible that the exam will change significantly in form. It could be updated to adaptive form from fixed-form or have a different set of questions or question types.

The intention of Microsoft is clearly not to make the exams more difficult by introducing unwanted change. Their intent is to create and maintain valid measures of the technical skills and knowledge associated with the different MCP credentials. Preparing for an MCP exam has always involved not only studying the subject matter, but also planning for the testing experience itself. With these changes, this is now more true than ever.

APPENDIX B

Glossary

In the age of information, buzz words and acronyms seem to grow on trees. Keeping up with all of them can be tiresome and annoying. This glossary covers terms related to TCP/IP and networking.

A

account A user ID and disk area (typically the home directory) restricted for the use of a particular person. Usually password protected.

ACK Acknowledgment. A response from a receiving computer to a sending computer to indicate successful reception of information. TCP requires that packets be acknowledged before it considers the transmission safe.

Active open An action taken by a client to initiate a TCP connection with a server.

Address classes A grouping of IP addresses with each class, defining the maximum number of networks and hosts available. The first octet of the address determines the class.

Address mask A 32-bit binary number used to select bits from an IP address for subnet masking.

Address resolution A translation of an IP address to a corresponding physical address.

Agent The software routine in a Simple Network Management Protocol (SNMP)–managed device that responds to get and set requests and sends trap messages.

alias A short name that represents a more complicated one. Often used for mail addresses or host domain names.

analog A form of electronic communication using a continuous electromagnetic wave, such as television or radio. Any continuous wave form, as opposed to digital on/off transmissions. See also *digital.*

anchor A hypertext link in the form of text or a graphic that, when clicked, takes you to the linked file.

annotation A Mosaic feature that enables you to add a comment to a viewed document.

anonymous FTP Enables you to download (and sometimes upload) files without requiring a password.

ANSI American National Standards Institute. The membership organization responsible for defining U.S. standards in the information technology industry.

API Application Programming Interface. A language and message format that enables a programmer to use functions in another program or in the hardware.

Archie A search engine that finds filenames on anonymous FTP services.

Archive A repository of files available for access at an Internet site. Also, a collection of files, often a backup of a disk or files saved to tape to allow them to be transferred.

Argument A parameter passed to a subroutine or function.

ARP Address Resolution Protocol. A protocol in the TCP/IP suite used to resolve an IP address to a physical hardware address.

ARPA Advanced Research Projects Agency. A government agency that originally funded the research on the ARPAnet (became DARPA in the mid-1970s).

ARPAnet The first network of computers funded by the U.S. Department of Defense Advanced Research Projects Agency. An experimental communications network funded by the government that eventually developed into the Internet.

Article Message submitted to a Usenet newsgroup. Unlike an email message that goes to a specific person or group of persons, a newsgroup message goes to directories (on many machines) that can be read by any number of people.

ASCII American Standard Code for Information Interchange. A standard character set of data that is limited to letters, numbers, and punctuation.

ATM Asynchronous Transfer Mode. A high-speed network technology based on transmitting cells of a small, fixed size. Currently, ATM supports network speeds from 25 to 622 megabits per second.

Attribute A form of a command-line switch as applied to tags in the HTML language. HTML commands or tags can be more specific when attributes are used. Not all HTML tags use attributes.

au An extension for audio files.

B

Backbone Generally very high-speed, T3 telephone lines that connect remote ends of networks and networks to one another; only service providers are connected to the Internet in this way. Can also be the main network segment that connects the network.

Bang A slang term for an exclamation point.

Bang address A type of email address that separates host names in the address with exclamation points. Used for mail sent to the (UNIX-to-UNIX copy) UUCP network, where specifying the exact path of the mail (including all hosts that pass on the message) is necessary. The address is in the form of `machine!machine!userID`, in which the number of machines listed depends on the connections needed to reach the machine that stores the account userID.

Baseband A network technology that requires all nodes attached to the network to participate in every transmission. Ethernet, for example, is a baseband technology.

Baseline A starting point.

Best-effort delivery A characteristic of a network technology that does not ensure link-level reliability. IP and UDP protocols work together to provide best-effort delivery service to applications.

BGP Border Gateway Protocol. An Internet protocol that allows groups of routers to share routing information. This protocol is defined in RFC 1771.

Binary A file or other data that may contain nonprintable characters, including graphics files, programs, and sound files.

BinHex A program that encodes binary files as ASCII so that they can be sent through email.

Bit A binary number that has the value of 0 or 1.

BITNET Because It's Time Network. A non-TCP/IP network for small universities without Internet access.

Block A group of statements enclosed in braces.

Bookmarks Term used by some World Wide Web browsers for marking URLs you access frequently.

Boolean logic Logic dealing with true/false values. (The operators AND, OR, and NOT are Boolean operators.)

BOOTP Bootstrap Protocol. A protocol used to configure systems across internetworks.

Bounce An email message you receive that tells you that an email message you sent wasn't delivered. Usually contains an error code and the contents of the message that wasn't delivered.

bps Bits per second. A measurement that expresses the speed at which data is transferred between computers.

Bridge A device that operates at the Data Link layer of the OSI model and connects one physical section of a network to another, often providing isolation.

Broadband A network technology that multiplexes multiple network carriers into a single cable.

Broadcast A packet destined for all hosts on the network.

Brouter A computer device that works as both a bridge and a router. Some network traffic can be bridged while other traffic is routed.

Browse list A dynamic list of resources available across the network

Browser A utility that lets you look through collections of things. For example, a file browser lets you look through a file system. Applications that let you access the World Wide Web are called browsers.

Browsing The ability to see other resources available across the network.

Buffer A storage area used to hold input or output data.

C

CAN Campus Area Network. A physical communications network that operates across a campus or similar geographic area. See also *MAN* (Metropolitan Area Network).

CERN The European Laboratory for Particle Physics, where the World Wide Web was first conceived of and implemented.

Checksumming A service performed by UDP that determines whether packets were changed during transmission.

Child A subprocess. A subprocess is a process that is launched by another process, called the parent process.

CIDR Classless Interdomain Routing. An IP addressing scheme designed to replace the current scheme based on class A, B, and C addresses. With CIDR, a single IP address can be used to designate many unique IP addresses.

Client A user of a service. Also often refers to a piece of software that retrieves information from a server. Additionally, client can refer to an application that makes a request of a service on a (sometimes) remote computer; the request can be, for example, a function call.

Client computer A computer that can access the resource from a host.

CMIP Common Management Information Protocol. An OSI network management protocol.

Community In SNMP, this is a logical grouping to which a system belongs.

Compress A program that compacts a file so it fits into a smaller space. Also can refer to the technique of reducing the amount of space a file takes up.

Concatenate To join two strings.

Connection A logical path between two protocol modules that provides a reliable delivery service.

Connectionless service A delivery service that treats each packet as a separate entity. Often results in lost packets or packets delivered out of sequence.

Context Many functions return either array values or scalar values depending on the context, that is, whether returning an array or a scalar value is appropriate for the place where the call was made.

Counters Statistical measurements on objects used by Performance Monitor.

CRC Cyclic Redundancy Check. A computation about a frame of which the result is a small integer. The value is appended to the end of the frame and recalculated when the frame is received. If the results differ from the appended value, the frame has presumably been corrupted and is therefore discarded. CRC is used to detect errors in transmission.

CSMA Carrier Sense Multiple Access. A simple media access control protocol that enables multiple stations to contend for access to the medium. If no traffic is detected on the medium, the station can send a transmission.

CSMA/CD Carrier Sense Multiple Access with Collision Detection. A characteristic of network hardware that uses CSMA with a process that detects when two stations transmit simultaneously. If that happens, both back off and retry the transmission after a random time period has elapsed.

Cyberspace Refers to the entire collection of sites accessible electronically. If your computer is attached to the Internet or another large network, it exists in cyberspace.

D

Daemon A program that runs automatically on a computer to perform a service for the operating system or for clients on the network.

DARPA Defense Advanced Research Projects Agency, originally ARPA. The government agency that funded the research that developed the ARPAnet.

Data transfer The ability provided by a utility to transfer a file from a remote host to a local host.

Database A structured way of storing data in a way often described in terms of a number of tables; each table is made up of a series of records, and each record contains a number of fields.

Datagram A packet of data and delivery information.

Debugging The process of tracking down errors in a program, often aided by examining or outputting extra information designed to help this process.

Decimal Notation A number taking the form of w.x.y.z such as 134.57.8.8.

Dedicated line See *leased line.*

Default Gateway The IP address of a router on the same network as the configured host. It is able to transpose traffic from one IP network to another, and is the router to use if the packet is not intended for the subnet.

DES Data Encryption Standard. An algorithm developed by the U.S. government to provide security for data transmitted over a network.

DHCP Dynamic Host Configuration Protocol. A protocol that provides dynamic address allocation and automatic TCP/IP configuration.

DHCP client A client that obtains TCP/IP configuration information from a DHCP server.

DHCP Manager A utility for administering scopes.

DHCP server A Dynamic Host Configuration Protocol server that issues TCP/IP configuration information.

Dial-up connection A connection to the Internet through a modem and telephone line that allows email and running processes to occur on a remote computer.

Digest A form of mailing list in which a number of messages are concatenated (linked) and sent out as a single message.

digital A type of communications used by computers, consisting of individual on and off pulses. Compare to *analog*.

Direct connection A connection to the Internet through a dedicated line, such as ISDN.

Directed broadcast address An IP address that specifies all hosts on the network.

Directory of Servers A service that describes what is available on servers throughout the world.

DNS See *Domain Name System (DNS)*.

DNS Name Server The server(s) that contain information about a portion of the DNS database.

Doc-ID In a wide area information server (WAIS), an ID that identifies a specific document in a database.

DOD Networking Model A 4-layer networking model that defines the TCP/IP protocol suite.

DOD Department of Defense. A U.S. government agency that originally sponsored the ARPAnet research.

Domain The highest subdivision of the Internet, for the most part by country (except in the United States, where it's by type of organization, such as educational, commercial, and government). Usually the last part of a host name; for example, the domain part of `ibm.com` is `.com`, which represents the domain of commercial sites in the United States.

Domain Name System (DNS) The system that translates between Internet IP addresses and Internet host names.

Dot address See *host address.*

Download To move a file from a remote computer to your local computer.

Dynamic routers Use interrouting protocols.

E

EBGP External Border Gateway Protocol. A form of Border Gateway Protocol that is used within a network. See also Border Gateway Protocol.

Effective GID The group identifier of the current process, which may have been changed from the original GID by various means.

Effective UID The user identifier of the current process, which may have been changed from the original UID by various means.

Election The process of determining roles each machine will play in the browsing process.

email An electronic message delivered from one computer user to another. Short for electronic mail.

email address An address used to send email to a user on the Internet, consisting of the username and host name (and any other necessary information, such as a gateway machine). An Internet email address is usually in the form `username@hostname`.

Encryption The process of scrambling a message so that it can be read only by someone who knows how to unscramble it.

Ethernet A type of local area network hardware. Many TCP/IP networks are ethernet based.

Eudora The most widely used email system.

Expire To remove an article from a Usenet newsgroup after a specified interval.

Extinction Interval The amount of time that must pass before the WINS server marks a released entry as extinct.

Extinction Timeout The amount of time WINS waits before removing (scavenging) entries that have been marked extinct.

F

Fair queuing A technique that controls traffic in gateways by restricting every host to an equal share of gateway bandwidth.

FAQ Frequently Asked Question(s). Often a question and answer approach to common problems. Most Usenet newsgroups have a FAQ to introduce new readers to popular topics in the newsgroup.

FCS Frame Check Sequence. A computation about the bits in a frame; the result is appended to the end of the frame and recalculated within the frame in which it is received. If the results differ from the appended value, the frame has presumably been corrupted and is therefore discarded. It is used to detect errors in transmission.

FDDI Fiber Distributed Data Interface. A set of ANSI protocols for sending digital data over fiberoptic cable. FDDI networks are based on token-passing technology and support transmissions up to 100 Mbps.

FDM Frequency Division Multiplexing. A technique of passing signals across a single medium by assigning each signal a unique carrier frequency.

Feed To send Usenet newsgroups from your site to another site that wants to read them.

FIFO First-in first-out. A queue in which the first item placed in the queue is the first item processed when the queue is processed.

File A basic unit of storage of computer data in a file structure; files can normally be binary or text only (ASCII).

Finger A program that provides information about users on an Internet host; may include a user's personal information, such as project affiliation and schedule.

Firewall A device placed on a network to prevent unauthorized traffic from entering the network.

Flame To communicate in an abusive or absurd manner. Often occurs in newsgroup posts and email messages.

Flow control A mechanism that controls the rate at which hosts may transmit at any time. It is used to avoid congestion on the network, which may exhaust memory buffers.

Flushing When data is output to a text file, it is usually buffered to make processing more efficient. *Flushing* forces any items in the buffer to be actually written to the file.

Forms Online data-entry sheets supported by some World Wide Web browsers.

FQDN Fully Qualified Domain Name. A combination of the host name and the domain name.

Fragment A piece that results when a datagram is partitioned into smaller pieces. It is used to facilitate datagrams that are too large for the network technology in use.

Frame A set of packets as transmitted across a medium. Differing frame types have unique characteristics.

Frame relay A type of digital data communications protocol.

Freeware Software that the author makes available at no cost to anyone who wants it (although the author retains rights to the software).

FTP File Transfer Protocol. A popular Internet communications protocol that allows you to transfer files between hosts on the Internet.

G

Gateway A device that interfaces two networks that use different protocols.

gif Graphics Interchange Format. An image format.

Gigabit Very high-speed (1 billion bits per second) data communications.

Gigabyte A unit of data storage approximately equal to one billion bytes of data.

Global option To set configuration items for all scopes on a DHCP server.

Global variables Variables that can be referred to anywhere within a package.

Gopher An application that allows you to access publicly available information on Internet hosts that provide gopher service.

gopher Provides menu descriptions of files on Internet servers; used primarily to find Internet information.

Gopherbook An application that uses an interface resembling a book to access Gopher servers.

Gopherspace Connected Gopher services.

GOSIP Government Open Systems Interconnection Profile. A U.S. government document that defines a specification of a set of OSI protocols that agencies may use.

Greenwich mean time An international time-standard reference, also known as Universal time.

GUI Graphical user interface. A computer interface based on graphical symbols rather than text. Windowing environments and Macintosh environments are GUIs.

H

Hacking Originally referred to playing around with computer systems; now often used to indicate destructive computer activity.

Hardware address The physical address of a host used by networks.

Hash lookup To find the value associated with a specified key in an associative array.

Hash table A method used for implementing associative arrays, which allows the keys to be converted to numbers for internal storage purposes.

HDLC High Level Data Link Control. A standard Data Link level protocol.

Header Data inserted at the beginning of a packet that contains control information.

Home page The document that serves as the entryway for all the information contained in a company's WWW service—your World Wide Web browser loads when it starts up.

Hop-check A utility that allows you to find out how many routers exist between your host and another Internet host. See also *Traceroute.*

Host A server connected to the Internet.

host address A unique number assigned to identify a host on the Internet (also called an *IP address* or a *dot address*). This address is usually represented as four numbers between 1 and 254 and separated by periods (for example, 192.58.107.230).

host computer The computer that has the resource you are trying to access.

Host ID The portion of an IP address that identifies the host in a particular network. It is used with network IDs to form a complete IP address.

Host name A unique name for a host that corresponds to the host address.

Hosts Individual computers connected to the Internet.

HOSTS file A text file that contains mappings of IP addresses to host names.

Hot list A list of your favorite World Wide Web sites that can be accessed quickly by your WWW browser.

HTML Hypertext Markup Language. The formatting language/protocol used to define various text styles in a hypertext document, including emphasis and bulleted lists.

html The extension for HTML files.

HTTP Hypertext Transfer Protocol The communications protocol used by WWW services to retrieve documents quickly.

Hyperlinks See *links.*

Hypertext An online document that has words or graphics containing links to other documents. Usually, selecting the link area onscreen (with a mouse or keyboard command) activates these links.

I

IAB Internet Architecture Board. An independent group responsible for policies and standards for TCP/IP and the Internet.

IBGP Internal Border Gateway Protocol. A form of Border Gateway Protocol that is used between networks. See also Border Gateway Protocol.

ICMP Internet Control Message Protocol. A maintenance protocol that handles error messages to be sent when datagrams are discarded or when systems experience congestion.

IEEE Institute of Electrical and Electronics Engineers. The professional society for electrical and computer engineers.

IETF Internet Engineering Task Force. A group of volunteers who help develop Internet standards.

IGMP Internet Group Management Protocol. A protocol used to carry group membership information in a multicast system.

IGP Interior Gateway Protocol. A generic term that applies to any routing protocol used within an autonomous system.

IIS Internet Information Server. A multifunction Web, FTP, NNTP, and SMTP server produced by Microsoft. IIS is shipped with Windows NT Server 4.0.

Index files Files created by waisindex that make up the WAIS source database. See also *waisindex.*

Internet The term used to describe all the worldwide interconnected TCP/IP networks.

InterNIC The NSFNET manager sites on the Internet that provide information about the Internet.

IP Internet Protocol. The communications protocol used by computers connected to the Internet.

IP address See *host address.*

IP forwarding The process of resending IP packets on one network after having been received on another.

IPCONFIG A command-line utility to view IP configuration information.

IPng Internet Protocol, next generation.

IPv4 Internet Protocol, version 4.

IPv6 Internet Protocol, version 6.

ISDN A dedicated telephone line connection that transmits digital data at the rate of 56Kbps.

ISO International Standards Organization. An organization that sets worldwide standards in many different areas.

ISP Internet Service Provider. A company that provides access to the Internet, usually for a monthly fee.

J–L

Java A programming language developed by Sun Microsystems that is platform independent.

JPEG Joint Photographic Experts Group. A compression standard.

LAN Local area network. A network of computers that is usually limited to a small physical area, like a building.

LATA Local Access and Transport Area.

Leased connection A connection to the Internet through a local phone company that allows your company to set up, for example, FTP, WWW, and Gopher services on the Internet at a permanent address.

leased line A dedicated phone line used for network communications.

LIFO Last-in first-out. A queue in which the last item placed in the queue is the first item processed when the queue is processed.

links The areas—words or graphics—in an HTML document that cause another document to be loaded when the user clicks them.

List A series of values separated by commas; lists are often enclosed in parentheses to avoid ambiguity and these parentheses are often necessary.

Listproc Software that automates the management of electronic mailing lists.

LISTSERV Software that automates the management of electronic mailing lists.

LLC Logical Link Control. A protocol that provides a common interface point to the media access control (MAC) layers.

LMHOSTS A static file used for NetBIOS name resolution.

Local host The computer you are currently using.

Local variables Local variables can be accessed only in the current block and in subroutines called from that block.

Logical operators Boolean operators: that is, those dealing with true/false values.

Logon The process of entering your user ID and password at a prompt to gain access to a service.

M

MAC Media Access Control. A protocol that governs the access method a station has to the network.

Mac address A unique number that is physically branded on every network interface card.

Mail bridge A gateway that screens mail between two networks to make certain they meet administrative constraints.

Mailers Applications that let you read and send email messages.

Mailing list A service that forwards to everyone on a list an email message sent to it, allowing that group of people to discuss a particular topic.

Majordomo Software that automates the management of electronic mailing lists.

MAN Metropolitan area network. A physical communications network that operates across a metropolitan area.

Match A string that fits a specified pattern.

Metacharacters Characters that have a special meaning and so may need to be escaped to turn off that meaning.

metric The associated cost or number of hops required to reach a remote network.

MIB Management Information Base. A database made up of a set of objects that represent various types of information about devices. It is used by SNMP to manage devices.

MIME Multipurpose Internet Mail Extension. A protocol that describes the format of Internet messages. Also, an extension to Internet mail that supports the inclusion of nontextual data such as video and audio in email.

modem An electronic device that allows digital computer data to be transmitted via analog phone lines.

moderator A person who examines all submissions to a newsgroup or mailing list and allows only those that meet certain criteria to be posted. Usually, the moderator makes sure that the topic is pertinent to the group and that the submissions aren't flames.

Mosaic A graphical interface for the World Wide Web that employs hypertext, images, video clips, and sound.

motd Message of the day. A message posted on some computer systems to let people know about problems or new developments.

MSS Maximum Segment Size. The largest amount of data that can be transmitted at one time; negotiated by sender and receiver.

MTU Maximum Transmission Unit. The largest datagram that can be sent across a given physical network.

Multihomed host A TCP/IP host that is attached to two or more networks, requiring multiple IP addresses.

N

Name resolution The process of mapping a computer name to an IP address. DNS and DHCP are two ways of resolving names.

NetBIOS The Microsoft computer name convention. Names are 15 characters long with a 16th in hexadecimal representing the service associated with the name.

Netiquette Network etiquette conventions used in written communications; usually referring to Usenet newsgroup postings but also applicable to email.

Netnews A collective way of referring to the Usenet newsgroups.

Netscape A popular commercial World Wide Web browser.

Network A number of computers physically connected to enable communication with one another.

Network ID The portion of an IP address that identifies the network. It is used with host IDs to form a complete address.

Newsgroups The electronic discussion groups of Usenet.

Newsreaders Applications that let you read (and usually post) articles in Usenet newsgroups.

NFS Network File System. A file system developed by Sun Microsystems that is now widely used on many different networks.

NIC Network Interface Card. An add-on card to allow a machine to access a LAN (most commonly an Ethernet card).

NIS Network Information Service. A naming service from SunSoft that provides a directory service for network information.

NNTP Network News Transport Protocol. The communications protocol that is used to send Usenet news on the Internet.

Nodes Individual computers connected to a network.

NSFNET Network funded by the National Science Foundation, now the backbone of the Internet.

NSLOOKUP A utility used to access DNS tables.

Null character A character with the value 0.

Null list An empty list represented as empty parentheses.

O

Objects Hardware and software components monitored with Performance Monitor.

Octet A set of eight bits.

OSF Open Software Foundation. A nonprofit organization formed by hardware manufacturers who attempt to reduce standard technologies for open systems.

OSI Open Systems Interconnection. A set of ISO standards that define the framework for implementing protocols in seven layers.

OSPF Open shortest path first protocol. A protocol that defines how routers share routing information. Unlike other routing protocols, OSPF is designed to transmit only routing information that has changed since the previous transfer, thus conserving bandwidth.

P–Q

Packet The unit of data transmission on the Internet. A packet consists of the data being transferred with additional overhead information, such as the transmitting and receiving addresses.

Packet switching The communications technology that the Internet is based on, in which data being sent between computers is transmitted in packets.

Parallel The means of communication in which digital data is sent multiple bits at a time, with each simultaneous bit being sent over a separate line.

Parameter An argument; a value that is passed to a routine.

Pattern An expression defining a set of strings that match the pattern and a set that do not.

Peer-to-peer Internet services that can be offered and accessed by anyone, without requiring a special server.

Perl Practical Extraction and Report Language. A language well suited to text-file processing as well as other tasks.

PGP Pretty Good Privacy. An application that allows you to send and receive encrypted email.

PID Process identifier. A number indicating the number assigned by the operating system to that process.

PING A utility that sends out a packet to an Internet host and waits for a response (used to check whether a host is up).

Pipe The concept in an operating system in which the output of one program is fed into the input of another.

Pipeline A complete Internet service package.

Plain text Unencrypted text, subject to interception by third parties.

POP Point of presence. Indicates availability of a local access number to a public data network.

Port (hardware) A physical channel on a computer that allows you to communicate with other devices (printers, modems, disk drives, and so on).

Port (network) An address to which incoming data packets are sent. Special ports can be assigned to send the data directly to a server (FTP, Gopher, WWW, Telnet, or email) or to another specific program.

Port ID The method used by TCP and UDP to specify which application is sending or receiving data.

Post To send a message to a Usenet newsgroup.

Postmaster An address to which you can send questions about a site (asking whether a user has an account there or whether it sells a particular product, for example).

PPP Point-to-Point Protocol. A driver that enables you to use a network communications protocol over a phone line; used with TCP/IP to enable you to have a dial-in Internet host.

PPTP Point-to-Point Tunneling Protocol. A secure extension of PPP.

Precedence The order in which operators are evaluated is based on their precedence.

Process In multitasking operating systems such as UNIX, many programs may be run at once, and each one as it is running is called a process.

Protocol The standard that defines how computers on a network communicate with one another.

Proxy A connection through a modem and telephone line to the Internet that enables you to use full-screen programs, such as Mosaic and Netscape, to browse the Internet.

Public domain software Software that is made available by the author to anyone who wants it. (In this case, the author gives up all rights to the software.)

Pull partner Receives entries from another WINS server.

Push partner Sends its entries to another WINS server.

R

RARP Reverse Address Resolution Protocol. A protocol that enables a computer to find its IP address by broadcasting a request. It is usually used by diskless workstations upon startup to find their logical IP address.

RAS Remote Access Service. The ability to access your network from a remote location.

Recursion Occurs when a subroutine makes a call to itself.

Regular expressions A way of specifying a pattern so that some strings match the pattern and some strings do not. Parts of the matching pattern can be marked for use in operations such as substitution.

Relay agent Performs the task of forwarding broadcasts to a DCHP server.

Relevance feedback In WAIS, a score between 0 and 1,000 that represents how closely a document satisfies search criteria.

Remote Pertaining to a host on the network other than the computer you are now using.

Remote execution The ability provided by a utility to run a process on another host over the network.

Remote host A host on the network other than the computer you currently are using.

Renewal Interval The interval given to a WINS client after it successfully registers its name.

Repeater Device that allows you to extend the length of your network by amplifying and repeating the information it receives.

Reservation A reserved IP address excluded from the scope.

Resolver Client software that enables access to the DNS database.

RFC Request for Comments. A document submitted to the Internet governing board to propose Internet standards or to document information about the Internet.

RIP Routing Information Protocol. A router-to-router protocol used to exchange information between routers. RIP supports *dynamic routing*.

rlogin A UNIX command that allows you to log on to a remote computer.

RMON Remote Network Monitor. A device that collects information about network communications.

Route The path that network traffic takes between its source and its destination.

route table A listing that describes the possible ways to reach a destination network.

Router Equipment that receives an Internet packet and sends it to the next machine in the destination path. Relays traffic based on layer 3 addressing (IP address, IPX address, and so on).

RPC Remote Procedure Call. An interface that allows an application to call a routine that executes on another machine in a remote location.

S

Scope A range of available addresses on a DHCP server.

Scope option Used to set configuration items only for a given scope on a DHCP server.

Script An interpreted set of instructions in a text file.

Segment A protocol data unit consisting of part of a stream of bytes being sent between two machines. It also includes information about the current position in the stream and a checksum value.

Serial Means of communication in which digital data is sent one bit at a time over a single physical line.

Server A provider of a service; a computer that runs services. It also often refers to a piece of hardware or software that provides access to information requested from it.

Service An application that processes requests by client applications, for example, storing data or executing an algorithm.

SGML Standard Generalized Markup Language. A language that describes the structure of a document.

Shareware Software that is made available by the author to anyone who wants it, with a request to send the author a nominal fee if the software is used on a regular basis.

Signal A means of passing information between the operating system and a running process; the process can trap the signal and respond accordingly.

Signature A personal sign-off used in email and newsgroup posts, often contained in a file and automatically appended to the mail or post. Often contains organization affiliation and pertinent personal information.

Site A group of computers under a single administrative control.

SLIP Serial Line Internet Protocol. A way of running TCP/IP via the phone lines to enable you to have a dial-up Internet host.

SmartList Software that automates the management of electronic mailing lists.

Smiley face An ASCII drawing such as :-) (look at it sideways) used to indicate an emotion in a message. Also called *emoticon.*

SMTP Simple Mail Transport Protocol. The accepted communications protocol standard for exchange of email between Internet hosts.

SNA System Network Architecture. A protocol suite developed and used by IBM.

SNMP Simple Network Management Protocol. A communications protocol used to control and monitor devices on a network.

Socket A means of network communications via special entities.

Source In WAIS, describes a database and how to reach it.

Source route A route identifying the path that a datagram must follow; determined by the source device.

Static entries Entries that require manual input into the WINS database. After these entries are added, they are permanent until removed.

Static routers Routers unable to discover networks other than those to which they have a physical interface.

String A sequence of characters.

Subnet Any lower network that is part of the logical network; identified by the network ID.

Subnet mask A 32-bit value that distinguishes the network ID from the host ID in an IP address.

Subscribe To become a member of a mailing list or newsgroup; also refers to obtaining Internet provider services.

Super Netting In a class C network, borrowing bits from the HOST id to expand the size of a network to be greater than 254 nodes. The product is applied as a subnet mask.

Supernet A compilation of different networks into one.

Surfing Jumping from host to host on the Internet to get an idea of what can be found. Also refers to briefly examining a number of different Usenet newsgroups.

Syntax A statement that contains programming code.

T

T1 A dedicated telephone line connection that transfers data at the rate of 1.544MB/sec.

T3 A dedicated telephone line that transfers data at the rate of 45MB/sec.

Tag A slang reference for annotations used by HTML, such as <H2>, </H2>.

TCP Transmission Control Protocol. The network protocol used by hosts on the Internet.

TCP/IP Transmission Control Protocol/Internet Protocol. A communications protocol that allows computers of any make to communicate when running TCP/IP software.

Telephony Telephone services used through a computer.

Telnet A program that allows remote logon to another computer.

Terminal emulation Running an application that enables you to use your computer to interface with a command-line account on a remote computer as if you were connected to the computer with a terminal.

TFTP Trivial File Transfer Protocol. A basic, standard protocol used to upload or download files with minimal overhead. TFTP depends on UDP and is often used to initialize diskless workstations, as it has no directory and password capabilities.

Thread All messages in a newsgroup or mailing list pertaining to a particular topic.

tiff Tag Image File Format. A graphics format.

TLI Transport Layer Interface. An AT&T-developed interface that enables applications to interface to both TCP/IP and OSI protocols.

Token ring A network protocol for LAN.

Traceroute A utility that enables you to find out how many routers exist between your host and another Internet host.

Traffic The information flowing through a network.

Transceiver A device that connects a host interface to a network. It is used to apply signals to the cable and sense collisions.

Trap A block of data that indicates that some request failed to authenticate. An SNMP service sends a trap when it receives a request for information with an incorrect community name.

TTL Time to Live. A measurement of time, usually defined by a number of hops, that a datagram can exist on a network before it is discarded. It prevents endlessly looping packets.

U–V

UDP User Datagram Protocol. A simple protocol that enables an application program on one machine to send a datagram to an application program on another machine. Delivery is not guaranteed, nor is it guaranteed the datagrams will be delivered in proper order.

Universal time An international time standard reference, also known as Greenwich mean time.

Upload To move a file from your local computer to a remote computer.

URL Universal Resource Locator. A means of specifying the location of information on the Internet for WWW clients.

Usenet An online news and bulletin board system accommodating more than 7,000 interest groups.

Username The ID used to log on to a computer.

UUDecode A program that lets you construct binary data that was UUEncoded.

UUEncode A program that enables you to send binary data through email.

Verify Interval The interval at which the WINS server verifies the validity of names in its database that came from other servers.

Veronica A tool that helps you find files on Gopher servers.

Viewer applications Software that gives you access to the images, video, and sounds stored on Internet servers.

Viewers Applications that are used to display non-text files, such as graphics, sound, and animation.

virus A computer program that covertly enters a system by means of a legitimate program, usually doing damage to the system; compare to *worm*.

VMS Virtual Memory System. An operating system used on hosts made by Digital Equipment Corporation (DEC).

VRML Virtual Reality Modeling Language. An experimental language that lets you display 3D objects in Web documents.

W

WAIS Wide area information server. A tool that helps you search for documents by using keywords or selections of text as search criteria.

WAIS client An application that formats user-defined search criteria to be used by waisserver; the goal is to find matches between search criteria and data files (of all types).

WAIS sources Databases created by waisindex that include, for example, a table of all unique words contained in a document.

waisindex A mechanism that extracts data from raw data files (of most types) to put into databases, called WAIS sources, which allow waisserver to match search criteria to data files quickly.

waisserver A mechanism that compares search criteria, supplied by a WAIS client, to WAIS sources.

WAN Wide area network. A network of computers that are geographically dispersed.

Web See *World Wide Web.*

Web chat An application that allows you to carry on live conversations over the World Wide Web.

Web Crawler A Web search tool.

WHOIS A service that enables you to look up information about Internet hosts and users.

WINS Windows Internet Name Service. A dynamic, distributed database system that resolves NetBIOS names to IP addresses on a Microsoft-based network.

WINS Manager A tool used to manage the local WINS server and remote WINS servers.

WINS replication The process used to copy one WINS server's database to another WINS server.

World Wide Web WWW or Web. A hypertext-based system that allows browsing of available Internet resources.

worm A computer program that invades other computers over a network, usually nondestructively; compare to *virus.*

X–Z

X.25 A CCITT standard for connecting computers to a network that provides a reliable stream transmission service, which can support remote logons.

X.400 A CCITT standard for message transfer and interpersonal messaging, such as electronic mail.

xbm X bitmapped. A graphics format.

XDR External Data Representation. A data format standard developed by Sun Microsystems that defines datatypes used as parameters and encodes these parameters for transmission.

Xmodem A communication protocol that lets you transfer files over a serial line. It works by sending blocks of data along with a checksum and waiting for an acknowledgment of the receipt. Xmodem is useful, however, only at speeds of less than 4800 bps. See also *Y-modem* and *Z-modem.*

Ymodem An enhanced version of Xmodem that increases the transfer block size and allows batch transfer of files. See also *X-modem* and *Z-modem.*

Zmodem Another enhanced version of Xmodem, Zmodem allows faster transfer rates, better error detection, and the ability to resume an aborted data transfer. See also *X-modem* and *Y-modem.*

APPENDIX C

Fast Facts

Last-Minute Studying for the TCP/IP Exam

Now that you have read through this book, worked through the exercises, and acquired as much hands-on experience by using TCP/IP on Windows NT Server as you could, you're ready for the exam. This last chapter is designed as a "final cram in the parking lot" before you walk into the exam. You can't reread the whole book in an hour, but you will be able to read this chapter in that time.

This chapter is organized by objective category, giving you not just a summary, but a review of the most important points from each chapter. Remember that this is meant to be a review of concepts and a trigger for you to remember those tidbits of information you'll need when taking the exam. If you know what is in here and the concepts that stand behind it, chances are the exam will be a snap.

Planning

Planning is limited to a single, general objective.

Objective: Given a scenario, identify valid network configurations.

- If two physical segments are separated by a router, each segment must have a unique subnet ID.
- If two physical segments are separated by a bridge or repeater, both segments must have the same subnet ID.

Installation and Configuration

The following 10 objectives reflect installation and configuration issues.

Objective: Given a scenario, select the appropriate services to install when using Microsoft TCP/IP on a Microsoft Windows NT Server computer.

- Microsoft Windows NT 4.0 includes the following TCP/IP services:

  Microsoft DNS Server—Provides domain name resolution services.

  Simple TCP/IP Services—Adds client programs such as DayTime and Echo.

  SNMP Service—Allows for monitoring and troubleshooting hosts.

  DHCP Relay Agent—Relays DHCP broadcast messages.

  Microsoft DHCP Server—Enables automatic TCP/IP configuration.

  Microsoft TCP/IP Printing—Adds the LPR and LPD services for integrating printing with UNIX and network hosts.

Windows Internet Name Service—Provides NetBIOS name resolution services.

RIP for Internet Protocol—Provides dynamic routing services.

- NetBT (NetBIOS over TCP/IP) allows NetBIOS data to be transferred over the TCP/IP protocol.
- Only two parameters are required to configure TCP/IP: the IP address and subnet mask.
- The default gateway parameter is required only for remote communication.
- ARP (Address Resolution Protocol) resolves the destination IP address to the destination MAC addresses for *local* hosts by using a local hardware broadcast.
- ARP (Address Resolution Protocol) resolves the next router's IP address to that router's MAC addresses for *remote* hosts by using a local hardware broadcast.
- ARP cache entries live for ten minutes if reused, two minutes if not.

Objective: On a Windows NT Server computer, configure Microsoft TCP/IP to support multiple network adapters.

- Your network cannot be assigned a network ID of 0, 127, or a number greater than 223 in the first octet.
- A network ID must be assigned to each subnet in an environment and each router interface.
- A host ID cannot be all 1s or all 0s.

Objective: Configure subnet masks.

- Subnet masks distinguish the network ID from the host ID by ANDing the IP address and subnet mask.
- Subnet masks are used to determine whether a destination host is on a local or remote network.
- The default subnet mask for a class A network is 255.0.0.0. The default subnet mask for a class B network is 255.255.0.0. The default subnet mask for a class C network is 255.255.255.0.
- Subnetting is the process of borrowing bits from the host ID and using them to identify a subnet ID.
- The more subnets you create, the fewer hosts per subnet that are available, and vice versa.
- To determine the number of subnets, use the calculator to figure 2^x (where x is the number of bits used in the subnet ID), and then subtract 2.
- To determine the number of valid hosts per subnet, use the calculator to figure 2^x (where x is the number of bits used in the host ID), and then subtract 2.

SUMMARY TABLE FOR CALCULATING SUBNET MASK, SUBNET IDS, AND NUMBER OF SUBNETS

PositionValue	64	32	16	8	4	2	1
Subnet bits	2	3	4	5	6	7	8
SubnetsAvailable	2^2-2 2	2^3-2 6	2^4-2 14	2^5-2 30	2^6-2 62	2^7-2 126	2^8-2 254
Subnet Mask	128+64=192	192+32=224	224+16=240	240+8=248	248+4=252	252+2=254	254+1=255
Host bits	6	5	4	3	2	1	0

Objective: Configure scopes by using DHCP Manager.

- DHCP automatically assigns to clients an IP address, subnet mask, and other optional parameters.
- In order to forward DHCP packets, a BOOTP Relay Agent (RFC 1542) must exist on every subnet that has DHCP clients. Otherwise, you will need a DHCP server on every subnet. A BOOTP relay agent can be implemented on a router, or on a Windows NT Server by adding the DHCP Relay Agent service.
- Only one scope can be created for each subnet on a single DHCP server.
- When implementing multiple DHCP servers, Microsoft recommends that you assign 75 percent of a subnet's available addresses to the closest server and 25 percent to the next closest for redundancy and fault tolerance.
- DHCP servers cannot communicate with one another.
- If creating scopes on different DHCP servers for the same subnet, only one server can include a given address.
- The DHCP server cannot be a DHCP client, and vice versa.
- Scopes must be activated before they distribute IP addresses.
- DHCP can also assign a router, DNS server, domain name, NetBIOS node type, WINS server, and NetBIOS scope ID to Microsoft clients.
- A WINS Server option requires a NetBIOS Scope ID option.
- User options override scope options, which override global options. All options are overridden by information manually configured on the client.
- Use Client Reservations to preassign an IP address to a client. The unique identifier in this configuration is the MAC address of the client.
- To create scopes on different DHCP servers for the same subnet, a client reservation must be duplicated to each DHCP server.
- IPCONFIG can be used to release and renew DHCP addresses.

Objective: Install and configure a WINS server.

- To enable a WINS client, simply configure a WINS server address in the TCP/IP properties either manually or by using a DHCP option.
- Only one WINS server is required in a TCP/IP environment.
- Microsoft recommends one primary WINS server and one secondary WINS server for every 10,000 clients. Two WINS servers provide fault tolerance.
- Install a WINS server by adding the Windows Internet Name Service in Network Properties.
- A WINS proxy agent allows non-WINS clients to retrieve information from the WINS database. A WINS proxy agent must exist on each subnet with non-WINS clients.
- A WINS proxy agent must be a WINS client and cannot be a WINS server.

Subobjective: Import LMHOSTS files to WINS.

- To import entries from an existing LMHOSTS file into the WINS database, click the Import Mappings button in the Static Mappings dialog box and specify the location of the LMHOSTS file.

Subobjective: Run WINS on a multihomed computer.

- Microsoft does not recommend running WINS on a multihomed computer in an environment with DOS clients.

Subobjective: Configure WINS replication.

- Configure replication between WINS server partners so that they can exchange database information.
- A WINS server notifies its *push partners* of changes to the database when a threshold is reached.
- A WINS server pulls information from its *pull partners* at a scheduled time.
- The Replicate Now button in the Replication Partners dialog box will replicate immediately with the partner highlighted, or with all partners if the local host is highlighted.

Subobjective: Configure static mappings in the WINS database.

- Static mappings allow WINS clients to locate non-WINS clients by using the WINS database.
- To configure static mappings, add the name and IP address mapping to the WINS database by using the Add Static Mapping dialog box in WINS Manager.
- Static mapping can be Unique (for a one-to-one mapping), Group (for broadcasting to the local subnet), Domain Name (for domain logon validation), Internet Group (for resources such as printers), and Multihomed (for computers with multiple IP addresses).

Objective: Configure a Windows NT Server computer to function as an IP router.

- IP is a connectionless protocol, and its packets are called *datagrams.*
- IP compares the source subnet ID with the destination subnet ID to determine whether the destination host is on the same subnet as the source host (local) or on a different subnet than the source host (remote). If the destination host is remote, IP begins the routing process.
- IP on routers decrements the TTL by at least one metric, fragments packets, and is responsible for all addressing. IP routing is used only if the destination host is remote.
- Windows NT checks the routing table for a known route before sending a packet to the default gateway (router).
- The IP address of the default gateway must be the router interface that is on the same subnet as the host.
- *Static routing* is a function of IP. Check the Enable IP Forwarding checkbox to implement it.
- *Dynamic routing* is a function of a routing protocol, such as RIP and OSPF, that exchanges routing tables with other routers. Install the RIP for Internet Protocol service to implement it.

- When integrating both dynamic and static routing in an environment, static routes must be configured on both the static and dynamic routers.
- The following command displays the routing table: ROUTE PRINT.
- The following command adds a static route: ADD *destination* MASK *netmask gateway.*
- The following command deletes a route: ROUTE DELETE *destination.*
- Use the –p switch with the ROUTE command to add a permanent route.
- ICMP Source Quench messages from a router tell a sending host to reduce both the frequency and amount of data it is generating. Microsoft NT can react to these messages, but it does not initiate them.
- *Dead gateway detection* can access an alternative default gateway when the primary is unresponsive (and if a second default gateway is configured).

Subobjective: Install and configure the DHCP Relay Agent.

- To install the DHCP Relay Agent, first add the service, and then configure it from the TCP/IP Properties sheet.
- Add the DHCP Relay Agent service to allow a Windows NT computer to forward DHCP packets to other subnets.
- The DHCP Relay Agent service must be configured with the IP address on a DHCP server to which it will relay messages.

Objective: Install and configure the Microsoft DNS Server service on a Windows NT Server computer.

- A *zone* file is the local database file. If a name server has the local database file (master copy) for a zone, the server is said to be *authoritative* for that zone.
- *Recursive* queries require the queried name server to respond with a resolution or an error. *Resolvers,* or clients, initiate recursive queries.
- *Iterative* queries allow name servers to give a best answer, often referring the querying host to another name server. Servers send iterative queries to each other.
- Microsoft stores all service information, including the boot configuration, in the registry.
- DNS files include the database, or zone, file; a reverse lookup file; the cache file; and, optionally, a boot file.
- Zone files are used to resolve Fully Qualified Domain Names (FQDNs) to IP addresses. Every zone file includes an SOA (Start of Authority) record, at least one NS (Name Server) record, multiple A records, or resource records. Zone files optionally include MX (Mail Exchange) and CNAME (Canonical Name) records. An example zone filename in Windows NT is microsoft.com.dns.
- A sample zone file called mcp.com.dns looks like the following:

```
@                  IN SOA
server1.mcp.com.admin.mcp.com.    (
                   2                ; serial
➥number
                   3600             ; refresh
```

```
                  600              ; retry
                  86400            ; expire
                  3600             ) ;
➥minimum TTL
@                 IN NS      server1
server1           IN A       10.10.10.50
mailsrv              IN      A
➥10.10.10.150
www               IN CNAME   server1
@                 IN MX      15
mailsrv.mcp.com.
```

- A reverse lookup file is used to find an FQDN for an IP address. An example reverse lookup filename in Windows NT is 10.168.192.in-addr.arpa.
- All DNS servers have a cache file that contains resource records for the DNS root servers.
- The boot file is primarily used for migrations from BIND implementations of DNS. This file contains boot information for the DNS server. Microsoft DNS server stores in the registry by default, but it can be configured to use the boot file.
- Multiple zone files can be created on a single name server. Configuring a zone under an existing zone in DNS Manager creates a subdomain.

Subobjective: Integrate DNS with other name servers.

- Because Microsoft DNS server is RFC-compliant, it can be integrated with any UNIX implementation of DNS.
- Microsoft DNS can be integrated with WINS servers to create "dynamic DNS" by using a WINS record in the zone file. The DNS server will then query the WINS server if it cannot resolve a query in a zone for which it is authoritative.
- Integrating a DNS server with a WINS server reduces the number of static resource records in the DNS zone file.

Subobjective: Connect a DNS server to a DNS root server.

- Each DNS server must be registered with a name server higher in the hierarchy. For example, both the primary and secondary name servers for mcp.com must register with the .com name server.

Subobjective: Configure DNS server roles.

- Each domain should have a *primary name server* that maintains the master zone files and at least one *secondary name server* that maintains a read-only copy of the zone file.
- When a *master name server* sends a copy of the zone file to another name server, it is called a *zone transfer*. A master name server can be either a primary or secondary name server.
- *Caching-only servers* do not maintain zone files. They can be used to reduce network traffic across WAN links because they do not participate in zone transfers but do maintain resolution information.

Objective: Configure HOSTS and LMHOSTS files.

- NetBIOS name resolution resolves a NetBIOS name, such as a computer name, to an IP address.
- Host name resolution resolves a host name, or alias, to an IP address.
- The four node types are b-node (broadcast), p-node (peer node, or WINS servers), m-node (mixed; or broadcast, then WINS server), and h-node (hybrid; or WINS server, then broadcast).

- The default node type is enhanced b-node (broadcast, then LMHOSTS file). If a WINS server is configured, the default node type is h-node.
- If all options are configured for NetBIOS name resolution, Windows NT will check the NetBIOS name cache, contact the WINS server, send a local broadcast, check the LMHOSTS file, check the HOSTS file, and then contact the DNS server.
- If all options are configured for host name resolution, Windows NT will check the local host name, check the HOSTS file, contact the DNS server, contact the WINS server, send a local broadcast, and then check the LMHOSTS file.
- The LMHOSTS file is a text file with no extension. The most common keywords are #PRE for preloading the cache and #DOM for specifying a domain name.
- A line in the LMHOSTS files looks like this:

```
131.107.2.200    Instructor    #PRE
➥#DOM:Classroom
```

- If multiple entries exist for one name in the LMHOSTS file, only the first one will be read.
- A HOST file is a text file with no extension. One must reside on each computer.
- A line from a HOSTS file looks like this:

```
131.107.2.200   instructor
➥instructor.mcp.com
```

- Both the LMHOSTS file and HOSTS file are stored in the *winntroot*/system32/drivers/etc directory.
- Comments in both the LMHOSTS and HOSTS file are indicated by a semicolon (;) and are ignored by Windows NT.

Objective: Configure a Windows NT Server computer to support TCP/IP printing.

- LPD (Line Printer Daemon) is a printing service that enables any client running TCP/IP and LPR (Line Printer Remote) to send print jobs to it.
- LPQ (Line Printer Query) allows you to view the files in the LPD print queue, as well as its status.
- A UNIX client can print to Windows NT server running LPD.
- Windows NT can print to a UNIX print server if Windows NT has LPR.
- A UNIX server can print to a Windows NT printer if Windows NT has an LPD printer configured.
- LPD, LPR, and LPQ are installed with the Microsoft TCP/IP Printing service.
- To print to a UNIX printer, you must add an LPR Port in Print Manager that indicates the IP address of the server running LPD and the name of the print queue; or use the command-line utility LPR.

Objective: Configure SNMP.

- Simple Network Management Protocol (SNMP) is used to monitor and communicate status information between SNMP managers and SNMP agents.
- The Microsoft SNMP server includes four commands: get, get-next, set, and trap.

- Get and get-next retrieve status information from an *SNMP agent*, or client.
- Set allows an *SNMP manager* to configure information on an SNMP agent, but it is rarely used.
- The SNMP Service included with Windows NT only creates an SNMP agent. SNMP manager software must be obtained from a third party.
- The only command an SNMP agent can initiate is a trap, which notifies an SNMP manager of a significant event, such as an "out of disk space" error or a potential security breach.
- Information that an SNMP agent tracks is stored as a manageable object in a MIB (Management Information Base).
- Windows NT Server includes four MIBs: Internet MIB II for general TCP/IP information, LAN Manager MIB II for Microsoft–specific information, DHCP MIB for DHCP Server activity, and WINS MIB for WINS Server activity.
- *SNMP communities* provide primitive security for the SNMP service. Agents and managers will communicate only with other hosts within their designated communities. Both agents and managers can belong to multiple communities. The default community name is Public.
- The SNMP agent service can be configured to send traps to a community or specific manager.
- A trap is configured with both the community name and IP address of the SNMP management station to which it sends the messages.
- The SNMP agent service can be configured as having one or more of the following services: Physical, if the computer manages a physical device; Datalink/Subnetwork, if the computer manages a bridge; Internet, if the computer is a router; End-to-End, if the computer acts as an IP host; and Applications, if the computer runs an TCP/IP application. End-to-End and Applications should always be selected.

Connectivity

Connectivity is addressed by three objectives.

Objective: Given a scenario, identify which utility to use to connect to a TCP/IP-based UNIX host.

- Windows NT server can connect to a non-Microsoft server with NetBIOS commands if both servers use the same transport protocol and the non-Microsoft server provides Server Message Block (SMB) connectivity.
- REXEC (Remote Execute), RSH (Remote Shell), and TELNET (Telecommunications Network) allow a Windows NT computer to run applications and commands on a non-Microsoft host that does not provide SMB connectivity.
- RCOPY (Remote Copy), FTP (File Transfer Protocol), TFTP (Trivial File Transfer Protocol), and Web browsers allow a Windows NT computer to copy files to and from a non-Microsoft host that does not provide SMB connectivity.

Objective: Configure a RAS server and dial-up networking for use on a TCP/IP network.

- To configure the RAS service, you must first install and configure a modem on the Windows NT Server, and then install and configure the Remote Access Service.
- For outbound communications, you need to configure Dialing Properties in Dial-Up Networking.
- From the Remote Access Service in Network Properties, select TCP/IP as the network protocol for the Server Settings in the Network Configuration dialog box.
- Select either the Use DHCP to Assign Remote TCP/IP Client Address or the Use Static Address Pool radio button in the RAS Server TCP/IP Configuration dialog box.
- Although it is not recommended, you may also select the Allow Remote Clients to Request a Predetermined IP Address in the RAS Server TCP/IP Configuration dialog box.

Objective: Configure and support browsing in a multiple-domain routed network.

- *Master browsers* maintain the master copy of the browse list. *Backup browsers* retrieve the read-only copy of the browse list and distribute it to clients that request it.
- A browse list is specific to a domain or workgroup.
- Browse lists (and, thus, browsing) is restricted to a single subnet unless WINS or LMHOSTS files are configured.
- To implement an LMHOSTS file solution for domain browsing, each master browser must have an LMHOSTS entry for the domain master browser with a #DOM tag, and vice versa.
- *Domain master browsers* consolidate subnet browse lists into a domainwide browse list and offer it to other domain master browsers. Domain master browsers are always the primary domain controller (PDC) of that domain.
- Logon issues in a domain apply to browsing in a domain; implement either WINS servers or LMHOSTS files.
- To allow domain logon across subnets by using LMHOSTS files, each client requires a line in the LMHOSTS file for each backup domain controller (BDC), including the #PRE and #DOM keywords.
- To allow account information to be updated between domain controllers by using LMHOSTS files, each domain controller requires a line in the LMHOSTS file for each other domain controller, including the #PRE and #DOM keywords.

Monitoring and Optimization

There is a single objective concerning monitoring and optimization.

Objective: Given a scenario, identify which tool to use to monitor TCP/IP traffic.

- Performance Monitor provides charting, alerting, and reporting capabilities that reflect both current activity and ongoing logging.
- Performance Monitor counters are enabled when the SNMP Service is installed on Windows NT Server.

- Network Monitor allows you to monitor, capture, and analyze network traffic, including individual packets. Capture filters can also be applied to locate specific types of packets.
- The SNMP Service allows a Windows NT computer to report its status to an SNMP manager.
- The NETSTAT command displays current protocol statistics and current TCP/IP connections.
- The NET command with the STATISTICS switch displays network statistics since the computer was last started.
- The NBTSTAT command displays current protocol statistics and current TCP/IP connections by using NetBIOS over TCP/IP (NetBT).
- The NET command displays information since the computer was last started; both NETSTAT and NBTSTAT display current statistics, or a snapshot.
- The registry setting TCPWindowSize can be used to improve TCP connections.

TROUBLESHOOTING

There are three troubleshooting objectives.

Objective: Diagnose and resolve IP addressing problems.

- All hosts on the same physical segment must be configured with the same subnet ID based on its subnet mask.

Objective: Use Microsoft TCP/IP utilities to diagnose IP configuration problems.

- IPCONFIG is the best utility to verify IP configuration.
- PING is the best utility to verify the availability of a host and to test network connectivity.

Subobjective: Identify which Microsoft TCP/IP utility to use to diagnose IP configuration problems.

- TRACERT is the best utility to verify the path to a remote host, and to troubleshoot WAN connections.
- Use the ROUTE PRINT command to add a view the local routing table.
- NSLOOKUP is used to query and troubleshoot a DNS server.
- Use Event Viewer to find and troubleshoot SNMP Service errors.
- The SNMPUTIL utility is included with the Windows NT Resource Kit and can be used to test the SNMP Service.

Objective: Diagnose and resolve name resolution problems.

- Use NBTSTAT to view the NetBIOS name cache.
- Use IPCONFIG to view the DNS servers, WINS servers, and node type of a TCP/IP client.
- The NSLOOKUP command is used to query DNS servers.

Good luck on the exam!

Index

SYMBOLS

A

B

C

E

F

G

H

J-L

M

N

O

P-Q

R

S

T

U

V-W

X-Z

TRAINING GUIDES

Complete, Innovative, Accurate, Thorough

Our next generation *Training Guides* have been developed to help you study and retain the essential knowledge that you need to pass the MCSE exams. We know your study time is valuable, and we have made every effort to make the most of it by presenting clear, accurate, and thorough information.

In creating this series, our goal was to raise the bar on how MCSE content is written, developed, and presented. From the two-color design that gives you easy access to content, to the new software simulator that allows you to perform tasks in a simulated operating system environment, we are confident that you will be well-prepared for exam success.

Our New Riders Top Score Software Suite is a custom-developed set of full-functioning software applications that work in conjunction with the Training Guide by providing you with the following:

Exam Simulator tests your hands-on knowledge with over 150 fact-based and situational-based questions.
Electronic Study Cards really test your knowledge with explanations that are linked to an electronic version of the Training Guide.
Electronic Flash Cards help you retain the facts in a time-tested method.
An Electronic Version of the Book provides quick searches and compact, mobile study.
Customizable Software adapts to the way you want to learn.

MCSE Training Guide: Networking Essentials, Second Edition

1-56205-919-X, $49.99, 9/98

MCSE Training Guide: TCP/IP, Second Edition

1-56205-920-3, $49.99, 11/98

MCSE Training Guide: Windows NT Server 4, Second Edition

1-56205-916-5, $49.99, 9/98

MCSE Training Guide: SQL Server 7 Administration

0-7357-0003-6, $49.99, Q2/99

MCSE Training Guide: Windows NT Server 4 Enterprise, Second Edition

1-56205-917-3, $49.99, 9/98

MCSE Training Guide: SQL Server 7 Design and Implementation

0-7357-0004-4, $49.99, Q2/99

MCSE Training Guide: Windows NT Workstation 4, Second Edition

1-56205-918-1, $49.99, 9/98

MCSD Training Guide: Solution Architectures

0-7357-0026-5, $49.99, Q2/99

MCSE Training Guide: Windows 98

1-56205-890-8, $49.99, 1/99

MCSD Training Guide: Visual Basic 6

0-7357-0002-8, $49.99, Q1/99

TRAINING GUIDES

FIRST EDITIONS

Your Quality Elective Solution

MCSE Training Guide: Systems Management Server 1.2, 1-56205-748-0

MCSE Training Guide: SQL Server 6.5 Administration, 1-56205-726-X

MCSE Training Guide: SQL Server 6.5 Design and Implementation, 1-56205-830-4

MCSE Training Guide: Windows 95, 70-064 Exam, 1-56205-880 0

MCSE Training Guide: Exchange Server 5, 1-56205-824-X

MCSE Training Guide: Internet Explorer 4, 1-56205-889-4

MCSE Training Guide: Microsoft Exchange Server 5.5, 1-56205-899-1

MCSE Training Guide: IIS 4, 1-56205-823-1

MCSD Training Guide: Visual Basic 5, 1-56205-850-9

MCSD Training Guide: Microsoft Access, 1-56205-771-5

TESTPREPS

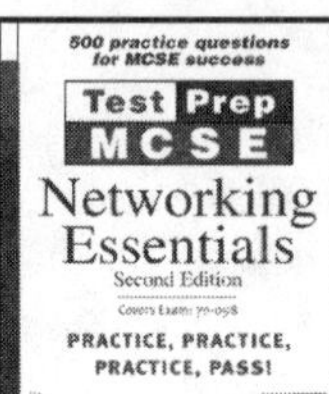

MCSE TestPrep: Networking Essentials, Second Edition

0-7357-0010-9, $19.99, 12/98

MCSE TestPrep: TCP/IP, Second Edition

0-7357-0025-7, $19.99, 12/98

MCSE TestPrep: Windows 95, Second Edition

0-7357-0011-7, $19.99, 12/98

MCSE TestPrep: Windows 98

1-56205-922-X, $19.99, 11/98

MCSE TestPrep: Windows NT Server 4, Second Edition

0-7357-0012-5, $19.99, 12/98

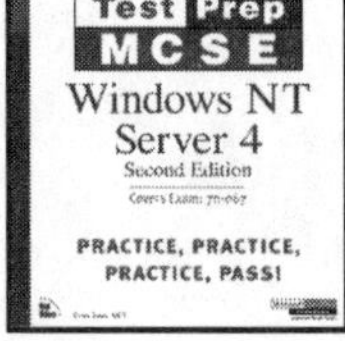

MCSE TestPrep: Windows NT Server 4 Enterprise, Second Edition

0-7357-0009-5, $19.99, 11/98

MCSE TestPrep: Windows NT Workstation 4, Second Edition

0-7357-0008-7, $19.99, 12/98

TESTPREPS

FIRST EDITIONS

Your Quality Elective Solution

MCSE TestPrep: SQL Server 6.5 Administration, 0-7897-1597-X

MCSE TestPrep: SQL Server 6.5 Design and Implementation, 1-56205-915-7

MCSE TestPrep: Windows 95 70-64 Exam, 0-7897-1609-7

MCSE TestPrep: Internet Explorer 4, 0-7897-1654-2

MCSE TestPrep: Exchange Server 5.5, 0-7897-1611-9

MCSE TestPrep: IIS 4.0, 0-7897-1610-0

FAST TRACK SERIES

The Accelerated Path to Certification Success

Fast Tracks provide an easy way to review the key elements of each certification technology without being bogged down with elementary-level information.

These guides are perfect for when you already have real-world, hands-on experience. They're the ideal enhancement to training courses, test simulators, and comprehensive training guides. *No fluff, simply what you really need to pass the exam!*

LEARN IT FAST

Part I contains only the essential information you need to pass the test. With over 200 pages of information, it is a concise review for the more experienced MCSE candidate.

REVIEW IT EVEN FASTER

Part II averages 50–75 pages, and takes you through the test and into the real-world use of the technology, with chapters on:

1) Fast Facts Review Section
2) The Insider's Spin (on taking the exam)
3) Sample Test Questions
4) Hotlists of Exam-Critical Concepts
5) Did You Know? (real-world applications for the technology covered in the exam)

MCSE Fast Track: Networking Essentials

1-56205-939-4, $19.99, 9/98

MCSE Fast Track: TCP/IP

1-56205-937-8, $19.99, 9/98

MCSE Fast Track: Windows 98

0-7357-0016-8, $19.99, 12/98

MCSE Fast Track: Internet Information Server 4

1-56205-936-X, $19.99, 9/98

MCSE Fast Track: Windows NT Server 4

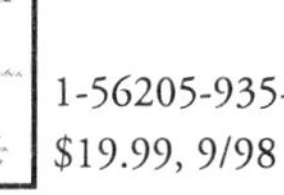

1-56205-935-1, $19.99, 9/98

MCSD Fast Track: Solution Architectures

0-7357-0029-X, $19.99, Q2/99

MCSE Fast Track: Windows NT Server 4 Enterprise

1-56205-940-8, $19.99, 9/98

MCSD Fast Track: Visual Basic 6, Exam 70-175

0-7357-0018-4, $19.99, 12/98

MCSE Fast Track: Windows NT Workstation 4

1-56205-938-6, $19.99, 9/98

MCSD Fast Track: Visual Basic 6, Exam 70-176

0-7357-0019-2, $19.99, 12/98

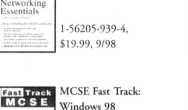

How to Contact Us

IF YOU NEED THE LATEST UPDATES ON A TITLE THAT YOU'VE PURCHASED:

1) Visit our Web site at www.newriders.com.
2) Click on the DOWNLOADS link, and enter your book's ISBN number, which is located on the back cover in the bottom right-hand corner.
3) In the DOWNLOADS section, you'll find available updates that are linked to the book page.

IF YOU ARE HAVING TECHNICAL PROBLEMS WITH THE BOOK OR THE CD THAT IS INCLUDED:

1) Check the book's information page on our Web site according to the instructions listed above, or
2) Email us at support@mcp.com, or
3) Fax us at (317) 817-7488 attn: Tech Support.

IF YOU HAVE COMMENTS ABOUT ANY OF OUR CERTIFICATION PRODUCTS THAT ARE NON-SUPPORT RELATED:

1) Email us at certification@mcp.com, or
2) Write to us at New Riders, 201 W. 103rd St., Indianapolis, IN 46290-1097, or
3) Fax us at (317) 581-4663.

IF YOU ARE OUTSIDE THE UNITED STATES AND NEED TO FIND A DISTRIBUTOR IN YOUR AREA:

Please contact our international department at international@mcp.com.

IF YOU WISH TO PREVIEW ANY OF OUR CERTIFICATION BOOKS FOR CLASSROOM USE:

Email us at pr@mcp.com. Your message should include your name, title, training company or school, department, address, phone number, office days/hours, text in use, and enrollment. Send these details along with your request for desk/examination copies and/or additional information.

We Want to Know What You Think

To better serve you, we would like your opinion on the content and quality of this book. Please complete this card and mail it to us or fax it to 317-581-4663.

Name ____________________

Address ____________________

City ____________ State ________ Zip ____________

Phone ____________ Email Address ____________

Occupation ____________________

Which certification exams have you already passed? ________

Which certification exams do you plan to take? ________

What influenced your purchase of this book?

- ❑ Recommendation
- ❑ Cover Design
- ❑ Table of Contents
- ❑ Index
- ❑ Magazine Review
- ❑ Advertisement
- ❑ Reputation of New Riders
- ❑ Author Name

How would you rate the contents of this book?

- ❑ Excellent
- ❑ Very Good
- ❑ Good
- ❑ Fair
- ❑ Below Average
- ❑ Poor

What other types of certification products will you buy/have you bought to help you prepare for the exam?

- ❑ Quick reference books
- ❑ Testing software
- ❑ Study guides
- ❑ Other

What do you like most about this book? Check all that apply.

- ❑ Content
- ❑ Writing Style
- ❑ Accuracy
- ❑ Examples
- ❑ Listings
- ❑ Design
- ❑ Index
- ❑ Page Count
- ❑ Price
- ❑ Illustrations

What do you like least about this book? Check all that apply.

- ❑ Content
- ❑ Writing Style
- ❑ Accuracy
- ❑ Examples
- ❑ Listings
- ❑ Design
- ❑ Index
- ❑ Page Count
- ❑ Price
- ❑ Illustrations

What would be a useful follow-up book to this one for you? ____________

Where did you purchase this book? ____________

Can you name a similar book that you like better than this one, or one that is as good? Why? ____________

How many New Riders books do you own? ____________

What are your favorite certification or general computer book titles? ____________

What other titles would you like to see New Riders develop? ____________

Any comments? ____________

Fold here and Scotch tape to mail

Place
Stamp
Here

New Riders
201 W. 103rd St.
Indianapolis, IN 46290